Best Practices for Legal Education

Roy Stuckey and Others

Cataloged at the Coleman Karesh Law Library at the University of South Carolina

Stuckey, Roy

> Best Practices for Legal Education / by Roy Stuckey and Others
> ISBN 0-9792955-0-5
> ISBN 978-0-9792955-0-8

Stuckey, Roy

Law – Study and Training
I. Title
KF272.S88 2007

First Edition

This book is dedicated to
The Honorable Rosalie Wahl,
Supreme Court of Minnesota,

and

Robert MacCrate, Esq.,
Sullivan and Cromwell, New York,

for their love of the legal profession
and their efforts to improve legal education.

Table of Contents

Foreword

Robert MacCrate, Esq.

Over the past 25 years, I have been privileged actively to participate in a rich dialogue, among law teachers, lawyers, and judges, regarding the education of lawyers. This report, BEST PRACTICES FOR LEGAL EDUCATION, is a fruit of that dialogue. It was authored by a group, aptly described by The Carnegie Foundation for the Advancement of Teaching as "a far-flung network of legal educators." The Carnegie Foundation in its own contemporaneous report, EDUCATING LAWYERS, views this time as an "historic opportunity to advance legal education," which it surely is following the dialogue we have had during the past 25 years.

Sparked by the Ford Foundation's CLEPR Project (during the 1960s and 70s), the American Bar Association convened a 1984 conference "Legal Education and the Profession: Approaching the 21st Century" at the McGeorge School of Law, which started the continuous dialogue that bears fruit today in the two reports. In 1987, Justice Rosalie Wahl of the Minnesota Supreme Court and Chair of the ABA Section of Legal Education and Admissions to the Bar, convened a "National Conference on Professional Skills and Legal Education." Professor Roy Stuckey, co-chair of that conference and leader of the Best Practices Project, stated the 1987 goal: "To develop through a dialogue a consensus understanding about the present state of professional skills instruction in American law schools." At the conference Justice Wahl rhetorically asked:

> Have we really tried in law school to determine what skills, what attitudes, what character traits, what quality of mind are required of lawyers? Are we adequately educating students through the content and methodology of our present law school curriculums to perform effectively as lawyers after graduation?

Justice Wahl went on to say that until the entire profession had a clearer vision of the answer to the questions, further progress in relating legal education to the needs of lawyers and judges and the advancement of the profession as a client-centered public calling would be thwarted.

To address the questions Justice Wahl had rhetorically raised, the Council of the Section of Legal Education in 1989 established the "Task Force on Law Schools and the Profession: Narrowing the Gap" comprised of law teachers, practicing lawyers, and sitting judges. Early in their deliberations the members of the Task Force concluded that the skills and values of competent and responsible lawyers are developed along a continuum that neither begins nor ends in law school, but starts before law school, reaches its most formative and intensive stage during the law school experience, and continues throughout the lawyer's professional career. At a time when the professional idea seemed overwhelmed by change both within the profession and in society at large, the Task Force developed a conceptual statement of the skills and values that all lawyers should seek to acquire. Over a period of three years, the Task Force in plenary sessions, in subcommittees, and in public hearings, carried on and expanded the dialogue on the education of lawyers.

The Task Force Report published in July 1992 was entitled LEGAL EDUCATION AND PROFESSIONAL DEVELOPMENT – AN EDUCATIONAL CONTINUUM. During the decade following publication of the report, bar associations in many parts of the country, in cooperation with law schools and the judiciary, convened conclaves in more than 25 states to continue the dialogue in discussion of how the educational continuum could best be built in a state or in a region of states.

Against this background, the leaders of the Clinical Legal Education Association in 2001 decided to establish a committee of scholars to develop a "Statement of Best Practices for Legal Education" and asked Professor Stuckey to chair that committee. Over the ensuing five years the authors of BEST PRACTICES have distilled out of the continuing dialogue a consensus of understanding of an alternative vision of all the components of legal education, based on educational research and scholarship: an integrated combination of substantive law, skills, and market knowledge, and embracing the idea that legal education is to prepare law students for the practice of law as members of a client-centered public profession.

The central message in both BEST PRACTICES and in the contemporaneous Carnegie report is that law schools should:
- broaden the range of lessons they teach, reducing doctrinal instruction that uses the Socratic dialogue and the case method;
- integrate the teaching of knowledge, skills and values, and not treat them as separate subjects addressed in separate courses; and
- give much greater attention to instruction in professionalism.

At the same time, the reports recognize that the program of instruction should reflect each law school's mission for developing competent and committed professionals.

With BEST PRACTICES and EDUCATING LAWYERS as guides, and now informed by the annual Law School Survey of Student Engagement (co-sponsored by the Association of American Law Schools and the Carnegie Foundation), there is indeed an "historic opportunity to advance legal education."

CLEA'S Best Practices Project

With approval of the CLEA Board of Directors, the Best Practices Project was initiated in August, 2001, by the 2001 President of CLEA, Professor Carrie Kaas of the Quinnipiac University School of Law and the 2002 President of CLEA, Professor Peter Joy of the Washington University School of Law, St. Louis. They asked Professor Roy Stuckey of the University of South Carolina School of Law to chair the project and then appointed the Steering Committee. Their charge to the Committee was to "develop a statement of best practices," leaving it up to the Committee to determine the scope and nature of that statement.

BEST PRACTICES FOR LEGAL EDUCATION was developed collaboratively over the course of almost six years, 2001-2007. Roy Stuckey is the principal author of the document, but many people contributed to the final product.

Each new draft was posted on the professionalism website at the University of South Carolina School of Law (http://professionalism.law.sc.edu), usually in late spring, August, and December. Notices of each posting were distributed via the internet to lists serving law professors (lawprof), clinical law teachers (lawclinic), externship teachers (lextern), and the Global Alliance for Justice Education (GAJE). Hard copies of each draft were mailed to leaders of the AALS, the ABA Section of Legal Education and Admissions to the Bar, and other leaders of the legal profession and legal academia. These drafts and intermittent requests for assistance on specific issues were also sent to the Steering Committee, an increasingly large number of people who expressed interest in the project, and people with expertise about specific topics. Ideas for improving the document were widely solicited, and many people made suggestions. As indicated in the document, a number of people drafted sections that were incorporated into the document.

As the document evolved, presentations about the project were made at a variety of meetings and conferences, and the Steering Committee held open meetings to discuss the project during AALS annual meetings and clinical teachers' conferences. The document was the subject of a national conference at Pace University School of Law in March, 2005, and several CLEA-sponsored workshops.

Steering Committee for CLEA's Best Practices Project

Professor Roy T. Stuckey, Chair
University of South Carolina School of Law

Professor Margaret Barry
The Catholic University of America
School of Law

Professor Robert D. Dinerstein
American University, Washington
College of Law

Professor Jon C. Dubin (2001 - 2004)
Rutgers, The State University of New
Jersey, S.I. Newhouse Center for Law &
Justice

Professor Russell Engler
New England School of Law

Professor John S. Elson
Northwestern University School of Law

Professor Gail Hammer (since 2003)
Gonzaga University School of Law

Professor Randy Hertz
New York University School of Law

Professor Peter Joy
Washington University School of Law,
St. Louis

Professor Carolyn Kaas
Quinnipiac University School of Law

Professor Vanessa Merton
Pace University School of Law

Professor Greg Munro (since 2003)
University of Montana School of Law

Professor Sandy Ogilvy
The Catholic University of America
School of Law

Dean Suellyn Scarnecchia (2001-2002)
University of New Mexico School of Law

Professor Michael Hunter Schwartz
(since 2005)
Washburn University School of Law

Presidents of CLEA During the Project

2001 Professor Carolyn Kaas
Quinnipiac University School of Law

2002 Professor Peter Joy
Washington University School of Law,
St. Louis

2003 Professor Annette Appell
University of Nevada, Las Vegas School
of Law

2004 Professor Antoinette Sedillo
University of New Mexico School of Law

2005 Professor Alex Scherr
University of Georgia School of Law

2006 Professor Susan Kay
Vanderbilt University Law School

2007 Professor Paulette J. Williams
University of Tennessee College of Law

Acknowledgments

I thank Carrie Kaas and Peter Joy for asking me to chair the Steering Committee. I also thank Carrie, Peter, and the other officers and Board members of CLEA for their unwavering support and encouragement. I appreciate the Steering Committee's guidance and tolerance as the project made numerous twists and turns. The inspiration to move forward and finish the project was provided by the participants in the remarkable best practices conference that was organized and facilitated by Vanessa Merton at Pace University School of Law on March 11-13, 2005.

This document has the fingerprints of hundreds of people who provided suggestions, sources, and even some drafting. Many people can legitimately claim to be contributing authors. The contributing authors who made the most substantial contributions are Sandy Ogilvy, Catholic University of America, Columbus School of Law, and Michael Schwartz, Washburn University School of Law.

It would have been impossible to describe best practices for legal education without relying on the work of dozens of scholars who care about the quality of legal education, a number of whom shared works in progress with us. Judith Wegner, University of North Carolina School of Law, deserves special recognition for allowing us to use drafts of her findings and conclusions from her study of legal education for the Carnegie Foundation for the Advancement of Teaching. Her insights led to significant changes at a critical stage of the project's evolution. The document was also enhanced by the generosity of Bill Sullivan and the Carnegie Foundation for the Advancement of Teaching who allowed us to incorporate material from the July, 2005, draft of EDUCATING LAWYERS (March, 2007), a report on Carnegie's study of legal education in the United States.

In the final editing stages, Louis Sirico, Villanova University School of Law, and Ruth Anne Robbins of Rutgers, The State University of New Jersey School of Law, Camden, provided expert editorial and formatting assistance in preparing the document for publication. The book may never have made it to the printer without the help of Beth Prendergast Hendrix, Faculty and Staff Computer Trainer and Technology Coordinator at the University of South Carolina School of Law. In the process of getting the book "camera ready," she fought and defeated many dragons that had taken up residence in the file.

I was aided by some very talented law student research assistants. Heather Shirley was with me at the beginning when we did not know how to start or where to go. She was followed by William Hughes, Camey Everhart, and Jodi Ramsey.

Finally, I want to acknowledge the broad and diverse range of people within and beyond the legal profession who encouraged us to see this project through. I am convinced today that more people care about the quality of legal education than I thought when I began. I am confident that by working together, people who care can make a positive difference for our students, their future clients, and ourselves.

Roy Stuckey
University of South Carolina
School of Law
stuckeyroy@gmail.com

Introduction

This book provides a vision of what legal education might become if legal educators step back and consider how they can most effectively prepare students for practice. It has several potential uses. It could serve as a road map for a partial or complete review of a law school's program of instruction. It could also help individual teachers improve course design, delivery of instruction, and assessment of student learning. Most of all, however, we hope the document will facilitate dialogue about legal education among law teachers and between law teachers and other members of the legal profession. A serious, thoughtful reconsideration of legal education in the United States is long overdue.

The principles of best practices described in this document are based on long-recognized principles of sound educational practices as well as recent research and scholarship about teaching and learning. Our conclusions are based on the most up-to-date information available. Such resources include EDUCATING LAWYERS, the report of a study of legal education conducted by the Carnegie Foundation for the Advancement of Teaching, and the unpublished drafts of chapters for a book being written by Judith Wegner, which contain her personal observations and conclusions as the principal investigator for the Carnegie Foundation's study.

Another resource is information produced from on-going empirical studies by Ken Sheldon and Larry Krieger about the negative effects that current legal educational practices can have on the emotional well-being of our students. Our work was also informed by the progress of the Law Society of England and Wales as it continues developing a new training framework for solicitors, including a description of the knowledge, skills, and values that new solicitors should have on their first day in practice. Additionally, we tracked and incorporated developments in the professionalism movement, a successful experiment using standardized clients to evaluate lawyer performance in Scotland, evolving theories from cognitive scientists and educational theorists about teaching and learning, current trends in evaluating institutional success, new techniques for assessing student learning, including electronic and other types of portfolios, and many other new initiatives.

The principles of best practices described in this document are based on the following assumptions about legal education in the United States:
1. Most new lawyers are not as prepared as they could be to discharge the responsibilities of law practice.
2. Significant improvements to legal education are achievable, if the issues are examined from fresh perspectives and with open minds.
3. The process for becoming a lawyer in the United States will not change significantly.[1]

The Best Practices Project was motivated in large part by our concern about the potential harm to consumers of legal services when new lawyers are not adequately prepared for practice. We are also concerned about helping law school

---

[1] If there is any possibility that the third assumption is invalid, we would encourage the legal profession to reconsider the entire continuum of educating and training lawyers in the United States. This book examines how the law school years might be used more effectively, but even the most effective law school program cannot fully prepare new lawyers for practice. Post graduate education and training needs to become more rigorous and sophisticated.

graduates to succeed in law practice and to lead satisfied, healthy lives.

Since its inception, the United States' model of legal education has been criticized as serving only some of the educational needs of new lawyers.[2] Since the 1970's, numerous groups of leaders of the legal profession and groups of distinguished lawyers, judges, and academics have studied legal education and have universally concluded that most law school graduates lack the minimum competencies required to provide effective and responsible legal services.[3] The depth and seriousness of defects in legal education in the United States were summarized by Greg Munro:

> These critics did not focus on peripheral matters, but rather identified defects that go to the core and structure of legal education. They are the problems of ignoring the constituencies a law school serves, not knowing what lawyers do, what law students need to learn, how law students learn best, what teaching methods are most effective, how to determine whether students have learned, what responsibilities the law school has to the profession and society, and how the school knows it is discharging these responsibilities. They are the same core problems that have plagued American higher education and have prompted demands for reform.[4]

Former Secretary of Education William J. Bennett said "we are uncertain what we think our students should learn, how best to teach it to them, and how to be sure when they have learned it."[5] Gary Bellow characterized the deficiencies in our system of legal education as "indefensible."

> Al Sacks once said to me: 'Well, it seems to me that what you're saying is that law school is empirically irrelevant, theoretically flawed, pedagogically dysfunctional, and expensive.' And I am, of course, saying just that. When you add to these deficiencies, the incoherence of the second- and third-year course offerings, the amount of repetition in the curriculum, the degree to which unacknowledged ideology pervades the entire law school experience and the fact that no graduate of an American law school is able to practice when graduated, you have a system of education which, I

---

[2] *See, e. g.*, William V. Rowe, *Legal Clinics and Better Trained Lawyers – A Necessity*, 11 ILL. L. REV. 591 (1917); SUSAN BOYD, THE ABA'S FIRST SECTION: ASSURING A QUALIFIED BAR (1993); ROBERT STEVENS, LEGAL EDUCATION IN AMERICA: FROM THE 1850'S TO THE 1980'S (1983).

[3] A fairly comprehensive discussion of the state of legal education and criticisms of it up to 1980 can be found in various footnotes in H. Russell Cort & Jack L. Sammons, *The Search for "Good Lawyering:" A Concept and Model of Lawyering Competencies*, 29 CLEV. ST. L. REV. 397 (1980). More recent articles are noted in Mitu Gulati, Richard Sander & Robert Sockloskie, *The Happy Charade: An Empirical Examination of the Third Year of Law School*, 51 J. LEGAL EDUC. 235, 238, n.4 (2001).

[4] GREGORY S. MUNRO, OUTCOMES ASSESSMENT FOR LAW SCHOOLS 46, n.113 (2000). A more recent book is PHILIP C. KISSAM, THE DISCIPLINE OF LAW SCHOOLS (2003). Kissam describes the paradoxes in legal education in which intentions and practices seem to be at cross-purposes, and he depressingly holds out little hope for significant change.

[5] William J. Bennett, *Foreword*, ASSESSMENT IN AMERICAN HIGHER EDUCATION: ISSUES AND CONTEXTS, at I (Clifford Adelman ed., 1986).

believe, is simply indefensible.[6]

In the history of legal education in the United States, there is no record of any concerted effort to consider what new lawyers should know or be able to do on their first day in practice or to design a program of instruction to achieve those goals. The Carnegie Foundation for the Advancement of Teaching conducted a study of legal education that ended in 2006. It "discovered that faculty attention to the overall purposes and effects of a school's educational efforts is surprisingly rare."[7]

The authors of the Carnegie Foundation's report recognized that some changes have occurred in legal education but not the comprehensive, systemic changes that are needed.

> And, indeed, over the past decade, important changes have been taking place. Compared to fifty years ago, law schools now provide students with more experience, more context, more student choice, and more connection with the larger university world and other disciplines. However, efforts to improve legal education have been more piecemeal than comprehensive. Few schools have made the overall practices and effects of their educational effort a subject for serious study. Too few have attempted to address these inadequacies on a systematic basis. This relative lack of responsiveness by the law schools, taken as a group, to the well-reasoned pleas of the national bar antedates our investigation.[8]

Legal educators generally ignore long-recognized basic principles of curriculum development, which involves four stages:

Stage 1: Identifying educational objectives that the school or course should seek to attain.

Stage 2: Selecting learning experiences that are likely to be useful in attaining those objectives.

Stage 3: Organizing the selected learning experiences for effective instruction.

Stage 4: Designing methods for evaluating the effectiveness of the selected learning experiences.[9]

The disinclination of law teachers to engage in critical thinking and debate about legal education is especially surprising when one considers that our model of legal education has not been in place very long. It was not until the 1960s that our structure of four years of college followed by three years of law school was firmly established.[10]

It is time for legal educators, lawyers, judges, and members of the public to reevaluate our assumptions about the roles and methods of law schools and to explore new ways of conceptualizing and delivering learner-centered legal education.

---

[6] Gary Bellow, *On Talking Tough to Each Other: Comments on Condlin*, 33 J. LEGAL EDUC. 619, 622-23 (1983).

[7] WILLIAM M. SULLIVAN, ANNE COLBY, JUDITH WELCH WEGNER, LLOYD BOND & LEE S. SHULMAN, EDUCATING LAWYERS 98 (Draft July, 2006).

[8] *Id.* at 243.

[9] *See, e.g.*, RALPH TYLER, BASIC PRINCIPLES OF CURRICULUM AND INSTRUCTION (1949).

[10] STEVENS, *supra* note 2, at 209.

We agree with the authors of the Carnegie Foundation's report that the changes we need to make are substantial.

> A more adequate and properly formative legal education requires a better balance among the cognitive, practical, and ethical-social apprenticeships. To achieve this balance, legal educators will have to do more than shuffle the existing pieces. It demands their careful rethinking of both the existing curriculum and the pedagogies law schools employ to produce a more coherent and integrated initiation into a life in the law.[11]

It is no easy task to consider how to improve legal education even if all concerned agree there is a need for improvement. Generations of debate have not resolved the relative merits of a liberal, general education versus a technical, professional orientation for the practice of law. Nor will we ever be able to reach universal agreement about the specific knowledge, skills, and values that law schools should teach if for no other reason than the vastly diverse practice settings in which our graduates work. There are some fundamental things about which we should be able to agree, however, and we should not refrain from trying to improve legal education simply because the task is difficult. Other countries are reforming their systems of legal education; our attention to improving the preparation of lawyers for practice in the United States is long overdue.

We undertook a thoughtful and deliberate search for ways to improve legal education that are consistent with sound educational theories and practices. We hope our final product has achieved these goals, though some of our proposals call for significant changes in the content and organization of the law school curriculum and in the attitudes and practices of law teachers.

This is a large document, unavoidably so because preparing students for practice is a complex project. Despite its size, it provides only a broad overview of most of the topics it addresses. Entire books have been written about the concepts contained in almost every page. Thus, reference to many outside sources is required to acquire a complete understanding of the problems and possible solutions.

Many of our recommendations do not have any cost or time implications, and others have none beyond the initial effort involved in making the transition from current practices.[12] Certainly, schools that decide to offer the best possible learning experiences for their students may want to have smaller student-faculty ratios than today's typical law school. Moreover, they might expect their faculties to devote more time to educating students than current practice.

Graduate professional education should have lower student-faculty ratios than the current norm in law schools in the United States. As one scholar wrote, "Langdell's perhaps greatest coup was his persuasion of universities that legal

---

[11] SULLIVAN ET AL., *supra* note 7, at 180.

[12] In fact, the law schools in the United States that appear to be the most student-centered and committed to preparing students for practice have relatively modest budgets. We considered naming schools that have made an institutional commitment to preparing students for practice and have taken significant steps toward that objective. We decided not to do so, however, because we did not have valid selection criteria.

education was inexpensive."[13] Sandy D'Alemberte observed that "[l]aw schools have not had the teaching resources of our other graduate programs, and they do not have the resources of the professional school programs – even those which terminate with a community college degree. This should suggest something to us – nobody does things the way we do. We're probably the group that's out of step."[14] Even without improving student-faculty ratios, however, we believe significant improvements are possible. One of our basic tenets is that law schools should become more student-centered and should recognize and reward good teaching more than most do today.

The changes we recommend should have a positive impact on legal scholarship. If law teachers begin giving more thought to how students learn as well as what lawyers do and how they do it, new avenues of legal scholarship will be opened beyond the traditional scholarship about doctrine and judging.[15] These new directions in scholarship are more likely to involve interdisciplinary work than traditional legal scholarship and strengthen law schools' claims that they are worthy members of research universities.

We hope the completion of the drafting phase will mark the beginning of a process of discussion, debate, and implementation of the principles discussed in this document – or other principles that will promote improvements in legal education. We also hope, as Gary Bellow did, that "our discourse be real discourse – concerned with normative values, not the justification of the system that currently exists."[16]

We acknowledge that any description of "best practices" will soon be eclipsed as we refine our understanding of the desirable goals of legal education and how to achieve them. That is how it should be.

---

[13] Christoph G. Courchesne, *"A Suggestion of a Fundamental Nature:" Imagining a Legal Education of Solely Electives Taught as Discussions*, 29 RUTGERS L. REC. 21, 60 (2005) (citing STEVENS, *supra* note 2, at 268).

[14] Talbot D'Alemberte, *Talbot D'Alemberte on Legal Education*, 76 ABA J. 52, 52 (Sep. 1990).

[15] For suggestions of where such scholarship may lead, see Gary L. Blasi, *What Lawyers Know: Lawyering Expertise, Cognitive Science, and the Functions of Theory*, 45 J. LEGAL EDUC. 313, 391-96 (1995); Carrie Menkel-Meadow, *The Legacy of Clinical Education: Theories About Lawyering*, 29 CLEV. ST. L. REV. 555 (1980).

[16] Bellow, *supra* note 6, at 623.

Executive Summary and Key Recommendations

Developing a Statement of Best Practices
(Introduction and Chapter One)

There is a compelling need to change legal education in the United States in significant ways. Law schools do some things well, but they do some things poorly or not at all. While law schools help students acquire some of the essential skills and knowledge required for law practice, most law schools are not committed to preparing students for practice. It is generally conceded that most law school graduates are not as prepared for law practice as they could be and should be. Law schools can do much better.

Our key recommendations for improving legal education are listed below. One can quickly grasp the full breadth of our recommendations by reviewing the table of contents.

We divide our discussion of best practices into seven categories: 1) setting goals, 2) organizing the program of instruction, 3) delivering instruction, generally, 4) conducting experiential courses, 5) employing non-experiential methods of instruction, 6) assessing student learning, and 7) evaluating the success of the program of instruction. We also include an example of a "model" best practices program of instruction.

We call on law schools to make a commitment to improve the preparation of their students for practice, clarify and expand their educational objectives, improve and diversify methods for delivering instruction, and give more attention to evaluating the success of their programs of instruction. The importance of accomplishing these goals was explained by Greg Munro:

> A law school can best achieve excellence and have the most effective academic program when it possesses a clear mission, a plan to achieve that mission, and the capacity and willingness to measure its success or failure. Absent a defined mission and the identification of attendant student and institutional outcomes, a law school lacks focus and its curriculum becomes a collection of discrete activities without coherence. If a school does not assess its performance, it can easily be deluded about its success, the effectiveness of its pedagogical methods, the relevance of its curriculum, and the value of its services to its constituencies. A law school that fails to assess student performance or its performance as an institution, or that uses the wrong measures in doing so, has no real evidence that it is achieving any goals or objectives. A law school that lacks evidence of achievement invites demands for accountability.[17]

It may not be possible to prepare students fully for the practice of law in three years, but law schools can come much closer than they are doing today. It is

---

[17] MUNRO, *supra* note 4, at 3-4.

especially important for law schools to make an institutional commitment to do the best they can to prepare their students for practice.

An important step is to articulate clear educational objectives for the program of instruction and, preferably, to describe those objectives in terms of desired outcomes. Outcomes-focused education is becoming the norm throughout higher education. In fact, regional accrediting agencies are requiring institutions of higher education, including some law schools, not only to state educational outcomes but also to prove that their students are attaining those outcomes.[18] Legal education programs in the United Kingdom and other countries have outcomes-focused curriculums, and a few law schools in the United States are making progress toward becoming outcomes-focused. It is time for all law schools to make the transition.

Descriptions of desired outcomes of legal education should include statements of what graduates should know, what they should be able to do, and how they should do it. We describe some general outcomes that all law schools should seek to achieve as they try to develop basic competence.

The key recommendations in this document are set forth below.

Setting Goals (Chapter Two)

1. Law schools should demonstrate a commitment to preparing their students for bar examinations and for law practice. They should engage in a continuing dialogue with academics, practitioners, judges, licensing authorities, and the general public about how best to accomplish this goal.

2. Law schools should clearly articulate their educational goals and share them with their students.

3. Law schools should shift from content-focused programs of instruction to outcomes-focused programs of instruction that are concerned with what students will be able to do and how they will do it, as well as what they will know on their first day in law practice.

4. The primary goal of legal education should be to develop competence, that is, the ability to resolve legal problems effectively and responsibly.

5. Law schools should help students acquire the attributes of effective, responsible lawyers including self-reflection and lifelong learning skills, intellectual and analytical skills, core knowledge and understanding of law, professional skills, and professionalism.

Organizing the Program of Instruction (Chapter Three)

6. Law schools should organize their curriculums to develop knowledge, skills,

---

[18] *See, e.g.*, Standards 2 & 4, WESTERN ASSOCIATION OF SCHOOLS AND COLLEGES, ACCREDITING COMMISSION FOR SENIOR COLLEGES AND UNIVERSITIES, HANDBOOK OF ACCREDITATION (2001), *available at* http://wacssenior.org/wasc/Doc_Lib/2001%20Handbook.pdf (last visited September 19, 2006) [hereinafter WESTERN ASSOCIATION ACCREDITATION HANDBOOK].

and values progressively; integrate the teaching of theory, doctrine, and practice; and teach professionalism pervasively throughout all three years of law school.

Delivering Instruction (Chapters Four, Five, and Six)

7.   Law schools should use teaching methods that most effectively and efficiently achieve desired educational objectives, employ context-based instruction throughout the program of instruction, and employ best practices when using any instructional methodology.

8.   Law schools should create and maintain healthy teaching and learning environments.

9.   Law schools should enhance the quality of their programs of instruction with technology and by making appropriate use of practicing lawyers and judges.

10.   Law schools should have effective teacher development programs and establish learning centers.

Assessing Student Learning (Chapter Seven)

11.   Law schools should use best practices for assessing student learning, including criteria-referenced assessments, multiple formative and summative assessments, and various methods of assessment.

Evaluating the Success of the Program of Instruction (Chapter Eight)

12.   Law schools should regularly evaluate their effectiveness and use best practices for conducting such evaluations.

Many of our recommendations do not have cost or time implications, and others have none beyond the initial effort involved in making the transition from current practices. It will require hard work and, perhaps, additional or reallocated resources to implement some of our recommendations. We are convinced, however, that the major impediment to reforming legal education is a lack of vision and commitment, not a lack of resources. Hopefully, this document provides some of the needed vision and will inspire more people to become committed to implementing positive changes in legal education.

Chapter One
Reasons for Developing a Statement of Best Practices

A.   **A Statement of Best Practices Can Help Evaluate the Quality of a Law School's Program of Instruction and Guide Efforts to Improve It.**

This document contains statements of principles of best practices in legal education. It also includes comments that more fully explain the meaning of each principle and how it relates to current practices, scholarship about learning and teaching, and recommendations of scholars and practitioners for improving legal education.

A comparison of principles of best practices with the actual practices of a given law school will help evaluate the quality of the school's program of instruction and provide guidance for improving it.

We are aware of Stanley Fish's clever dissection of the term "best practices" in which he concluded that invoking "best practices" is all about saying something incredibly obvious and banal. He included "best practices" among those administrative pieties that should be banned from polite conversation.[19]

We concede that many of the best practices described in this document are banal and obvious. But that is the problem. Although they seem obvious, most law schools do not employ the best practices for educating lawyers. Thus, with due deference to Fish's opinion that discussions of best practices should be banned from polite conversation, we believe there is value in describing best practices for legal education and encouraging debate about them.

B.   **The Need to Improve Legal Education is Compelling.**

1.   **The Licensing Process is Not Protecting the Public.**

This document describes best practices for legal education, particularly the initial phases of legal education that occur in law schools. The conundrum that law schools face is that even the most well-designed program of instruction will not prepare students to provide a full range of legal services competently upon graduation after three years. Law school instruction will always be only one segment of the continuum of learning in the life of a lawyer. Lawyers learn throughout their careers from experience, collaboration, self-study, reflection, and continuing legal education. Law school education is only the first step in the process of becoming an effective, responsible lawyer.

The burden of preparing students for law practice should not rest solely on the law schools. Other segments of the legal profession should assume more of the responsibility. For example, bar admissions authorities could impose additional requirements on law school graduates to ensure that they are prepared to provide

---

[19] Stanley Fish, *Keep Your Eye on the Small Picture*, CHRONICLE OF HIGHER EDUCATION, February 1, 2002.

professional legal services before they are eligible for licenses to provide such services. Although this is the reality in some other countries, it is not yet the reality in the United States.[20]

Currently, a person's ability to practice law in the United States typically requires only graduating from law school and passing a state licensing examination, the bar examination. For the most part, bar examinations evaluate the ability of an examinee to recognize legal problems embedded in a written fact scenario and to draft a short essay that addresses each problem identified, drawing on the examinee's memory of legal doctrine and ability to communicate to the reader an understanding of the problem and the doctrine.

Bar examinations require applicants to demonstrate only a small amount of the knowledge, skills, and values that are needed for participation in the legal profession. They are not valid indicators of a new lawyer's ability to practice law effectively and responsibly. The nature and effectiveness of bar examinations are widely criticized.[21] Among other shortcomings, bar examinations require students

---

[20] Vermont and Delaware require new lawyers to spend a period of time working for experienced lawyers before they are fully licensed, but there is no assessment or certification of competency at the end of the experience, just a certification that the requisite time was put in and the requisite tasks were performed. We encourage other states to follow the lead of Vermont and Delaware, even if the quality of the learning experiences cannot be guaranteed. Another effort to improve the transition to practice is being made in Georgia where the Supreme Court authorized a mandatory Transition Into Law Practice Program that went into effect in January, 2006. The core of the program is to assign every beginning lawyer with a mentor for the first year after bar admission. A CLE component will lay the groundwork for and support the mentorships. Commission on Continuing Lawyer Competency, State Bar of Georgia, Transition Into Law Practice Program: Executive Summary (2005), *available at* http://www.gabar.org/public/pdf/tilpp/7-G.pdf.

[21] *See, e.g., Society of American Law Teachers Statement on the Bar Exam: July 2002*, 52 J. LEGAL EDUC. 446 (2002) (concluding that bar examinations as currently administered fail to adequately measure competence to practice law, negatively affect law school curricular development and the law school admission process, and are a significant barrier to achieving a more diverse bench and bar). *See also* Clark D. Cunningham, *The Professionalism Crisis: How Bar Examiners Can Make a Difference*, 74 THE BAR EXAMINER 6 (Nov. 2005); William C. Kidder, *The Bar Examination and the Dream Deferred: A Critical Analysis of the MBE, Labor Market Control, and Racial and Ethnic Performance Disparities*, 29 LAW & SOC. INQUIRY 547 (2004); Robert MacCrate, *Yesterday, Today and Tomorrow: Building the Continuum of Legal Education and Professional Development*, 10 CLINICAL L. REV. 805 (2004); Roy T. Stuckey, *Why Johnny Can't Practice Law – and What We Can Do About It: One Clinical Law Professor's View*, 72 THE BAR EXAMINER 32 (2003); Adrian Evans & Clark D. Cunningham, *Specialty Certification as an Incentive for Increased Professionalism: Lessons from Other Disciplines and Countries*, 54 S.C. L. REV. 987 (2003); Andrea A. Curcio, *A Better Bar: Why and How the Existing Bar Exam Should Change*, 81 U. NEB. L. REV. 363 (2002); Beverly Moran, *The Wisconsin Diploma Privilege*, 2000 WISC. L. REV. 645 (2002); Kristin Booth Glen, *When and Where We Enter: Rethinking Admission to the Legal Profession*, 102 COL. L. REV. 1696 (2002); Lawrence M. Grosberg, *Medical Education Again Provides a Model for Law Schools: the Standardized Patient Becomes the Standardized Client*, 51 J. LEGAL EDUC. 212 (2001); Deborah J. Merritt, Lowell L. Hargens & Barbara F. Reskin, *Raising the Bar: A Social Science Critique of Recent Increases to Passing Scores on the Bar Exam*, 69 U. CINN. L. REV. 929 (2000); MUNRO, *supra* note 4; Joan Howarth, *Teaching in the Shadow of the Bar*, 31 U. SAN FRAN. L. REV. 927 (1997); Daniel R. Hansen, Note, *Do We Need The Bar Examination? A Critical Evaluation of the Justifications for the Bar Examination and Proposed Alternatives*, 45 CASE WES. L. REV. 1191 (1995); Lawrence M. Grosberg, *Should We Test for Interpersonal Lawyering Skills?*, 2 CLINICAL L. REV. 349 (1996); Cecil B. Hunt, *Guests in Another's House*, 23 FLA. ST. U. L. REV. 721 (1996). The Georgia State

to demonstrate much more substantive legal knowledge than new lawyers need for successful law practice,[22] much of which is memorized in commercial cram courses and quickly forgotten once bar examinations end.

A law school graduate who passes a bar examination and a character and fitness review receives an unrestricted license to practice law in the licensing jurisdiction. A newly licensed lawyer is permitted to accept any client and provide representation in any type of matter, no matter how complex, guided only by his or her own sense of responsibility and the remote threat of tort liability or disciplinary action for intentionally or negligently mishandling the matter. Without any restriction on a novice lawyer's ability to practice law, there is no mechanism for protecting clients from new lawyers while they try to acquire, on the job, the specialized knowledge and skills required for providing competent legal services.

We encourage the legal profession to develop statements of best practices for bar examinations, licensing regulations, transitions to practice, and continuing legal education programs. Members of the legal profession and others who are concerned about the public's interests should ask why licensing authorities continue to issue unrestricted licenses to practice law without testing for minimal competency in the broad range of skills and values required for the basic practice of law. Moreover, they should investigate why more licensing authorities do not require a period of supervised practice before full licensure, significant post-graduate training,[23] and demonstrations of competency through assessment during and after post-graduate training and experience.

We believe the public would be better served by a process that begins sooner, lasts longer, and includes a mandatory period of supervised practice before full admission to the legal profession, perhaps adapted from the best traditions of British Commonwealth jurisdictions.

Licensing authorities should consider alternatives to the traditional bar exam. For example, Judith Wegner proposed a three part bar examination that would be administered over a period of years. The first part would assess students' abilities to "think like lawyers" and their command of traditional common law subjects; the second would require students to demonstrate more breadth and depth of knowledge and ability to work with more complex legal problems; and the third would evaluate professional skills and values through more in-depth performance testing and a professionalism review.[24] In Wegner's three part bar examination:

University School of Law published a symposium issue devoted to examining alternatives to the bar exam, 20 GA. ST. U. L. REV. vii (2004), *available at* http://gsulaw2.gsu.edu/lawreview/archives/symposium.php. A series of alternatives to the bar examination are also discussed in 74 THE BAR EXAMINER (Nov. 2005).

[22] The issue of how much substantive legal doctrine law students need to know is discussed in Chapter Two.

[23] Although many states have implemented mandatory "bridge-the-gap" programs that provide new lawyers with practical information about law practice, we are not aware of any that require new lawyers to participate in intensive, hands-on "practice modules" as recommended in ALI-ABA COMMITTEE ON CONTINUING PROFESSIONAL EDUCATION, A MODEL CURRICULUM FOR BRIDGE-THE-GAP PROGRAMS (1988).

[24] Judith Wegner, Thinking Like a Lawyer About Law School Assessment (Draft 2003) (unpublished manuscript on file with Roy Stuckey) [hereinafter Wegner, Assessment]. This material and other related manuscripts by Wegner contain preliminary findings from a study of legal education conducted as part of the Preparation for the Professions Program of the

Part one would test knowledge and skills learned in the first year curriculum. Students would take this test during the summer after their first or second year.

Part two would be administered after graduation, and would concentrate on more in-depth examination using "working files" of materials such as those currently employed for simple "performance-based" tests. Applicants could be asked to select two general areas out of perhaps six available so that they could demonstrate their knowledge in areas with which they had become relatively familiar (perhaps through concentrated work in elective courses in law school). Rather than being asked to rely on memory or face exceedingly constrained time limits, they would be given three-hour blocks to complete each of the two "file" exercises, with evaluation to be based on the quality of their work, not just their speed. A range of essays on subjects relevant to the specific jurisdiction could be posed, while also providing some opportunity for applicants to demonstrate more in-depth thinking and expertise in areas where they may hope to work without the artificial constraints of relying on memory alone. After completing the first two parts of the exam and satisfying character and fitness requirements, applicants would receive a license for the limited interval of two years.

Part three would be administered following two years of practice experience. Satisfactory completion would result in a full license. It would provide a more meaningful assessment of applicants' performance skills and professionalism, using an "assessment center" system in which applicants could be asked to perform an "in basket" exercise (involving priority setting and relatively quick judgments) and conduct an interview with a simulated client, conduct a negotiation, or prepare a discovery plan. One or more of such tasks could include issues of professional responsibility that the applicant would need to address. In addition, applicants could be required to present a more full-blown portfolio of professional references, a description of their major professional experience to date, and a simple self-assessment regarding their strengths and areas in which they are continuing to focus efforts at professional development. This portfolio could serve as part of the basis for a structured interview designed to determine how applicants have made the transition into practice and how well they understand the increasing weight of professional responsibilities they will face in the years ahead. Applicants who successfully passed part three would receive a full license, while those who fared poorly could continue their provisional licensure until taking this portion of the bar exam once more.

As Wegner explained, in addition to other virtues, "[t]he proposal also has the virtue of creating a bifurcated licensing system that recognizes the level of professional development attained at the time of law school graduation, while focusing afresh on the important process of transition into the early stages of lawyers'

Carnegie Foundation for the Advancement of Teaching. The Preparation for the Professions Program investigates the preparation for various professions offered by academic institutions and compares across the professions the approaches to teaching and learning that these institutions use to ensure the development of professional understanding, skills, and integrity. As a Senior Carnegie Scholar, former AALS President and Dean Judith Wegner led a two year study of legal education which included intensive fieldwork at 16 United States and Canadian law schools in 1999-2001. Wegner is completing a book describing her findings and conclusions, and the Carnegie Foundation will publish its own book, EDUCATING LAWYERS, in the Spring of 2007. The drafts produced by Wegner reflect her views, not necessarily the Carnegie Foundation's.

professional careers."[25]

Such a system may also give bar examiners needed flexibility in dealing with complex issues of character and fitness that have led some jurisdictions to adopt conditional licensure rules. The proposal in this respect more closely parallels the Canadian system, which in most instances requires a period of "articling" and additional practice-oriented training before bar admission, yet retains greater flexibility regarding the nature of practice experience gained during the early years of practice that is associated with the American system as it exists today.[26]

Until licensing authorities face the reality that law schools cannot fully prepare students to represent clients in three years, consumers of new lawyers' services will remain at risk no matter what law schools accomplish.

2.   Law Schools Are Not Fully Committed to Preparing Students for Bar Examinations.

Until bar examiners reform bar examinations, we encourage law schools to improve the odds of their students passing existing bar examinations. The law school curriculum is dictated to a significant degree by the subjects tested on the bar examination, and law schools purport to teach what bar examiners test. However, law schools are not doing a particularly good job of preparing students to pass bar examinations. Bar examination pass rates for first time takers in 2004 ranged from 60% in California to 91% in Mississippi. The average pass rate was 75% in 2004, and over a ten year span was never higher than 79%.[27] Thus, one out of every four law school graduates in the United States did not pass a bar examination on his or her first attempt, even though most bar applicants participated in commercial bar cram courses after graduating from law school.

We encourage law schools to reexamine their current practices and make adjustments to enhance their students' chances of passing a bar examination on their first attempt and without having to pay for and participate in bar preparation courses between law school and the bar examination. At the very least, law schools should help students understand what they are expected to know to succeed on bar examinations and help them locate treatises that contain that information.

Law schools may want to offer bar preparation courses as part of the third year curriculum for credit. The accreditation standards of the ABA allow law schools to offer academic credit for bar examination preparation courses, but they prohibit law schools from requiring students to take such courses or from counting such credits toward the minimum requirements for graduation established in the standards.[28] This seems illogical to us. If the knowledge and skills that students are expected to demonstrate on a bar examination are considered essential to the

---

[25] *Id.* at 79.

[26] *Id.*

[27] *Revised Ten-Year Summary of Bar Passage Rates 1995-2004*, 74 THE BAR EXAMINER 33-35 (Aug. 2005).

[28] Interpretation 302-7, AMERICAN BAR ASSOCIATION, SECTION OF LEGAL EDUCATION AND ADMISSIONS TO THE BAR, STANDARDS AND RULES OF PROCEDURE FOR APPROVAL OF LAW SCHOOLS 19 (2006-2007) [hereinafter ABA STANDARDS].

practice of law by bar admission authorities, law schools should not only be allowed, but should be encouraged to prepare students for bar examinations in the most effective and efficient manner possible for credit and have those credits counted toward the minimum required for graduation by the accrediting authorities. We also see no reason to prohibit a school from requiring students to take such courses if it is inclined to do so.

We are not suggesting that the third year of law school should become one large cram course for the bar examination.[29] Law schools still need to concern themselves with helping students develop the additional knowledge, skills, and values required for law practice but not evaluated by bar examiners. All we are saying is that it seems hypocritical for law schools to collect three years of tuition while failing to prepare most students for law practice and while failing to prepare one in four students for the bar examination.

3.   Law Schools Are Not Fully Committed to Preparing Students for Practice.

There is general agreement today that one of the basic obligations of a law school is to prepare its students for the practice of law. "With formal legal education maintaining a virtual monopoly over preparation for entry into the legal profession, it is assumed that law schools are or ought to be the primary source of the skills and knowledge requisite to the practice of law."[30]

The responsibility of law schools to prepare students for practice was not made clear in the accreditation standards until 1996 after the 1992 MacCrate Report[31] prompted this clarification. Accreditation Standard 301(a) requires an approved law school to "maintain an educational program that prepares its students for admission to the bar *and effective and responsible participation in the legal profession.*"[32] Unfortunately, the implications of this mandate are not fully developed in the accreditation standards.

Law schools serve a number of important functions, but we are concerned only with one in this document – the preparation of new lawyers for practice. From our perspective, a law school can do anything it wants with students who attend law school for purposes other than entering the legal profession. A law school should not, however, try to use the presence of such students as an excuse for not preparing *any* students for the practice of law.

> While people educated in the law may fill a variety
> of societal roles, the principal mission of law school is to
> prepare students for the practice of law, no matter what

---

[29] This would not be a risk, as discussed earlier, if bar examiners were more realistic about the amount of substantive knowledge that lawyers really need before beginning practice. The issue of how much substantive legal doctrine law students need to know is discussed in Chapter Two.

[30] F. Zemans & V. Rosenblum, The Making of a Public Profession 123 (1984).

[31] American Bar Association, Section of Legal Education and Admissions to the Bar, Legal Education and Professional Development – An Educational Continuum, Report of the Task Force on Law Schools and the Profession: Narrowing the Gap [hereinafter MacCrate Report].

[32] Standard 301(a), ABA Standards, *supra* note 28, at 17.

the spillover benefits are for those who will go on to careers as
law teachers, judges, politicians, community organizers, or
business executives.[33]

Without clearer guidance from the accrediation standards and without any
significant internal or external motivators to change the *status quo*, law schools have
been slow to consider the implications of the ABA's mandate to prepare students
for effective and responsible participation in the legal profession. Nevertheless, a
growing number of legal educators is beginning to understand the compelling need to
reexamine the goals and methods of legal education, and some law schools are taking
steps to improve the preparation of their students for practice. This is a trend that
we expect to continue and accelerate.

The Carnegie Foundation's study of legal education found "signs that
education for practice is moving closer to the center of attention in the legal academy,
a positive development and a trend to be encouraged."[34]

Making part of the standard legal curriculum students'
preparation for the transition to practice is likely to make law school
a better support for the legal profession as a whole by providing
more breadth and balance in students' educations. Educational
experiences oriented toward preparation for practice can provide
students with a much-needed bridge between the formal skills of legal
analysis and the more fluid expertise needed in much professional
work. In addition, we think that practice-oriented courses can
provide important motivation for engaging with the moral dimensions
of professional life, a motivation that is rarely accorded status or
emphasis in the present curriculum.[35]

The preparation of students for practice involves much more than simply
training students to perform mechanical lawyering tasks. In reflecting on his
students' suggestion that the sole, or virtually sole, purpose of a law school should be
to provide training for the practice of law, Alan Watson wrote:

There is so much more to the law, even for the practice of law,
than that: issues such as the social functions of law, the factors that
influence legal development, patterns of change, the interaction of
law with other forms of social control such as religion, and, of course,
the relationship of law and ethics. Law students should be trained
to have a greater awareness of their role in society. Law school is *the*
obvious place and time for presenting the greater dimension of law.
Law teachers should cater to the needs of the lawyer philosopher as
well as the lawyer plumber. Both types of lawyer are necessary for a
healthy society.[36]

---

[33] Mark Neal Aaronson, *Thinking Like a Fox: Four Overlapping Domains of Good Lawyering*, 9 Clinical L. Rev. 1, 42 (2002).

[34] Sullivan et al., *supra* note 7, at 96.

[35] *Id.*

[36] Alan Watson, *Legal Education Reform: Modest Suggestions*, 51 J. Legal Educ. 91, 93 (2001) (proposing replacing casebooks with books that would be an amalgam of the standard British legal textbook and the American casebook – and other reforms).

We concur with Watson's comments about the value of broad-based legal education. We also agree with his statement that "most law teachers that I am acquainted with deny that law schools are "trade schools." But to some extent law schools are and must be trade schools. The result of the denial is that law schools are poor trade schools . . . ."[37] We hope this statement of best practices will help law schools become better trade schools, in the best sense of the term.

4.   Law Students Can be Better Prepared for Practice.

Even though it is unrealistic to expect law schools to prepare students fully for practice in three years, law schools can significantly improve their students' preparation for their first professional jobs.

Our system of legal education achieves some worthwhile goals. Some students are prepared for the jobs that await them, especially the top students who are hired by appellate judges or by large law firms, government agencies, and corporations that have the resources and patience to complete their education and training, although even these employers are increasingly forcing their new hires to sink or swim.

The unfortunate reality is that law schools are simply not committed to making their best efforts to prepare all of their students to enter the practice settings that await them. This concern is not a recent development.

> [L]aw schools must accept responsibility for every graduate to whom they award degrees. Karl Llewellyn's assessment a half-century ago is generally still true:
>
>> What has not been done as yet on any important scale at any individual law school is to . . . seek to set up, within the available time, a reasonably rounded, reasonably reliable body of training for a whole student body. That is, as the question of social responsibility raises its head, a sustained effort to make the law school's law degree become a reliable mint mark.
>
> Not long before his death, Llewellyn concluded that anyone "who proposes to practice a liberal art must be technically competent" and that "this minimum competence of each mint-marked law graduate does not appear, as yet, in these United States."[38]

In order to improve the preparation of law students for practice, law schools should expand their educational goals, improve the competence and professionalism of their graduates, and attend to the well-being of their students.

---

[37] *Id.* at 96.

[38] Byron D. Cooper, *The Integration of Theory, Doctrine, and Practice in Legal Education, in* ERASING LINES: INTEGRATING THE LAW SCHOOL CURRICULUM 51, 62-63 (Pamela Lysaght et al. eds., 2002) [hereinafter ERASING LINES] (citations and emphases omitted).

a.   Law schools should expand their educational goals.

Law schools need to expand their educational goals. In 1950, Arthur Vanderbilt wrote that "[t]he keynote we should strike is that all education in the last analysis is self-education . . . that in law schools we are only going to attend to two things, giving them the art of legal reasoning and some of the main principles of law."[39] Some would say this remains a reasonably accurate description of what law schools actually accomplish today, and some academics would probably be content to pursue only these goals. These goals, however, are too limited to meet the needs of law students and the legal profession in today's world.

Historically, law schools have taken their bearings from a conception of the legal world developed at the end of the last century. This was a world composed of legal doctrines with lines drawn between property, contracts, torts, and other "fields" of law. Law schools ever since have given their students a map of this landscape.

But the landscape encountered in law practice is different. It is not populated with cases and doctrine, but with clients and their problems. The lines between the fields of law are blurred or missing altogether. The landscape is messy and unfamiliar. Not surprisingly, new lawyers report being disoriented and unprepared for this world. Some feel cheated by their legal education as they are left to construct a new map and to do so often without the help of an experienced guide.[40]

The core goal of legal education should be the same as all other forms of professional education, which are, according to the authors of the Carnegie Foundation's report on legal education, "to initiate novice practitioners to think, to perform, and to conduct themselves (that, is to act morally and ethically) like professionals."[41] The Carnegie authors observed that toward the goal of knowledge, skills, and attitude, education to prepare professionals involves six tasks:

1. Developing in students the fundamental knowledge and skill, especially an academic knowledge base and research.
2. Providing students with the capacity to engage in complex practice.
3. Enabling students to learn to make judgments under conditions of uncertainty.
4. Teaching students how to learn from experience.
5. Introducing students to the disciplines of creating and participating in a responsible and effective professional community.
6. Forming students able and willing to join an enterprise of public service."

The Carnegie Foundation's report concluded that it is important for law schools to address all of these purposes. "Since in essence, these tasks of professional education represent commonplaces of professional work, a normative model in which

---

[39] SUSAN K. BOYD, THE A.B.A.'s FIRST SECTION: ASSURING A QUALIFIED BAR 59 (1993).

[40] John O. Mudd, *Beyond Rationalization: Performance-Referenced Legal Education,* 35 J. LEGAL EDUC. 189, 197 (1986).

[41] SULLIVAN ET AL., *supra* note 7, at 2.

each feature is essential, we believe that the more effective the preparation for the profession is to be, the more consciously the educational program must actually address all these purposes."[42]

The authors of the Carnegie Foundation's report determined that the near-exclusive focus of law schools on systematic abstraction from actual social contexts suggests two major limitations of legal education:

> One limitation is the casual attention that most law schools give to teaching students how to use legal thinking in the complexity of actual law practice. Unlike other professional education, most notably medical school, legal education typically pays little attention to direct training in professional practice. The result is to prolong and reinforce the habits of thinking like a student rather than an apprentice practitioner, conveying the impression that lawyers are more like competitive scholars than attorneys engaged with the problems of practice.
>
> . . . . .
>
> The second limitation is law schools' failure to complement the focus on skill in legal analysis with effective support for developing the ethical and social dimensions of the profession. Students need opportunities to learn about, reflect on, and practice the responsibilities of legal professionals.[43]

Tony Amsterdam made the following observations about the narrowness of the law school curriculum.

> Legal education is often criticized for being too narrow because it fails to teach students how to practice law – it fails to develop in them practical skills necessary for the competent performance of lawyers' work. But I think this criticism, while just to some extent, conceals a deeper, more important problem, a problem that I think Judge Wallace was alluding to when he said we should be training law students to be problem-solvers. Legal education is too narrow because it fails to develop in students ways of thinking within and about the role of lawyers – methods of critical analysis, planning and decision-making that are not themselves practical skills but rather the conceptual foundations for practical skills and for much else, just as case reading and doctrinal analysis are foundations for practical skills and for much else.[44]

Carrie Menkel-Meadow produced the following description of some of the abilities that law school graduates will need in law practice, in addition to

---

[42] *Id.* at 3.

[43] *Id.* at 240.

[44] Anthony G. Amsterdam, *Clinical Education – Modes of Thinking, in* A Dialogue About Legal Education As It Approaches the 21st Century 12 (1987). Amsterdam went on to describe three kinds of analytic thought that are taught in law schools – case reading and interpretation, doctrinal analysis and application, and logical conceptualization and criticism – and "three of perhaps fifteen or twenty that are not" – ends-means thinking, hypothesis formulation and testing in information acquisition, and decision-making in situations where options involve differing and often uncertain degrees of risks and promises of different sorts.

substantive knowledge, research and writing skills, and traditional analytical skills:

> The lawyer of the next century will need to be able to
> diagnose and analyze problems, to talk to and listen to people, to
> facilitate conversations, to negotiate effectively, to resolve disputes,
> to understand and present complex material, to use ever-changing
> technologies, to plan, to evaluate both economic and emotional
> components and consequences of human decision-making, and to be
> creative – to use tried and true methods when they are appropriate,
> but not to fear new and category-smashing ideas or solutions.[45]

Few of these skills and capacities are given much attention in the traditional law school curriculum even though they are obviously critical for success in law practice.

Law schools should begin by expanding the educational goals of the first year curriculum. The traditional first year curriculum has some strengths, but it also has some shortcomings. Judith Wegner produced the following description of what students learn in the first year curriculum and what they could learn but typically do not.

> *Intellectual Tasks.* "Thinking like a lawyer" involves an
> array of sophisticated intellectual tasks that are generally not named
> or described explicitly, but which correspond to widely-recognized
> cognitive tasks associated with higher-order thinking often familiar
> to those students with strong earlier academic preparation and less
> well-known to others with more non-traditional backgrounds.

> *Legal Literacy.* Students are trained to develop legal
> literacy through emphasis on vocabulary, close reading, and textual
> interpretation, all of which contribute to their ability to develop
> their knowledge and comprehension of the field. Faculty often model
> important ways of "thinking about thinking" particularly with regard
> to testing one's own knowledge and understanding, but rarely cue
> students explicitly about what they are doing or elaborate on the
> importance of such skills.

> *Legal Analysis.* Students are taught a structured form of
> analysis that focuses on individual cases or lines of cases within
> a doctrinal context and emphasizes certain questions relating to
> relevant facts, doctrinal holdings, lines of argumentation, judicial
> reasoning, and the use of cases as precedent.

> *Application.* Students learn to apply abstract principles of
> legal doctrine through experience working with simple hypothetical
> fact-patterns, consideration of current events, and occasional role-
> plays, but there is little apparent effort to stretch their thinking by
> applying the law to more complex problems over time.

> *Synthesis.* Although the abilities to observe complex patterns
> and construct aggregated "chunks" of knowledge are of considerable

---

[45] Carrie Menkel-Meadow, *Taking Problem-Solving Pedagogy Seriously: A Response to the Attorney General*, 49 J. Legal Educ. 14, 14 (1999).

importance, students generally receive little formal instruction about or practice in synthesizing complex ideas, other than through the process of comparing individual cases or observing the models provided by their teachers.

Evaluation. Students are taught to engage in limited forms of evaluation that consider the logic and consistency of doctrinal developments and their relation to conceptual themes developed within a particular course, but are rarely asked to engage in external critiques of the law emphasizing such considerations as fairness or justice, leaving the impression that these topics are of little concern or importance, and providing little chance for them to develop their abilities to evaluate such matters on their own.

Implicit Messages. Students receive subtly different cues regarding the process of learning, the relation of law to the outside world, and the collaborative or competitive nature of professional interaction, depending on instructional strategies used, including classroom roles and forms of dialogue employed.

Learning in Context. Students who receive instruction that is contextualized by reference to problems or professional settings seem to believe that more is expected of them, and treat associated intellectual tasks with a greater seriousness of purpose and a higher level of engagement.

Notable Gaps: The Profession and Perspectives. Students generally receive little systematic grounding in the roles and responsibilities of lawyers, the interrelation between cases and statutes or doctrinal areas, and the broader intellectual and social context in which law operates, with the possible result that these matters are devalued or misimpressions of them are formed.[46]

The first year curriculum gives students a skewed and inaccurate vision of the legal profession and their roles in it. Wegner made the following observations about the negative impact of our failure to give more attention to the issues of role assumption and professional norms in the first year curriculum.

Students wonder, very early, what carefully structured questions and reasoning, the legal universe and its language signify for their future lives as lawyers. As they confront the directive to "think" and function intellectually "like lawyers" they must confront at least two associated types of uncertainty: what it means to assume the role of "lawyer," as distinguished from their ordinary self-concept, and what responsibilities and values are associated with that role. The notion of "thinking like a lawyer," strikingly skirts these questions, in contrast to its treatment of other uncertainties that it meets head on. Instead, uncertainties are blunted as a result of persistently superficial treatment of the exceedingly complex issues of

---

[46] Judith Wegner, Theory, Practice, and the Course of Study – The Problem of the Elephant 51 (Draft 2003) (unpublished manuscript on file with Roy Stuckey) [hereinafter Wegner, Theory and Practice].

role assumption and professional norms. By taking professional roles and values as givens rather than probing the depths of associated quandaries, faculty members avoid troubling uncertainties they often feel uncertain in addressing because of their own inexperience with the practicing profession and their discomfort in negotiating different value claims. As a result, students' underlying uncertainties are held in abeyance, postponing the inevitable confrontations between personal commitments and professional responsibilities in problematic and unhealthy ways.[47]

Wegner further pointed out that "[s]uperficial exposure to the work of lawyers and judges who populate first-year casebooks causes students to absorb professional expectations and norms while putting aside more deep-seated personal uncertainty about future professional roles for the time being" and that narrowing the forms of evaluative judgment that can acceptably be brought to bear, raises "concerns that marginalizing legitimate forms of social criticism may in due course cause personal values gradually to fade from view."[48]

"[T]his is by no means an even contest for the hearts and minds of law students. The first year experience as a whole, without conscious and systematic efforts at counterbalance, tips the scales, as Llewellyn put it, away from cultivating the humanity of the student and toward the student's re-engineering into a 'legal machine.'"[49]

Wegner noted that some first year teachers are making efforts to integrate broader intellectual conceptions of the law and its relation to it into first year classes "in order to provide thematic unity, provide comparative insights from other cultures, bring to bear new theoretical critiques, or integrate aspects of their scholarship into their teaching."[50] She lamented, however, the absence in first year classes of "efforts to link ideas or legal doctrine from one subject to the next."[51]

> Even within single courses it appears difficult for students to grapple with the relationship between case law, statutes, regulations, and rules. There was rarely a sense that faculty members worked together to convey a coherent sense of the field of law to their students or shared such views among themselves, even though it is certainly conceivable that common first-year subjects could be seen to contribute in unique and complementary ways to an overall vision of the field . . . . [52]

Wegner also discovered that "[s]urprisingly, given its relevance, jurisprudence is rarely introduced in a meaningful way."[53]

---

[47] Judith Wegner, "Law is Gray:" "Thinking Like a Lawyer" in the Face of Uncertainty 25-26 (Draft 2003) (unpublished manuscript on file with Roy Stuckey) [hereinafter Wegner, Thinking Like a Lawyer].

[48] *Id.* at 31.

[49] SULLIVAN ET AL., *supra* note 7, at 91.

[50] Judith Wegner, Thinking Like a Lawyer: the Lessons of Experience 48 (Draft 2003) (unpublished manuscript on file with Roy Stuckey) [hereinafter Wegner, Experience].

[51] *Id.*

[52] *Id.*

[53] *Id.*

Programs of instruction during the second and third year at most law schools are little more than a series of unconnected courses on legal doctrine. The educational goals of the programs of instruction and most courses in them are unclear, and no effort is made to help students progressively acquire the knowledge, skills, and values needed for law practice.

After the first year, some teachers continue to stress the development of basic analytical skills, rather than incorporating "some additional mental stretch to higher levels of cognitive functioning or other modalities of learning and knowing. Absent such progression in the nature of learning or knowing, students who have mastered introductory 'thinking' are apt to be bored, while those who are still struggling are apt to tune out and relinquish expectations of becoming engaged."[54] By and large, the focus of instruction after the first year turns toward content.

> While the first year of law school gives pride of place to particular forms of legal reasoning (with the goal of developing higher level cognitive capabilities against the backdrop of common law subject matter), the later years reverse this priority, emphasizing content with forms of knowing or reasoning taking second place.[55]

We encourage law schools to expand their educational objectives to more completely serve the needs of their students and to provide instruction about the knowledge, skills, and values that will enable their students to become effective, responsible lawyers. Specific proposals are discussed later.

b. Law schools should improve the competence and professionalism of their graduates.

Law schools are not producing enough graduates who provide access to justice, are adequately competent, and practice in a professional manner.

(1) Access to justice is lacking.

The legal profession, due in part to the shortcomings of legal education, is failing to meet its obligation to provide access to justice.

> According to most estimates, about four-fifths of the civil legal needs of low income individuals, and two- to three-fifths of the needs of middle-income individuals, remain unmet. Less than one percent of the nation's legal expenditures, and fewer than one percent of its lawyers assist the seventh of the population that is poor enough to qualify for aid. Our nation prides itself on a commitment to the rule of law, but prices it out of reach for the vast majority of its citizens.[56]

> Many of the nation's biggest law firms – inundated with more business than they can often handle and pressing lawyers to raise their billable hours to pay escalating salaries – have cut back on pro bono work so sharply that they fall far below professional guidelines

---

[54] Wegner, Theory and Practice, *supra* note 46, at 7.

[55] *Id.* at 5.

[56] Deborah Rhode, *Access to Justice: Connecting Practices to Principles*, 17 GEO. J. OF LEGAL ETHICS 369, 371 (2004).

for representing people who cannot afford to pay. The roughly 50,000 lawyers in the nation's 100 highest-grossing firms spent an average of just eight minutes a day on pro bono cases in 1999 . . . [or] about 36 hours a year, down significantly from 56 hours in 1992 . . . .[57]

"The best available research finds that American lawyers average less than half an hour work per week and under half a dollar a day in support of pro bono legal assistance. . . . And only 18 of the nation's 100 most financially successful firms meet the Model Rules' standard of 50 hours per year of pro bono service. The approximately 50,000 lawyers at these firms averaged less than 10 minutes per day on pro bono activities."[58] "And seventeen firms were so embarrassed by their pro bono commitment that they refused to share pro bono statistics with *The American Lawyer* at all, even though they proudly shared their income and revenue figures."[59]

The failure of our system to provide adequate legal services to poor people is not a new problem, of course, but it remains an important issue for our society to resolve. Perhaps the importance of providing access to justice for those who cannot afford it was best explained by William Rowe in 1917.

> Our system is highly legalistic. Based as it is upon individual liberty and freedom of justice, all citizens are constantly forced into contact with the law in order to advance their liberty by an ascertainment and protection of individual legal rights, in other words, by seeking justice under law. In this process, lawyers are an absolutely essential element, but, for a majority of our people, the expense of the process, especially under the complicated conditions of modern life, is prohibitive. Hence, the righteous complaint that the liberty and rights of the mass of the people are now crushed and lost beneath the weight of the system. The remedy is plain. The public must, where necessary, bear these particular burdens of government. The people at large and their government must take over and organize the work of legal aid societies, not as a charity or social-service enterprise, but as a necessary and long-neglected government function. For those who cannot bear the burden of expense, legal advice and justice must be free. Otherwise, our boast of freedom, our whole system, indeed, becomes a mockery.[60]

Law schools do not even produce lawyers who meet the needs of the middle class. "The academy has failed to train lawyers who provide legal services to the middle and working classes, which, of course, constitute the overwhelming majority of American society."[61]

> Delivering affordable legal services to the middle class is a challenge that the legal profession has been unable to meet. Advice

---

[57] Greg Winter, *Legal Firms Cutting Back on Free Services to Poor*, N.Y. TIMES, Aug. 17, 2000, at A1.

[58] DEBORAH RHODE, PRO BONO IN PRINCIPLE AND IN PRACTICE 20 (2005) (citations omitted). *See also*, Lawrence J. Fox, *Should We Mandate Doing Well by Doing Good?*, 33 FORDHAM URB. L.J. 249, 250 (2005) (reporting similar data).

[59] Fox, *supra* note 58, at 250.

[60] Rowe, *supra* note 2, at 592.

[61] John B. Attanasio, *Out-of-the-Box Dialogs: Foreword*, 52 J. LEGAL EDUC. 473, 475 (2002).

on topics of daily importance in the lives of individuals, such as
landlord/tenant law, child custody disputes, and testamentary
dispositions is priced beyond the reach of millions of working
Americans. Equal Justice Under the Law is an ideal whose pursuit
is becoming increasingly futile. Wealthy individuals and large
organizations have the financial means to purchase the legal services
they need, while members of the middle class and small business
owners are left to struggle in a legal maze from which extrication is
almost impossible.[62]

Law schools should give more attention to educating students about the importance
of providing access to justice and to instilling a commitment to provide access to
justice in their students.

(2)   Graduates are not sufficiently competent.

Most law school graduates are not sufficiently competent to provide legal
services to clients or even to perform the work expected of them in large firms.
The needs and expectations of the workplaces awaiting law school graduates have
changed since the traditional law school curriculum was developed, even in the large
law firms that serve the legal needs of corporate America. Research conducted by the
American Bar Foundation in the early 1990's reached the following conclusion:

The [hiring] partners today, in contrast to the mid-1970s,
expect relatively less knowledge about the content of law and much
better developed personal skills. It appears that the law firms in
the 1970s could afford to hire smart, knowledgeable law graduates
with as yet immature communication and client skills, place them
in the library, and allow them to develop. Today there is much
less tolerance for a lack of client and communication skills; there
is perhaps more patience with the development of substantive and
procedural expertise in a world of increasing specialization.[63]

Potential clients should be able to hire any licensed lawyer with confidence
that the attorney has demonstrated at least minimal competence to practice law.
Doctors' patients reasonably expect that their doctors have performed medical
procedures multiple times under the supervision of fully qualified mentors before
performing them without supervision. Clients of attorneys should have similar
expectations, but today they cannot.

Legal education today is effectively an indoctrination into
the ideology of the rule of law, seen as the law of rules. Maybe
that was fine fifty years ago. Maybe then, a time that Anthony
Kronman unaccountably waxes romantic about it didn't matter what
students were taught. Like some students today, they could ignore
the normativity, keep their nice doctrinal outlines, and pass the
bar. Thereafter they would find someone who would teach them to
practice law. But, as Kronman recognizes, today the world where

---

[62] Mary C. Daly, *The Structure of Legal Education and the Legal Profession, Multidis-ciplinary Practice, Competition, and Globalization*, 52 J. LEGAL EDUC. 480, 484 (2002).

[63] Bryant G. Garth & Joanne Martin, *Law Schools and the Construction of Competence* 27 (Am. B. Found., Working Paper No. 9212, 1992).

new associates were getting patiently taught how to practice law is long past, if it ever existed for those at the bottom of the profession. Today's world is one where, even in the biggest firms, mentoring is hit or miss at best, and associates are hired in quantities and put to work in ways that ought to remind one of riflemen at Gettysburg or Passendale. In less fancy practices, conditions are even worse, if that is possible.[64]

We encourage law schools to do more to prepare their graduates for the jobs they are likely to have and the contexts they are likely to encounter as new lawyers.

(3)   Too many graduates conduct themselves unprofessionally.

The public has lost much of its trust in lawyers and respect for them. "Survey after survey of public opinion shows lawyers gradually slipping below politicians and journalists, and even approaching car salesmen and advertising executive levels in the public's esteem."[65] "Public opinion polls and surveys indicate that lawyers are poorly viewed by the public and that lawyers' public image has been worsening in the past decade or so. It has been said that attorneys 'have become symbols of everything crass and dishonorable in American public life.'"[66]

In 1984, the ABA established a Commission on Professionalism to study the professionalism of lawyers at the suggestion of United States Supreme Court Chief Justice Warren E. Burger. He observed that the Bar "might be moving away from the principles of professionalism and that it was so perceived by the public."[67] In 1999, the National Conference on Public Trust and Confidence in the Justice System reported that "poor customer relations with the public and the role, compensation and behavior of the bar in the justice system were ranked in the top ten 'Top Priority National Agenda Issues' affecting public trust and confidence in the justice system."[68] Also in 1999, the National Conference of Chief Justices developed a national action plan on lawyer conduct and professionalism in "response to concerns about a perceived decline in lawyer professionalism."[69]

Walter Bennett has stated that changes in legal education are essential if the legal profession is to regain its ideals and identity as a moral community.

In order to restore ideals to the practice of law and rebuild the profession as a moral community, the legal academy must find ways to recontextualize its educational process. This does not mean abandoning

---

[64] John Henry Schlegal, *Walt Was Right*, 51 J. Legal Educ. 599, 608 (2001) (citation omitted).

[65] W. William Hodes, *Truthfulness and Honesty Among American Lawyers: Perception, Reality, and the Professional Reform Initiative*, 53 SC L. Rev. 527, 528 (Spring 2002) (citing multiple sources).

[66] Susan Swain Daicoff, Lawyer Know Thyself 5 (2004) (citations omitted).

[67] American Bar Association, Commission on Professionalism, . . . In the Spirit of Public Service: A Blueprint for the Rekindling of Professionalism (1986).

[68] Conference of Chief Justices, Implementation Plan for the Conference of Chief Justices' National Action Plan on Lawyer Conduct and Professionalism 3 (2002) (citing *the National Conference on Public Trust and Confidence in the Justice System, National Action Plan: A Guide for State and National Organizations* 16 (1999)).

[69] *Id.* at 7.

the teaching and practice of rigorous legal analysis. Rather, it requires undertaking something far more difficult: continuing to teach rigorous legal analysis as well as other lawyerly skills, such as the emerging curricula in alternative dispute resolution, while making all of it morally relevant.

. . . . .

The first step toward making the legal academy operate as a moral community is for it to begin to perceive itself as a community that is part of the larger moral community of the profession. For many law faculties and faculty members, this will require a reorientation on the purpose of legal education. An essential purpose of legal education should be to teach the Holmesian skills of legal analysis and prediction. But it should also be to teach and practice professional ideals. Both law students and faculty should feel the presence of those ideals in the work of law school. At present, ideals receive intermittent attention in law school, and some aspects of legal education actually work to defeat ideals and the promotion of community.[70]

After noting that "[l]awyers have come to be the all-too-frequent butt of mean spirited humor," Bill Sullivan observed that American society needs the professions today as examples of ethical work. "The ethical dimension – living 'as within a larger life,' as Lawrence Haworth has put it – is what is institutionalized in the professions' social contract. This is the essential, but jeopardized, civic dimension of professionalism."[71] Sullivan further explained that the core of professionalism is to recognize that we have a civic identity that comes with duties to the public.

Chief among these duties is the demand that a profession work in such a way that the outcome of the work contributes to the public value for which the profession stands.

What has been missing, then, is not understanding or even appreciation of the value of professionalism so much as trust that professional groups are serious about their purposes. It is not that assertions of good faith on the part of the organized bar or medicine have been lacking in recent years. Rather, the public has seen these professions (in the other sense) as gestures that must be redeemed by concerted action. What has been missing is action in which the professions take public leadership in solving perceived public problems, including the problems of abuse and privilege and refusal of public accountability.[72]

It is not clear to what extent law schools have contributed to the public's loss of trust in lawyers, but we should be trying to be part of the cure by educating students about the traditions and values of the legal profession, by serving as role models, and by striving to infuse in every student a commitment to professionalism.

---

[70] WALTER BENNETT, THE LAWYER'S MYTH: REVIVING IDEALS IN THE LEGAL PROFESSION 169-70 (2001).

[71] WILLIAM M. SULLIVAN, WORK AND INTEGRITY 23 (2005).

[72] *Id.*

Ours is an era marked by a growing body of lawyers trained by an increasing number of law schools who then enter unstable and highly competitive domains of practice. Under these conditions, it has proven hard to make the old ideals of independent public service the basis of everyday legal practice. The result has been confusion and uncertainty about what goals and values should guide professional judgment in practice, leaving many lawyers "wandering amidst the ruins of those [past] understandings."

Not in spite of but precisely because of these social pressures, legal education needs to attend very seriously to its apprenticeship of professional identity. Professional education is highly formative. The challenge is to deploy this formative power in the authentic interests of the profession and the students as future professionals. Under today's conditions, students' great need is to begin to develop the knowledge and abilities that can enable them to understand and manage these tensions in ways that will sustain their professional commitment and personal integrity over the course of their careers. In a time of professional disorientation, the law schools have an opportunity to provide direction. Law schools can help the profession become smarter and more reflective about strengthening its slipping legitimacy by finding new ways to advance its enduring commitments.[73]

Many legal scholars have encouraged law schools to change,[74] and some law schools are making greater efforts to provide instruction about professionalism.[75] So far, however, not enough is being done to change the outcomes at most law schools. All legal educators should take leadership roles in making professionalism instruction a central part of law school instruction.

c.   **Law schools should attend to the well-being of their students.**

The problems with legal education extend far beyond educational shortcomings. There are clear and growing data that legal education is harmful to the emotional and psychological well-being of many law students.[76]

---

[73] SULLIVAN ET AL., *supra* note 7, at 153-54 (citations omitted).

[74] Annotated lists of books and articles about the need to improve professionalism instruction are located on the Professionalism of Lawyers and Judges website at http://professionalism.law.sc.edu. *See also, Symposium Issue: Therapeutic Jurisprudence in Clinical Education and Legal Skills Training*, 17 ST. THOMAS L. REV. (2005). An especially creative and insightful article is Joseph G. Allegretti, *In a Dark Wood: Dante as a Spiritual Guide for Lawyers*, 17 ST. THOMAS L. REV. 875 (2005).

[75] Some of the professionalism programs at law schools are described on the Professionalism of Lawyers and Judges website, http://professionalism.law.sc.edu. The Professionalism Committee of the American Bar Association conducted a survey and published a report on law school professionalism programs in 2006, *available at* http://www.abanet.org/cpr/reports/LawSchool_ProfSurvey.pdf.

[76] The following list includes some of the more well-known articles about the negative impacts of legal education. They include cites to many studies, some of which are ongoing. Lawrence S. Krieger, *The Inseparability of Professionalism and Personal Satisfaction: Perspectives on Values, Integrity and Happiness*, 11 CLINICAL L. REV. 425 (2005) [hereinafter, Krieger, *Professionalism and Personal Satisfaction*]; Lawrence S. Krieger, *Institutional Denial About the Dark Side of Law School, and Fresh Empirical Guidance for Constructively Breaking the*

It is well-known that lawyers suffer higher rates of depression, anxiety and other mental illness, suicide, divorce, alcoholism and drug abuse, and poor physical health than the general population or other occupations.[77] These problems are attributed to the stress of law practice, working long hours, and seeking extrinsic rather than intrinsic rewards in legal practice.[78]

It is less well-known that these problems begin in law school. Although law students enter law school healthier and happier than other students, they leave law school in much worse shape. "It is clear that law students become candidates for emotional dysfunction immediately upon entry into law school and face continued risks throughout law school and subsequent practice."[79]

The harm to students is caused by the educational philosophies and practices of many law school teachers. Educational theorists tell us that we should strive to create classroom experiences where "[t]he classroom is and must be a protected place, where students discover themselves and gain knowledge of the world, where they are free of all threats to their well-being, where all received opinion is open to evaluation, where all questions are legitimate, where the explicit goal is to see the world more openly, fully, and deeply."[80] Instead, too many law school classrooms, especially during the first year, are places where students feel isolated, embarrassed, and humiliated, and their values, opinions, and questions are not valued and may even be ridiculed.

Daisy Hurst Floyd vividly described the impact that current educational practices have on many law students.

> Students come to law school with an idea that being a lawyer is something meaningful, something important and valuable. They are drawn to a vision that includes a job undertaken in relationship with and on behalf of other people, helping clients to solve problems or move through difficult times. While they may not have a detailed or even realistic picture of what lawyers do, students envision themselves engaged in professional work that is intellectually challenging and that has value and meaning. They arrive at law school with hope and expectation that their work as lawyers will have a positive impact for society as a whole.

. . . . .

Silence, 52 J. LEGAL EDUC. 112 (2002) [hereinafter, Krieger, *Institutional Denial*]; Gulati et al., *supra* note 3; Patrick J. Schiltz, *On Being a Happy, Healthy, and Ethical Member of an Unhappy, Unhealthy, and Unethical Profession*, 52 VAND. L. REV. 871 (1999); Ann L. Iijima, *Lessons Learned: Legal Education and Law Student Dysfunction*, 48 J. LEGAL EDUC. 524 (1998); Lawrence S. Krieger, *What We're Not Telling Law Students (and Lawyers) That They Really Need to Know: Some Thoughts in Action Toward Revitalizing the Profession from its Roots*, 13 J. LAW AND HEALTH 1 (1998) [hereinafter, Krieger, *What We're Not Telling*]; Note, *Making Docile Lawyers: An Essay on the Pacification of Law Students*, 111 HARV. L. REV. 2027 (1998); R. GRANFIELD, MAKING ELITE LAWYERS (1992); Barbara A. Glesner, *Fear and Loathing in the Law Schools*, 23 CONN. L. REV. 627 (1991).

[77] *See, e.g.*, Schiltz, *supra* note 76.

[78] *See, e.g., id.*

[79] Iijima, *supra* note 76, at 526.

[80] JAMES M. BANNER, JR. & HAROLD C. CANNON, THE ELEMENTS OF TEACHING 37 (1997).

Upon beginning law school, students quickly learn that law school values rational, objective analysis to the exclusion of other qualities, such as self-awareness and interpersonal relationships. They also learn that winning – as measured by the prizes of grades, law review membership, and certain jobs – is the most important goal. They believe that they must adopt those values as part of their changing professional identities. They believe that their personal visions of lawyering are naive and unrealistic. As a result, students replace their hopeful expectations for finding meaning and purpose in their work. They will accept unfulfilling work environments because they think there is no other option.[81]

Hurst's conclusion is that "law school causes students to lose the sense of purpose that made them want to become lawyers. This loss is not only harmful to individual students, but it also has enormous negative consequences for the profession and for those served by the profession."[82]

Susan Daicoff described similar negative consequences produced by legal education.

Although everyone who has been through it knows that law school has dramatic effects, there is empirical evidence to flesh out what actually changes when one learns to "think like a lawyer." People who come to law school with a rights orientation either keep it or it becomes more ingrained. Many of those who come to law school with an ethic of care appear to lose it and adopt a rights orientation by the end of the first year. Law students become less interested in community, intimacy, personal growth, and inherent satisfaction and more interested in appearance, attractiveness, and garnering the esteem of others. Cynicism about the legal profession increases and opinions of lawyers and the legal system become more guarded and negative by the end of the first year of law school, but an elitist protectiveness of the profession also emerges. Interest in public interest and public service work decreases as a result of law school. Students also become less intellectual (i.e., less philosophical and introspective and less interested in abstractions, ideas, and the scientific method) perhaps in favor of more realistic, practical values. Law school inadvertently discourages collaborative peer relationships, instead fostering more competitive interactions. It unintentionally rewards introversion and pessimistic attitudes.[83]

There are empirical data that the law school experience can cause psychological harm. A substantial empirical study of psychological distress in law students was conducted in 1986 by G. Andrew Benjamin and others. The study found that "[l]evels of psychological distress rose significantly for first year students and persisted throughout law school and for two years after graduation. The results are especially strong because they remained consistent regardless of age, gender, and

---

[81] Daisy Hurst Floyd, *Reclaiming Purpose – Our Students' and Our Own*, 10 THE LAW TEACHER 1 (2003).

[82] *Id.*

[83] DAICOFF, *supra* note 66, at 76-77.

law school grades."[84] Symptoms of distress included depression, obsessive-compulsive behavior, interpersonal sensitivity (feelings of inadequacy and inferiority), anxiety, hostility, paranoia, and psychoticism (social alienation and isolation).

"Many students report that the law school environment results in loss of self-esteem and alienation. Large percentages believe that they were more articulate and intelligent before beginning their legal education and that they felt pressure to put aside their values in law school. These negative effects appear to be especially prevalent among women and people of color."[85]

Christophe Courchesne concluded that "[b]y and large, one can attribute this range of disastrous outcomes, namely the severance of supportive social ties, eventual disengagement with academics, and marginalization of women and minorities, to institutional failures of the law school in adapting the Langdellian model, particularly its fixation with grades-based elitism and its lack of attention to non-academic student needs."[86]

Gerry Hess identified the sources of law student distress and alienation as the grading and ranking system that serve as gatekeepers to the reward system during and after law school; the high cost of legal education, which pressures students to qualify for the best paying jobs; the overwhelming workload of law school that leaves little time for sleep, relaxation, and relationships with friends and family; and the narrowly focused curriculum that concentrates on analytical skills while minimizing the development of the interpersonal skills that are critical for law practice.[87]

> [The curriculum] teaches that tough-minded analysis, hard facts, and cold logic are the tools of a good lawyer, and it has little room for emotion, imagination, and morality. For some students, "learning to think like a lawyer" means abandoning their ideals, ethical values, and sense of self.[88]

Kirsten Edwards placed some of the blame on professors who intimidate students, demean their opinions and insult their values.

> [I]t can be argued that the problem stems not from what is being said to the students, nor even the method by which it is said, but rather the attitude of the people doing the talking. ... Is it possible that students' sense of justice, humanity and common good are harmed less by the lack of certainty of legal principle, or lack of reverence for the traditions of the law, than by teachers who deliberately and systematically undertake to ruin students' sense of

---

[84] Gerald F. Hess, *Heads and Hearts: The Teaching and Learning Environment in Law School*, 52 J. LEGAL EDUC. 75, 77 (2002) (citing *The Role of Legal Education in Producing Psychological Distress Among Law Students and Lawyers*, 1986 AM. B. FOUND. RES. J. 225).

[85] *Id.* at 77 (citing Joan M. Drauskopf, *Touching the Elephant: Perceptions of Gender Issues in Nine Law Schools*, 44 J. LEGAL EDUC. 311, 328 (1994); Suzanne Homer & Lois Schwartz, *Admitted But Not Accepted: Outsiders Take an Inside Look at Law School*, 5 BERKELEY WOMEN'S L. J. 52 (1990)).

[86] Courchesne, *supra* note 13, at 31. *See also* GRANFIELD, *supra* note 76, at 71 (reaching similar conclusions).

[87] Hess, *supra* note 84, at 78.

[88] *Id.* at 79.

self-worth and the value of their own ideas?[89]

Larry Krieger and Ken Sheldon recently undertook a longitudinal study of law students, and the data produced from their study provide new insights into the harm that legal education in the United States does to many students, particularly how it undermines the values and motivation that promote professionalism.

> [I]ncoming students were happier, more well-adjusted, and more idealistic/intrinsically oriented than a comparison undergraduate sample. This refutes the idea that problems in law schools and the profession may result from self-selection by people with skewed values or who are already unhappy.

> Well-being and life satisfaction fell very significantly during the first year. More fundamentally, the general intrinsic values and motivations of the students shifted significantly towards the more extrinsic orientations. These shifts have distinct negative implications for the students' well-being. In the sample followed for the final two years of law school, these measures did not rebound. Instead, students experienced a further and troubling diminution of all of their valuing processes (both intrinsic and extrinsic) beginning in the second year, suggesting a sense of disinterest, disengagement, and loss of enthusiasm. This loss of valuing is a serious occurrence and a likely cause of the continued loss of well-being measured among these students. It may well mark the beginning of the destructive "values-neutral" approach of many lawyers.

> The findings that students became depressed and unhappy in the first year and remained so throughout law school are consistent with previous studies. Our further investigation of values and motivation was the first such study of which I am aware. All of the data provides empirical support for the concern that our legal training has precisely the opposite impact on students from that suggested by our rhetoric – it appears to undermine the values and motivation that promote professionalism as it markedly diminishes life satisfaction. All indications are that when students graduate and enter the profession, they are significantly different people from those who arrived to begin law school: they are more depressed, less service-oriented, and more inclined toward undesirable, superficial goals and values.[90]

Kreiger and Sheldon concluded from their data that "[s]omething distinctly bad is happening to the students in our law schools."[91] While calling on law teachers and other researchers to review their attitudes and educational practices to identify those most likely to have a deleterious effect on the basic needs of law students, Krieger suggests that some of the likely culprits include the belief held by many

---

[89] Kirsten Edwards, *Found! The Lost Lawyer*, 70 FORDHAM L. REV. 37, 70 (2001).

[90] Krieger, *Professionalism and Personal Satisfaction*, supra note 76, at 433-34 (citations omitted). Krieger and Sheldon also determined that the students who made the highest grades in law school "suffered losses in well-being and life satisfaction to the same extent as the rest of their class." Krieger, *Institutional Denial*, supra note 76, at 123.

[91] Krieger, *Institutional Denial*, supra note 76, at 115.

students that success in law school is measured by being in the top ten percent of the class, appointment to a law review, and similar academic honors; the corollary sense that personal worth depends on one's place in the hierarchy of academic success; the belief that the American dream is achieved by financial affluence and other external indicia of achievement (and that success in law school will secure the dream); and the emphasis on one form of "thinking like a lawyer" converts students into people who define people primarily according to their legal rights, who learn to resolve legal problems by linear application of legal rules to those rights, and using competitive approaches to resolving problems. "Thinking 'like a lawyer' is fundamentally negative; it is critical, pessimistic, and depersonalizing. It is a damaging paradigm in law schools because it is usually conveyed, and understood, as a new and superior way of thinking, rather than an important but strictly limited legal tool."[92]

> All of these paradigms share a powerful, atomistic worldview and a zero-sum message about life in the law and in law school. For every winner there is a loser, and if anything beyond winning or losing matters, it doesn't matter much. The theme for law students is constant: you must work very, very hard, and you must excel in the competition for grades and honors, in order to feel good about what you have done, have the respect of your teachers and peers, get a desirable job, and generally be successful.[93]

Krieger has proposed that law schools should "investigate our predilection to work students exceptionally hard," because "it teaches students to accept constant stress and to associate it with a law career."[94] The contingent-worth and top-ten-percent paradigms, coupled with mandatory grade curves and law schools' over reliance on the Socratic dialogue and case method, produce constant tension and insecurity about outperforming other students, and create the impression that personal values, ideals, and intentions are largely irrelevant to law school or law practice. "One could hardly design purposely a more effective belief system for eroding the self-esteem, relatedness, authenticity, and security of an affected population."[95]

While Steven Hartwell agrees with Krieger that law school unnecessarily harms some students, he believes that depression among law students is primarily caused by the negative impact that legal education has on students' moral development. "Attending law school arrests the moral development of many if not most students, a halt that most likely would not occur if these same students had attended a different graduate program."[96] Hartwell begins his article with "a quote from Carl Jung to the effect that neurosis, that is, a 'psychiatric disorder characterized by depression, anxiety and hypochondria,' is the suffering of a soul, that is, the suffering of one's 'essence, the deepest and truest nature' that has not discovered its meaning."[97]

---

[92] *Id.* at 117.

[93] *Id.*

[94] *Id.* at 124.

[95] *Id.*

[96] Steven Hartwell, *Moral Growth or Moral Angst? A Clinical Approach,* 1 Clinical L. Rev. 115, 118-19 (2004).

[97] *Id.* at 115.

"Meaning" here refers to an "inner importance" in a psychological, spiritual or moral sense. Law students in great numbers are classically neurotic, suffering from alarmingly high levels of reported depression and anxiety. Many suffer, in my view, because law school education arrests student moral development such that law students fail to advance towards postconventional moral reasoning as they might anticipate in attending a graduate program. They remain mired at the same level of conventional moral reasoning at which they entered law school. They have not discovered their moral meaning. The reason students fail to advance may result from the nature of law as a subject matter, from the way law is taught, from the moral development level of the instructors, from some combination of these reasons or from other reasons I have not understood.[98]

Hartwell does not think his theory is inconsistent with Krieger's conclusions.

In other ways, Krieger's assessment that students fall into depression because of their shift to extrinsic motivation and my assessment that they fall into depression because their expectations of continued development in their moral reasoning are not that different. As individuals move from basing moral decisions on personal interest to conventional and then to postconventional moral thinking, they also move from extrinsic moral motivators to intrinsic moral motivators. Personal interest motivators are completely extrinsic. They involve avoiding punishment and obtaining awards. The motivators of conventional moral thinking are a mix of extrinsic and intrinsic. On the one hand, they entail the extrinsic motivators of social acceptance for being seen as a "good person" as well as the intrinsic motivation of incorporating civic rules in support of society. Postconventional moral thinking is almost entirely intrinsically motivated. Postconventional motivators entail the conscious choice of rational values that will lead to a healthier and more just society.[99]

Hartwell proposed that law schools can promote moral development and reduce the degree of depression among students by being more candid with students about the nature and risks of legal education and by using more experiential teaching methods. Experiential teaching is student centered, takes clients seriously, and values feelings as much as thinking, whereas the Socratic dialogue and case method is teacher centered, gives little consideration to clients, and treats feelings as irrelevant.

I see two ways to help these students. One way would be for law school faculty and administrations to be more candid in warning law school applicants about the real "meaning" of a law school education. Students would be healthier if the law schools were not in denial. A second way would be for law schools to change their pedagogy so as to encourage growth in moral reasoning. The data reported in this article from experientially taught professional responsibility courses suggest that students can make dramatic

---

[98] *Id.* at 146 (citations omitted).
[99] *Id.* at 140 (citations omitted).

strides towards postconventional moral reasoning over the course of a single semester.[100]

Whatever the causes, something about legal education in the United States is unnecessarily harming students. For law schools to provide students with the knowledge, skills, and values they will need to participate effectively and responsibly in the legal profession and live satisfied, healthy lives, legal educators should reexamine their attitudes and paradigms, as well as their methods of instructing students.

5.   Principles of Accountability and Consumer Protection Require Change.

The accountability movement in higher education is likely to force law schools to improve the preparation of students for practice, whether or not all law teachers want to move in this direction.

> The assessment movement is knocking at the door of American legal education. Legal education in the United States is renowned for its adherence to traditional case books, Socratic teaching method, single end-of-the-semester final exams, and an unwillingness to change. Now, regional accrediting bodies, acting under the aegis of the U.S. Department of Education, are demanding that law schools, as units of accredited colleges and universities, state their missions and outcomes, explain how their curricula are designed to achieve those outcomes, and identify their methods for assessing student performance and institutional outcomes.[101]

Consumerism is the driving force behind the accountability movement. If law schools cannot find ways to improve their performance on their own, they can expect increasing pressure from outside forces seeking to protect the consumers of law schools' products – students, employers, and clients.

> For most of its 366-year history, American higher education has been a largely self-regulated industry of nonprofit, private, and public institutions. Colleges and universities have been accountable principally to colleagues and peers in regional and specialized accrediting groups and state and federal departments of higher education. In recent years, however, the level and type of accountability have changed. Colleges and universities are now increasingly responding to questions and criticisms from non-educational groups including political leaders and elected representatives at the state and federal level, from various non-educational agencies including the Internal Revenue Service, the Environmental Protection Agency, the Federal Bureau of Investigation, the Justice Department, the Human Rights Commission, and so on, as well as the media and general public. In addition, the accreditation groups and educational bodies traditionally responsible for evaluating higher education are also under attack for their ineffectiveness in protecting the consumer.

---

[100] *Id.* at 147.

[101] MUNRO, *supra* note 4, at 3.

And to make matters worse, as we well know in legal education, when accrediting groups have attempted to uphold standards and accountability, they have been assailed and even sued by institutions that did not agree with their decisions.

In an age of increasing consumerism, one thing is certain: higher education will be closely watched, evaluated, and criticized by more people and from more quarters in the future than at any other time in its history. To what extent the balance of this evaluation will be shifted from the traditional collegial peer evaluation to extend to groups including politicians, non-educational governmental agencies, the media, and the general public remains to be seen.[102]

The Best Practices Project was undertaken in the spirit of fixing our own house before reform is imposed from the outside. Hopefully, the product of our work will help law schools broaden their educational goals, improve the preparation of students for practice, and become more accountable for their products and more consumer-oriented in their educational practices.

---

[102] John L. Lahey & Janice C. Griffith, *Recent Trends in Higher Education: Accountability, Efficiency, Technology, and Governance*, 52 J. LEGAL EDUC. 528, 528-29 (2002) (citations omitted).

Chapter Two
Best Practices for Setting Goals of the Program of Instruction[103]

A.   Be Committed to Preparing Students for Practice.

Principle: The school is committed to preparing its students to practice law effectively and responsibly in the contexts they are likely to encounter as new lawyers.

Comments:

Law schools should demonstrate their commitment to preparing students for practice. They should begin with mission statements that include a commitment to prepare students to practice law effectively and responsibly in the contexts they are likely to encounter as new lawyers.

Most law schools have multiple missions. At its core, however, legal education is a professional education, and part of the mission of every law school is to prepare its students to enter the legal profession. It is why law schools exist.

The accreditation standards of the American Bar Association require law schools to prepare their students for practice. All ABA-approved law schools must "maintain an educational program that prepares its students for admission to the bar and *effective and responsible participation in the legal profession*."[104] Thus, it seems self-evident that a law school should include this objective in its mission statement.

A mission statement explains to prospective students, alumni, and contributors how the school views its reasons for existing.

Ideally, the articulated mission of the school will be the result of a dialogue between members of the law faculty and representatives of the constituencies of the law school. Such a group can identify the functions that the school should serve. The process of articulating a mission will likely identify functions that the school already performs. But it may reveal other roles that the group feels ought to be undertaken, or it may uncover a consensus that the school should no longer perform a particular function. The group should distinguish mission from outcomes and teaching methods. . . .

The resulting mission statement should reflect the values of the particular institution.

. . . . .

In the end, the articulated mission should be a brief statement of the overall goals and objectives of the law school in its

---

[103] "Program of instruction" includes all curricular and co-curricular components that are developed by a law faculty to support the educational mission of a law school.
[104] Standard 301(a), ABA STANDARDS, *supra* note 28, at 17 (emphasis added).

role of serving society. Ideally, it is concisely and perhaps elegantly drafted to inspire in others a desire to support the mission.[105]

More important than words on paper, of course, is that the institution actually be committed to doing the best job it can to prepare its graduates to practice law effectively and responsibly in the contexts they are likely to encounter as new lawyers. Evidence of such commitment could be the extent to which a school employs best practices for legal education, as described in this document or elsewhere.

B.   Clearly Articulate Educational Goals.

Principle: The school clearly articulates its educational goals.

Comments:
There is nothing more important for any educational institution than to have clearly articulated educational goals. A law school cannot determine whether it is achieving its educational goals unless the goals are clear and specific. A law school's educational objectives should be published and made available to prospective and current students, alumni, and employers.

The educational goals of most law schools in the United States are articulated poorly, if at all. This is one of the primary reasons why most law school curriculums can best be described as chaotic: they lack cohesion, coordination, and common purpose, especially after the first year.

Law teachers have consistently rejected calls to define their objectives more clearly. In 1971, the Carrington Report encouraged law teachers to be more precise about their educational objectives.

> While most law teachers would assert that they are teaching much beside legal doctrine, few are eager to say precisely what. Some have been content to describe their work as teaching students "to think like lawyers," although that phrase is so circular that it is essentially meaningless. Perhaps the reluctance to be more specific is borne in part by a distaste for platitudes. Or perhaps it reflects the instinct of lawyers (shared by others who are experienced in human conflict) that it is more difficult to secure approval of goals than means. This reluctance should be overcome, partly to try to help students get a better sense of direction, but also in order to direct attention to the "hidden curriculum" which serves to transmit professional traits and values by the process of subliminal inculturation.[106]

---

[105] MUNRO, *supra* note 4, at 87.

[106] AALS Curriculum Study Project Committee, *Training for the Public Professions of the Law: 1971*, *reprinted in* HERBERT L. PACKER & THOMAS EHRLICH, NEW DIRECTIONS IN LEGAL EDUCATION 93, 129 (1972) [hereinafter PACKER & EHRLICH] (concluding that "[l]aw teachers are confused about legal education and the form that it has been forced to take by the interplay of bar admission requirements, professional organization, and the law schools. They are unclear about the goals of the second and third years of legal education. They are often frustrated in their scholarship and uncertain about their professional and academic roles. Increasingly disappointed and impatient students interact with increasingly frustrated and confused teachers and emerge with a patchwork professional education and an ambivalent view of themselves as

In addition to clarifying what we are trying to teach, it is important that we explain our teaching objectives to our students. Part of the stress and confusion that first year students experience is caused by our failure to explain why we are having them read appellate cases and wrestle with questions that do not seem to have any correct answers. This is a problem that can be easily cured by developing transparent teaching objectives and helping students understand what we are trying to accomplish.

In her examination of the process of learning to "think like a lawyer," Judith Wegner determined that most first year students reach a point where they master the concept and a "phase shift" occurs in their understanding of knowledge and the process of knowing. She notes, however, that the progressive development of legal reasoning skills and the ultimate "phase shift" could be accomplished more quickly with less stress if the educational objectives were made clear to students. "Unfortunately, the critical underlying 'phase-shift' associated with legal 'thinking' is rarely recognized and articulated, when it might better be rendered visible and addressed."[107]

Part of the problem with clarifying the goals of legal education is that the world of increased specialization, coupled with the innumerable fields of law that await law school graduates, makes it impossible for three years of law school to prepare students to practice competently in every field of law. The requisite knowledge and skills are simply too diverse. There are several logical responses to the disconnect between law schools' general education mission and the legal market's demand for lawyers with very specific and extremely diverse types of competencies. Law schools could either:
  • prepare students to provide a limited range of legal services,
  • prepare students for very specific areas of practice, or
  • help students develop fundamental competencies common to multiple practice areas, counting on students to acquire specialized knowledge and skills after graduation.

Law schools in the United States have long asserted that they are achieving the third objective, but in fact we mostly teach basic principles of substantive law and a much too limited range of analytical skills and other competencies, such as legal research and writing.

There is a place in legal education for "niche" law schools that seek to prepare students for very specific areas of practice, or even for specialty tracks in any law school's curriculum.[108] The creation of more niche schools or specialty tracks would

---

professionals.").

[107] Wegner, Thinking Like a Lawyer, *supra* note 47, at 11.

[108] Alfred Reed predicted in 1921 that law schools would inevitably begin teaching lawyers to be specialists rather than generalists. He noted that even in 1921 most lawyers confined their practices to a few areas of practice, though they were initially trained as generalists. He believed there was already too much law for law schools to possibly teach thoroughly. "As there seems to be no practicable means of reducing the volume of the law in the near future, and nobody wants the law to be less thoroughly taught, the only available remedy is the direction of specialized schools leading into specialized branches of the profession. This development will probably not occur very soon. It will probably not occur as soon as it ought. Sooner or later, as the existing unitary organization of legal education, and of the profession itself, proves inadequate to meet the requirements of actual practice, the organization will be changed to correspond." Alfred Z. Reed, Training for the Public Profession of the Law (1921),

be a particularly appealing development if legal education would become more affordable for some and produce lawyers who are proficient in areas where unmet legal needs are greatest. As explained by Deborah Rhode:

> It makes no sense to require the same training for the Wall Street securities specialist and the small town matrimonial lawyer. While some students may want a generalist degree, others could benefit from a more specialized advanced curriculum or from shorter, more affordable programs that would prepare graduates for limited practice areas. ... Almost no institutions require students to be proficient in areas where unmet legal needs are greatest, such as bankruptcy, immigration, uncontested divorces, and landlord-tenant matters.[109]

While specialized programs of instruction may be appropriate for some schools, most law schools, especially state-supported schools, have missions that require them to try to prepare students for a wide range of practice options. Thus, they have little choice than to try to help students develop the fundamental competencies common to most practice areas and the characteristics of effective and responsible lawyers.

C.   Articulate Goals in Terms of Desired Outcomes

Principle: The school articulates its educational goals in terms of desired outcomes, that is, what the school's students should know, understand, and be able to do, and the attributes they should have when they graduate.

Comments:
        1.   What "Outcomes" Means.

A statement of educational goals should describe, to the extent possible, what the school's students will be able to do after graduating and how they will do it in addition to what they will know, that is, it should describe the school's desired outcomes. The importance of clearly specifying the desired outcomes for curriculum planning purposes is well-recognized by educational theorists:

---

reprinted as edited by Kate Wallach in Packer & Ehrlich, *supra* note 106, at 163, 186. Reed recognized, however, that "[p]rospective practitioners of different vocations must receive part of their education in common, for reasons of economy: the community cannot afford to establish specialized machinery for more than the final stage of training. They must do so for what is technically known as "orientation": when they start their education, they do not know what they will eventually do, and it is against public policy that they should be forced to make a too early decision. They must do so in order to establish an equipoise to the narrowing tendencies of training for one particular end: the late war has fortified in this country the English tradition that education which conduces in no way, that human calculation can foresee, to the efficient discharge of our particular duties, whether as citizens or as individuals, may nevertheless have a value of its own, by widening our sympathies, teaching us toleration of another's point of view, freeing us from the temptation to subordinate humanitarian impulses to the demands of ruthless logic." *Id.*

[109] Deborah L. Rhode, In the Interests of Justice 190 (2000).

When objectives are not made explicit, the result is almost certainly a preoccupation with specific knowledge.

If students are expected to develop a degree of independence in pursuit of learning, reach a satisfactory level of skill in communication, demonstrate sensitivity to their own values and those of their associates, become capable of collaborating with peers in defining and resolving problems, be able to recognize the relevance of their increasing knowledge to the current scene, and seek continually for insightful understanding and organization of their educational experience, these outcomes must be specifically stated. In addition, they must be made explicit in relation to learning experiences and by providing opportunities for demonstration of the developing behavior and for evaluation of it.

Content, subject matter, and behavior are interrelated and must be so construed by teachers, students, and evaluators. This requires an interrelated trinity of conceptual statements defining the objectives of operational statements, indicating how the behavior is to be evoked and appraised, and providing standards for deciding whether progress is evident and whether accomplishment is finally satisfactory. If this approach is fully implemented, the traditional distinctions between majors and distribution (or between depth and breadth) become meaningless.

No matter what the elements involved in planning a curriculum, it must involve content and learning experiences chosen to produce the ultimate capabilities desired in those whose educational experiences it provides.[110]

Educational theorists most frequently describe outcomes as having three components: knowledge, skills, and values. "Statements of intended educational (student) outcomes are descriptions of what academic departments intend for students to know (cognitive), think (attitudinal), or do (behavioral) when they have completed their degree programs . . . ."[111] As indicated in the preceding quote, educational theorists usually refer to "attitudes" instead of "values." Either word would suffice, but we prefer using "values" because attitudes are the products of value systems. Values are the bases from which preferences arise and on which all decisions are made. They guide human action and decisions in daily situations.[112]

Currently, when law schools articulate educational goals, they almost universally refer to what students will do in class, what they will learn about the law,

---

[110] PAUL L. DRESSEL, HANDBOOK OF ACADEMIC EVALUATION: ASSESSING INSTITUTIONAL EFFECTIVENESS, STUDENT PROGRESS, AND PROFESSIONAL PERFORMANCE FOR DECISION MAKING IN HIGHER EDUCATION 316-17 (1976).

[111] JAMES O. NICHOLS, THE DEPARTMENTAL GUIDE AND RECORD BOOK FOR STUDENT OUTCOMES ASSESSMENT AND INSTITUTIONAL EFFECTIVENESS 17 (1995).

[112] MILTON ROKEACH, THE NATURE OF HUMAN VALUES 14 (1973). "Values are determinants of virtually all kinds of behavior that could be called social behavior – of social action, attitudes and ideology, evaluations, moral judgments and justifications of self and others, comparisons of self with others, presentations of self to others, and attempts to influence others." *Id.* at 24.

or what specific skills they will acquire, not what they will be able to do with their knowledge and skills or how they should do it.

The ABA accreditation standards also describe curriculum requirements in terms of course content. The standards require law schools to provide instruction encompassing a broad range of topics, although these are described in general terms for the most part and are content-focused rather than outcomes-focused.

> A law school shall require that each student receive substantial instruction in:
> (1) the substantive law generally regarded as necessary to effective and responsible participation in the legal profession;
> (2) legal analysis and reasoning, legal research, problem-solving, and oral communication;
> (3) writing in a legal context, including at least one rigorous writing experience in the first year and at least one additional rigorous writing experience after the first year;
> (4) other professional skills generally regarded as necessary to effective and responsible participation in the legal profession; and
> (5) the history, goals, structure, values, and responsibilities of the legal profession and its members.[113]

On the other hand, the Preamble to the Standards, which is not part of the accreditation mandates, contains the following statement that expresses curricular objectives in a more outcomes-focused manner:

> . . . [A]n approved law school must provide an opportunity for its students to study in a diverse educational environment, and in order to protect the interests of the public, law students, and the profession, it must provide an educational program that ensures that its graduates:
>
> (1) understand their ethical responsibilities as representatives of clients, officers of the courts, and public citizens responsible for the quality and availability of justice;
> (2) receive basic education through a curriculum that develops:
>> (i) understanding of the theory, philosophy, role, and ramifications of the law and its institutions;
>> (ii) skills of legal analysis, reasoning, and problem solving; oral and written communication; legal research; and other fundamental skills necessary to participate effectively in the legal profession;
>> (iii) understanding of the basic principles of public and private law; and
> (3) understand the law as a public profession calling for performance of pro bono legal services.[114]

---

[113] Standard 302, ABA STANDARDS, *supra* note 28, at 17-18.
[114] *Preamble, id.* at viii.

We encourage law schools to describe their desired outcomes in terms of what their students will know, be able to achieve, and how they will do it upon graduation. We also encourage the ABA Section of Legal Education and Admissions to the Bar to rewrite the accreditation standards in outcomes-focused language. The standards should describe the core knowledge, skills, and values that all law schools should strive to teach.

2. The Global Movement Toward Outcomes-Focused Education.

A transition from content-focused to outcomes-focused instruction is underway in legal education programs in other countries and in professional education in other disciplines. Prior calls for a similar transition among law schools in the United States had some impact, but not much.[115] It is an idea that warrants aggressive implementation.

Scotland, Northern Ireland, and England and Wales have made a transition to outcomes-focused systems of legal education, both in law schools and in the graduate programs operated by professional organizations.

The Law Society of England and Wales is developing a new framework of desired outcomes. This was motivated in part by a decision of the Court of Justice of European Communities that requires professional regulatory bodies such as the Law Society to assess on an individual basis, and to give credit for, any equivalent qualifications and experience held by European Union (EU) nationals.[116] The case was brought by Christine Morgenbesser, a French woman living in Italy, who completed most of her legal education in France and desired to enroll in the Italian "registro dei praticanti" which is a necessary prerequisite for taking the aptitude test for practicing law in Italy. Her application was denied on the basis that she did not hold a law degree that was awarded in Italy. The court held that Italy could not refuse to enroll her solely on the ground that her law degree was not obtained in Italy. What is important, in the court's opinion, is whether the knowledge and skills acquired by an applicant sufficiently meet the qualifications for practice in Italy. Italy, of course, has the right to measure whether an applicant has the requisite knowledge and skills.

As a result of the Morgenbesser case, the Law Society cannot prescribe how or where applicants for admission to practice law in England and Wales must study and prepare for qualification, but it can set the standard they must reach. Additional motivation for developing a new framework came from age and disability discrimination legislation that requires licensing regulations to be reasonably related to the attributes necessary to perform the job for which a license is required.[117]

---

[115] *See, e.g.,* Munro, *supra* note 4; Gregory S. Munro, *Integrating Theory and Practice in a Competency-Based Curriculum: Academic Planning at the University of Montana,* 52 Mont. L. Rev. 345 (1991); Mudd, *Beyond Rationalization, supra* note 40.

[116] Case C-313/01, Christine Morgenbesser v Consiglio dell'Orinde degli avvocati di genova 2003 E.C.R. I-(13.11.2003).

[117] The Law Society, Qualifying as a Solicitor – A Framework for the Future: A Consultation Paper 6 (March 2005) [hereinafter Law Society Framework], *available at* http://www.lawsociety.org.uk/documents/downloads/becomingtfr05consultppr.pdf. (last visited May 23, 2005). The first and second consultation papers are also on the Law Society's website at http://www.lawsociety.org.uk/documents/downloads/becomingfrconsultation1.pdf and http://www.lawsociety.org.uk/documents/downloads/becomingfrconsultation2.pdf.

Whereas law teaching in the United Kingdom previously focused heavily on content, the current approach is to focus on what a student should be able to do as a result of his or her studies. The Quality Assurance Agency established benchmarks that set minimal standards for undergraduate law degrees.[118] Each law school is expected to establish its own standards at a modal level, that is, to describe what a typical student should be able to do rather than what the weakest students can do. Thus, the QAA benchmarks are not standards to measure up to, but standards below which students cannot fall.

After obtaining their undergraduate law degrees, students who want to practice law in the United Kingdom are still several years away from being licensed to practice. For example, in England and Wales, the next step for aspirant solicitors is the year-long Legal Practice Course. This is followed by a two year period of work-based learning under the supervision of an experienced solicitor, the "training contract." During this time, the trainee must also enroll in the Professional Skills Course for a minimum of seventy-two hours of instruction. These programs are very outcomes-focused. Their goal is to teach students what they need to know, understand, and be able to do and the attributes they should have on their first day as practicing lawyers.

The Law Society of England and Wales began the process of developing a new outcomes-focused training framework for solicitors in 2001. Three consultation papers, most recently in March, 2005, contributed to a statement of the core values, professional skills, and legal understanding that solicitors should have on their first day in practice, and the Law Society is developing new forms of examination and assessment of those values, skills, and knowledge.[119] The proposals are intended "to ensure that qualification to practice law is based on an individual's knowledge and understanding of law and legal practice and their ability to deliver legal services to a high quality, rather than on their ability to complete a particular course or courses of study."[120] The new framework for the Legal Practice Course will be implemented in 2008/2009. The Law Society is also seeking to modernize the training contract arrangements. It plans to undertake a two year pilot of a new framework for assessment of work-based learning beginning in September, 2007.

The Law Society of Scotland is also reexamining its current program of instruction for prospective Scottish solicitors, which is already outcomes-focused. In June, 2004, the Society released a working draft of "A Foundation Document" for the future development of professional legal training in Scotland.[121] The document described the fundamental values of the legal profession and the fundamental principles of professional legal education, taking as its core educational concept the benchmark of competence in legal practice. The document defined competence

---

[118] For a description of the impact of benchmarking on undergraduate legal education in England and Wales and N. Ireland, see *John Bell, Benchmarking: A Pedagogically Valuable Process?*, http://webjcli.ncl.ac.uk/1999/issue2/bell2.html. Further information can be obtained from the websites of the various universities, law societies, bar councils, and, in Scotland, the Faculty of Advocates.

[119] Law Society Framework, *supra* note 117, at Annex 1, § A.

[120] *Id.* at 8.

[121] The Foundation Document is no longer available on-line. It was taken off the website of the Law Society of Scotland, http://www.lawscot.org.uk, because as of September, 2006, the Law Society had undertaken another, much more comprehensive consultation with the profession about legal education. Presumably, the results of this consultation will be made available on the Law Society's website.

in entry level professional legal practice as "the distinguishing but minimum performance standards characteristic of the performance of a novice legal professional."

The Scottish Foundation Document recognized that the ongoing revolution in business practice and communication creates the prospect of continuously changing requirements for law practice. Thus, it tried to identify how best to prepare lawyers to cope with and manage all the changes they will encounter during their careers. The document endorsed the concept of "deep learning" that is designed to foster understanding, creativity, and an ability to analyze material critically. It challenges the philosophy of "coverage" which asserts that new lawyers should not be permitted to practice unless and until they have demonstrated knowledge of the key provisions of numerous branches of Scottish law. It viewed the "coverage" philosophy as encouraging passive, unreflective learning, while discouraging analysis, reasoned argument, and independent research. In addition to continuing its emphasis on skills training in the three years between the granting of a law degree and the grant of a full Practising Certificate, the Society joined the Joint Standing Committee on Legal Education in Scotland and the Quality Assurance Agency in calling on undergraduate law programs to increase their emphasis on teaching generic, transferable skills such as communication, reasoning and analysis, problem-solving, teamwork, and information technology.

Australia is also considering a transition towards outcomes-focused legal education. In 2000, the Australian Law Reform Commission completed a four year study of the federal civil justice system, including legal education, and published its report.[122] Recommendation 2 of the report states that "[i]n addition to the study of core areas of substantive law, university legal education in Australia should involve the development of high level professional skills and a deep appreciation of ethical standards and professional responsibility." The following observation is included among the Commission's findings in support of this recommendation.

> It is notable that where the MacCrate Report focuses on providing law graduates with the high level professional skills and values they will need to operate in a dynamic work environment, and assumes that lawyers will keep abreast of the substantive law as an aspect of professional self-development, the equivalent list – the 'Priestly 11' – focuses entirely on specifying areas of substantive law. In other words, MacCrate would orient legal education around *what lawyers need to be able to do*, while the Australian position is still anchored around outmoded notions of *what lawyers need to know*.[123]

---

[122] AUSTRALIAN LAW REFORM COMMISSION, MANAGING JUSTICE: A REVIEW OF THE FEDERAL CIVIL JUSTICE SYSTEM, Rep. No. 89 (1999) [hereinafter AUSTRALIAN LAW REFORM COMMISSION], available at http://www.austlii.edu.au/au/other/alrc/publications/reports/89/. An article that discusses the sections of the report relating to legal education is David Weisbrot, *What Lawyers Need to Know, What Lawyers Need to be Able to Do: An Australian Experience, in* ERASING LINES, *supra* note 40, at 21.

[123] AUSTRALIAN LAW REFORM COMMISSION, *supra* note 122, at ¶ 2.21. The 'Priestly 11' referred to in this quotation is a list of eleven compulsory doctrinal areas for academic legal study which individuals must complete in order to fulfil admission requirements. It was endorsed by the Consultative Committee of State and Territorial Admitting Authorities headed by Mr. Justice Lancelot Priestly, but roundly criticized by the Australian Law Reform Commission. *See* Weisbrot, *supra* note 124, at 122.

Other professions in the United States are far ahead of legal education in shifting to outcome-focused programs of instruction.

The Accreditation Council of Graduate Medical Education (ACGME) has an ongoing initiative, the Outcome Project, by which ACGME is increasing its emphasis on educational outcomes assessment in the accreditation process.[124] Rather than measuring the potential of a graduate medical education program to educate residents, the Outcome Project emphasizes a program's actual accomplishment through assessment of program outcomes.

ACGME identifies the following six general competencies for graduates of graduate medical schools:
1. Medical knowledge.
2. Interpersonal and communication skills.
3. Professionalism.
4. Patient care.
5. Practice-based learning and improvement.
6. Systems-based practice.[125]

All Residency Review Committees (RRCs) were required to include the General Competencies, and their evaluation, in their respective program requirements by July, 2002. A "full" version of the General Competencies is being drafted by a Joint Initiative of ACGME and the American Board of Medical Specialties (ABMS) to reflect the uniqueness of each specialty.

Explaining why it chose to concentrate on outcomes, ACGME reported that it was "playing catch up" to other accrediting bodies in the health professions, education, and business that have focused on educational outcomes since the 1980's. At that time, the U.S. Department of Education mandated a movement aimed at making greater use of outcomes assessment in accreditation. As a result, efforts were begun by many organizations to expand their use of outcomes measures in accreditation. ACGME further explained that the impetus to emphasize educational outcomes assessment in graduate medical education accreditation is based on the following goals: 1) to increase accountability to the public; 2) to improve

---

[124] Accreditation Council for Graduate Medical Education, The Outcome Project (2005) [hereinafter, ACGME Outcome Project], *available at* http://www.acgme.org/Outcome/.

[127] *Id*. at General Competencies, version 1.3 (9.28.99), http://www.acgme.org/Outcome/ comp/compFull.asp. We were so impressed with the ACGME's work product that, in our first attempt to describe desirable outcomes for legal education, we took its statement of six competencies and converted them into terms that fit legal profession. The resulting list was:
1. Legal knowledge.
2. Lawyering skills;
   a. research and analysis of laws and facts,
   b. interpersonal and communication skills,
   c. client services,
   d. practice-based learning and improvement, and
   e. contexts- and systems-based practice, including practice organization and management.
3. Professional values.
This list was concise, seemed to be comprehensive, and was based on ACGME's well-funded and professionally developed description of professional competencies. In the end, however, we decided that the description of outcomes being developed by the Law Society of England and Wales was a better fit for legal education.

measurements of program quality; and 3) to inform discussions with policymakers and others who are focused on funding for medical education and public safety.

So far, most law schools in the United States have largely ignored the outcomes movement. We encourage law schools and those who regulate legal education and attorney licensing to shift the focus of legal education from content to outcomes. Legal education should strive to develop the competencies and characteristics of effective and responsible lawyers. Law schools should describe their learning objectives in terms of what graduates will be able to do and how they will do it when they enter the legal profession, and not just in terms of what they will know.

3.   Principles for Developing Statements of Outcomes.

The following seven principles provide guidance for developing statements of outcomes:[126]

1.   A faculty should formulate outcomes in collaboration with the bench, bar, and perhaps other constituencies [including students]. The practicing profession, for instance, can assist in identifying what graduates need to be able to do to serve clients and society.

2.   Outcomes should be consistent with and serve the school's mission.

3.   A faculty should adopt an outcome only upon arriving at consensus after dialogue and deliberation. By this means, an outcome gains acceptance and permanence. Outcomes adopted on an *ad hoc* basis on the whim of individual professors or members of the bench and bar may present problems of inconsistency with mission, lack of acceptance, and lack of credibility.

4.   Outcomes should be measurable. It is self-defeating to state an outcome which cannot be assessed. At the same time, it is important not to be bound by the expectations of objective decimal-place accuracy. In this context, "measurable" means "a general judgment of whether students know, think, and can do most of what we intend for them."[127] For example, if MacCrate's fundamental skill "Recognizing and Resolving Ethical Dilemmas"[128] was among a school's desired outcomes, it would be difficult, if not impossible, to measure with mathematical accuracy. Yet, clinical faculty members who work with a student for a semester report with some confidence that they are able to form a general judgment as to whether the student has the ability to recognize and resolve ethical dilemmas.

5.   An outcome should be stated explicitly, simply, in plain English, and without educational and legal jargon. The strength of a program based on students' abilities is that the outcomes are clear to students, the faculties, and the constituencies, so that all focus on common goals. The explicit statement of outcomes assures continuity in the

---

[126] These principles were copied from MUNRO, *supra* note 4, at 94-95.

[127] NICHOLS, *supra* note 111, at 22.

[128] MACCRATE REPORT, *supra* note 31, at 140.

academic program. Lack of explicit statements makes it more likely that outcomes will be ignored by new or visiting faculty members.

6.   There is no "correct" number of outcomes for a law school. Outcomes are suggested by the mission statement: their number is a function of mission, resources, and time. Faculty need to consider how many outcomes they can reasonably address and assess during law school.[129] It is worth noting that a Senior Scholar with the American Association of Higher Education (AAHE) recommends that educational institutions embarking on an outcomes-focused approach start small and focus on articulating, assessing and insuring student acquisition of core skills, values, and knowledge and gradually build towards a more robust list of skills, values, and knowledge.[130]

7.   The demands which outcomes make on students and faculty should be reasonable in light of the abilities of the students and the faculty.

The task of developing descriptions of specific outcomes for the program of instruction is neither simple nor easy. It is, however, an important task to undertake if legal education is to realize its full potential. The process of articulating outcomes is not something that any law school should necessarily attempt on its own. Collaboration among all law schools would make the transition easier and improve the quality of the results. Perhaps teams of law professors from multiple schools could work together preparing proposed statements and illustrations of outcomes. Perhaps it is time to reconsider the MacCrate Task Force's recommendation to establish an "American Institute for the Practice of Law" to help coordinate research into and implementation of ways to improve the preparation of lawyers for practice.[131]

4.   Various Statements of Desirable Outcomes.

While it is easy to conclude that legal educators should seek to achieve outcomes, it is difficult to determine how best to describe desirable outcomes. We are convinced, however, that it is essential for legal educators in the United States to make the effort to describe the desired outcomes of legal education, even if our initial efforts are imperfect. Only when we articulate the objectives of legal education can we evaluate the extent to which we are achieving those objectives.

There are many tenable ways to define and organize statements of desired outcomes. Some of the proposed descriptions of the core general characteristics and abilities that we might want new lawyers to possess include the following proposals, presented in chronological order with the most recent coming first.

---

[129] NICHOLS, *supra* note 111, at 20.

[130] Peggy L. Maki, *Developing an Assessment Plan to Learn About Student Learning*, J. ACAD. LIBRARIANSHIP, Jan. 2002, at 8, *available at* http://www.lanecc.edu/inservice/fall05/DevelopingAssessmentPlan.pdf. ("Initially, limiting the number of outcomes colleagues will assess enables them to determine how an assessment cycle will operate based on existing structures and processes or proposed new ones.")

[131] MACCRATE REPORT, *supra* note 31, at 140.

LSAC Project to Create a New LSAT

The Law School Admission Council (LSAC) is supporting a project that might result in a very different Law School Admissions Test (LSAT). The LSAT is a cognitive exam that uses multiple-choice questions to measure logical and analytical reasoning skills as well as reading comprehension. The LSAT does not, however, predict success as a lawyer. Rather, it predicts law school performance and is only partly effective at that. The goal of the current project is to create a new test that will evaluate a broader range of factors related to effectiveness as a lawyer. The principal investigators of the project are Marjorie M. Shultz and Sheldon Zedeck.

The project was initiated in 2000. The first phase identified twenty-six factors related to effectiveness as a lawyer (see below). The second phase developed tests that are designed to determine if law school applicants have the potential to perform effectively on the twenty-six factors. For example, the new tests will try to measure situational and practical judgment.

The third phase of the project, which began in August, 2006, is to find out if the new tests work. The tests are being administered to practicing lawyers. Their supervisors and peers will then evaluate these lawyers on a subset of the twenty-six effectiveness characteristics. Shultz and Zedeck will review the data to determine if the tests are valid and reliable.[132]

The factors listed below are randomly ordered; they are not in order of importance.
1. Problem solving.
2. Practical judgment.
3. Passion and engagement.
4. Analysis and reasoning.
5. Creativity/innovation.
6. Integrity/honesty.
7. Writing.
8. Community involvement and service.
9. Building client relationships and providing advice and counsel.
10. Organizing and managing (own) work.
11. Fact finding.
12. Self-development.
13. Researching the law.
14. Speaking.
15. Ability to see the world through the eyes of others.
16. Strategic planning.
17. Networking and business development.
18. Stress management.
19. Listening.
20. Influencing and advocating.
21. Questioning/interviewing.
22. Negotiation skills.
23. Diligence.
24. Organizing and managing others (staff/colleagues).
25. Evaluation, development, and mentoring.
26. Developing relationships.

---

[132] An informational website that includes links to articles about the project is at http://www.law.berkeley.edu/beyondlsat/.

Rogelio Lasso's Description

Rogelio Lasso concluded that good lawyers possess four competencies:
1. *Knowledge* which includes technical and general knowledge. This competency involves the cognitive and analytical skills that have been the principal focus of legal education since the advent of law schools.
2. *Skill* which includes two types of lawyering skills: "those needed to obtain and process information and those which enable the lawyer to transform existing situations into those that are preferred."
3. *Perspective* which is the ability to consider the historical, political, ethical, and moral aspects of a legal problem and its possible solutions.
4. *Personal attributes* which refers to qualities of character that pertain to the way lawyers go about their professional activities and relate to others.[133]

Teaching and Learning Professionalism Report's Description

The Professionalism Committee of the ABA Section of Legal Education and Admission to the Bar described the "essential characteristics of the professional lawyer" as:
1. Learned knowledge.
2. Skill in applying the applicable law to the factual context.
3. Thoroughness of preparation.
4. Practical and prudential wisdom.
5. Ethical conduct and integrity.
6. Dedication to justice and the public good.

Supportive elements are:
1. Formal training and licensing.
2. Maintenance of competence.
3. Zealous and diligent representation of clients' interests within the bounds of law.
4. Appropriate deportment and civility.
5. Economic temperance.
6. Subordination of personal interests and viewpoints to the interests of clients and the public good.
7. Autonomy.
8. Self-regulation.
9. Membership in one or more professional organizations.
10. Cost-effective legal services.
11. Capacity for self-scrutiny and for moral dialogue with clients and other individuals involved in the justice system.
12. A client-centered approach to the lawyer-client relationship that stresses trust, compassion, respect, and empowerment of the client.[134]

---

[133] Rogelio Lasso, *From the Paper Chase to the Digital Chase; Technology and the Challenge of Teaching 21st Century Law Students*, 43 SANTA CLARA L. REV. 1, 12-13 (2002).

[134] AMERICAN BAR ASSOCIATION, SECTION OF LEGAL EDUCATION AND ADMISSIONS TO THE BAR, TEACHING AND LEARNING PROFESSIONALISM: REPORT OF THE PROFESSIONALISM COMMITTEE 6-7 (1996)

Judith Younger's Description

Judith Younger identified eight abilities that law school graduates should possess:
1. Put problems into their appropriate places on substantive legal map; in other words, spot the issues, characterize or affix the right legal labels to facts.
2. Plumb the law library to its greatest depth and come up with buried treasure.
3. Write grammatically, clearly, and with style.
4. Speak grammatically, clearly, and with style.
5. Find, outside the library, the facts they decide they need to know. This includes the ability to listen.
6. Use good judgment.
7. Find their way around courts, clerks, legislatures, and governmental agencies.
8. Approach any problem with enough social awareness to perceive what nonlegal factors bear on its solution.[135]

Jack Mudd's Description

Jack Mudd described four "dimensions" that are prerequisites for effective lawyer performance:
1. Knowledge.
2. Skill.
3. Perspective.
4. Character.[136]

Bayless Manning's Description

Dean Bayless Manning is credited with the following list:
1. Analytic skills.
2. Substantive legal knowledge.
3. Basic working skills.
4. Familiarity with institutional environment.
5. Awareness of total non-legal environment.
6. Good judgment.[137]

5. Statement of Outcomes Chosen for This Document.

We considered each of the preceding descriptions of desirable outcomes, and others. We decided that the most useful approach would be to adopt, with a few changes, the statement of outcomes being pursued in England and Wales, at least as a starting point for discussion. The Law Society of England and Wales has proposed the following statement of the core general characteristics and abilities that solicitors

---

[hereinafter TEACHING AND LEARNING PROFESSIONALISM].

[135] Judith T. Younger, *Legal Education: An Illusion*, 75 MINN. L. REV. 1037, 1039 (1990) (concluding that law schools "are successfully teaching only one of these qualities – the first on the list").

[136] Mudd, *Beyond Rationalization, supra* note 40.

[137] PACKER & EHRLICH, *supra* note 106, at 23-24 (citing Dean Bayless Manning).

should have on day one in practice.[138] Collectively, these are the components of entry level competence.

1. Demonstrate appropriate behavior and integrity in a range of situations, including contentious and non-contentious areas of work.
2. Demonstrate the capacity to deal sensitively and effectively with clients, colleagues and others from a range of social, economic and ethnic backgrounds, identifying and responding positively and appropriately to issues of culture and disability that might affect communication techniques and influence a client's objectives.
3. Apply techniques to communicate effectively with clients, colleagues and members of other professions.
4. Recognize clients' financial, commercial and personal constraints and priorities.
5. Effectively approach problem-solving.
6. Effectively use current technologies and strategies to store, retrieve and analyze information and to undertake factual and legal research.
7. Demonstrate an appreciation of the commercial environment of legal practice, including the market for legal services.
8. Recognize and resolve ethical dilemmas.
9. Use risk management skills.
10. Recognize personal and professional strengths and weaknesses, to identify the limits of personal knowledge and skill and to develop strategies that will enhance their personal performance.
11. Manage their personal workload and manage efficiently and concurrently a number of client matters.
12. Work as part of a team.[139]

We decided to use the Law Society's statement of desirable outcomes for two reasons. First, we think it provides a reasonable description of the knowledge, skills, and values that a client should be able to expect a novice lawyer to possess. Our second reason is our hope that, if legal educators in the United States can agree on a reasonably similar statement, we can also study how legal educators in the United Kingdom are producing and assessing those outcomes.

We develop and explain our statement of desired outcomes later in this Chapter. It is necessarily general. It would be inappropriate and fruitless to try to describe in detail the specific outcomes that every law school should seek to achieve because these will necessarily differ depending on the mission of each school and the needs of its students, and it would be inefficient to attempt to suggest even an intermediate level of specificity until we agree that the proposed general statement of outcomes is appropriate.

There are, of course, much more detailed descriptions of the knowledge, skills, and values that lawyers need to practice law. Three such descriptions are

---

[138] The Law Society, Second Consultation on a New Training Framework for Solicitors, § 4, ¶ 46 (Sept. 2003) [hereinafter Law Society Second Consultation], *available at* http://www.lawsociety.org.uk/documents/downloads/becomingtfranalysisfirms.pdf. *See also*, Law Society Statement on the Training Framework Review, http://www.ukcle.ac.uk/quality/lawsoc.html (last visited July, 2004). The proposed statement of outcomes was organized into five categories which were modified slightly during the third consultation, the results of which are contained in the Law Society Framework, *supra* note 117.

[139] Law Society Framework, *supra* note 117, at 15-16.

in David R. Barnhizer, "An Essay on Strategies for Facilitating Learning" 12 (June 2006), Cleveland-Marshall Legal Studies Paper No. 06-127, available at SSRN: http://ssrn.com/abstract=906638; the MacCrate Report;[140] and H. Russell Cort & Jack L. Sammons, *The Search for "Good Lawyering:" A Concept and Model of Lawyering Competencies*, 29 Clev. St. L. Rev. 397, 439-44 (1980).

The Law Society of England and Wales is preparing a more detailed statement of its outcomes "to a level of detail that would enable the qualification requirements to be transparent."[141] However, the current descriptions of the desired outcomes of the Legal Practice Course provide examples of how to describe desired outcomes for professional legal education in more detail.[142]

D.   Articulate Goals of Each Course in Terms of Desired Outcomes.

Principle: The school articulates what its students should know, understand, and be able to do, and the attributes they should develop in each course or other component of the program of instruction.

Comments:
Law schools should describe the specific educational goals of each course or other component of the program of instruction in terms of what students will know, understand, and be able to do, and what attributes they will develop by completing that component.

A formidable obstacle every teacher faces is how to analyze the content of a course, predetermine the outcomes desired, and communicate the necessary performance expectations to the learners in a detailed, congruous syllabus that logically connects goals to the measures for grades. That is, the objectives follow from the goals, the requirements are demonstrations of performance of those objectives, and the evaluation methods reflect attainment of the objectives to measurable criteria. This is rarely simple – at times teachers need their own cooperative learning groups in order to solve the myriad of problems in coordinating course goals, uncovering the traditional discontinuities between goals and grading, and clarifying assessment.[143]

Setting specific educational goals and determining how best to achieve them is an unfamiliar task for most law teachers in the United States. We can be guided by the work that our colleagues are doing in the United Kingdom and elsewhere. For example, clear learning objectives have been established for each course in the Diploma in Legal Practice Program at the Glasgow Graduate School of Law in Scotland.[144] Some examples are set forth below to illustrate how one

---

[140] MacCrate Report, *supra* note 31.

[141] Law Society Framework, *supra* note 117, at 8.

[142] Law Society of England and Wales, Legal Practice Course: Written Standards, Version 10 (September 2004) [hereinafter Legal Practice Course], *available at* http://www.lawsociety.org.uk/documents/downloads/becominglpcstandards.pdf.

[143] Tom Drummond, A Brief Summary of the Best Practices in Teaching 6 (1994, 2002), http://northonline.sccd.ctc.edu/eceprog/bstprac.htm.

[144] Glasgow Graduate School of Law, Course Handbook: Diploma in Legal Practice 17-25 (2003-2004) (copy on file with Roy Stuckey).

might describe learning outcomes for particular courses. It should be noted that the Diploma in Legal Practice Program is a year long program that follows four years of undergraduate law study and precedes two years of supervised work experience and additional professional education.

Accountancy for Lawyers

Aim: To develop knowledge and understanding of information contained in accounts.

Learning Objectives: By the end of the course, students should be able to:
• Understand basic accounting concepts, the form and content of the annual accounts of trading enterprises and the workings of a standard accounting system.
• Interpret simple accounting information.
• Give basic advice to the different users of accounts, having regard to their particular interest in such accounts.

Conveyancing

Aim: To develop knowledge and understanding of basic domestic and commercial conveyancing transactions including the purchase, sale and leasing of residential and commercial properties.

Learning Objectives: By the end of the course students should be able to:
• Understand the mechanics of a straightforward purchase and sale transaction of a domestic property, including the importance of missives, the documentation required to be drafted to complete the conveyance and the responsibilities undertaken by the selling and purchasing solicitors.
• Understand the formalities required in revising a commercial lease, and drafting the appropriate documents.
• Understand how to create assured and short-assured tenancies, to draft the appropriate documentation, and the role which any lender to a landlord would have, and explain and discuss the practice rules, money laundering and accounts rules applicable to conveyancing transactions and the practice management and client care implications of conveyancing, including letters of obligation and accounting to the client.

Civil Court Practice: Civil Procedure and Civil Advocacy & Pleadings

Aim: To develop skills in relation to the conduct, funding and resolution of civil litigation.

Learning Objectives: By the end of the course, students should be able to:
• Interview and advise clients in relation to straightforward or relatively straightforward problems.
• Take basic precognitions.
• Draft basic pleadings.
• Demonstrate a practical working knowledge of the rules of civil procedure in the sheriff court.

• Explain and discuss the different ways in which civil litigation may be funded.
• Explain and discuss how actions are settled, including the role played by negotiation.
• Conduct a basic negotiation.
• Explain and discuss the rules of professional ethics and conduct applicable to civil litigation and dispute resolution.

Criminal Court Practice: Criminal Procedure and Criminal Advocacy & Pleadings

Aim: To develop skills in relation to criminal advocacy and procedure.

Learning Objectives: By the end of the course, students should be able to:
• Understand summary criminal procedure.
• Identify issues of competency, relevancy, and other preliminary matters in connection with summary criminal complaints.
• Explain and discuss what is involved in preparing for a summary criminal trial, and how such a trial is conducted.
• Demonstrate an understanding of the nature of criminal advocacy, including the ethical considerations applicable to it.
• Explain and discuss the rules of professional practice applicable to criminal advocacy, including registration for the provision of criminal legal assistance.
• Demonstrate an awareness of the different appellate procedures applicable to summary criminal procedure, and the sentencing powers available to the summary criminal courts.
• Understand the basics of solemn procedure and appeals advocacy skills.

Financial Services and Tax

Aim: To develop knowledge and understanding of the provision and regulation of financial services.

Learning Objectives: By the end of the course, students should be able to:
• Explain and discuss the various forms of financial services available for clients, the regulation of the provision of financial services, including investment protection, complaints procedures and compensation.
• Advise clients in relation to basic investment decisions, including concepts of risk, advantages/disadvantages, flexibility, portfolio planning and charging structures.
• Explain and discuss the taxation implications in relation to investments, and the general economic environment and context against which advice should be considered.
• Explain, discuss and problem solve typical ethical difficulties arising in everyday provision of financial services.

Practice Management

Aim: To develop knowledge and understanding of practice management skills required in professional practice, including financial and accounting issues associated with the running of a law practice.

Learning Objectives: By the end of the course, students should be able to:
• Identify and understand the issues involved in the concepts of client care, risk management, time management, file management and case load management.
• Identify and understand the role played by information technology in a legal practice.
• Identify and understand the role of a trainee in a legal office in relation to its partners, employees, clients and outside agencies with which it deals.
• Demonstrate a basic understanding of the accounts rules, cash room procedures, the money laundering regulations, credit control, outlays on behalf of clients, charging fees to clients and arrangements for payment of fees and outlays.

Private Client

Aim: To develop the practical skills of taking instructions, preparing wills, administering executries, trusts and curatories.

Learning Objectives: By the end of the course, students should be able to:
• Take instructions from a client for the preparation of a will.
• Advise the client on basic matters including the giving of simple tax planning advice.
• Draft a suitable will for a client avoiding legal pitfalls and taking account of the tax implications.
• Investigate the estate and prepare the inventory of a simple estate, calculate inheritance tax on death and lifetime gifts, make over the estate to the beneficiaries, produce an account of the executor's intromissions with the funds in the estate, demonstrate an awareness of the implications of income tax and capital gains tax on the executries and beneficiaries, and demonstrate an ability to ascertain those entitled to prior rights, legal rights and the free estate under the law of intestacy.
• Draft a deed appropriate to the various types of *inter vivos* and *mortis causa* trusts, taking account of the tax implications of each.
• Prepare basic trust accounts.

Professional Ethics

Aim: To develop knowledge and understanding of the ethical principles governing the conduct of lawyers in Scotland enabling the identification of ethical problems as they arise in everyday legal practice.

Learning Objectives: By the end of the course, students should be able to:
• Explain and discuss the systems, practice rules and voluntary codes which regulate the legal profession in Scotland.
• Explain and discuss the concepts of: risk management; negligence; incompetence; inadequate professional service and misconduct; conflict of interest; client care in the context of the professional obligations of a solicitor to a client; the duties of a solicitor to the court and to professional colleagues; professional responsibilities in society; and methods of dealing with ethical problems.
• Explain and discuss and problem solve typical ethical difficulties arising in everyday legal practice.

As mentioned earlier regarding the need to articulate outcomes for the program of instruction, articulating course specific outcomes is not an easy task and law teachers may want to work collaboratively to develop them and seek help from our more experienced colleagues in the United Kingdom and elsewhere.

As a starting point, law teachers may want to ask practicing lawyers what new lawyers need to know, understand, and be able to do when they begin practice. We could then examine the content of our courses, perhaps with the aid of practicing lawyers, and ask what beginning lawyers really need to know and be able to do.

E.   Aim to Develop Competence – The Ability to Resolve Legal Problems Effectively and Responsibly.[145]

Principle: The program of instruction aims to develop competence, and graduates demonstrate at the point of admission the ability to solve legal problems effectively and responsibly, including the ability to:
• **work with clients to identify their objectives, identify and evaluate the merits and risks of their options, and advise on solutions;**
• **progress civil and criminal matters towards resolution using a range of techniques and approaches;**
• **draft agreements and other documentation to enable actions and transactions to be completed; and**
• **plan and implement strategies to progress cases and transactions \ expeditiously and with propriety.**[146]

---

[145] The Law Society included "effective approaches to problem solving" as one of the skills that law school should teach. We do not think it belongs in a list of skills because it is "the" skill of lawyering. We also removed the "ability to complete legal transactions and progress legal disputes towards resolution" from the Law Society's list of five core competencies because we believe this is a statement about the central goal of a program of legal education that aims to prepare students for practice, not just one of the categories of competence. We think a lawyers' ability to resolve disputes and process legal transactions are encompassed within the framework of "problem-solving."

[146] Law Society Framework, *supra* note 117, at Annex 1, § B. The Law Society also included in its list of requisite abilities "the ability to establish business structures and transact the sale or purchase of a business," "the ability deal with various forms of property ownership and transactions," and "the ability to gain a grant of representation and administer an estate," but we thought these were too specific to include on a list of competencies that all law graduates should possess on day one in practice.

Comments:

The primary reason why all law schools in the United States exist is to prepare students for entry into the legal profession. "Amid the useful varieties of mission and emphasis among American law schools, the formation of competent and committed professionals deserves and needs to be the common unifying purpose."[147]

Achieving this goal requires schools to design and offer programs of instruction that aim to take novice learners, help them develop basic competence, and equip them to develop into expert problem-solvers. "The mark of professional expertise is the ability to both act and think well in uncertain situations. The task of professional education is to facilitate novices' growth into similar capacities to act with competence, moving toward expertise."[148]

The following definition of professional competence for lawyers was adapted with very few changes from a definition of professional competence for physicians.

> Professional competence is the habitual and judicious use of communication, knowledge, technical skills, legal reasoning, emotions, values, and reflection in daily practice for the benefit of the individual, organization, or community being served. Competence builds on a foundation of basic professional skills, legal knowledge, and moral development. It includes a cognitive function – acquiring and using knowledge to solve real life problems; an integrative function – using legal and factual data in legal reasoning;[149] a relational function – communicating effectively with clients, colleagues, and others; and an affective/moral function – the willingness, patience, and emotional awareness to use these skills judiciously and humanely. Competence depends on habits of mind, including attentiveness, critical curiosity, self-awareness, and presence. Professional competence is developmental, impermanent, and context-dependent.[150]

Competence requires the integrative application of knowledge, skills, and values. "Professional competence is more than a demonstration of isolated competencies, when we see the whole, we see its parts differently than when we see them in isolation."[151] Competence requires client-centered behaviors such as responding to client's emotions and participatory decision-making. It has affective and moral dimensions. "Competence depends on habits of mind that allow the practitioner to be attentive, curious, self-aware, and willing to recognize and correct errors."[152] Competence is context dependent in that it is a statement of relationship between an ability (in the person), a task (in the world), and the legal framework and specific contexts in which those tasks occur. Competence is developmental, and it is difficult to determine which aspects of competence should be acquired at which stage of professional education or how best to measure it.

---

[147] SULLIVAN ET AL., *supra* note 7, at xvii.

[148] *Id.* at xii.

[149] The physicians' version says "using biomedical and psychosocial data in clinical reasoning," instead of "using legal and factual data in legal reasoning."

[150] Ronald M. Epstein, MD, & Edward M. Hundert, MD, *Defining and Assessing Professional Competence*, JAMA, Jan. 9, 2002, at 226, 226-27.

[151] *Id.* at 227.

[152] *Id.* at 228 (citation omitted).

The Carnegie Foundation's report on legal education refers to the "three apprenticeships of professional education" to explain its understanding of professional competence.

As understood in contemporary learning theory, the metaphor of apprenticeship sheds useful light on the practices of professional education. In these recent Carnegie Foundation studies and reports on professional education, we use the metaphor but extend it to the whole range of imperatives confronting professional education. So, we speak of three apprenticeships. The signature pedagogies of each professional field all have to confront a common task: how to prepare students for the complex demands of actual professional work – to think, to perform, and to conduct themselves like professionals. The common problem of professional education is how to teach the complex ensemble of analytic thinking, skillful practice, and wise judgment upon which each profession rests.

Drawing upon contemporary learning theory, one can consider law, medical, divinity, or engineering schools as sites to which students come to be inducted into all three of the dimensions of professional work: its way of thinking, performing, and behaving. For the sake of their future practice, students must gain a basic mastery of specialized knowledge, begin acquiring competence at manipulating this knowledge under the constrained and uncertain conditions of practice, and identify themselves with the best standards and in a manner consistent with the purposes of the profession. Yet within the professional school, each of these aspects of the whole ensemble tends to be the province of different personnel, who often understand their function differently and may be guided by different, even conflicting goals.

The first apprenticeship, which we call intellectual or cognitive, focuses the student on the knowledge and way of thinking of the profession. Of the three, it is most at home in the university context since it embodies that institution's great investment in quality of analytical reasoning, argument, and research. In professional schools, the intellectual training is focused on the academic knowledge base of the domain, including the habits of mind that the faculty judge most important to the profession.

The students' second apprenticeship is to the forms of expert practice shared by competent practitioners. Students encounter this practice-based kind of learning through quite different pedagogies from the way they learn the theory. They are often taught by different faculty members than those through whom they are introduced to the first, conceptual apprenticeship. In this second apprenticeship, students learn by taking part in simulated practice situations, as in case studies, or in actual clinical experience with real clients.

The third apprenticeship, which we call the ethical-social apprenticeship, introduces students to the purposes and attitudes that are guided by the values for which the professional community is responsible. Its lessons are also ideally taught through dramatic pedagogies of simulation and participation. But because it opens the student to the critical public dimension of the professional life, it also shares aspects of liberal education in attempting to provide a wide, ethically sensitive perspective on the technical knowledge and skill that the practice of law requires. The essential goal, however, is to teach the skills and inclinations, along with the ethical standards, social roles, and responsibilities that mark the professional.[153]

In order to develop competent graduates, therefore, law schools need to emphasize the development of students' expertise in three different areas: legal analysis, training for practice, and development of professional identity.[154] They must attend to all three areas of emphasis, and do so in an integrative fashion, or their graduates will not be prepared for practice. "The students must learn abundant amounts of theory and vast bodies of knowledge, but the 'bottom line' of their efforts will not be what they know, but what they can do. They must come to understand well in order to act competently, and they must act competently in order to serve responsibly."[155]

According to the authors of the Carnegie Foundation's report, the goals of legal education should be to give students the fundamental techniques, as well as the patterns of reasoning, that make up the craft of law; the ability to grasp the legal significance of complex patterns of events; the skills of interviewing, counseling, arguing, and drafting of a whole range of documents; and the intangible qualities of expert judgment: the ability to size up a situation well, discerning the salient features relevant not just to the law but to legal practice, and, most of all, knowing what general knowledge, principles, and commitments to call on in deciding on a course of action.[156]

Therefore, the goal of professional education cannot be analytic knowledge alone or, perhaps, even predominately. Neither can it be analytic knowledge plus merely skillful performance. Rather, the goal has to be holistic: to advance students toward genuine expertise as practitioners who can enact the profession's highest levels of skill in the service of its defining purpose.[157]

In practice, competence is the ability to resolve problems, using legal knowledge and skills and sound professional judgment. The core function of practicing lawyers is to help people and institutions resolve legal problems. This includes helping clients avoid legal problems, as well as helping them resolve disputes, process legal transactions, and engage in planning. The central goal of legal education, therefore, should be to teach students how to resolve legal problems.[158] "Educational programs have the important ultimate purpose of teaching

---

[153] SULLIVAN ET AL., *supra* note 7, at 9-11.

[154] *Id.* at xviii-xix.

[155] *Id.* at 4.

[156] *Id.* at 135.

[157] *Id.* at 199.

[158] The notion that developing problem-solving skills is the end goal, and other aspects of legal education are simply the means to this end is not a novel concept. Gary Blasi wrote "[a]t bottom, lawyering entails solving (or making worse) problems of clients and others, under conditions of extraordinary complexity and uncertainty, in a virtually infinite range of set-

students to solve problems."[159]

> [M]ost lawyers spend most of their time trying to solve
> problems. Those problems consist of raw facts (not yet distilled into
> the short, coherent story laid out in the appellate court opinion)
> – facts presented by clients, along with some question like "Legally
> speaking, how do I get myself out of this mess?" or "How do I plan my
> affairs to avoid getting into a mess in the first place?"
>
> If our job is to teach students how to "think like lawyers,"
> then we should train them to solve such a problem, because that is
> the kind of thinking that lawyers must actually do. But – you reply
> – law schools cannot spend their scarce academic resources teaching
> students every single skill they will need in law practice – how to
> bill clients, how to manage a law office, how to find the courthouse.
> True, but problem-solving is not like any of those activities. Problem-
> solving is the single intellectual skill on which all law practice is
> based.[160]

Students arrive in law school with problem-solving skills they developed
dealing with problems before law school. Although these skills provide a foundation
on which students can build their legal problem-solving skills, legal problems require
specialized skills that must be acquired after entering law school.

> [P]roblem solving focuses on the "whole picture" of what
> lawyers do, and thus provides a wonderful compendium of skills
> taught in law school. Any problem solver must have competencies
> or, at minimum, an awareness of the skills of legal analysis, legal
> writing, negotiation, client counseling, and mediation. Thirdly,
> creative problem solving involves not only legal skills, but also
> development of our cognitive, heuristic thought processes. The
> ambiguous situations of law practice require more original thought
> than is taught through appellate cases. In fact, the narrow analysis
> of appellate cases, particularly in the second and third years, may
> stifle students' development of original thinking.[161]

Law schools give students some of the tools they need to solve legal problems.
Students acquire legal analytical, writing, and research skills, and an overwhelming
amount of doctrinal knowledge. However, law teachers typically do not explain that
the purpose of learning the knowledge of the domain "is not on acquiring information
as such so much as learning the concepts and procedures that enable the expert to

---

tings." Blasi, *supra* note 15, at 317. Stephen Nathanson made the ends-means analogy in
The Role of Problem-Solving in Legal Education, 39 J. LEGAL EDUC. 167, 182 (1989). He also
concluded that problem-solving is "the essence of what lawyers are supposed to do" and that
"the development of problem-solving skill should be made the primary goal of legal education."
Id. at 168, 182. Tony Amsterdam discussed the central importance of teaching problem-solving and "ends-means thinking" in Amsterdam, *supra* note 46, at 613-14.

[159] ROBERT M. GAGNE, THE CONDITIONS OF LEARNING AND THEORY OF INSTRUCTION 195
(1985).

[160] Myron Moskovitz, *Beyond the Case Method: It's Time to Teach With Problems*, 42 J.
LEGAL EDUC. 241, 245 (1992) (citations omitted).

[161] Linda Morton, *Teaching Creative Problem Solving*, 34 CAL. W. L. REV. 375, 379
(1998) (citations omitted).

use knowledge to solve problems."[162]

Nor do law schools give much direct attention to helping students develop problem-solving skills. As Linda Morton observed, law "students are well versed in legal analysis, but not in creative thinking that the demands of law practice now require. It used to be that an educated lawyer could develop many of the skills of creative problem solving in practice but, with our current state of increasing globalization and interdisciplinary interaction, this is no longer true. In order to better equip our students for future practice, teaching methods and principles of creative problem solving is essential."[163]

Mark Aaronson describes a problem-solving approach for making good decisions with roots in business education and an easy to remember acronym.

> That approach, which is intended for a general audience but is easily adaptable to different lawyering tasks, sets out and discusses in ordinary language and with everyday examples eight critical elements in making good decisions. The first four elements are the touchstone of any sound problem-solving methodology: problem definition; setting objectives; identifying alternatives; and evaluating consequences. In setting out what is meant by each, the architects of this approach underscore the importance of perspective and framing in how problems are defined and the centrality of using objectives both to refine initial problem definitions and in identifying alternatives and assessing their consequences. The fifth element entails structuring how to make tradeoffs among alternatives and objectives before making a final decision. The other three elements are not so much specific steps in a problem-solving process as essential considerations that need to be taken into account at critical, decision-making junctures. They involve coming to grips with uncertainty in a rational fashion, acknowledging subjective differences in risk tolerance, and accounting for the linkages between and among decisions. The easy-to-remember acronym that summarizes this approach is PrOACT (Problems, Objectives, Alternatives, Consequences, Tradeoffs).[164]

Thus, a key part of problem-solving skill is the ability to use an analytic methodology that focuses on the process of how to identify objectives and ways for accomplishing them – "ends-means thinking." This "problem analysis" methodology, however, is part of an overall problem-solving process that also involves the use of decision-making techniques and the exercise of sound practical judgment.

> [T]he progression from novice to expert is the opposite of the common belief that learners simply move from concrete examples toward gradually more abstract conceptions. Instead, the Dreyfuses show that mature skill acquisition moves from a distanced manipulation of clearly delineated elements of a situation according to formal rules toward involved behavior based on an accumulation of concrete experience. Over time, the learner gradually develops

---

[162] SULLIVAN ET AL., *supra* note 7, at 8.

[163] Morton, *supra* note 161, at 379 n.17.

[164] Aaronson, *supra* note 33, at 22 (citations omitted).

the ability to see analogies, to recognize new situations as similar to whole remembered patterns, and, finally, as an expert to grasp what is important in a situation without proceeding through a long process of formal reasoning. Sometimes called expert "intuition" or judgment," such ability is the goal of professional training.[165]

Developing competence in novice lawyers is a daunting challenge, but one well worth pursuing.

Research validates the widespread belief that developing professional judgment takes a long time, and much experience, to develop. It cannot typically be achieved within three years of law school, no matter how well crafted the students' experience. But those years in law school can give students a solid foundation and, as they begin their careers in the law, useful guidance on what they need to continue to develop – if the curriculum and teaching in law school are conceived and carried out with the intentional goal of promoting growth in expertise. Knowing the end is an essential step toward figuring out the best means for getting to it. If the final aim of legal education is to foster the development of legal expertise and sound professional judgment, then educators' awareness of the basic contours of the path from novice to expert, along with appropriate steps along the way, are very important.[166]

The kind of careful instruction, study, practice, and reflection that will help students more quickly become effective, responsible problem-solvers can and should occur in law school, even though students' problem-solving expertise will not fully develop until years after graduating from law school. Helping students acquire an understanding of legal problem-solving and to begin developing their expertise as problem-solvers is the most important task of legal education.

F.   Help Students Acquire the Attributes of Effective, Responsible Lawyers.

Principle: Graduates have and are able to demonstrate at the point of admission to practice the attributes of effective, responsible lawyers, which include the following knowledge, understandings, skills, and abilities:
- **self-reflection and lifelong learning skills,[167]**
- **intellectual and analytical skills,**
- **core knowledge of the law,**
- **core understanding of the law,[168]**

---

[165] SULLIVAN ET AL., *supra* note 7, at 136.

[166] *Id.* at 135.

[167] The Law Society included "problem-solving skills" which we are treating as the central goal of legal education. We added "self-reflection and lifelong learning skills" which are probably implicitly included within the Law Society's statement, but we believe such skills should be explicitly emphasized.

[168] The Law Society combined core legal knowledge and understanding as a single competency, but described the components of them separately, as we show here. The Law Society explained that the distinction between knowledge and understanding is suggested to indicate the emphasis to be placed, pre qualification, on the different aspects and the required capabilities of individuals to work with and manipulate their knowledge base. Knowledge

- **professional skills, and**
- **professionalism.**[169]

The following sections expand and comment on these attributes of effective, responsible lawyers.

1.   Self-Reflection and Lifelong Learning Skills.

Principle: Graduates demonstrate self-reflection and lifelong learning skills.

Comments:

All professionals must be lifelong learners. "Legal employers, clients and others expect that, because the young lawyer has a law degree, she . . . possesses the ability to engage in self-regulated learning after law school."[170]

Law school graduates should be skillful in planning their learning by setting goals and identifying strategies for learning based on the task, their goals, and self-awareness of their personal learning preferences. They should be able to implement those strategies, monitoring and reflecting on their learning efforts as they work, and making any necessary adjustments in those strategies.

The key skill set of lifelong learners is reflection skills.[171] The entire law school experience should help students become expert in reflecting on their learning process, identifying the causes of both successes and failures, and using that knowledge to plan future efforts to learn with a goal of continuous improvement.[172] The United Kingdom Centre for Legal Education explains self-regulated, lifelong learning in similar terms:

> Lifelong learning demands . . . the ability to think
> strategically about your own learning path, and this requires the
> self-awareness to know one's own goals, the resources that are
> needed to pursue them, and your current strengths and weaknesses

---

indicates familiarity with an area, recollection of key facts, rules, methods and procedures. Understanding indicates a higher level capacity to work with, manipulate and apply knowledge including in unfamiliar situations.

[169] The term used by the Law Society is "a practical understanding of the values, behaviors, attitudes, and ethical requirements of a lawyer." We think "professionalism" captures this, but it also implies that the goal should be not only to give students an "understanding" of professionalism, but also to instill a commitment to perform in a professional manner. Two factors determine whether a lawyer will perform in a professional manner: whether the lawyer is *capable* of performing professionally (which requires understanding) and whether the lawyer is *committed* to performing professionally (which requires motivation).

[170] Alice M. Thomas, *Laying the Foundation for Better Student Learning in the Twenty-First Century: Incorporating an Integrated Theory of Legal Education into Doctrinal Pedagogy*, 6 WIDENER L. SYMP. J. 49, 76 (2000). *See also* Michael Hunter Schwartz, *Teaching Law Students to be Self-Regulated Learners*, 2003 MICH. ST. D.C.L. L. Rev. 447.

[171] *See* U.K. Ctr. for Legal Educ., Higher Educ. Acad., *What's Reflection Got to Do With It?*, http://www.ukcle.ac.uk/resources/reflection/reflection.html (last visited June 27, 2006).

[172] The best known works on reflective learning by professionals are by Donald A. Schön: THE REFLECTIVE PRACTITIONER: HOW PROFESSIONALS THINK IN ACTION (1983), and *Educating the Reflective Legal Practitioner*, 2 CLINICAL L. REV. 231 (1995). *See also* Schwartz, *supra* note 170, at 452-66.

in that regard . . . . You have to be able to monitor your progress; if necessary even to measure it; to mull over different options and courses of development; to be mindful of your own assumptions and habits, and to be able to stand back from them and appraise them when learning gets stuck; and in general to manage yourself as a learner – prioritizing, planning, reviewing progress, revising strategy and if necessary changing tack.[173]

It is unlikely that three years of law school will fully prepare students for practice, but law schools can protect their graduates' clients by helping students become proficient lifelong learners who can realistically evaluate their own level of performance and develop a plan for improving.

2. Intellectual and Analytical Skills.

Principle: **Graduates demonstrate the intellectual and analytical skills required to:**
  • **apply methods and techniques to review, consolidate, extend, and apply knowledge and understanding and to initiate and carry out projects; and**
  • **critically evaluate arguments, assumptions, abstract concepts and data to make judgments and to frame appropriate questions to achieve a solution, or identify a range of solutions to a problem.[174]**

Comments:
The intellectual and analytical skills required to practice law effectively and responsibly include practical judgment, analytical skills, and self-efficacy.

a. Practical judgment.

Principle: **Graduates demonstrate practical judgment.**

Comments:
In order to succeed as lawyers, students must acquire the habit of mind needed for competent law practice, which in medical education is referred to as "clinical judgment" and by some legal scholars as "practical judgment" or "practical wisdom."

> This twofold aspect of professional expertise [fluency in both the engaged mode of narrative thinking characteristic of everyday practice and the detached mode of analytical thinking emphasized in case-dialogue teaching] is captured by Eliot Freidson when he describes medical education's aim as forming a "clinical" habit of mind so that physicians could "work as consultants who must intervene [with specialized, esoteric knowledge] in everyday, practical

---

[173] *What's Reflection Got to Do With It?*, *supra* note 171 (quoting G. Claxton, Wise Up: The Challenge of Lifelong Learning 14 (1999)).

[174] Law Society Framework, *supra* note 117, at Annex 1, § A. The Law Society also included in this section "communication skills," which it defined as the ability to "communicate information, ideas, problems, and solutions to both specialist and non-specialist audiences." We consider communication skills to be among the professional skills that a lawyer should possess. Professional skills needed for competent law practice are described later in this Chapter.

affairs." In order to treat the patient, the clinician must be able
to move back and forth between detached analysis of the medical
condition and emphatic engagement with the distressed patient.
Medical education clearly demonstrates that this clinical habit of
mind can, like analytic thinking, also be developed within a formal
education program.[175]

Practical judgment is "the key faculty needed when lawyers seek to identify,
assess, and propose concrete solutions in particular and often complex social
circumstances."[176] In law practice, it is the norm rather than the exception for
lawyers to encounter situations where it is not clear what outcomes would best serve
clients' interests and where lawyers must weigh multiple and complex options to find
the most appropriate means for achieving any outcome. Determining the best course
of action in such situations requires the exercise of practical judgment.

Although skill in legal reasoning is not as closed a process
of reasoning as sometimes supposed, everyday lawyering activities
are even less subject to formally structured deliberation. The
factual situations are almost always fraught with complications,
contingencies, and uncertainties. The areas of inquiry have no
pre-definable limits and include small and large matters. Whether
gathering information, communicating with others, planning courses
of action, or contemplating client options, attorneys constantly make
judgment calls. A lawyer's reliance on judgment runs the gamut from
how to order and frame questions when interviewing or counseling
clients, to what research leads to follow, to how to decide major issues
of legal strategy, to how to identify and seek to reconcile conflicting
moral obligations. What the client regards as the problem may or
may not be the problem. There may be a legal solution, but it is not
clear that it would be the best solution. In short, in the practice of
law, how best to proceed and what exactly to say and do are almost
always problematic.

In such situations, it is the lawyer's capacity for reflective,[177]
not determinant, judgment that is regularly tested. One's ability to
identify and apply the law is but one skill and one form of reasoning
needed, and often enough not the most important. The critical
attribute is not the attorney's legal knowledge but his or her ability to
bring to bear, competently and sensibly, the appropriate breadth and
depth of knowledge, whether rooted in schooling or experience, that
best addresses the particular matter at-hand. The high development
of this capacity for reflective judgment is what accounts for good
practical judgment in lawyering. It is a process of deliberation that
involves the contextual synthesizing and prioritizing of a range of

---

[175] SULLIVAN ET AL., *supra* note 7, at 109.

[176] Mark Neal Aaronson, *We Ask You to Consider: Learning About Practical Judgment
in Lawyering*, 4 CLINICAL L. REV. 247, 249 (1998). Other important articles related to teaching
professional judgment are Paul Brest & Linda Krieger, *On Teaching Professional Judgment*,
69 WASH. L. REV. 527 (1994); Blasi, *supra* note 15.

[177] "Reflective judgment is that process of reasoning we use to give coherence and
direction to our thinking when matters are confusing and unsettled, and there is no initially
obvious course of action to take or set formula to apply." Aaronson, *supra* note 33, at 31.

factors, including facts, feelings, values, and general and expert knowledge, all at once. It is what is needed intellectually to reach a cohesive and balanced conclusion when there is no straightforward method for resolving competing concerns. When we have hard knowledge and are able to arrange key elements in a standardized and systematic fashion, we are back in the domain of formalized decision making, where the judgments made are determinant in nature.[178]

Mark Aaronson described "six key characteristics and dynamics regarding the nature of practical judgment, as a concise overview of the kinds of considerations and perspectives that help to explain what accounts for good judgment generally, and in lawyering specifically."[179]

1. Practical judgment entails the application and tailoring of general knowledge to particular circumstances.

2. Practical judgment involves a dialogic process of deliberation or reasoning. Even when not engaged in discussions with others, one has to take into account how an event or situation looks from plural perspectives.

3. The critical dynamic in developing good lawyering judgment is the ability to be empathetic and detached at the same time. Empathy involves imaginatively putting oneself in someone else's shoes.

4. Because the focus of practical judgment is on the just achievement of human ends, knowledge is not valued abstractly for its own sake but instrumentally in terms of how it can be used equitably for the betterment of humanity.

5. Practical lawyering judgment develops over time and with experience. Its nurturing and maturation require exposure to a variety of problem situations and repetitive practice.

6. Practical judgment intertwines intellectual and moral attributes. The connection originates with Aristotle's concept of phronesis or practical wisdom, which he construed as both an intellectual and moral virtue.[180]

It is particularly important for law schools to help students explore and understand the ethical and moral dimensions of legal work. "[T]here is obviously much more to lawyering than the instrumental solving of client problems. Lawyering also entails moral reason and ethical sense, just as law reflects and constitutes the

---

[178] *Id.* at 32-33.

[179] *Id.* at 34-37.

[180] In another article, Aaronson further explains the concept that practical wisdom has both intellectual and moral dimensions.

Aristotle's capsule definition is as follows: "Practical wisdom is a rational facility exercised for the attainment of truth in things that are humanly good and bad" [citing Aristotle, the Ethics of Aristotle: The Nicomachean Ethics, Book VI, at 177 (J.A.K. Thomson, trans., 1953)]. Like other cognitive faculties, practical wisdom involves how we know, perceive, reason, and think, but it also calls on our moral sensibilities. . . . The point is that how we exercise judgment in legal practice depends on both our mental development and our moral development. The impact of what we do is not just a matter of scholarly and experiential knowledge and acumen. It is also a reflection of our moral character and its effects on others.

Aaronson, *supra* note 176, at 258.

normative order of those who make and interpret it."[181] Only by attending to such matters can students acquire the ability to exercise practical judgment, a critical intellectual skill of effective, responsible lawyers.

Students arrive in law school with varying abilities to exercise judgment, but they do not have the professional knowledge or experience to exercise practical judgment in legal settings. Law schools have a special obligation to help students begin to develop practical judgment in legal settings, though the task neither begins nor ends in law school. For law schools "[t]o make judgment a curricular focus, rather than just an aside, requires coming to grips with not only what it means to say someone has and uses good judgment, but also to what extent and under what circumstances practical judgment is a skill and disposition that can be learned."[182]

b.   Analytical skills.

Principle: Graduates demonstrate analytical skills.

Comments:
        The ABA accreditation standards require law schools to provide all students instruction in the "legal analysis and reasoning" skills generally regarded as necessary for effective and responsible practice of law.[183] Law schools in the United States are particularly effective at teaching students how to engage in legal reasoning and helping them develop the skill that is described by many as "thinking like a lawyer."

        The form of "thinking like a lawyer" that most first year teachers strive to develop in their students is a way of analytical thinking that "provides an overarching framework that helps students construct complex forms of working knowledge about particular ways to reason, understand the law, and appreciate lawyers' roles, while at the same time confronting them with subtle forms of uncertainty embedded in each of these major facets of a lawyer's life."[184] "Over time . . . this broadly encompassing, multi-faceted construct provides a framework through which students are taught to confront, engage, accept, and embrace the complex uncertainties that lawyers must ultimately accommodate and perhaps come to love."[185]

        [A]t heart, "thinking like a lawyer" describes a unique educational process through which law faculty aid students in negotiating fundamental educational processes associated with legal reasoning, the law, and lawyers themselves. In particular, it forces students to "domesticate doubt" and offers pragmatic strategies

---

        [181] Blasi, *supra* note 15, at 396 (citations omitted). In a footnote following the first sentence, Blasi said, "[t]his point is made by critics of the MacCrate Report, who see it as interpreting lawyering only as an instrumental activity." *Id.* at n.239. In a footnote following the second sentence, Blasi wrote, "[i]n my view, developments in cognitive science may have significant implications for our understanding of these areas as well. Two noteworthy examples are MARK JOHNSON, MORAL IMAGINATION: IMPLICATIONS OF COGNITIVE SCIENCE FOR ETHICS (1993), and Steven L. Winter, *Transcendental Nonsense, Metaphoric Reasoning, and the Cognitive Stakes for Law*, 137 U. PA. L. REV. 105 (1989)." *Id.* at n.240.
        [182] Aaronson, *supra* note 176, at 249.
        [183] Standards 302(a)(2) and (a)(4), ABA STANDARDS, *supra* note 28, at 17-18.
        [184] Wegner, Thinking Like a Lawyer, *supra* note 47, at 9.
        [185] *Id.*

to do so: the recurring use of questions, a structured approach to reasoning, a phase shift in the nature of knowledge, conventions of legal literacy, an abstracted legal world, and superficial exposure to lawyers' roles and professional norms."[186]

"Thinking like a lawyer" involves:
 • recurrent use of questions that are gradually internalized,
 • structured forms of reasoning that become routine,
 • new concepts of "knowing" that integrate uncertainty at their root,
 • exposure to a limited universe of law and the legal system,
 • development of "legal literacy" involving careful reading, mastery of vocabulary, and conventions for textural interpretation,
 • treating professional roles as a given, rather than exploring their depth, and
 • exposure to professional norms to foster adaptation without confronting student views.[187]

The analytical and thinking skills described above are essential for law students to develop. Law schools, however, tend to continue teaching these skills in the second and third year of law school, after most students have become competent in this form of analysis, rather than helping students develop other important skills and values. The analytical skills taught in the first year are the skills that appellate judges use in deciding cases, rather than the ends-means analytical skills that lawyers use in solving clients' problems.

Ends-means thinking is at the heart of how to develop and apply a problem-solving approach, no matter what the context. Anthony Amsterdam classically describes ends-means thinking as follows:

> This is the process by which one starts with a factual situation presenting a problem or an opportunity and figures out the ways in which the problem might be solved or the opportunity might be realized. What is involved is making a thorough, systematic, and creative canvass of all the possible goals or objectives in the situation – the "end points" to which movement from the present state of affairs might be made – then making an equally systematic and creative inventory of the possible means or routes to each goal, then analyzing the ways in which and the extent to which the various means and goals are compatible or incompatible with one another, seeking means to reconcile them or to prioritize them to the extent that they are irreconcilable.
>
> The purpose of ends-means thinking is to introduce newcomers in a profession to how they initially might go about thinking through a problem. For Amsterdam, it provides important guidance on

---

[186] *Id.* at 1.
[187] *Id.* at 10.

answering the question "how on earth do I get started
in dealing with this situation?"

This kind of thinking – this kind of problem solving – is not
something that we should assume students pick up on their own.[188]

As the Carnegie Foundation's report on legal education put it, "[t]o 'think like
a lawyer' emerges as the ability to translate messy situations into the clarity and
precision of legal procedure and doctrine and then to take strategic action through
legal argument in order to advance a client's cause before a court or in negotiation."[189]

Law schools should continue teaching students the form of "thinking like a
lawyer" they have taught for generations, but they should expand the scope of their
instruction to help students learn more ways of thinking like a lawyer.

c.   **Self-efficacy.**

Principle: **Graduates demonstrate self-efficacy.**

Comments:
An important aspect of helping students develop their intellectual skills is
the concept of "self-efficacy." "Self-efficacy refers to students' beliefs about whether
they have the ability to successfully master an academic task."[190] Self-efficacy is "an
individual's estimate of his or her capability of performing a specific set of actions
required to deal with task situations."[191] Four factors influence the strength of a
student's perceptions of her self-efficacy for performing a task: (1) the student's
current skill level, (2) the extent to which she has witnessed modeling from peers
and from teachers (if the student has not yet become skilled at the task), (3)
verbal persuasion regarding the difficulty of the task, and (4) the student's current
psychological state.[192]

Students with high self-efficacy are better learners. Albert Bandura is
the national expert in this field. He and many other educational researchers have
consistently found a relationship between self-efficacy and academic achievement
even after controlling for traditional measures of ability, such as the SAT or LSAT.
Anastacia Hagan and Claire Ellen Weinstein summarize this research by saying,
"[s]tudents with high self-efficacy have been shown to actively participate in
learning activities, show greater effort and persistence and achieve higher levels of
academic performance than students with low self-efficacy."[193] In fact, in a synthesis
and analysis of thirty-nine past self-efficacy studies, including studies at every

---

[188] Aaronson, *supra* note 33, at 21 (quoting Anthony G. Amsterdam, *Clinical Legal
Education – A 21st-Century Perspective*, 34 J. LEGAL EDUC. 612, 614 (1984)).

[189] SULLIVAN ET AL., *supra* note 7, at 46-47.

[190] Anastasia S. Hagen & Claire Ellen Weinstein, *Achievement Goals, Self-Regulated
Learning, and the Role of Classroom Context, in* NEW DIRECTIONS FOR TEACHING AND LEARNING:
UNDERSTANDING SELF-REGULATED LEARNING No. 63, at 43, 45 (Paul R. Pintrich ed., 1995).

[191] Robert E. Wood & Edwin A. Locke, *The Relation of Self-Efficacy and Grade Goals
to Academic Performance*, 47 EDUCATIONAL AND PSYCHOLOGICAL MEASUREMENT 1013, 1014 (1987).
See also id.

[192] Gregory Schraw & David W. Brooks, *Helping Students Self-Regulate in Math and
Science Courses: Improving the Will and the Skill*, http://dwb.unl.edu/Chau/SR/Self_Reg.html
(last visited June 27, 2006).

[193] Hagan & Weinstein, *surpa* note 190, at 45.

education level from elementary school through college, investigators found that self-efficacy facilitates both performance and persistence.[194] In a set of four studies of undergraduates, researchers found that "self-efficacy has a significant relationship to academic performance, even with ability controlled."[195]

Unfortunately, the competitive atmosphere in United States law schools and negative messages to students about their competence and self-worth undermines rather than enhances students' self-efficacy. Traditional teaching methods and beliefs that underlie them undermine "the sense of self-worth, security, authenticity, and competence among students. Law students get the message, early and often, that what they believe, or believed, at their core, is unimportant – in fact 'irrelevant' and inappropriate in the context of legal discourse – and their traditional ways of thinking and feeling are wholly unequal to the task before them."[196]

Law teachers should clearly articulate our educational goals, help students understand the techniques we are using to accomplish them and be careful not to ask students to demonstrate knowledge and skills until they have a fair opportunity to acquire them.

Particularly given the intellectual demands of the skills and values law students are learning, law professors should sequence instruction so that students have early success and therefore build self-efficacy.[197] In other words, law professors interested in teaching students case analysis skills would order their syllabi so that the students start with easier cases and build to more difficult ones. Likewise, all law professors should consider the order in which they teach the concepts under study. Perhaps, highly theoretical and difficult concepts such as estates in property law, personal jurisdiction in civil procedure, and consideration in contract law are not good places to start for new law school learners.

3.   Core Knowledge of the Law.
• the jurisdiction, authority, and procedures of the legal institutions and the professions that initiate, develop, interpret, and apply the law of relevant jurisdictions, including knowledge of constitutional law and judicial review;
• the rules of professional conduct (including the accounts rules); and
• the regulatory and fiscal framework within which business and other legal transactions and financial services are conducted.

4.   Core Understanding of the Law.
• the law of contract and tort and of parties' obligations, rights, and remedies;
• criminal law;
• the legal concept of property and the protection, disposal, acquisition, and transmission of proprietary interests;

---

[194] Karen D. Multon, Steven D. Brown & Robert W. Lent, *Relationship of Self-Efficacy Beliefs to Academic Outcomes: A Meta-Analytic Investigation*, J. Counseling Psychol. 30, 34 (Jan. 1991).

[195] Wood & Locke, *supra* note 191, at 1021 & 1023.

[196] Krieger, *Institutional Denial, supra* note 76, at 125.

[197] Patricia L. Smith & Tillman J. Ragan, Instructional Design 118, 139 and 202 (2d ed. 1999).

• **equitable rights, titles, and interests;**
• **the range of legal protections available to the individual in society in civil and criminal matters and with regard to their human rights;**
• **legal personality[198] and business structures; and**
• **the values and principles on which professional rules are constructed.[199]**

Principle: Graduates demonstrate adequate core knowledge and understanding of the law.

Comments:

Law schools must give students "an adequate level of knowledge of the applicable legal doctrine. Before a novice lawyer can embark on solving any legal problem, she has to have a knowledge base to organize her experience, to communicate her ideas to others, to rely on for handling difficult situations, and to develop creative solutions."[200] While everyone would agree that students should acquire a body of knowledge before practicing law, reasonable people would disagree about the particulars. This principle broadly describes the requisite body of knowledge to put something on the table to consider.

As noted earlier, the Law Society of England and Wales combined core legal knowledge and understanding as a single competency, but described the components of them separately. The Law Society explained that the distinction between knowledge and understanding is suggested to indicate the emphasis to be placed, pre-qualification, on the different aspects and the required capabilities of individuals to work with and manipulate their knowledge base. Knowledge indicates familiarity with an area, recollection of key facts, rules, methods and procedures. Understanding indicates a higher level capacity to work with, manipulate, and apply knowledge including in unfamiliar situations.

In the United Kingdom, students acquire their core legal knowledge as undergraduate students in law school, and additional subjects are covered in graduate programs operated by the professional organizations. In England and Wales, the "foundations of legal education" taught by law schools include seven substantive courses in addition to legal research: Criminal Law, Equity and Trusts, Law of the European Union, Obligations I (contract); Obligations II (tort), Property Law, and Public Law. In Ireland, there are eight core courses similar to those in England, except they include Company Law and replace Public Law with Constitutional Law. In Scotland, there are eight "qualifying subjects:" Public Law and the Legal System, Scots Private Law, Scots Criminal Law, Scots Commercial Law, Conveyancing, Evidence, Taxation, and European Community Law.

---

[198] According to BLACK'S LAW DICTIONARY 1163 (7th ed. 1999), "personality" is "[t]he legal status of one regarded by the law as a person; the legal conception by which the law regards a human being or an artificial entity as a person. – Also termed *legal personality*." BLACK'S also includes the following quote. "Legal personality . . . refers to the particular device by which the law creates or recognizes units to which it ascribes certain powers and capacities," citing GEORGE WHITECROSS PATON, A TEXTBOOK OF JURISPRUDENCE 393 (G.W. Paton & David P. Derham eds., 4th ed. 1972).

[199] Law Society Framework, *supra* note 117, at Annex 1, § A.

[200] *See* Stefan H. Krieger, *Domain Knowledge and the Teaching of Creative Legal Problem Solving*, 11 CLINICAL L. REV. 149, 207 (2004).

The accreditation standards for law schools in the United States do not require law schools to teach many specific subjects. The standards do not designate any specific substantive law topics that should or must be taught by law schools. Instead, they require law schools to offer instruction in "the substantive law generally regarded as necessary to effective and responsible participation in the legal profession."[201]

The accreditation standards do require law schools to provide all law students instruction in "the history, goals, structure, values, and responsibilities of the legal profession and its members."[202] The Carnegie Foundation's report encourages law schools to include instruction in "the history of American legal education, legal practice, and professions more broadly. Like landmark cases, biographies of notable figures in the law are valuable as concrete manifestations of the principles under discussion."[203]

Although the accreditation standards give law schools a great deal of flexibility in curriculum design and coverage, the reality is that most law school curriculums are very similar and emphasize teaching substantive law far beyond core knowledge and understanding and far beyond what typical law school graduates need to know and understand on their first day in law practice. It is precisely this emphasis on substantive law, driven in part by the emphasis given to substantive law by bar examiners, that weakens the curriculum in most United States law schools.

Gerry Hess and Stephen Gerst conducted a survey of the Arizona Bar in 2005 and asked those lawyers and judges to assess the importance of various categories of legal knowledge to the success of an associate at the end of the first year of practice in a small, general practice firm.[204] Only four courses were rated by more than 70% of the respondents as "essential" or "very important:"
1. Civil Procedure (87%).
2. Professional Responsibility (Arizona and Model Rules) (82%).
3. Contracts (80%).
4. Evidence (74%).

Only three other subjects received a rating higher than 50%:
1. Remedies (damages, injunctions, enforcement of judgments) (68%).
2. Torts (67%).
3. Property (real, personal, landlord) (62%).

The lawyers and judges in Arizona apparently agree with Harry Edwards that "we should stop attempting to teach so much substance in the basic law school program. We should not attempt to prepare someone to practice labor law,

---

[201] Standard 302(a)(1), ABA STANDARDS, *supra* note 28, at 17-18.

[202] Standard 302(a)(5), *id.* at 18. Bob MacCrate suggested that a goal for a program of law school instruction should be stated as "'making students aware' of such things as 'the organization of the profession' in bar associations, the articulation by professional organizations of 'professional values,' the relation of those values to the rule of law and lawyers' public service role and the regulation of the profession by the Courts." Letter from Robert MacCrate, Esq., to Professor Roy Stuckey (Sept. 15, 2004) (on file with Roy Stuckey).

[203] SULLIVAN ET AL., *supra* note 7, at 16.

[204] Gerry Hess & Stephen Gerst, Phoenix Int'l School of Law, Arizona Bench and Bar Survey and Focus Group Results (2005) (on file with Roy Stuckey). As discussed later, the survey also asked members of the bar to assess the importance of various skills and values.

environmental law, commercial transactions and the many other subjects that we teach."[205] Although people can reasonably disagree about which doctrinal subjects should be required for all students, Judge Edwards is not alone in reaching the following conclusion: "Nor does doctrinal education require three years of law school. Absent specialist training, it probably requires only the first year and part of the second; the remaining time should be used for clinical courses, as well as doctrinal and theoretical electives."[206]

In 2000, the Australian Law Reform Commission made the following observations concerning the amount of substantive legal knowledge that law students should acquire before beginning law practice.

> [A] requirement that students must "master" (or at least "know") large bodies of substantive law ignores the stark reality that this substance changes dramatically over time – sometimes in a very short time. Where once it was possible to trace the slow and careful development of the common law, and identify with either the "bold" or "timorous" judges of the English superior courts, Justice Paul Finn has described Australians as "born to statutes". . . .[207]

> Thus, a student who "masters" taxation law or environmental law or social security law, but does not then work in these areas for a time, would find the substance of law almost unrecognizable a decade later; and a practitioner who relied significantly on what he or she learned in law school would soon, if unwillingly, become acquainted with the law of professional negligence.[208]

> Accompanied by a commitment to facilitating "lifelong learning" for professionals, Australian law schools might consider adoption of an underlying philosophy which holds that "[i]n a changing environment, the best preparation that a law school can give its students is one which promotes intellectual breadth, agility and curiosity; strong analytical and communications skills; and a (moral/ethical) sense of the role and purpose of lawyers in society."[209]

We endorse the observations and philosophy of the Australian Law Reform Commission. We encourage law schools and bar admissions authorities to reconsider the extent of substantive legal knowledge that lawyers should have on day one of law practice.

---

[205] Harry T. Edwards, *The Growing Disjunction Between Legal Education and the Legal Profession*, 91 MICH. L. REV. 34, 57 (1992).

[206] *Id.* at 63.

[207] AUSTRALIAN LAW REFORM COMMISSION, *supra* note 122, at para. 2.83.

[208] *Id. at* ¶ 2.84.

[209] *Id. at* ¶ 2.89.

5.   **Professional Skills.**

• **the application of techniques to communicate effectively with clients, colleagues, and members of other professions;**
• **the ability to recognize clients' financial, commercial, and personal constraints and priorities;**
• **the ability to advocate a case on behalf of others, and to participate in trials to the extent allowed upon admission to practice;[210]**
• **effective use of current technologies and strategies to store, retrieve, and analyze information and to undertake factual and legal research;**
• **an appreciation of the commercial environment of legal practice, including the market for legal services;**
• **the ability to recognize and resolve ethical dilemmas;**
• **effective skills for client relationship management and knowledge of how to act if a client is dissatisfied with the advice or service provided;**
• **employment of risk management skills;**
• **the capacity to recognize personal and professional strengths and weaknesses, to identify the limits of personal knowledge and skill, and to develop strategies that will enhance professional performance;**
• **the ability to manage personal workload and to manage efficiently, effectively, and concurrently a number of client matters; and**
• **the ability to work effectively as a member of a team.[211]**

Principle: Graduates demonstrate adequate professional skills.

Comments:

This principle calls on law schools to help students develop a variety of skills, including concern about and skills for delivering legal services efficiently. It also points out the importance of teaching students to think about the effects of their actions on our society at large, the administration of justice, and the overall performance and reputation of the legal profession.

The scope and depth of skills instruction called for in this principle are somewhat greater than what the American Bar Association requires through its accreditation process. The ABA requires law schools to ensure that each student receive substantial instruction in "legal analysis and reasoning, legal research, problem solving and oral communication, . . . writing in a legal context, including at least one rigorous writing experience in the first year and at least one additional rigorous writing experience after the first year," and "other professional skills generally regarded as necessary for effective and responsible practice of law."[212] The ABA lists the following professional skills as some of the skills generally regarded as necessary for law practice: "[t]rial and appellate advocacy, alternative methods

---

[210] The Law Society's language for the second part of this statement is "and to exercise the rights of audience available to all solicitors on admission."

[211] Law Society Framework, *supra* note 117, at Annex 1, § B. The Law Society included "effective approaches to problem solving" among the descriptive components of this competency, but we took it out because we believe that helping students become effective and responsible problem-solvers is the primary goal of legal education, not just a component of one category of competency.

[212] Interpretation 302-2, ABA STANDARDS, *supra* note 28, at 17-18.

of dispute resolution, counseling, interviewing, negotiating, problem solving, factual investigation, organization and management of legal work, and drafting."[213]

It does not appear, however, that the ABA's rules will ensure that students receive instruction in all of the skills listed in the Standards or to any level of proficiency, because the accreditation standards also state that a school may satisfy the standard by "requiring students to take one or more courses having substantial professional skills components."[214] One course cannot equip students with the professional skills needed to practice law effectively and responsibly.

As mentioned earlier, in 2005 Gerry Hess and Stephen Gerst conducted a survey of the Arizona Bar.[215] They asked those lawyers and judges to assess the importance of various professional skills to the success of an associate at the end of the first year of practice in a small, general practice firm. Twelve skills were rated by more than 70% of the respondents as "essential" or "very important," and three more were rated that highly by more than 50% of the respondents.
1.   Legal analysis and reasoning (96%).
2.   Written communication (96%).
3.   legal research (library and computer) (94%).
4.   Drafting legal documents (92%).
5.   Listening (92%).
6.   Oral communication (92%).
7.   Working cooperatively with others as part of a team (90%).
8.   Factual investigation (88%).
9.   Organization and management of legal work (88%).
10. Interviewing and questioning (87%).
11. Problem solving (87%).
12. Recognizing and resolving ethical dilemmas (77%).
13. Pretrial discovery and advocacy (64%).
14. Counseling (58%).
15. Negotiation (57%).

The importance and purposes of teaching skills in law school were described by William Twining:

> One of the main objectives of legal training is to enable intending practitioners to achieve minimum standards of competency in basic skills before being let loose on the public; what constitutes such skills depends on a job analysis of what lawyers of different kinds in fact do: lawyer-jobs can be analysed into transactions or operations, which can be further broken down into tasks or sub-operations; a skill or skill-cluster denotes the ability to carry out a task to a specified standard. Minimum, acceptable competence is to be distinguished from excellence. It is the main function of primary legal education and training to ensure that all entrants to the profession exhibit minimum competence in a range of skills, measured by actual performances which satisfy articulated criteria under specified conditions.[216]

---

[213] Standard 302(a)(2), (3), and (4), *id.* at 18.

[214] Interpretation 302-3, *id.* at 19.

[215] Hess & Gerst, *supra* note 204.

[216] WILLIAM TWINING, BLACKSTONE'S TOWER: THE ENGLISH LAW SCHOOL 168 (1994).

As Twining mentions, the basic objective is for all lawyers to achieve minimum standards of competence in basic skills before being let loose on the public. It is not clear whether law schools in the United States can bring students to an adequate level of proficiency to represent clients without supervision in three years. Even if they cannot, however, graduates and their clients would still benefit from more emphasis on skills instruction.

While it is easy to conclude that law students should be made aware of and receive instruction in all professional skills during law school, it is more difficult to determine which skills are the most important to develop during law school to a level of proficiency that will enable a school's graduates to provide effective, responsible legal services upon admission to the bar.

It is likely that law schools are currently doing an adequate job of helping students develop some forms of law-related reading skills, legal analysis and reasoning skills,[217] and legal writing and research skills, but they are giving much less attention to other important skills. Many students graduate without even an introduction to many of the basic skills of the legal profession, such as how to learn from experience, managing legal work, interviewing, counseling, negotiation and other forms of advocacy, and preparing pleadings and other legal documents. An expanded discussion of the most important skills for law students to acquire is in Chapter Five.

> **6.   Professionalism.**[218]
> **• appropriate behaviors and integrity in a range of situations;**
> **• the capacity to deal sensitively and effectively with clients, colleagues, and others from a range of social, economic, and ethnic backgrounds, identifying and responding positively and appropriately to issues of culture and disability that might affect communication techniques and influence a client's objectives.**[219]

Principle: Graduates demonstrate professionalism.

Comments:
This principle calls on law schools to give students an understanding of the values, behaviors, attitudes, and ethical requirements of a lawyer and to infuse a commitment to them. In other words, it highlights the importance of teaching professionalism.[220] Professionalism encompasses the formal rules of professional

---

[217] *See* earlier discussion of intellectual, analytical, and lifelong reasoning skills.

[218] A collection of descriptions of professionalism is located on the Professionalism of Lawyers and Judges website, http://professionalism.law.sc.edu.

[219] Law Society Framework, *supra* note 117, at Annex 1, § C.

[220] In an earlier version of this document, we adapted the ACGME descriptions of competency related to professional values and formulated the following principle:
> Graduates understand and are committed to the values of the legal profession, as manifested through a commitment to professional responsibilities, adhering to ethical principles, and being sensitive to a diverse client population. Graduates:
> -demonstrate respect, compassion, and integrity; a responsiveness to the needs of clients and society that supercedes self-interest; accountability to clients, society, and the profession; and a commitment to excellence and on-going professional development,
> -demonstrate a commitment to ethical principles pertaining to provision or with holding of legal services, confidentiality of client information, informed consent,

conduct, that is, the minimally required conduct of lawyers, but it also encompasses "what is more broadly *expected* of them, both by the public and by the best traditions of the legal profession itself."[221]

"Professionalism" is "the conduct, aims, or qualities that characterize or mark a profession or a professional person."[222] Another definition is: "Professionalism is conduct consistent with the tenets of the legal profession as demonstrated by a lawyer's civility, honesty, integrity, character, fairness, competence, ethical conduct, public service, and respect for the rule of law, the courts, clients, other lawyers, witnesses, and unrepresented parties."[223]

The Supreme Court of Washington and the Washington State Bar define professionalism as follows:

> "Professionalism" is no more, and no less, than conducting one's self at all times in such a manner as to demonstrate complete candor, honesty, courtesy and avoidance of unnecessary conflict in all relationships with clients, associates, courts and the general public. It is the personification of the accepted standard of conduct that a lawyer's word is his or her bond. It includes respectful behavior towards others, including sensitivity to substance abuse prevention, anti-bias or diversity concerns. It encompasses the fundamental belief that a lawyer's primary obligation is to serve his or her clients' interests faithfully and completely, with compensation only a secondary concern, acknowledging the need for a balance between the role of advocate and the role of an officer of the court, and with ultimate justice at a reasonable cost as the final goal.[224]

Our society expects lawyers to provide competent legal services that achieve their clients' goals. In providing such services, a professional lawyer will comply with the law as well as with the rules and values of the legal profession. A professional lawyer will be trustworthy and honest, work cooperatively with opposing counsel, judges, colleagues, and clients, perform on schedule, keep promises, respond promptly to telephone calls, answer questions courteously, and charge a fair price. A professional lawyer will be accountable for the quality of his or her work.[225]

We are not born with values.[226] Values are learned. They are derived from

---

and business practices, and
-demonstrate sensitivity and responsiveness to clients' culture, age, gender, and disabilities.

[221] Allen K. Harris, *The Professionalism Crisis – The "Z" Words and Other Rambo Tactics: The Conference of Chief Justices' Solution*, 53 SC L. REV. 549 (2002).

[222] MERRIAM-WEBSTER'S COLLEGIATE DICTIONARY (10th ed. 1999).

[223] Adopted by the New Mexico Commission on Professionalism, November 28, 2000 (www.nmbar.org/statebar.professionalism.html).

[224] Wash. State Ct. A.P.R. 11 Reg. 101(n).

[225] For a more complete list of the attitudes and values necessary for competence, see Neil Gold, *Competence and Continuing Legal Education, in* ESSAYS ON LEGAL EDUCATION 23, 32-34 (Neil Gold ed., 1982).

[226] Values are sometimes confused with basic human needs. Abraham Maslow developed a hierarchical theory of human motivation based on basic human needs in 1954. ABRAHAM MASLOW, MOTIVATION AND PERSONALITY (2d ed. 1970). Maslow described categories of basic human needs that influence human behavior in descending order of importance: 1. physiological

our life experiences and are transmitted in successive generations through society's institutions.[227] Teaching values is considered to be an unavoidable part of all educators' functions.

> *Ethical teaching means teaching ethics.* Beyond setting examples, teaching requires active efforts to teach about and instill good character. To be sure, in an age of relativism, when rival camps battle over the teaching of virtues and values, it is not easy to know how to teach ethics to students; and teachers are often confused and uncertain even about whether they should attempt to do so. But that decision is already made when they exemplify the worth and use of knowledge, service to others, or compassion. They must therefore be conscious of the moral qualities and dimensions of their work and not hesitate to teach about ethics and character.[228]

It is especially appropriate for law teachers to teach about professional values. One can assume that law students' knowledge and understanding of the values of the legal profession are undeveloped when they begin law school. Thus, the teaching of professional values is an appropriate and important topic for attention by law schools. "Law school is where most students first come into contact with issues relating to legal professionalism."[229] The failure of law schools to give more attention to teaching students about professional values is increasingly criticized by scholars.[230]

> [I]n most law schools, the apprenticeship of professionalism and purpose is subordinated to the cognitive, academic apprenticeship. In fact, in the minds of many faculty, ethical and social values are subjective and indeterminate and, for that reason, can potentially even conflict with the all-important values of the academy, values that underlie the cognitive apprenticeship: rigor, skepticism, intellectual distance, and objectivity.

> However, if law schools would take the ethical-social apprenticeship seriously, they could have a significant and lasting impact on many aspects of their students' professionalism. This is not widely understood by faculty, who often argue that by the time students enter law school it is too late to affect their ethical commitment and professional responsibility.[231]

> Although some people believe that law school cannot affect

---

needs (sexual desire, sleep, activity and exercise, tastes, smells); 2. safety and security needs (security, stability, dependency, protection); 3. love and belonging needs; 4. esteem needs (self-respect; self-esteem; esteem of others); and 5. needs for self-actualization (inner motivation, to become what one is capable of becoming). *Id.* at 36.

[227] "[C]ulture, society, and personality are the major antecedents of values . . . ." MILTON ROKEACH, THE NATURE OF HUMAN VALUES 326 (1973). "Insights from various directions permit our pointing to a number of influences in shaping people's values – family, peers, school and college, religion and church, folk story, personal experience, and other." RICHARD W. KILBY, THE STUDY OF HUMAN VALUES 109 (1993).

[228] BANNER & CANNON, *supra* note 80, at 40.

[229] TEACHING AND LEARNING PROFESSIONALISM, *supra* note 134, at 13.

[230] *See, e.g.*, Russell G. Pearce, *MacCrate's Missed Opportunity: The MacCrate Report's Failure to Advance Professional Values*, 22 PACE L. REV. 575 (2003).

[231] SULLIVAN ET AL., *supra* note 7, at 160.

students' values or ethical perspectives, in our view law school cannot help but affect them. For better or worse, the law school years constitute a powerful moral apprenticeship, whether or not this is intentional. Law schools play an important part in shaping their students' values, habits of mind, perceptions, and interpretations of their legal world; their understanding of their roles and responsibilities as lawyers; and the criteria by which they define and evaluate professional success.[232]

The objective of teaching professional values to law students is consistent with Jack Sammons' suggestion that, instead of focusing on competencies, that is, what a graduate should be able to do, "a law school should start thinking about its curriculum by seeking faculty agreement on what kind of lawyers it wants its students to be. I do not mean what they, the students, should be able to do, although that is part of it, but what they should be."[233]

Helping students understand and develop a commitment to professionalism can have important long terms benefits for the students, the profession, and the public.

> [W]e can make the practice of law more satisfying and more fun. Instead of worrying about our image, we should focus on two concepts – one, the full performance of our duty to practice our profession in the interest of the public, and two, the practice of our profession consistent with personal values and satisfaction. If we are faithful to these fundamentals, we will be better lawyers, citizens, and humans, and our standing will grow accordingly.[234]

The values of the legal profession can be described in various ways and reasonable people can disagree about how best to prioritize the list, but there is general, if not universal, agreement about many aspects of professional values. The MacCrate Report described four "fundamental values of the profession:" 1) provision of competent representation; 2) striving to promote justice, fairness, and morality; 3) contributing to the profession's fulfillment of its responsibility to enhance the capacity of law and legal institutions to do justice; and 4) professional self-development.[235]

The following components of professionalism also represent professional values:
Handle cases professionally:
> • recognize the broader implications of your work,
> • consider interests and values of clients and others,
> • provide high quality services at fair cost,
> • maintain independence of judgment,

---

[232] *Id.* at 169.

[233] Jack L. Sammons, *Traditionalists, Technicians, and Legal Education*, 38 GONZ. L. REV. 237, 245 (2002/03).

[234] Former Attorney General Benjamin Civiletti as quoted in THE NATIONAL LAW JOURNAL, Feb. 7, 2000, at A16.

[235] MACCRATE REPORT, *supra* note 31, at 140-41. Some critics have complained that the MacCrate Report did not give first priority to values over skills and that the Report inadequately describes and explains professional values. *See, e.g.,* Pearce, *supra* note 230.

- embody honor, integrity, and fair play,
- be truthful and candid,
- exhibit diligence and punctuality,
- show courtesy and respect towards others, and
- comply with rules and expectations of the profession.

Manage law practice effectively and efficiently.

Engage in professional self-development.

Nurture quality of life.

Support aims of legal profession:
- provide access to justice,
- uphold the vitality and effectiveness of the legal system,
- promote justice, fairness, and morality,
- foster respect for the rule of law, and
- encourage diversity.[236]

The 2005 survey of the Arizona Bar conducted by Gerry Hess and Stephen Gerst[237] also asked those lawyers and judges to assess the importance of various values to the success of an associate at the end of the first year of practice in a small, general practice firm. Sixteen values were considered "essential" or "very important" by over 70% of the respondents, and one more was rated that highly by over 50% of the respondents.

1. Act honestly and with integrity (99%).
2. Show reliability and willingness to accept responsibility (97%).
3. Strive to provide competent, high quality legal work for each client (97%).
4. Treat clients, lawyers, judges, and staff with respect (95%).
5. Show diligence and ethic of hard work (90%).
6. Demonstrate maturity, autonomy, and judgment (90%).
7. Demonstrate self-motivation and passion (88%).
8. Show self-confidence and earn others' confidence (88%).
9. Commitment to continued professional growth and development (82%).
10. Demonstrate tolerance, patience, and empathy (82%).
11. Commitment to critical self-reflection (77%).
12. Commitment to personal growth and development (75%).
13. Engage in healthy stress management (75%).
14. Strive to promote justice, fairness, and morality (73%).
15. Demonstrate creativity and innovation (71%).
16. Commitment to a balanced life (70%).
17. Strive to rid the profession of bias (55%).

An earlier version of this document proposed that law schools should strive to help students develop the characteristics of "good lawyers." We changed the

---

[236] These components of professionalism were gleaned from numerous standards and codes of professionalism developed by state bars and other professional organizations, and they were used as the organizational framework for the professionalism website created and maintained by the Nelson Mullins Riley & Scarborough Center on Professionalism at the University of South Carolina School of Law, http://professionalism.law.sc.edu. The professionalism website was developed by the Center with a grant from the Open Society Institute. The site contains information about and links to materials, organizations, and initiatives related to professionalism in the legal profession.

[237] Hess & Gerst, *supra* note 204.

language after receiving comments that this term may be politically incorrect. Bob MacCrate reminded us, however, that the moral concept of the good lawyer was promoted by Professor David Hoffman as early as 1836, and that Judge George Sharswood concluded his 1854 lecture on professional ethics with the admonition, "[l]et it be remembered and treasured in the heart of every [law] student, that no man [or woman] can ever be a truly great lawyer, who is not, in every sense of the word, a good man [or woman]."[238]

The remainder of this section discusses five professional values that we believe deserve special attention during law school: a commitment to justice; respect for the rule of law; honor, integrity, fair play, truthfulness and candor; sensitivity and effectiveness with diverse clients and colleagues; and nurturing quality of life.

a.   A commitment to justice.[239]

Principle: Graduates strive to seek justice.

Comments:
All professional values deserve attention by law schools, but teaching students to strive to seek justice may be the most important goal of all. Andrew Boan concluded that "[t]he integration of skills and knowledge should assist practitioners in achieving the good of legal professions; achieving justice. The development of virtues consistent with this social good must be a central goal of legal education."[240] Richard Burke reached similar conclusions:

> Truth, justice, and fairness, both in means and ends, are paramount on the scale of legal values, and when those are at stake, the other values must yield.[241]

. . . . .

> First, we should say that truth and justice are our goals; that, though we may never find totally objective truth or achieve perfect justice, we will seek and strive for them to the best of our professional ability. Second, we should make clear that this quest for truth and justice is a professional responsibility upon which rests the reliability and integrity of the entire legal system. Hence, an individual client's desires and objectives must be subordinate to that quest. Third, our rules of conduct should specifically prohibit lawyer or lawyer participation in lying, falsification, misrepresentation, or deception in every aspect of practice from courtroom advocacy to office

---

[238] MacCrate, *supra* note 21, at 824.

[239] An annotated list of books and articles discussing the lawyer's duty to promote justice, fairness, and morality is located on the Professionalism of Lawyers and Judges website, http://professionalism.law.sc.edu.

[240] Andrew Boon, *History is Past Politics: A Critique of the Legal Skills Movement in England and Wales, in* TRANSFORMATIVE VISIONS OF LEGAL EDUCATION 151, 154-55 (Anthony Bradney & Fiona Cownie eds., 1998), *published simultaneously in* 25 J. LAW & SOC. 151 (1998) (citing Ronald Dearing, The National Committee of Inquiry into Higher Education, Report of the National Committee (1997)).

[241] Richard K. Burke, *"Truth in Lawyering:" An Essay on Lying and Deceit in the Practice of Law*, 38 ARK. L. REV. 1, 22 (1984).

consultation and practice.[242]

Calvin Woodward also concluded that teaching students to seek justice should be the central focus of legal education. Woodward considered the impact of the centuries-long process of secularization and concluded that this process had undermined the influence of religion and discredited legality as a social sanction, especially in western democratic societies. He also determined, however, that "the course of secularization has been led, almost without exception, by men seeking substantial justice. And therein lies the clue – a straw in the wind – for modern law schools. In a world populated by ultra-rational men, Law must find its strength in Justice, not Legality."[243] Woodward called on law schools to train students to regard themselves as agents of Justice as well as officers of the court.

> Law schools must rid themselves of the vestiges of mysticism that, in days past, held laymen in awe of law and legality; and students must be trained to regard themselves as agents of Justice as well as officers of the court. More important, they must be shown precisely what this responsibility entails. And establishing a course of instruction that will serve this purpose should be the great issue with legal education today.[244]

Woodward proposed two governing maxims for law schools. "First, within the House of the Law there are many mansions – in which practitioners of all kinds, counsellors, judges, public servants, scholars and philosophers work in their several ways to further the course of, and to implement, Justice. Second, legal education, as an adjunct of Justice, must start with the proposition that the greater includes the lesser, the higher the lower, and not *vice versa*. That is, law schools must assume, as their basic premise, that the man who first understands his obligations to Justice will be better able to fulfill his legal 'function,' whatever it might be. Justice, in a word, must take precedence over law."[245]

b. Respect for the rule of law.[246]

Principle: Graduates foster respect for the rule of law.

Comments:
It is impossible for a democracy to function unless most citizens generally abide by the laws of the society. Moral codes are one influence on individual behavior, but perhaps the most significant situational constraint on individual behavior is the legal system crafted by the society.

> The society's laws set forth rules of behavior that are enforced by the formal institutions of government. But in a democratic society, individual obedience to the law requires more than mere fear

---

[242] *Id.* at 3-4.

[243] Calvin Woodward, *The Limits of Legal Realism: An Historical Perspective, in* PACKER & EHRLICH, *supra* note 106, at 329, 380.

[244] *Id.*

[245] *Id.* at 381.

[246] A collection of books and articles discussing the lawyer's duty to foster respect for the rule of law is located on the Professionalism of Lawyers and Judges website, http://professionalism.law.sc.edu.

of punishment for violations. For the law to serve as an effective constraint on behavior, the members of the society must respect the substance of the laws and the process by which they are created and enforced. This condition of respect will be referred to as the existence of the Rule of Law in a society.[247]

The rule of law not only constrains individual behavior, it also protects the human rights of individuals and prevents governments from acquiring unbridled power or acting arbitrarily.

> [T]his concept has been built from various aspects of all legal systems. In France they will talk about l'état de droit, in Germany they will talk about rechts staat, in Italy they will talk about stati di diritto. But all these are variations of what we call the rule of law, and they are aimed at achieving the same objective – the establishment of individual freedoms and the protection against any manifestation of arbitrary power by the public authorities.

> The experiences of many generations of jurists from highly diverse nationalities have enabled certain basic conditions and principles to be elaborated without which the rule of law cannot be sustained. These conditions and principles are: the separation of powers, judges' independence, respect for individual fundamental rights and freedoms, the legality of administrative action, control of legislation and administration by independent judges, and, most importantly, the need for a bar which maintains its independence from the authorities and which is devoted to defending the notion of the rule of law.

> This notion is, therefore, intended to submit the administration to respect of the law. Legislation passed by the parliament, which represents the electorate, is the instrument through which the people's sovereignty is imposed on the administration, preventing the administration from becoming an autocracy.[248]

The importance of the rule of law in maintaining order in a society cannot be overstated. The Preamble of the Universal Declaration of Human Rights states that "[h]uman rights have to be protected by the rule of law, and where the rule of law is not observed, finally people may resort to rebellion against tyranny and oppression."[249]

---

[247] Richard Lavoie, *Subverting the Rule of Law: The Judiciary's Role in Fostering Unethical Behavior*, 75 U. Colo. L. Rev. 115, 138 (2004) (citing Margaret J. Radin, *Reconsidering the Rule of Law,* 69 B. U. L. Rev. 781, 790 (1989) who explained that the Rule of Law is grounded not on the bare claim of efficacy of behavioral control, but on the specific political vision of traditional liberalism. Liberty is the core value; over-reaching by Leviathan is the danger on one hand, and disintegration of social cooperation because of the prisoner's dilemma is the danger on the other).

[248] Adama Dieng, *Role of Judges and Lawyers in Defending the Rule of Law*, 21 Fordham Int'l L. J. 550, 550-51 (1997).

[253] Preamble, Universal Declaration of Human Rights, G.A. Res. 217A, at 1, U.N. GAOR, 3d Sess., 1st plen. mtg., U.N. Doc. A/810 (Dec. 12, 1948).

Lawyers play a central role in maintaining the rule of law in every democracy. As gate keepers to the judicial system which upholds and enforces the rule of law, lawyers have a special obligation to respect and foster respect for the rule of law, irrespective of their personal opinions about particular aspects of the law. The basic integrity of our system of law is the "long range good" that justifies the activities of lawyers generally.[250] "[I]f an independent judiciary is the backbone of the rule of law, as it has been often described, then an independent legal profession is the catalyst that helps achieve it."[251]

Moreover, our respect for the rule of law in society should be an active one.

> Part of our responsibility as legal professionals must be to work to maintain the law's ability to structure relationships appropriately and efficiently, and to resolve disputes fairly and as harmoniously as circumstances and litigants will allow. We must recognize that the social usefulness of the law, and in turn the esteem in which lawyers are held, depends ultimately on the respect the law receives from non-lawyers. But that objective can only be achieved if we lead by example. Only if lawyers take seriously their special responsibility to hold the law in respect themselves will others understand fully its importance to our culture. And only with that understanding will others accept that the professional independence of lawyers is necessary to the adequate functioning of the legal system.[252]

Law schools should ensure that their students understand the importance of the rule of law and their roles in maintaining it, and they should infuse students with a commitment to foster respect for the rule of law.

c.   **Honor, integrity, fair play, truthfulness, and candor.[253]**

Principle: Graduates embody honor, integrity, and fair play and are truthful and candid.

Comments:
It is important for lawyers to embody honor, integrity, and fair play and to be truthful and candid. It may be especially important for lawyers to embody integrity. "Integrity is clearly a foundation of professionalism, but its effect on personal well-being is perhaps even more direct. In fact, integrity is conceptually synonymous with health . . . a person's level of personal integrity affects his physical health and well-being directly."[254] Law students who understand the relationship between professionalism and their own health and well-being are more likely to be committed

---

[250] Timothy P. Terrell & James H. Wildman, *Rethinking "Professionalism,"* 41 EMORY L. J. 403, 426 (1992).

[251] Dieng, *supra* note 248, at 550 (crediting Fali Nariman for making the statement).

[252] Terrell & Wildman, *supra* note 250, at 426-27.

[253] Annotated lists of books and articles discussing the lawyer's duty to embody honor, integrity, and fair play and to be truthful and candid is located on the Professionalism of Lawyers and Judges website, http://professionalism.law.sc.edu.

[254] Krieger, *Professionalism and Personal Satisfaction, supra* note 76, at 431.

to professionalism.

> We may certainly discourage lying, deception, manipulation of fact or law, or abuse of people or process because such behavior is "unprofessional." But the impact will be multiplied if we also explain that such behavior erodes integrity by separating the lawyer from key parts of her self – her conscience, sense of decency, and/or intrinsic values. The results are likely to include loss of her professional reputation along with the physical and emotional stress that will undermine her health.[255]

It is well-documented that the decline in public respect for lawyers is in significant measure attributable to the public's sense that lawyers are not trustworthy.[256] While the public's perception of lawyers may not be entirely accurate, there are surely some reasons for the public to doubt the integrity and truthfulness of lawyers. "The disheartening reality is that among lawyers – who once claimed honesty and integrity as their stock-in-trade, and who once proudly asserted that their word was their bond – too many are *rightly* seen as untrustworthy."[257]

The Professional Reform Initiative (PRI), an Open Society-funded project of the National Conference of Bar Presidents, is seeking to increase public trust and confidence in the justice system. The PRI is identifying those aspects of lawyer conduct that affect public trust and confidence and formulating reforms and solutions for improving respect for the legal profession. As its first project, the PRI is emphasizing truthfulness, honesty, and integrity as fundamental core values of the legal profession. The PRI initiative is based on the view that lack of truthfulness by lawyers is a problem that requires the systematic and long-term attention of the organized bar. The PRI is reaching out to the judiciary, law schools, and bar admissions authorities to help implement curative plans of action.[258]

d. Sensitivity and effectiveness with diverse clients and colleagues.

Principle: **Graduates deal sensitively and effectively with diverse clients and colleagues.**

Comments:

It is important for law schools to help students develop their capacity to deal sensitively and effectively with clients and colleagues from a range of social, economic, and ethnic backgrounds. Students should learn to identify and respond positively and appropriately to issues of culture and disability that might affect communication techniques and influence a client's objectives. Cross-cultural competence is a skill that can be taught.[259]

---

[255] *Id.* at 431-32.

[256] Hodes, *supra* note 65, at 528.

[257] *Id.* at 533.

[258] The information about the PRI was taken from a collection of materials captioned "The Professional Reform Initiative: A Project of the National Conference of Bar Presidents," that was distributed during the 2004 ABA Annual Meeting. Additional details about the PRI and its integrity initiative are provided in Hodes, *supra* note 68. More current information about the PRI can be obtained from W. Seaborn Jones, Esq., tel. 404/688-2600, email jones@og-law.com.

[259] Susan Bryant, *The Five Habits: Building Cross-Cultural Competence in Lawyers,* 8

One way in which law schools can enhance their students' abilities to deal sensitively and effectively with diverse groups of clients and colleagues is by serving as a model for promoting diversity in law practice and the community, including having in the law school community a critical mass of students, faculty, and staff from minority groups that have traditionally been the victims of discrimination. As students progress through law school, they identify and analyze their conscious and subconscious biases regarding race, culture, social status, wealth, and poverty through discourse with their teachers and fellow students. They test their own perceptions against those of their peers and teachers. If the law school community is racially, culturally, and socio-economically diverse, students develop better understandings of the ways in which race and culture can affect clients' and lawyers' world views and influence their objectives and decisions.[260]

Students can improve their cross-cultural skills by practicing and honing throughout their professional careers the five habits of cross-cultural lawyering developed by Susan Bryant and Jean Koh Peters.[261]

Habit One: Degrees of Separation and Connection. Ask students to list and diagram similarities and differences between themselves and their clients and then explore the significance of these similarities and differences.

Habit Two: The Three Rings. Ask students to identify and analyze the possible effects of similarities and differences on the interaction between the client, the legal decision-maker, and the lawyer – the three rings.

Habit Three: Parallel Universes. Teach students to explore alternative explanations for clients' behaviors that might be based in cultural differences.

Habit Four: Pitfalls, Red Flags and Remedies. Teach students to identify before and during communications with clients potential cross-cultural pitfalls that may impede communication, understanding, and rapport.

Habit Five: The Camel's Back. Encourage students to explore themselves as cultural beings who have and are influenced by biases and stereotypes, to create settings in which bias and stereotype are less likely to govern, and to seek to eliminate bias.

CLINICAL L. REV. 33 (2001), citing R.W. Terry, *Authenticity: Unity Without Uniformity, in* THE PROMISE OF DIVERSITY: OVER 40 VOICES DISCUSS THE STRATEGIES FOR ELIMINATING DISCRIMINATION IN ORGANIZATIONS 113-14 (E. Y. Cross, J. H. Katz, F. A. Miller & E. W Seashore, eds., 1994).

[260] *See* Suellyn Scarnecchia, *Gender & Race Bias Against Lawyers: A Classroom Response,* 23 U. MICH. J. L. Reform 319, 331 (1990) (setting out student reactions to discussions of race or gender issues in law school classes); Mary Jo Eyster, *Analysis of Sexism in Legal Practice: A Clinical Approach*, 38 J. LEGAL EDUC. 183 (1988) (discussing confronting racism and sexism through clinical education).

[261] Bryant, *supra* note 259, at 64-78.

e.   **Nurturing quality of life.**[262]

Principle: **Graduates nurture quality of life.**

Comments:

As a group, lawyers do not do very well at nurturing the quality of their lives. Lawyers suffer higher rates of depression, anxiety, and other mental illness, suicide, divorce, alcoholism and drug abuse, and poor physical health than the general population or other occupations.[263]

These problems often begin in law school. As discussed in Chapter One, law school has negative effects on many students' health.[264] Although law students enter law school healthier and happier than other students, they leave law school in much worse shape.

> The findings that students became depressed and unhappy in the first year and remained so throughout law school are consistent with previous studies. Our further investigation of values and motivation was the first such study of which I am aware. All of the data provides empirical support for the concern that our legal training has precisely the opposite impact on students from that suggested by our rhetoric – it appears to undermine the values and motivation that promote professionalism as it markedly diminishes life satisfaction. All indications are that when students graduate and enter the profession, they are significantly different people from those who arrived to begin law school: they are more depressed, less service-oriented, and more inclined toward undesirable, superficial goals and values.[265]

Law school communities would be heathier, happier places if we help each other understand the nature of the problems that legal education and law practice can cause and jointly search for solutions for preventing damage to our students' sense of self-worth, security, authenticity, and competence.

Law schools can help students understand that "well-being results from experiences of *self-esteem, relatedness to others, autonomy, authenticity, and competence.* Fulfillment of any of these needs provides a sense of well-being and thriving, while lack of such experiences produces distress, depressed mood or loss of vitality. Self-esteem and relatedness shows the very strongest correlation to happiness."[266] The message law schools should send to our students is, "[i]f you

---

[262] An annotated list of books and articles discussing the importance of lawyers nurturing quality of life is located on the Professionalism of Lawyers and Judges website, http://professionalism.law.sc.edu.

[263] *See, e.g.,* Schiltz, *supra* note 76.

[264] The following list includes some of the more well-known articles about the negative impacts of legal education. They include cites to many studies, some of which are ongoing. Krieger, *Professionalism and Personal Satisfaction, supra* note 76; Krieger, Institutional Denial, *supra* note 76; Gulati et al., *supra* note 3; Schiltz, *supra* note 76; Krieger, *What We're Not Telling, supra* note 76; *Making Docile Lawyers, supra* note 76; GRANFIELD, *supra* note 76; Glesner, *supra* note 76.

[265] Krieger, *Professionalism and Personal Satisfaction, supra* note 76, at 433-34 (citations omitted).

[266] *Id.* at 430.

focus your life on growth of self, relationships, and community, your life will feel meaningful and satisfying. You will avoid the frustration, confusion, isolation, depression and addictions common to so many in our profession."[267]

Unfortunately, as discussed earlier, the attitudes, paradigms, and teaching methods at most law schools are sending the opposite message. Consequently, law students are suffering unnecessary harm during law school which negatively impacts their professionalism as well as their health and happiness. If we do not teach and enable students to nurture the quality of their lives during law school, it is unlikely they will do so when confronted with the demands and pressures of law practice.

---

[267] *Id.* at 437-38.

Chapter Three
Best Practices for Organizing the Program of Instruction

A.   Strive to Achieve Congruence.[268]

Principle: **The school strives to achieve congruence in its program of instruction.**

Comments:

Educational effectiveness requires law schools to aspire not only to comply with best practices related to each topic discussed in this document but also to aspire to achieve congruence among all topics. Congruence, in fact, is a defining characteristic of effective educational programs, and to achieve congruence, law schools need to harmonize:

- their educational programs with their missions in the sense that the educational outcomes derive from the missions,
- their curricula with their educational outcomes in the sense that the curricula have been structured to build students toward mastery of the outcomes, and
- their course-by-course instructional objectives with their curricula in the sense that the curricular design dictates course objectives.

Likewise, legal education would be improved if law schools employed educational practices that are congruent with the course-by-course educational objectives in that they facilitate student achievement of the objectives.

Evaluation processes should be employed that are congruent with all of the above in order for schools to determine if their objectives are being accomplished. Congruent evaluation processes allow schools to assess whether their instructional practices, taken together, constitute curricula that produce graduates who possess the skills, knowledge, and values described in Chapter Two and to adjust the practices and curricula as needed. By ensuring that graduates attain the desired educational outcomes, law schools fulfill their missions.

In order to achieve congruence, law schools will need to know when, where, and how each desired outcome will be accomplished in the overall program of instruction. Curriculum and co-curriculum maps are helpful in accomplishing this task. A curriculum map is a wide-angle view of a program of instruction. For each outcome, a curriculum map identifies where in the curriculum students will be introduced to the skill, value, or knowledge; where in the curriculum the students will practice it; and at what point in the curriculum students can be expected to have attained the desired level of proficiency. For example, a law school may decide that legal research skills can be introduced, practiced, and mastered by the end of the first year of law school, whereas problem-solving skills are introduced and practiced in the first year, practiced again in the second year, and not mastered until the third year.

Law schools should not ignore the potential value of co-curricular programs

---

[268] This section was drafted by Michael Hunter Schwartz.

to the development of knowledge, skills, and values. A co-curricular map can help identify opportunities for student learning in co-curricular settings, such as, journals, moot court, competitions, pro bono programs, Inns-of-Court, and speakers programs.

Peggy L. Maki, a Senior Scholar with the American Association of Higher Education, explains the benefits of curriculum mapping:

> To assure that students have sufficient and various kinds of educational opportunities to learn or develop desired outcomes, faculty and staff often engage in curricular and co-curricular mapping. During this process, representatives from across an institution identify the depth and breadth of opportunities inside and outside of the classroom that intentionally address the development of desired outcomes. Multiple opportunities enable students to reflect on and practice the outcomes an institution or program asserts it develops. Furthermore, variation in teaching and learning strategies and educational opportunities contributes to students' diverse ways of learning. Column B provides a list of possible opportunities that might foster a desired outcome. That is, an institution has to assure itself that it has translated its mission and purposes into its programs and services to more greatly assure that students have opportunities to learn and develop what an institution values. If the results of mapping reveal insufficient or limited opportunities for students to develop a desired outcome, then an institution needs to question its educational intentionality. Without ample opportunities to reflect on and practice desired outcomes, students will likely not transfer, build upon, or deepen the learning and development an institution or program values.[269]

Curriculum maps are crucial to institutional advancement, because they can reveal both curricular redundancy and curricular gaps and inadequacies. For example, a law school may discover that its curriculum re-teaches certain skills, such as issue-spotting, applying rules to facts, and applying and distinguishing cases, over and over again. At the same time, the curriculum may fail to provide students with sufficient opportunities to handle the complex, multi-disciplinary client issues necessary to student development of problem-solving skills and no opportunity to develop self-regulated learning skills.

B.   Progressively Develop Knowledge, Skills, and Values.

Principle: The program of instruction is organized to provide students coordinated educational experiences that progressively lead them to develop the knowledge, skills, and values required for their first professional jobs.

Comments:

The importance of organizing the program of instruction to develop desired outcomes progressively is promoted by the Association of American Colleges and Universities:

---

[269] Maki, *supra* note 130, at 3.

> Well-designed curricula are more than just collections of
> independent courses; they are pathways for learning. Graduating
> intentional learners – empowered, informed, and responsible – calls
> for curricula designed to further learning goals in a sequential
> manner . . . .[270]

Paul Dressel described the curricular organization that one would expect to
find in a professional graduate school as follows.

> In professional and technical fields, the overall goal of
> preparing the individual for a definite career has encouraged the
> faculty to think about the curriculum as a well-planned and organized
> course of study. Requirements tend to be heavy, and electives are
> limited. . . . [T]he fact that the students are being educated for a job
> forces a degree of unity and coherence in the program.[271]

The organization of most law schools' curriculums falls somewhere between
that of a typical professional graduate school and that of a typical program of
instruction for preparing liberally-educated students. There are many required
courses, especially if we count bar exam subjects that students feel pressured to take,
but most law schools' programs of instruction lack coherence, coordination, or focus
toward the goal of preparing students for law practice.

At most law schools, individual members of the faculty operate with a
few moments of reflection and fewer yet of considered choice in matters related
to the overall curriculum, approaches to teaching and learning, and institutional
frameworks for legal education, especially beyond the first year.

> Too often faculty members do the expected, offering
> autonomous courses with little regard to the overall curriculum or
> the seemingly unbridgeable chasm between "traditional" faculty
> committed to "theory" and "skills" faculty who teach in clinics and
> legal writing programs. Similarly, students often take the path
> of least resistance, drifting through the later years of law school
> with little intellectual drive or recognition of responsibility for
> key choices that will shape the professionals they hope to become.
> Yet, . . . they could stop and reflect before making individual and
> collective choices that could shape legal education for the better.
> New patterns are emerging such as a rich, collaborative "laboratory"
> model that now, unrecognized, underlies the best of legal writing,
> clinical, and specialized substantive specialties, creating coherence
> and progression within focused contexts and broader implications if
> attention is paid. Fresh perspective on the balance of the curriculum
> suggests that clear-eyed attention to the goal of knowledge transfer,
> higher expectations of students, and new forms of inter-institutional
> cooperation could result in more well-defined educational progression
> and better use of faculty time.[272]

---

[270] *Principles of Good Practice in the New Academy, in* Ass'n of Am. Colleges and Universities, Greater Expectations: A New Vision for Learning as a Nation Goes to College 30 (2002) [hereinafter Greater Expectations].

[271] Dressel, *supra* note 110, at 298.

[272] Wegner, Theory and Practice, *supra* note 46, at 3.

One of the reasons why law school curriculums lack coordination is the tradition of trying to accommodate faculty preferences and student requests. "Often curricular decisions are made in an incremental fashion, through negotiations between associate deans and individual faculty members or students. Varying dynamics characterize different schools and the resulting curriculum is often a patchwork that reflects favors given one or denied another faculty member, pragmatic compromises and negotiations that rarely proceed systematically or see the light of day."[273]

Curriculum design should be guided by a school's educational goals. Existing courses and new course proposals should be evaluated in light of how each course helps the school achieve its educational objectives. Each faculty member should be expected to demonstrate why each course is needed, and course approval should be based on whether the course meets students' needs and interests, not just the teacher's.

Legal writing teachers at many institutions and collectively through their national organization are encouraging and engaging in the kinds of coordination, sharing, and collaboration that would benefit all components of legal education. Noting that many law school courses are isolated from one another as a result of the high value accorded traditional faculty autonomy, Judith Wegner found that within the legal writing community "[t]he commitment to shared design and coordination of coverage, the exchange of lesson plans, the use of grading templates, among other aspects shows how sharply such offerings contrast to classes of other sorts."[274]

We encourage law schools to engage in more systematic *institutional* planning of their programs of instruction to achieve greater coherence. We endorse the following recommendation of the Cramton Report.

> Recommendation 7: Law schools should seek to achieve greater coherence in their curriculum. Even if it entails the loss of some teacher autonomy, the three-year program should build in a structured way: to present students with problems of successively broader scope and challenge, to enable students to teach themselves, and to utilize skills and knowledge acquired earlier.[275]

Some progress with coordination has been made since the Cramton Report was released in 1979, but not very much. All law schools structure segments of their programs of instruction to ensure that students receive basic instruction in some subjects before taking more advanced courses. Law schools have not made much effort, however, to consider how best to coordinate the delivery of instruction about knowledge, skills, and values throughout the entire curriculum.[276]

---

[273] *Id.* at 12-13.

[274] *Id.* at 32.

[275] AMERICAN BAR ASSOCIATION, SECTION OF LEGAL EDUCATION AND ADMISSIONS TO THE BAR, REPORT AND RECOMMENDATIONS OF THE TASK FORCE ON LAWYER COMPETENCY: THE ROLE OF THE LAW SCHOOLS 4 (1979) [hereinafter CRAMTON REPORT].

[276] An exception to this is the growing trend to offer "tracks" in which students concentrate in specific fields of law, especially those with components that give students real life experiences. Some such programs provide a progressive series of educational experiences that cover skills and values in addition to legal knowledge.

C.   Integrate the Teaching of Theory, Doctrine, and Practice

Principle: The program of instruction integrates the teaching of theory, doctrine, and practice.

Comments:

Law schools have a tradition of emphasizing instruction in theory and doctrine over practice and of treating theory and doctrine as distinct, separate subjects from practice. The separation of theory and doctrine from practice in the law curriculum was an unfortunate fluke of history that hinders the ability of law schools to prepare students for practice.

> The separation of theory and practice in legal education may have originated in Thorstein Veblen's wisecrack in 1918 that "in point of substantial merit the law school belongs in the modern university no more than a school of fencing or dancing," or even Christopher Columbus Langdell's claim that the content of legal education must be scientific to be worthy of study in a university. John Dewey traced the origins of the dualism of theory and practice to the distinction drawn in Near Eastern cultures between higher and lower kinds of knowledge for purposes of social status. This distinction was unfortunately perpetrated by the Greeks, who confined experiential knowledge to the artisan and trader classes and hindered the development of scientific knowledge for more than one and a half millennia. Whether arising from a desire for social status or respectability within the university or from some other cause, the determined separation of theory from practice has severely limited the scope of modern legal education.[277]

Judith Wegner acknowledged the continuing dichotomy between theory and practice in legal education, but she encouraged legal educators to recognize the value of both as important subjects for teaching and scholarship.

> [L]egal educators and other university faculty have engaged in debate over the relative role of "theory" and "practice" for many years. It has long been common in academia to look down on "practice," carrying forward the Aristotelian preference for the intellectual life (and associated forms of declarative, written knowledge) to which academics commit themselves. Much like the blind men and the elephant, however, they have often been blind to the multiple dimensions of these concepts or assumed in error that the terms employed refer to similar things. Like George Orwell, academics are often drawn to shoot the elephant referred to as "practice" rather than to reflect on the reasons for and implications of such a choice.[278]

---

[277] Cooper, *supra* note 38, at 21.

[278] Wegner, Theory and Practice, *supra* note 46, at 7-8 (citing Aristotle, Nichomecean Ethics). *See also* Blasi, *supra* note 15, at 315-16 (explaining that "law professors know quite a lot about how lawyers acquire expertise in solving doctrinal problems. But we know virtually nothing about how lawyers acquire the other abilities most valued by clients: expertise, judgment, problem-solving abilities in areas beyond doctrine. Legal academics have largely ignored

One of the impediments to merging instruction in theory and practice has been the perception that context-based learning is useful for teaching "practical skills" but not substantive law or theoretical reasoning associated with "thinking like a lawyer." In fact, the opposite is true. In discussing her conclusions from studying legal writing and clinical programs, Wegner made the following observations:

> The evidence suggests quite strongly, however, that legal writing programs at their core reinforce instruction in traditional legal reasoning, using work with cases and statutes to push students' individual capacities to comprehend and analyze, then posing complex problems requiring not only these capabilities, but also ability to apply and synthesis legal concepts and to evaluate their bearing from competing points of view. Legal writing programs in fact provide a much better opportunity to judge students' development of advanced cognitive abilities than is afforded in large classes, where a single examination is generally offered and few opportunities for feedback or improvement exist.

> On the other hand, there are significant educational differences between legal writing and clinical instruction that have often been blurred. As discussed more fully later in this chapter, "practical judgment" in the useful sense described by Aristotle, is context-dependent, linked to intensive interplay between theory and a human problem, as relevant knowledge is developed through reflection in light of the surrounding circumstances and brought to fruition through action. This special modality of reasoning and knowing lies at the heart of "lawyering" courses and other courses that engage students intensively with solving problems in particular substantive fields, but is only superficially involved in legal writing courses in the first year. Instead, legal writing courses seem to fill the gap too often evident in first year curricula, providing students with a more concrete sense of lawyers and the world in which they operate, particularly when instructors with prior or ongoing practice experience are used. In interesting ways, legal writing programs have moved away from traditional instructional patterns found within the first-year core, favoring collaborative learning designs that more closely approximate the practice communities in which lawyers generally work. These similarities should not, however, confuse the differences in educational goals and forms of reasoning that lie at legal writing programs' hearts.[279]

Wegner's overall thesis is "that the disquiet associated with portions of the curriculum outside the first year core stems from legal educators' difficulty in seeing the full picture and the tendency to 'shoot the elephant' of practice-oriented instruction rather than to explore the context from which that impulse stems."[280] The following statement provides a vision of the kind of legal education we should be striving to provide:

---

these other aspects of lawyering practice, seeing them as either uninteresting or unfathomable").

[279] Wegner, Theory and Practice, *supra* note 46, at 29.

[280] *Id.* at 28.

[L]aw schools must serve the goal of teaching fundamental legal concepts, but this is only the beginning of a first-rate legal education. The MacCrate Commission and other critics argue that legal educators must avoid being too narrow, devoting too much time to honing the ability to analyze doctrine and too little to developing other abilities that are relevant to competent practice. We are sympathetic to this criticism. Unfortunately, however, the criticism has been misunderstood to set doctrinal analysis apart from all other kinds of lawyering work. This misunderstanding undermines reform efforts, for the doctrine-versus-other-skills dichotomy makes it difficult to appreciate the integration of capacities that occurs when one practices law successfully. We take a slightly different approach, arguing for development of an intellectual versatility that enriches doctrinal analysis as much as it expands the number of lawyering activities that students are led to consider. Legal education needs to be broad-ranging in its approaches to the analysis of doctrine as well as in its approaches to other tasks like counseling, negotiation, business planning, or advocacy. We therefore seek to develop a range of intellectual capacities and to teach students to integrate the use of those capacities across the various categories of lawyering work.

[H]igh quality, responsible lawyering requires integrated development of a broad range of intellectual capacities. . . . The analysis of doctrine is deeper if one has the intrapersonal intelligence to grasp multiple perspectives; the conduct of a mediation is more successful if one has the logical-mathematical intelligence to calculate prospective gains and losses; advocacy is more convincing if one has the strategic intelligence to assess both the efficacy of a move in the small world of litigation and the policy implications of a legal interpretation in the larger world.[281]

The authors of the Carnegie Foundation's report on legal education agree that law schools should integrate the teaching of theory, doctrine, and practice.

A fuller and more adequate legal education, one that would provide a broader – and, therefore, more realistic as well as more ethically appealing – understanding of the various vocations in the law, could not be based solely on most schools' current pedagogical and assessment practices. This fuller and more adequate preparation for the profession would, from the beginning, introduce students to lawyering and clinical work as well as concern with ethical and professional responsibility – in short, the cognitive, practical, and ethical-social apprenticeships would be integrated.[282]

Law schools cannot prepare students for practice unless they teach doctrine, theory, and practice as part of a unified, coordinated program of instruction.[283]

---

[281] Peggy Cooper Davis & Elizabeth Ehrenfest Steinglass, *A Dialogue About Socratic Teaching*, 23 N.Y.U. Rev. L. & Soc. Change 249, 251 (1997) (proposing improvements in the use of Socratic dialogue in law school teaching) (citations omitted).

[282] Sullivan et al., *supra* note 7, at 231.

[283] *See* Karen Gross, *Process Reengineering and Legal Education: an Essay on Daring to Think Differently*, 49 N.Y.L. Sch. L. Rev. 435 (2004-2005) (discussing ways to integrate

"Although theory and practice are distinct concepts, the resolution of lawyering problems involves a mixture of theoretical and practical concerns."[284]

> [T]he threefold movement between law as doctrine and precedent (the focus of the case-dialogue classroom) to attention to professional skills (the aim of the apprenticeship of practice) and then to responsible engagement with solving clients' legal problems – a back and forth cycle of action and reflection – also characterize most legal practice. The separation of these phases into distinct areas of the curriculum, or as separate apprenticeships, is always an artificial "decomposition" of practice. The pedagogical cycle is not completed unless these segregated domains are reconnected.[285]

"[W]e believe legal education requires not simply more additions, but a truly integrative approach in order to provide students with broad-based yet coherent beginning for their legal careers."[286]

D. Teach Professionalism Pervasively Throughout All Three Years of Law School.

Principle: **The school provides pervasive professionalism instruction and role modeling throughout all three years of law school.**

Comments:

Law schools do not currently foster professional conduct; just the opposite. Some fundamental changes are needed if law schools want to teach professionalism effectively. The competitive atmosphere and negative messages to students about their competence and self-worth impede the development of the attributes of professional lawyers. "The law school experience is a competition between students for limited rewards that foster unprofessional conduct."[287] "[U]nprofessional behavior among law students and lawyers typically proceed from a loss of integrity – a disconnection from intrinsic values and motivations, personal and cultural beliefs, conscience, or other defining parts of their personality and humanity."[288]

Law schools can and should have a positive impact on students' professional and personal values. As discussed in more detail in Chapter One, however, researchers have documented that existing law school goals, organization, and methods of teaching and evaluation tend to move students toward poor habits and inclinations to engage in unprofessional conduct. These negative effects are not inevitable.

---

instruction in doctrine, theory, and practice); Margaret Martin Barry, Jon C. Dubin & Peter A. Joy, *Clinical Education for this Millennium: The Third Wave*, 7 CLINICAL L. REV. 1, 19-28 (2000) (describing existing courses and programs that integrate instruction in doctrine, theory, and practice).

[284] Aaronson, *supra* note 176, at 287-88.

[285] SULLIVAN ET AL., *supra* note 7, at 147-48.

[286] *Id.* at 53.

[287] Roger I. Abrams, *Law School as a Professional Community, in* AMERICAN BAR ASSOCIATION, SECTION OF LEGAL EDUCATION AND ADMISSIONS TO THE BAR, TEACHING AND LEARNING PROFESSIONALISM: SYMPOSIUM PROCEEDINGS 53, 55 (1996).

[288] Krieger, *Professionalism and Personal Satisfaction, supra* note 76, at 426.

Law school experiences, if they are powerfully engaging, have the potential to influence the place of moral values such as integrity and social contribution in students' sense of self. This is especially likely to take place in relation to the students' sense of professional identity, which is of course an important part of the individual's identity more broadly. Professional identity is, in essence, the individual's answer to questions such as "Who am I as a member of this profession?" "What am I like and what do I want to be like in my professional role?" and "What place do ethical-social values have in my core sense of professional identity?" Since law school represents a critical phase in the transition into the profession, it is inevitable that it will influence students' image of what kind of lawyers they want to be.[289]

The culture and environment of the law school community should foster professional conduct. "A law school must have a culture of respect, civility, responsibility, and honor."[290] A culture of professionalism is promoted when the faculty, staff, and administrators model professional values and attitudes. Students will do as we do more frequently than they will do as we say. "For most students law school professors are their first and most important role models of lawyers. Professionalism ideals can either be enhanced or undermined by the behavior of faculty in and out of the classroom."[291]

An increased emphasis on instruction in and assessment of professionalism in legal education sends an important message to students. Often this might involve simply maintaining high standards for conscientious and respectful work in clinics, issues that are uncontroversial from an ethical point of view. Even when the questions being confronted are more complex and subject to multiple interpretations, however, teaching for and assessing professionalism need not entail the imposition of individual faculty members' own moral views on their students. Nor must all students agree on what the "right" or ethically defensible behavior is in ambiguous or complicated situations. Rather, the infusion of ethical concerns into teaching and assessment in legal education conveys a profoundly important message that, as future stewards of the profession, students must figure out for themselves an ethically defensible approach to their work; and that, as officers of the court and citizens, lawyers should not ignore the larger consequences of their professional behavior and conduct.[292]

Students should be expected to conduct themselves professionally upon entering law school, however, law students do not know intuitively what constitutes professional or unprofessional behavior. They learn how to act either by being taught or through their experiences. Law schools can help students understand the expectations placed on them as members of the legal profession by defining the components of professionalism when students enter school (or even before they

---

[289] Sullivan et al., *supra* note 7, at 163.

[290] Abrams, *supra* note 287, at 59.

[291] Teaching and Learning Professionalism, *supra* note 134, at 13.

[292] Sullivan et al., *supra* note 7, at 224-25.

arrive on campus) and by making it clear what the school considers to be appropriate professional conduct during law school and afterwards.

Instruction about professionalism would be more effective if it is provided pervasively and continuously.

> [A]s a general rule, law schools have treated professionalism issues as being part of legal ethics, to be covered in whatever course or courses deal explicitly with the subject. Although there has been a great deal written about the pervasive method of teaching legal ethics throughout the entire curriculum, law schools have, for the most part, merely given lip service to this approach. Thus, the basic course in legal ethics or professional responsibility has become, by design or by lack of time, the main, if not the only, place in the law school curriculum where students are exposed in a systematic manner to professionalism issues.[293]

We are not proposing that pervasive instruction in professionalism should replace courses in professional responsibility or other professionalism-focused courses. Rather, we are proposing that all members of a law faculty should embrace their collective responsibility to contribute to their students' understanding of and commitment to professional behavior.

> Law students need concrete ethical training. They need to know why pro bono work is so important. They need to understand their duties as "officers of the court." They need to learn that cases and statutes are normative texts, appropriately interpreted from a public-regarding point of view, and not mere missiles to be hurled at opposing counsel. They need to have great ethical teachers, and to have every teacher address ethical problems where such problems arise.[294]

Deborah Rhode is the most prominent proponent of teaching professional responsibility pervasively.[295] We believe she will concur with our conclusion that professionalism, which encompasses professional responsibility, should be taught pervasively. We agree with Rhode that the task will not be easy but the potential rewards warrant making the effort.

> This is neither to underestimate the difficulties in implementing a comprehensive approach nor to overstate its likely impact. The experience of law schools that have claimed to teach ethics by the pervasive method offers sobering case studies. But even if the aspiration of an integrated curriculum may be difficult to realize, it holds far more promise than the prevailing alternative. To ignore issues of professional responsibility as they arise in particular substantive areas marginalizes the ethical dimensions of daily practice. All too often, students will view their mandatory course as an add-on, a public relations digression from what is really

---

[293] TEACHING AND LEARNING PROFESSIONALISM, *supra* note 134, at 14 (citations omitted).
[294] Edwards, *supra* note 205, at 38.
[295] Deborah Rhode, *Ethics by the Pervasive Method*, 42 J. LEGAL EDUC. 32 (1996).

important. Every law school does, in fact, teach some form of ethics by the pervasive method, and pervasive silence speaks louder than formal policies and commencement platitudes.[296]

Walter Bennett encourages all law professors to embrace the challenges posed by teaching professionalism. After describing the importance of helping law students begin the process of viewing themselves as members of a noble profession and acting accordingly, Bennett wrote:

> And law professors should not be exempt from this process. In fact, the professor in the class described above will be competent to lead it and to read and grade student papers if, and only if, above all she views herself as a professional and fellow pilgrim on the personal and professional myth-way. The notion that law professors (and law schools) are somehow exempt from the process of inculcating professionalism because they are engaged in more lofty and arcane pursuits is an attitude the legal profession can no longer afford (if it ever could). A professional school should be staffed by people who think of themselves as professionals with perhaps an even greater obligation than practicing lawyers to pass on the professional creed.[297]

We endorse the following recommendations for improving law school professionalism training in Teaching and Learning Professionalism, and we encourage more law schools to make their implementation a priority.
- faculty must become more acutely aware of their significance as role models for law students' perception of lawyering.
- greater emphasis needs to be given to the concept of law professors as role models of lawyering in hiring and evaluating faculty.
- adoption of the pervasive method of teaching legal ethics and professionalism should be seriously considered by every law school.
- every law school should develop an effective system for encouraging and monitoring its ethics and professionalism programs.
- the use of diverse teaching methods such as role playing, problems and case studies, small groups and seminars, story-telling, and interactive videos to teach ethics and professionalism, should be encouraged.
- law book publishers should consider adopting a policy requiring that all new casebooks and instructional materials incorporate ethical and professionalism issues. Law book publishers should also publish more course-specific materials on legal ethics and professionalism issues as part of new casebooks, new editions of old casebooks, supplements to casebooks, compilations of supplemental readings, and compendiums.
- law schools need to develop more fully co-curricular activities, policies, and infrastructures that reflect a genuine concern with professionalism.[298]

Many of the problems with the legal profession begin with the explicit and implicit education provided by law schools. Law teachers should become more

---

[296] *Id.*

[297] Bennett, *supra* note 70, at 178.

[298] Teaching and Learning Professionalism, *supra* note 134, at 16-25 (citations and narrative omitted).

informed of the negative impacts that law school can have on students and consider how law school can more effectively help students develop the positive attributes of professional lawyers.

Chapter Four
Best Practices for Delivering Instruction, Generally

A. **Know Your Subjects Extremely Well.**

Principle: **The teachers know their subjects extremely well.**

Comments:
This almost goes without saying. "Without exception, outstanding teachers know their subjects extremely well."[299]

The most knowledgeable teachers, however, are not necessarily excellent teachers.

> [The best teachers], unlike so many others, have used their knowledge to develop techniques for grasping fundamental principles and organizing concepts that others can use to begin building their own understanding and abilities. They know how to simplify and clarify complex subjects, to cut to the heart of the matter with provocative insights, and they can think about their own thinking in the discipline, analyzing its nature and evaluating its quality. That capacity to think metacognitively drives much of what we observed in the best teaching.[300]

So, although one cannot become a great teacher without knowing the subject extremely well, more than knowledge is required to excel.

B. **Continuously Strive to Improve Your Teaching Skills.**

Principle: **The teachers continuously strive to improve their teaching skills, aided by the school's teacher development program.**

Comments:
This principle is consistent with the accreditation standards for law schools which require law schools to have a faculty that "possesses a high degree of competence, as demonstrated by its . . . Experience in teaching . . ., teaching effectiveness . . . ." The standards also require law schools "to ensure effective teaching by all persons providing instruction to students."[301] An interpretation of the standards provides that:

> Efforts to ensure teaching effectiveness may include: a faculty committee on effective teaching, class visitations, critiques of videotaped teaching, institutional review of student evaluation of teaching, colloquia on effective teaching, and recognition of creative scholarship in law school teaching methodology. A law school shall provide all new faculty members with orientation, guidance,

---

[299] KEN BAIN, WHAT THE BEST COLLEGE TEACHERS DO 15 (2004).
[300] *Id.* at 16.
[301] Standard 401, ABA STANDARDS, *supra* note 28, at 28.

mentoring, and periodic evaluation.[302]

The skills, values, and commitment of the people who deliver instruction to law students are, more than any other factor, the essential ingredients for preparing students for law practice. The accreditation standards require a law school to "have a faculty that possesses a high degree of competence, as demonstrated by its education, *classroom teaching ability, experience in teaching or practice*, and scholarly research and writing."[303]

> The most effective teachers have the following characteristics:
> - they exhibit genuine enthusiasm for teaching,
> - they follow good practices in planning and preparing entire courses and individual classes,
> - they stimulate student thought and interest,
> - they ascertain when their students are confused and use examples to diffuse students' confusion, and
> - they know and love their subjects and communicate that love to their students.[304]

Susan Hatfield described some of the attributes of effective teachers.

> The substantial body of research on effective teaching, upon which most systems for evaluating college teaching are based, emphasizes teacher behavior that actively engages students in learning. In addition to other traits such as command of subject matter, clear communication of expectations, enthusiasm, and expressiveness, effective teachers are often identified as those who encourage classroom interaction, establish rapport with students, and provide individualized feedback and reinforcement of student performance. Good teachers are further described as approachable, interested in students' learning and well-being, accessible, open to students' ideas and questions, and concerned about students' progress.[305]

Although the core mission of most law schools is to educate students, virtually no legal educators have educational training or experience when they are hired, and few law schools provide more than cursory assistance to help new faculty develop their teaching skills. As Deborah Rhode observed, "[w]e do not effectively educate legal educators. Most law professors get no formal training in teaching. Nor have legal academics shown much interest in building on broader educational research about how students learn."[306]

Some law schools organize sessions for their faculty where learning theory and teaching techniques are discussed, but these are generally minimal in scope and non-mandatory. At most law schools, new professors' classes are observed once or twice a year during their first few years of teaching by some of their more

---

[302] Standard 403(b), *id.* at 30.

[303] Interpretation 403-2, *id.* (emphasis added).

[308] GERALD F. HESS & STEVEN FRIEDLAND, TECHNIQUES FOR TEACHING LAW 12-14 (1999).

[305] THE SEVEN PRINCIPLES IN ACTION: IMPROVING UNDERGRADUATE EDUCATION 11-12 (Susan Rickey Hatfield ed., 1995) [hereinafter SEVEN PRINCIPLES IN ACTION].

[306] RHODE, *supra* note 109, at 196-97.

experienced colleagues who also had no formal education in teaching. While some peer reviews are very helpful, their value depends on the commitment and skills of the reviewers. After achieving tenure in six or fewer years, most law professors' classroom performances are seldom, if ever, evaluated again other than through end-of-the-semester student evaluations.

As a consequence of legal education's traditions of putting untrained teachers into classrooms, not establishing teacher development programs, and not effectively monitoring what occurs in classrooms, the quality of law students' educational experiences can vary greatly from teacher to teacher.

Despite many calls from the profession for law schools to give more weight to a person's potential and performance as a teacher in making hiring, retention, and tenure decisions and in rewarding faculty achievements,[307] most law schools continue to place more value on a new faculty member's potential for scholarly research and writing and to reward law professors almost exclusively for their scholarly activities. Many law schools assert that they expect excellence in both teaching and scholarship, but the primary criterion for tenure and promotion is usually scholarship, and most faculty make the perfectly rational decision to commit more time to scholarship than teaching.[308]

> There is much evidence that, institutionally, law schools care little about the quality of teaching. No overseeing body measures whether individual law schools have met previously defined factors regarding what constitutes effective teaching. Neither the ABA nor the AALS have defined what constitutes effective teaching. Moreover, law schools have not developed reliable methods to assess teaching. To the extent that schools engage in teaching assessment, they rely almost exclusively on student evaluations. Tellingly, hiring and promotion decisions in law schools are almost exclusively based on scholarship, and "most schools make no adverse decisions on the basis of teaching." In a perverse way, law schools' emphasis on scholarship further diminishes the already compromised quality of teaching by diverting faculty investment of time and effort away from the schools' teaching mission.[309]

It is not clear why this situation persists at so many law schools. Most law professors sincerely want to be good teachers, and many are, but too few study and practice effective educational philosophies and techniques. Tom Drummond's hypothesis about why good teaching in college is not adequately rewarded seems to fit legal education as well. "Instead of directly addressing learning to teach well, we often erroneously assume new teachers

---

[307] One task force recommended "that law school appointments, promotion, and tenure should place substantial emphasis on teaching performance." American Bar Association, Task Force on Professional Competence, Final Report and Recommendations of the Task Force on Professional Competence 12 (1983). This was consistent with the recommendation of an earlier task force's recommendation that "[l]aw school policies and practices of faculty appointment, promotion, and tenure should pay greater rewards for commitment to teaching, including teaching by techniques that foster skills development." Cramton Report, *supra* note 275, at 26.

[308] Gerald F. Hess, *Seven Principles for Good Practice in Legal Education: Principle 3: Good Practice Encourages Active Learning*, 49 J. Legal Educ. 401, 403 (1999).

[309] Lasso, *supra* note 133, at 56 n.281 (citations omitted).

know how to teach because they used to be students."[310]

If law schools really want their faculties to be excellent teachers, law school deans and faculties would "readjust institutional priorities so that teaching and scholarship have equal value."[311] In fact, law schools that are serious about teaching would reward professors whose students demonstrate greater levels of mastery on examinations.

> High expectations for teaching is a necessary prerequisite to increasing the expectations of students. For example, how would our teaching change if we defined ourselves by quality teaching and then set about to measure it in ourselves and others? What if, along with student evaluations of our teaching, we measured student mastery of course material against external, objective standards? What if our own professional success as teachers was measured by our students' success? How would our decisions about salary, promotion, and tenure, endowed chairs, or other tangible benefits be affected if we expected great teaching from all faculty? How would the curriculum structure change? Many faculty who care deeply about teaching become mired in negative expectations about the status of teaching in legal education.[312]

An important part of becoming an effective teacher is to learn how to conduct valid, reliable, and pedagogically meaningful assessments of student learning, but very few law professors receive any training in assessment theory or practice. We agree with Ron Aizen that such training should be provided, even mandated.

> Although any training would be welcome, the more extensive and formal the training, the more effective it likely would be. To truly maximize their abilities to assess students, professors should probably complete at least the equivalent of one college-level course in assessment design and grading. Law schools could work together to develop such a course, thus allowing the schools to share expertise and resources. Perhaps a group such as the AALS could coordinate such an effort – the association already offers educational workshops and conferences to its members.

> Training in assessment construction and grading should probably be made mandatory for both new and experienced law professors, and it should perhaps even be required as a condition of law school accreditation. Alternatively, the training could be kept voluntary, in which case it would be helpful to award a certificate to those who successfully completed the training. Certification would not only serve as proof that the training participants had acquired basic competency in crafting and grading assessments, but it also would provide one measure of the quality of a law school's assessments. This information would help prospective students, who might prefer to attend a school with a relatively high proportion of

---

[310] Drummond, *supra* note 143.

[311] Hess, *supra* note 308, at 403.

[312] Barbara Glesner-Fines, *The Impact of Expectations on Teaching and Learning*, 38 GONZ. L. REV. 89, 112 (2003) (citation omitted).

certified professors.[313]

Improving the quality of teaching in United States' law schools will not happen quickly or easily. A collective national effort is required as well as collaborative efforts within each law school.[314] Law teachers should seek "consensus on an ever-evolving definition of what constitutes best practices in this amorphous and complex endeavor"[315] and employ best practices in teaching, such as those set out in this document.

Ken Bain considered how to fashion a better summative evaluation of teaching.[316] He concluded that properly constructed "teaching portfolios" would be the best approach. The teaching portfolios envisioned by Bain would include student and peer evaluations, but the key component would be an analysis by the teacher of his or her goals and strategies, degree of success, and plans for the future.[317] The portfolio would be "the pedagogic equivalent of the scholarly paper, a document intended to capture the scholarship of teaching."[318]

> In short, a teacher should think about teaching (in a single session or an entire course) as a serious intellectual act, a kind of scholarship, a creation; he or she should then develop a case, complete with evidence, exploring the intellectual (and perhaps artistic) meaning and qualities of that teaching. Each case would lay out the argument in an essay.[319]

In this vision of teacher development, student learning drives legal education and faculty training, and evaluation is crucial. This vision also finds support from the American Association of Colleges and Universities (AACU). The AACU believes that faculty development has a critical role in the future of higher education; however, the AACU makes it clear that educational institutions must themselves invest in faculty development.

> Colleges and universities with learning as the center of their work provide professors with every means possible to teach, advise and mentor their students well. User friendly and extensive programs of faculty development help them become professional educators.[320]

Many of the principles for excellent teaching of students apply with equal force to training novice teachers. For example, communicating high expectations

---

[313] Ron M. Aizen, *Four Ways to Better 1L Assessments,* 54 Duke L.J. 765, 790-91 (2004).

[314] Pace University regularly updates a list of resources related to teaching effectiveness on its Faculty Development Collection web page, http://www.pace.edu/library/pages/links/facevcollection.html. A promising resource is the International Journal for the Scholarship of Teaching & Learning (IJ-So TL), http://www.georgiasouthern.edu/ijfotl/, that will be published by the Center for Excellence in Teaching at Georgia Southern University with the inaugural issue scheduled for January, 2007.

[315] Drummond, *supra* note 143.

[316] Bain *supra* note 299, at 166-72.

[317] For the specific questions that Bain proposes, see *id.* at 168-69.

[318] *Id.* at 169.

[319] *Id.*

[320] Greater Expectations, *supra* note 270, at 36.

to new teachers, providing them with high quality and frequent feedback, creating opportunities for new faculty to work with peers, and encouraging self-efficacy and mastery goals are all more likely to produce master teachers.

There is no quick and easy way to improve the quality of teaching in law schools, but we owe it to our students, their clients, and their employers to take our teaching responsibilities seriously.

C.   Create and Maintain Effective and Healthy Teaching and Learning Environments.

Principle: The teachers create and maintain effective and healthy teaching and learning environments.

Comments:

We are indebted to Gerry Hess for synthesizing four models of effective teaching and learning environments and providing the organizational structure and much of the content of this section.[321] Hess describes eight components of effective and healthy teaching and learning environments: respect, expectation, support, collaboration, inclusion, engagement, delight, and feedback."[322] We added one that is implicit in Hess' components – do no harm to students.[323]

Hess' conclusions are similar to Ken Bain's who wrote that the best teachers often try to create a "natural critical learning environment." The environment is "natural" because students encounter the skills, habits, attitudes, and information they are trying to learn embedded in questions and tasks they find fascinating – authentic tasks that arouse curiosity and become intrinsically interesting. The environment is "critical" because students learn to think critically, to reason from evidence, to examine the quality of their reasoning using a variety of intellectual standards, to make improvements while thinking, and to ask probing and insightful questions about the thinking of other people.[324]

The learning environments in the best teachers' classrooms provide "challenging yet supportive conditions in which learners feel a sense of control over their education; work collaboratively with others; believe that their work will be considered fairly and honestly; and try, fail, and receive feedback from expert learners in advance of and separate from any summative judgment of their effort."[325]

The practices described in this section will help law teachers construct healthy, effective teaching and learning environments, but [t]he magic does not lie in any one of these practices. I cannot stress enough the simple yet powerful notion that the key to understanding the best teaching

---

[321] Hess, *supra* note 84, at 87.

[322] *Id.*

[323] Law teachers would also benefit from studying Tom Drummond's summary of best practices in teaching which gives specific examples of useful techniques related to the following topics: lecture practices, group discussion triggers, thoughtful questions, reflective responses to learner contributions, rewarding learner participation, active learning strategies, cooperative group assignments, goals to grades connections, modeling, double loop feedback, climate setting, and fostering learner responsibility. Drummond, *supra* note 145.

[324] Bain, *supra* note 299, at 99.

[325] *Id.* at 18.

can be found not in particular practices or rules but in the *attitudes* of the teachers, in their *faith* in their students' abilities to achieve, in their *willingness* to take their students seriously and to let them assume control of their own education, and in their *commitment* to let all policies and practices flow from central learning objectives and from a mutual respect and agreement between students and teachers.[326]

In the end, therefore, the single most important keys to effective teaching are a teacher's desire to be an excellent teacher and a willingness to work hard at becoming one.

1.   Do No Harm to Students.

Principle: The teachers are aware of the potential damage they can do and they try not to harm students.

Comments:
James Banner and Harold Cannon described various aspects of ethical teaching, the first rule of which is to do no harm to students.

> *The first rule of ethical teaching is to do no harm to students.*
> This is not merely, in the spirit of Hippocrates' admonition to doctors, a negative admonition. Instead, it implies teachers' obligations to protect students actively from threats to their well-fare arising from such appealing blandishments as popularity or peer pressure. Students' sense of self and image is easily injured by embarrassment or punishment that appears excessive, or by teachers' abuse of their authority, and this is as much the case with older as with younger students. The abuse of authority, which can take many forms, such as prejudice, favoritism, and intimacy, is especially threatening to students' welfare.[327]

As established in Chapter One, there are clear and growing data that legal education is actually harmful to the emotional and psychological well-being of many law students.

> A growing body of research suggests that the highly competitive atmosphere of law schools, coupled with the inadequacy of feedback and personal support structures, leaves many students with personal difficulties that set the stage for problems in their future practice. Although the psychological profile of entering students matches that of the public generally, an estimated 20 to 40 percent leave with some psychological dysfunction including depression, substance abuse, and various stress-related disorders. These problems are not inherent by-products of a demanding professional education; medical students do not experience similar difficulties.[328]

---

[326] *Id.* at 78-79.

[327] BANNER & CANNON, *supra* note 80, at 37.

[328] RHODE, *supra* note 109, at 197 (citations omitted). The harm that the abuse of the Socratic dialogue and case method can cause to students is discussed more fully in Chapter One in the section on "Law Schools Should Attend to the Well-Being of Their Students" and in

It is important, therefore, for law teachers to be aware of the potential harm they can do to students and to reexamine their educational philosophies and practices to reduce the likelihood that they will unnecessarily harm students.

Although a teacher can harm students using any method of instruction, complaints about classroom abuse of students primarily involve misuse of the Socratic dialogue and case method. Deborah Rhode complained that the Socratic dialogue and case method leaves students confused, teachers often use it poorly, and it contributes to a hostile, competitive classroom environment that is psychologically harmful to a significant percentage of students.

> Under conventional Socratic approaches, the professor controls the dialogue, invites the student to "guess what I'm thinking," and then inevitably finds the response lacking. The result is a climate in which "never is heard an encouraging word and . . . thoughts remain cloudy all day." For too many students, the clouds never really lift until after graduation, when a commercial bar review cram course supplies what legal education missed or mystified. Highly competitive classroom environments can compound the confusion. All too often, the search for knowledge becomes a scramble for status in which participants vie with each other to impress rather than inform. Combative classroom styles also work against cooperative collaborative approaches that can be essential in practice. That is not to suggest that Socratic techniques are entirely without educational value. In the hands of an adept professor, they cultivate useful professional skills, such as careful preparation, reasoned analysis, and fluent oral presentations. But large class Socratic formats have inherent limits. They discourage participation from too many students, particularly women and minorities, and they fail to supply enough opportunities for individual feedback and interaction, which are crucial to effective education.[329]

The Socratic dialogue and case method has been a fixture in legal education in the United States for over 100 years. When properly used, it is a good tool for developing some skills and understanding in law students. If used inartfully, it can harm students.

Law teachers need to create and maintain student-friendly climates in their classrooms and other interactions with students. Students need to feel safe and free from fear of in-class humiliation. Only then will they be willing to take academic risks. The atmosphere in the classroom should be one of mutual respect and collaborative learning.

Many of the best practices described in this section and throughout the document will help create healthier classrooms and enhance student learning.

Chapter Four in the section on "Use Multiple Methods of Instruction and Reduce Reliance on the Socratic Dialogue and Case Method."

[329] *Id.* (citations omitted).

2.   **Support Student Autonomy.**

Principle: **The school and teachers support student autonomy.**

Comments:
     Law schools that value the opinions and priorities of their students give students as much autonomy as possible and explain why students do not have autonomy in some things. These schools are likely to have students who are happier, healthier, more motivated, and more successful than schools that are less supportive of student autonomy.

     The self-determination theory of human motivation holds that the development of positive motivation is importantly forwarded or impeded by the characteristics of the social environment.

          Specifically, when authorities provide "autonomy support" and acknowledge their subordinates' initiative and self-directedness, those subordinates discover, retain and embrace their intrinsic motivations and at least internalize non-enjoyable but important extrinsic motivations. In contrast, when authorities are controlling or deny the self-agency of subordinates, intrinsic motivations are undermined and internalization is forestalled.

          . . . . .

          According to self determination theory, all human beings require regular experiences of autonomy, competence, and relatedness in order to thrive and maximize their positive motivation. In other words, people need to feel that they are good at what they do, or at least can become good at it (competence); that they are doing what they choose and want to be doing – i.e., what they enjoy or at least believe in (autonomy); and that they are relating meaningfully to others in the process – i.e., connecting with the selves of others (relatedness). These needs are considered so fundamental that Ryan (1995) has likened them to a plant's need for sunlight, soil and water.[330]

     Ken Sheldon and Larry Krieger completed a longitudinal study of law students in 2006 which suggests that students who perceive that the school and faculty support their autonomy experience "less radical declines in need satisfaction, which in turn predicted better well-being in the third year, and also a higher GPA, better bar exam results, and more self-determined motivation for the first job after graduation."[331]

     Sheldon and Krieger explain that autonomy support has three features:
1.   *Choice provision*, in which the authority provides subordinates with as much choice as possible within the constraints of the task and situation;
2.   *Meaningful rationale provision*, in which the authority explains the situation in cases where no choice can be provided; and
3.   *Perspective-taking* in which the authority shows that he/she is aware of,

---

[330] *Id.* at 5.
[331] *Id.* at 2.

and cares about, the point of view of the subordinate.[332]

Law schools and teachers that want to provide autonomy support should, therefore, involve students in curricular and other institutional decisions that affect students; give students as much choice as possible within the constraints of providing effective educational experiences; explain the rationale for teaching methodologies and assignments, assessments, school policies and rules, and anything else that affects students' lives in which they have no choice; and demonstrate in word, deed, and spirit that the point of view of each student is welcomed and valued.

The reported autonomy support at one of the schools in the Sheldon/Krieger study was significantly greater. The students at the more supportive school were less negatively affected psychologically by their law school experience and had greater self-determined motivation to start their careers.[333] The statistical analysis demonstrated that the increased autonomy support was responsible for all of these better outcomes, as well as for providing greater satisfaction of fundamental psychological needs (for competence, relatedness, and autonomy).

The study also suggests that students who attended the more supportive school actually learned better than students at the other school. When law school grades were standardized for grade curves and for undergraduate grade point average, they were found to be higher for students experiencing higher autonomy support. Also, although students at both schools had equivalent academic qualifications upon entering law school, the students at the more supportive school scored substantially higher on the Multi-State Bar Examination.[334] "While these results are institution-wide, they are strongly suggestive that the teaching and learning at LS2 may be more effective. In sum, although it appears that the more autonomy-supportive teaching at LS2 may ultimately have produced better learning mastery among LS2 students, further research is needed to conclusively determine this."[335]

3. Foster Mutual Respect Among Students and Teachers.

Principle: **The students and teachers have mutual respect for each other.**

Comments:

The key component of a positive teaching and learning environment is for teachers and students to have respectful and caring attitudes. "A fundamental feature of effective facilitation [of learning] is to make participants feel that they are valued as separate, unique individuals deserving of respect."[336] "It is difficult to define caring and respect, but most people know when they are present and when they are not."[337]

---

[332] *Id.* at 5-6.

[333] *Id.* at 31.

[334] *Id.* at 25.

[335] *Id.*

[336] Stephen D. Brookfield, *Adult Learners: Motives for Learning and Implication for Practice, in* TEACHING AND LEARNING IN THE COLLEGE CLASSROOM 137, 143 (Kenneth A. Feldman & Michael B. Paulsen eds., 1993).

[337] Hess, *supra* note 84, at 87.

A respectful environment is one in which teachers and students participate in a dialog, explore ideas, and solve problems creatively. Intimidation, humiliation, and denigration of others' contributions are disrespectful, cause many students to withdraw from participation, and hinder their learning. But mutual respect does not mean that the participants avoid conflict, hard work, and criticism. To grow, teachers and students must engage in critical reflection and be willing to challenge and be challenged.[338]

Certain behaviors can help establish and maintain respect. These include:[339]

Learn students' names. This is perhaps the single most important thing a teacher can do to create a positive climate in the classroom. Call students by name in and out of the classroom. Do not allow them to be anonymous, to feel they can fade out without anyone's knowing or caring.

Learn about students' experiences and use them in class. Ask students to provide you with information about themselves: where they are from, undergraduate school and major, graduate degrees, work experience, other experience related to the course, hobbies, and anything else they want you to know. Ask students to share their experiences at relevant times in the course.

Let students get to know you. Introduce yourself at the beginning of the course, letting students know about your professional and personal interests. Fill out the same informational survey you ask the students to complete. Go to lunch with students and attend student events.

The results of the 2006 Law School Survey of Student Engagement reinforced the importance of student-faculty interaction. The report stated that "[p]rofessors are important role models. The nature of the student-faculty relationship affects students' perceptions of the degree to which they have developed a sense of professional ethics, how much they study, and their overall satisfaction with law school." The report reached the remarkable conclusion that "[s]tudent-faculty interaction was more strongly related to students' self-reported gains in analytical ability than time spent studying, cocurricular activities, or even the amount of academic effort put forth."[340]

Be considerate of students' time. Treat their time as a precious commodity. Come to class early and stay late to enable students to talk to you at a time convenient for them. Starting and ending class on time demonstrates your cognizance of students' busy lives. Set convenient office hours and do not miss them.

Define and model respect in the classroom. At the beginning of the course, you can articulate the critical role of mutual respect in the classroom and define with students "respectful behavior."

---

[338] *Id.*

[339] This list and most of the accompanying text come from *id.* at 88-90.

[340] Law School Survey of Student Engagement, Engaging Legal Education: Moving Beyond the Status Quo 13 (2006) [hereinafter 2006 LSSSE].

As Ken Bain put it, "[a]bove all, [the best teachers] tend to treat students with what can only be called simple decency."[341]

4.   Have High Expectations.

Principle: The teachers have high expectations.

Comments:
"A teaching and learning environment steeped in mutual respect between teachers and students does not imply low standards and minimal expectations. Indeed, high expectations are an important element of respect."[342]

The premise behind this principle is that we tend to get what we expect from students. Our expectations become self-fulfilling prophecies.

> Expect more and you will get it. High expectations are important for everyone – for the poorly prepared, for those unwilling to exert themselves, and for the bright and motivated. Expecting students to perform well becomes a self-fulfilling prophecy when teachers and institutions hold high expectations of themselves and make extra efforts.[343]

Having high expectations does not mean piling on the work. Assigning excessive work is likely to produce low student ratings and probably less learning because the students will become exhausted and alienated.[344] A combination of things goes into high expectations, most notably an appreciation of the value of each student and great faith in each student's ability to achieve.[345]

> The best teachers we encountered expect "more" from their students. Yet the nature of that "more" must be distinguished from expectations that may be "high" but meaningless, from goals that are simply tied to the course rather than to the kind of thinking and acting expected of critical thinkers. That "more" is, in the hands of teachers who captivate and motivate students and help them reach unusually high levels of accomplishment, grounded in the highest intellectual, artistic, or moral standards, and in the personal goals of the students. We found that the best teachers usually have a strong faith in the ability of students to learn and in the power of a healthy challenge, but they also have an appreciation that excessive anxiety and tension can hinder thinking.[346]

"[I]f the students' learning is a priority for the teacher, it will be a priority for the students themselves. They can achieve high expectations only if they believe that learning is important enough to invest time, energy, and commitment."[347] In

---

[341] BAIN, *supra* note 299, at 18.

[342] Hess, *supra* note 84, at 90.

[343] SEVEN PRINCIPLES IN ACTION, *supra* note 305, at 79.

[344] BAIN, *supra* note 299, at 71.

[345] *Id.* at 72.

[346] *Id.* at 96.

[347] Okianer Christian Dark, *Seven Principles for Good Practice in Legal Education: Principle 6: Good Practice Communicates High Expectations*, 49 J. LEGAL EDUC. 441, 442 (1999).

fact, law teachers must emphasize learning over grades, precisely because it will help students learn better. Studies of student goal setting show that students who set narrow, challenging and well-defined mastery learning goals obtain higher grades than students who set grade goals. And students who set grade goals get higher grades than students who set no goals or simply set goals focused on completing an assigned task.[348]

Law teachers' expectations of their students can be negatively influenced by two biases: the credential bias and the generational bias.[349] The credential bias is triggered by prior experiences with students and mandatory grade curves. These can lead us to expect that entire classes as well as individual students will perform similarly to their prior academic achievement. "When teachers speak of students' grades as though they have become immutable characteristics, they condition themselves to look for similar achievement in the future, thus sustaining and even amplifying the performance outcomes of their students."[350] Teachers should continue believing we can reach all of our students, even those who have not previously excelled.

The generational bias is created by opinions that Generation X students are disengaged, disrespectful, and suspicious of authority, and thus arrive in law schools unmotivated and lazy. Barbara Glesner-Fines encourages us to keep in mind that, though law students may arrive with poor study habits, as a group they are the most successful undergraduate students and do not necessarily fit the stereotype of Generation X. Most want to learn. Even if some students fit the Generation X stereotype, we should maintain high expectations for their academic performance.

> To create a positive expectancy effect, we must reconsider the assumption that past behavior and attitudes will continue in the law school setting. There is good reason to assume that students will undergo significant cognitive and social development during law school. Once again, however, we are best situated to believe that our students can be engaged as active learners if we believe we know how to teach them to do so.[351]

Gerry Hess explains that it is important to have high expectations of all students, clearly communicate expectations, and model high expectations.[352]

> *Have high expectations of all students.* You can show students you believe all of them can succeed by seeking participation from many students each class, by spreading difficult questions and assignments to all students, and by finding opportunities to celebrate student accomplishments publicly and privately.

> *Clearly communicate expectations.* In the first class, you should inform students orally and in writing of the course goals and your expectations

---

[348] *See* Wood & Locke, *supra* note 191, at 1013; Hagan & Weinstein, *supra* note 190, at 44-45.

[349] Glesner-Fines, *supra* note 312, at 104-09.

[350] *Id.* at 106.

[351] *Id.* at 108 (citation omitted). This article includes many simple, helpful techniques for communicating and maintaining high expectations of students.

[352] Hess, *supra* note 84, at 91-92.

regarding preparation for class, attendance, class participation, respect in the classroom, and teaching and evaluation methods. On daily assignments, tell students what focus questions to consider while reading the assigned materials.

Model high expectations. Give students models of outstanding student work. Be demanding on yourself. Be prepared; work hard.

We encourage law teachers to have high expectations of all students and try not to give up on any student's ability to practice law effectively and responsibly.

5.   Foster a Supportive Environment.

Principle: The teachers foster a supportive teaching and learning environment.

Comments:
      "A supportive teaching and learning environment is tied closely to respect and expectations. . . . Elements of a supportive environment include teachers' attitudes, student-faculty contact, and role-model and mentor relationships."[353]

      Teachers' supportive attitudes. The most helpful attitudes are *concerned, caring, encouraging, and helpful.* "Those teacher attitudes have strong positive effects on student motivation to excel."[354]

      Frequent student-faculty contact. Substantial research documents the importance of student-faculty contact.

> Frequent student-faculty contact in and out of class is the most important factor in student motivation and involvement. Faculty concern helps students get through rough times and keep on working. Knowing a few faculty members well enhances students' intellectual commitment and encourages them to think about their own values and future plans.[355]

      Contact with faculty can also have a positive impact on students' intellectual and personal development. "Students who were identified as having more frequent contact with faculty scored higher on tests designed to measure intellectual development, defined as including a higher tolerance for ambiguity and uncertainty as well as intellectual independence."[356] "Informal contact with faculty . . . may be particularly helpful in moving students away from notions of black-letter law to the more nuanced process of legal analysis. Contact with faculty may also motivate a student to think more deeply."[357]

      Law teachers may find it beneficial to initiate contact with students themselves. "An offer to meet with groups of students may attract students who

---

[353] *Id.* at 92.
[354] *Id.*, citing JOSEPH LOWMAN, MASTERING THE TECHNIQUES OF TEACHING 29 (2d ed. 1995).
[355] SEVEN PRINCIPLES IN ACTION, *supra* note 305, at 9.
[356] Susan B. Apel, *Seven Principles for Good Practice in Legal Education: Principle 1: Good Practice Encourages Student-Faculty Contact,* 49 J. LEGAL EDUC. 371, 374 (1999).
[357] *Id.* at 378.

think of themselves as too shy to maintain a one-to-one conversation."[358] Also, it may be helpful to initiate contact via the computer. "[M]any students prefer e-mail, either as an initial contact or for ongoing purposes."[359] Course web page discussion boards provide another, non-threatening, low workload mechanism for student-faculty contact.

Faculty time constraints are another impediment to faculty-student contact. "Teachers who signal their availability often find themselves overwhelmed with student demands for their time."[360] However, resolving time constraints often involves little more than simple planning, both short and long-term. Teachers can plan to arrive in class early or stay late to talk with students. Additionally, keeping regular office hours helps ensure that time is available for students.[361]

Role-model and mentoring relationships. "Role models and mentors are crucial for students' professional development. Through their actions, law professors teach students legal ethics and values."[362] They also teach students about the culture of the legal profession.

> For law students, understanding the legal culture is as
> important as learning any doctrine; it requires a form of learning
> that is less deliberate, more subtle, characterized to some extent
> by observation and osmosis . . . . Contact with faculty can help
> students learn the nuances of a life in the legal profession. . . . [N]ot
> only do law teachers disseminate the norms of the law school, they
> communicate the norms of the legal profession as well.

> . . . . .

> Values are difficult if not impossible to teach in the abstract.
> Individual contact with faculty not only allows for more intimate
> discussion of these issues, it also provides the student with a positive
> model . . . of the values that the law professes: "our students watch
> us to see whether we mean what we say."[363]

The importance of modeling professional behavior is also discussed in Chapter Three in the section, "Teach Professionalism Pervasively Throughout all Three Years of Law School."

6.   Encourage Collaboration.

Principle: **The teachers encourage collaboration among students and teachers.**

Comments:

Encourage collaboration among students. "An extensive body of research documents the benefits of cooperative learning methods. Over the past 100 years,

---

[358] *Id.* at 384.
[359] *Id.* at 385.
[360] *Id.* at 380.
[361] *Id.* at 383.
[362] Hess, *supra* note 84, at 93.
[363] Apel, *supra* note 356, at 379.

more than 600 studies have demonstrated that cooperative learning produces higher achievement, more positive relationships among students, and psychologically healthier students than competitive or individualistic learning."[364]

This principle is consistent with a recommendation of the Cramton Task Force. "Since lawyers today commonly work in teams or in organizations, law schools should encourage more cooperative law student work."[365]

Engaging pairs or teams of students in activities such as group projects, presentations, papers, study groups, peer tutoring, peer teaching, and peer evaluation can improve learning. "Learning is enhanced when it is more like a team effort than a solo race. Good learning, like good work, is collaborative and social, not competitive and isolated. Working with others often increases involvement in learning. Sharing one's ideas and responding to others' reactions improves thinking and deepens understanding."[366]

Carole Buckner documented the benefits to students of all races, ethnicities, and of both genders from highly structured cooperative learning experiences. Buckner reported on the hundreds of studies showing that cooperative learning "leads to higher achievement at all levels of education . . . higher quality problem solving . . . more higher level reasoning, more frequent generation of new ideas and solutions, . . . greater transfer of what is learned within one context to another . . . more in-depth analysis of the material and a longer lasting memory of the information processed."[367]

One of the values associated with encouraging student collaboration is academic excellence. Collaborative learning involves placing students in a wide variety of team projects and group assignments which allows the students to "compare and challenge perspectives, add insights, and strengthen their grasp of academic material. In the role of law firm partners and supervisors, they put pressure on each other to meet deadlines, to produce their best work, and to be accountable to affected third parties."[368]

Collaborative learning also heightens student awareness of the need for public service and the value of pro bono work. Collaboration helps students realize "the discrepancy between the reality of the legal system and the dream of social justice in our pluralistic American Culture. Students better understand legal rules and procedures as cultural phenomena, as complex compromises between competing social, political, and economic agendas."[369]

---

[364] Hess, *supra* note 85, at 94 (citing DAVID W. JOHNSON ET AL., COOPERATIVE LEARNING: INCREASING COLLEGE FACULTY INSTRUCTIONAL PRODUCTIVITY 1 (1991); Vernellia R. Randall, *Increasing Retention and Improving Performance: Practical Advice on Using Cooperative Learning in Law Schools*, 16 T. M. COOLEY L. REV. 201, 218 (1999)).

[365] CRAMTON REPORT, *supra* note 275, at 4.

[366] SEVEN PRINCIPLES IN ACTION, *supra* note 305, at 24.

[367] Carole J. Buckner, *Realizing Grutter v. Bollinger's "Compelling Educational Benefits of Diversity" – Transforming Aspirational Rhetoric Into Experience*, 72 UMKC L. REV. 877, 924-25 (2004). On pages 939-46 Buckner describes in detail how she integrates cooperative learning experiences into her first-year Civil Procedure classes.

[368] David Dominguez, *Seven Principles for Good Practice in Legal Education: Principle 2: Good Practice Encourages Cooperation*, 49 J. LEGAL EDUC. 386, 387 (1999).

[369] *Id.*

Involve students in collaborative course design with the teacher.[370] Invite students to help make decisions about course goals, learning activities, and evaluation methods. Consider giving students options on due dates for assignments, and choices of writing assignments. Design a simple form to gather feedback from students about the effectiveness of your instruction, e.g., what activities work best for you? These steps will enhance student commitment and foster mutual respect. They can also reduce student stress associated with feelings of powerlessness and paranoia. "Empirical research demonstrates that student-and-teacher collaboration in deciding classroom policies, course objectives, instructional methods, and evaluation schemes enhances student learning and student attitudes toward the course, the law school, and the teacher."[371]

7.   Make Students Feel Welcome and Included.

Principle: The teachers make students feel welcome and included.

Comments:

Making all students feel welcome and included enhances their motivation.

The quality of a student's learning is closely tied to their motivation. Motivation is enhanced more by the chance to achieve rewards than the desire to avoid punishment. For example, students whose primary motivation is to avoid a bad grade tend to exert less effort and perform less well on exams than students with positive motivation. Motivation can be extrinsic (motivation for grades, money, or other rewards) or intrinsic (motivation based on curiosity, interest, and the desire to learn). Although both types of motivation can aid learning, students perform better when their motivation is intrinsic.[372]

Feeling welcome and included is an important motivator for all students, but particularly for women, older students, minorities, and others who may tend to feel unwelcome or excluded for whatever reasons. Teachers can help students feel more welcome and included by responding to their goals and interests, valuing diverse perspectives, and teaching to a wide variety of learning styles.[373]

Responding to students' goals and interests. Students are motivated by knowing and sharing the educational goals of the course. "You can increase students' motivation by having them participate in generating goals for the course and by having them articulate their personal goals as well. Then you can shape your course to help students achieve course goals and personal goals."[374]

It also enhances motivation if the course includes topics and skills that match students' interest and values. "You can increase students' motivation and improve

---

[370] These ideas are developed more fully in Hess, *supra* note 84, at 96-98.

[371] *Id.* at 97 (citing GERALD F. HESS, *Student Involvement in Improving Law Teaching and Learning*, 67 UMKC L. REV. 343, 355-61 (1998)).

[372] *Id.* at 99 (citing Cameron Fincher, *Learning Theory and Research, in* TEACHING AND LEARNING IN THE COLLEGE CLASSROOM 47 (Kenneth A. Feldman & Michael B. Paulsen eds., 1993)).

[373] *Id.* at 99-101.

[374] *Id.* at 99.

their learning by finding out about their backgrounds, interests, and experiences and using that information when designing learning activities."[375] At least do not downplay issues that are important to students' lives.

   Valuing diverse perspectives. Students come from a variety of backgrounds and life experiences. Having a diverse community with diverse ideas, experiences, and values enriches the entire learning environment.[376] "You can facilitate and welcome diverse perspectives by choosing material that reflects a variety of viewpoints, by acknowledging at the beginning of the course the value of differing opinions, and by validating students who raise divergent views in class."[377]

   Teaching to a wide variety of learning styles. "Theories about learning styles indicate that learners have a preferred mode of learning, that people learn in different ways, that a variety of learning styles will be present in any classroom, and that no one teaching method is effective for all students."[378]

> There are many roads to learning. People bring different talents and styles of learning to college. Brilliant students in the seminar room may be all thumbs in the lab or art studio. Students rich in hands-on experience may not do so well with theory. Students need the opportunity to show their talents and learn in ways that work for them. Then they can be pushed to learning in ways that do not come so easily.[379]

   The majority of law schools emphasize and measure only the logical-mathematical type of intelligence rather than any other forms of intelligence. This is because "the usual method of evaluating student performance is a single exam that asks students to analyze a complex set of facts, in a limited time period, in writing."[380] Effective teachers find ways to teach and evaluate a larger range of intelligences, while encouraging their students to master more than merely one type. Effective teachers consider the various learning styles of students and employ a variety of teaching and learning methods.[381]

---

[375] *Id.*

[376] Paula Lustbader, *Seven Principles for Good Practice in Legal Education: Principle 7: Good Practice Respects Diverse Talents and Ways of Learning*, 49 J. Legal Educ. 448, 453 (1999).

[377] Hess, *supra* note 84, at 100 (citing *id.* at 456; Wilbert J. McKeachie, McKeachie's Teaching Tips; Strategies, Research, and Theory for College and University Teachers 218-24 (10th ed., 1999)).

[378] Lustbader, *supra* note 376, at 455.

[379] Seven Principles in Action, *supra* note 305, at 93.

[380] Lustbader, *supra* note 376, at 455.

[381] Vernellia Randall describes how cooperative learning methods can improve the effectiveness of teaching groups of law students with diverse abilities and characteristics in Randall, *supra* note 364, at 102.

8.   Engage Students and Teachers.

Principle: The learning environment engages teachers and students.

Comments:
   Students learn better when they are interested in what the teacher wants them to learn.

> Investigators have also found that performance – not just motivation – can decrease when subjects believe that people are trying to control them. If students study only because they want to get a good grade or be the best in the class, they do not achieve as much as they do when they learn because they are interested. They will not solve problems as effectively, they will not analyze as well, they will not synthesize with the same mental skill, they will not reason as logically, nor will they ordinarily even take on the same kinds of challenges.[382]

"Teachers demonstrate their engagement through their attentive presence with students in and out of the classroom. Students become engaged in learning when they actively participate in their own education."[383]

Teacher presence. Teaching and learning is enhanced by teacher immediacy. "Immediacy refers to verbal and nonverbal communication that brings teacher and students close together."[384]

Verbal behaviors that enhance learning include "soliciting alternative viewpoints and opinions from students; praising student work; calling on students by name; posing questions and encouraging students to talk; using humor; having discussions outside of class; and asking students how they feel about assignments."[385]

"Two nonverbal behaviors significantly affected learning for all four ethnic groups: maintaining eye contact and smiling at students."[386] Carefully listening to students is also important.

> Active listening takes effort. After asking a question or posing a discussion prompt, listen to what students actually say, rather than look for the responses you expect. When students ask questions and make comments, listen actively by waiting till the student is finished talking (rather than interrupting), by responding directly to the student's questions, and by checking with the student to be sure you have understood the student's comment or question.[387]

Engage the students in active learning. "Students learn better when they are actively engaged in the learning process."[388] "It has long been known that active

---

[382] Bain, *supra* note 299, at 34.
[383] Hess, *supra* note 84, at 101.
[384] *Id.*
[385] *Id.*
[386] *Id.*
[387] *Id.* at 102.
[388] *Id.*

methods of learning are more effective than passive ones. Indeed, conference papers demonstrating that fact no longer reach the research journals."[389]

Active learning requires students to share responsibility for acquiring knowledge, skills, and values. "The object of active learning is to stimulate lifetime habits of thinking."[390] "[Students] must make what they learn part of themselves."[391] "Active learning recognizes that, during classroom time, students should be engaged in behavior and activities other than listening. Active learning requires students to undertake higher order thinking, forcing them to engage in analysis, synthesis, and evaluation."[392]

> There are several levels at which active learning can occur, ranging from a particular approach to completing an assignment in a class to the overall design of a college. . . . A common element in all of these diverse events is that something happens to stimulate students to think about *how* as well as *what* they are learning and to increasingly take responsibility for their own education.
>
> . . . .
>
> Among the many dimensions of active learning are writing, discussion, peer teaching, research, internships, and community experiences. These kinds of active experiences help students understand and integrate new information.[393]

There are many values associated with active learning. For instance, active learning helps law students develop and improve thinking skills by teaching critical thinking and higher-level cognitive skills.[394] Active learning also enhances content mastery.

> Active learning helps students grasp, retain, and apply content. The more frequently students work with content and ideas in new situations, the more likely they will retain their understanding and be able to apply it on exams and in real life. By "discovering" ideas and knowledge through active learning . . . students often reach a deeper level of understanding.[395]

Socratic dialogue does not promote active learning, except for the student who happens to be on the hot seat, and perhaps not even then. Other students do not participate in the dialogue but are expected to learn vicariously by watching the interchange. This is not active learning.[396]

---

[389] DONALD A. BLIGH, WHAT'S THE USE OF LECTURES? 254 (2000).

[390] SEVEN PRINCIPLES IN ACTION, *supra* note 305, at 40.

[391] *Id.* at 39.

[392] Paul L. Caron & Rafael Gely, *Taking Back the Law School Classroom: Using Technology to Foster Active Student Learning*, 54 J. LEGAL EDUC. 551, 552 (2004) (explaining how technology can enhance active learning and why Socratic dialogue does not).

[393] SEVEN PRINCIPLES IN ACTION, *supra* note 305, at 40.

[394] Hess, *supra* note 308 at 402.

[395] *Id.*

[396] For additional discussion of the absence of active learning in many traditional law classes, see Caron & Gely, *supra* note 392, at 554-55; Michael Hunter Schwartz, *Teaching Law by Design: How Learning Theory and Instructional Design Can Inform and Reform Law Teach-*

9.   Take Delight in Teaching.

Principle: **The teachers take delight in teaching.**

Comments:
Gerry Hess explained the importance of showing that we are delighted to be teaching students.

> The teacher's attitude, enthusiasm, and passion are main ingredients of an effective teaching and learning environment. Students regularly identify teacher enthusiasm as the most important component of effective instruction. In Lowman's model of exemplary teaching, the most common descriptor of excellent teachers from students and other faculty was *enthusiastic*. A teacher's passion for both teaching and the subject is a critical factor in student motivation.
>
> Personal attitudes tend to produce reciprocal attitudes in others. When teachers display their delight in teaching and in the subject, students pick up that positive attitude. But when teachers appear bored and disengaged, students will too. If teachers convey to students that they love to be with them in and out of the classroom, students will not only reflect that attitude back to the teacher, they will be receptive to learning and will forgive many mistakes in the classroom.[397]

You can communicate your enthusiasm for teaching by expressly describing your interest in the subject and teaching and what energizes you. Enthusiasm **is** also communicated by "speaking in an expressive manner; using humor; not reading from notes or texts."[398] Nonverbal behavior can also demonstrate enthusiasm, for example, by moving while teaching, smiling at students, walking up the aisles, hand and arm gestures, and facial expressions.[399]

10.   Give Regular and Prompt Feedback.[400]

Principle: **The teachers give regular and prompt feedback.**

Comments:
Educational theorists agree on the importance of providing prompt feedback. Prompt feedback allows students to take control over their own learning by obtaining necessary remediation for identified deficiencies in their understanding and to adjust their approaches to future learning endeavors.

> Knowing what you know and don't know focuses learning. Students need appropriate feedback on performance to benefit from courses. In getting started, students need help in assessing existing

---

ing, 38 SAN DIEGO L. REV. 347, 351-53 (2001).

[397] Hess, *supra* note 84, at 104 (citations omitted).

[398] MARYELLEN WEIMER, IMPROVING YOUR CLASSROOM TEACHING 19 (1993).

[399] *Id.*

[400] The importance of giving prompt and regular feedback is also discussed in Chapter Seven: Best Practices for Assessing Student Learning.

knowledge and competence. In classes, students need frequent opportunities to perform and receive suggestions for improvement. At various points during [the semester], and at the end, students need chances to reflect on what they have learned, what they still need to know, and how to assess themselves.[401]

Students who are called on in a typical law school class receive prompt feedback on their performance. However, such opportunities are infrequent because of the large size of most law school classes, and the nature of the feedback is only minimally helpful in assessing a student's existing knowledge and competence. Law students seldom receive any feedback after taking final examinations. They are given a grade, but few law teachers encourage students to review their exams or provide any other feedback that would help a student understand how to improve.

The 2005 report of the Law School Survey of Student Engagement found that "students who frequently receive prompt oral or written feedback from faculty were more positive about their overall law school experience," but it also reported that "[a]bout one in six students 'never' received prompt written or oral feedback from faculty members."[402] The 2006 report concluded that "[s]tudents who have more opportunities to assess their own progress and refocus their studying in light of feedback tend to gain more in higher level thinking skills."[403] The report indicated that students who receive feedback reported greater gains in their ability to synthesize and apply concepts and ideas, spent more time preparing for class, and were more likely to say they worked harder than they thought they could to meet the expectations of faculty members.

Although providing prompt feedback is important, not everything a student receives feedback about needs to be graded.

First, the research on teaching methods that use frequent quizzes suggests that immediate feedback is superior to delayed feedback, whether the feedback comes from faculty grading of quizzes or students' grading of quizzes. It may be that this principle is most applicable to situations in which students' primary task is assimilating information, as opposed to problem-solving. Second, the research on intrinsic motivation suggests that informational feedback "provided in the context of relative autonomy" is more useful for maintaining intrinsic motivation than controlling, externally oriented feedback "intended or experienced as pressure to perform, think, and feel in a particular way," such as grades. Research suggests that feedback should be "(1) informative in terms of pinpointing the probable source of students' errors, (2) encouraging, and (3) provided in a natural context that displays performance recognition by a source student respects." Third, some research suggests that feedback coming from "the self is more valued and better recalled than feedback from any other source," implying that self-guided self-assessment may be a desirable strategy. Finally, more is not always better. Large quantities of feedback may be excessive, simply

---

[401] Seven Principles in Action, *supra* note 305, at 55.

[402] Law School Survey of Student Engagement, The Law School Years: Probing Questions, Actionable Data 7, 18 (2005).

[403] 2006 LSSSE, *supra* note 340.

overwhelming students. I suspect this may be particularly true of students who are struggling.

What implications can we draw from this research? I suggest the following. Prompt feedback is important, but grading each exercise is not necessarily the most useful way to provide it. The feedback should be encouraging where possible; if errors must be corrected, an explanation should be given. If private feedback is not possible, feedback in a small group is better than feedback in front of a large class, and might come in part from self-assessment or from peers.[404]

"To be most helpful, feedback normally should be prompt, indicate the direction of change desired, be specific to the particular circumstances and be given in a quantity that can be understood and acted upon by the learner."[405] Feedback can come from other students, faculty, and even self-evaluations.

11.   Help Students Improve Their Self-Directed Learning Skills.

Principle: The program of instruction is designed to help students improve their self-directed learning skills throughout their law school experience.

Comments:
Law school graduates will continue learning for the rest of their professional careers. After graduation, however, students will not always be able to depend on others to provide critique and feedback. For this reason, law schools must produce graduates who possess excellent self-directed learning skills.

This skill set is referred to self-directed learning, self-regulated learning, or autonomous learning. It involves a cyclical process in which self-directed learners appropriately classify the demands of a learning task, plan strategies for learning what needs to be learned, implement those strategies while self-monitoring the effectiveness and efficiency of the chosen strategies, and reflect on the success of the process afterwards, especially how the learner will handle a similar, future task.[406]

Within British legal education self-directed learning is one of the seven skills with which all undergraduate law students are expected to graduate. "A student should demonstrate a basic ability, with limited guidance, to reflect on his or her own learning, and to seek and make use of feedback."[407] "A student should be able not only to learn something, but to reflect critically on the extent of her or his learning.

---

[404] Deborah Maranville, *Infusing Passion and Context Into the Traditional Law Curriculum Through Experiential Learning*, 51 J. Legal Educ. 51, 73 (2001) (citations omitted).

[405] Seven Principles in Action, *supra* note 305, at 59.

[406] *See* Michael Hunter Schwartz, Expert Learning for Law Students (2005). Schwartz' text explains the self-regulated learning cycle in detail and demonstrates its application to law school learning.

[407] Quality Assurance Agency for Higher Education, Draft Statement Benchmark Standards for Law (England, Wales, N. Ireland), at Guidance Note for Law Schools on the Benchmark Standards for Law Degrees in England, Wales and Northern Ireland, item 5, http://www.qaa.ac.uk/academicinfrastructure/benchmark/evaluation/law.asp (last visited August 31, 2006).

At a minimum, a student should have some sense of whether s/he knows something well enough or whether s/he needs to learn more in order to understand a particular aspect of the law."[408]

Students should, therefore, be taught to value self-reflective evaluation and acquire essential habits and techniques for engaging in self-reflective evaluation. Students should be given explicit instruction in self critique and provided with opportunities to practice self critique, which then is itself the subject of peer and instructor critique and feedback. Michael Schwartz's "Expert Learning for Law Students" curriculum is one of the first attempts by a United States law professor to explain how to teach first year students these skills.[409]

In the context of experiential education courses in law schools, the value of helping students develop their self-directed learning skills has long been recognized. As Paul Bergman, Avrom Sherr, and Roger Burridge explained, "[l]earning does not result only from experience: 'Only experience that is reflected upon seriously will yield its full measure of learning . . . . Our duty as educators is both to provide the experiential opportunity and . . . a framework for regularly analyzing the experience and forming new concepts.'"[410] The value of experiential education for helping students develop self-directed learning skills is developed further in Chapter Five.

Students should be required, or at least encouraged, to keep journals in which they regularly record their reactions to their experiences and try to articulate what they are learning. By taking time to organize their thoughts and write them down, they will improve their self-reflective skills. Gary Blasi explained that "[j]ust as there is a sound and empirical basis for requiring law students to engage in the active process of extracting the common patterns in appellate cases, there is an equally sound basis for requiring clinical students to keep and maintain journals reflecting on the initial experience of practice."[411]

Although Blasi was focusing on the use of journals to enhance the development of problem-solving expertise in experiential education courses, journals can also help students organize and better understand what they are learning in any course. After all, law school itself is a life-altering experience. It would be useful for students to keep a reflective journal in at least one course during the first semester of law school.

Ideally, teachers would review the journals and provide feedback on them. If this is impractical, a teacher may want to offer to review journals at the students' option. Even if no feedback is provided, however, the act of keeping reflective journals can help students improve their self-directed learning skills.

---

[408] *Id.* at Guidance Note for Law Schools on the Benchmark Standards for Law Degrees in England, Wales and Northern Ireland, item 18.

[409] SCHWARTZ, *supra* note 406.

[410] Paul Bergman, Avrom Sherr & Roger Burridge, *Learning From Experience: Non-legally-Specific Role Plays*, 37 J. LEGAL EDUC. 535, 547 (1987) (quoting Austin Doherty, Marcia Mentkowski & Kelly Conrad, *Toward a Theory of Undergraduate Experiential Learning, in* LEARNING BY EXPERIENCE: WHAT, HOW 25 (Morris Keeton & Pamela Tate eds., 1978)).

[411] Blasi, *supra* note 15, at 360.

12. Model Professional Behavior.

Principle: **The teachers, administrators, and staff model professional behavior.**

Comments:

Law schools will be unable to instill a commitment to professionalism in their students if a commitment to professionalism is not evident in the words and conduct of the faculty, administration, and staff, especially the faculty. Members of the faculty influence students' perceptions of what the profession stands for and what qualities are important for a member of that profession. They inadvertently convey explicit and implicit messages in their teaching and also by the values and standards they personally exhibit.

Students not only perceive what the people who run the law school say and do relative to the legal profession but also relative to basic moral attitudes and values, including how to treat other people.

Perhaps the most significant quality faculty demonstrate over and over to students is how to use power and authority. From the first day of class onward, law students are vividly aware of the power faculty wield over their future prospects. There are real analogies here to the attorney-client relationship that faculty ignore to the detriment of law school's formative mission. Inspiration is an important part of moral motivation, and faculty have many opportunities to inspire their students toward ethical and socially responsible practice, beginning at home, so to speak.[412]

We join Tom Morgan in calling on law teachers to model the six qualities that Teaching and Learning Professionalism[413] labeled the "essential characteristics of professional lawyers:" (1) learned knowledge, (2) skill in applying the applicable law to the factual context, (3) thoroughness of preparation, (4) practical and prudential wisdom, (5) ethical conduct and integrity, and (6) dedication to justice and the public good.[414] We, like Morgan, recognize that modeling professional life as a task is difficult if not impossible to do perfectly, but as Morgan concluded, "[i]t is impossible to model *life* and *living* in an entirely satisfactory way, but it is a challenge worth a professional lifetime."[415]

---

[412] Sullivan et al., *supra* note 7, at 195.

[413] Teaching and Learning Professionalism, *supra* note 134, at 6.

[414] Thomas D. Morgan, *Law Faculty as Role Models, in* Professionalism Committee, ABA Section of Legal Education and Admissions to the Bar and Standing Committees on Professionalism and lawyer Competence of the ABA Center for Professional Responsibility, Teaching and learning Professionalism: Symposium Proceedings 37, 41 (1997).

[415] *Id.* at 52.

D.   Explain Goals and Methods to Students.

Principle: The school and teachers explain the educational goals of the program of instruction and each course, and they explain why they use particular methods of instruction and assessment.

Comments:

Students are more motivated to learn as part of a community of learners if they understand the long term and intermediate objectives of the program of instruction. Learning is also enhanced when students understand why certain instructional and assessment methods are employed. It is especially important that new law students understand that the development of professional expertise is the ultimate objective and that it will take time and hard work to achieve it.

> It is important that novices understand at the outset that they are embarking on a long and difficult path, but that the reward is great. The end point is expertise, the ability to achieve goals dependably without either working through complex problem-solving or devising explicit plans. Since this level of performance cannot be fully reduced to rules and context-free procedures, it often appears to the novice – or lay person – as a kind of magical know-how. It is in fact the result of long training and practice, during which feedback and coaching are essential. The expert, such as the skilled surgeon, the great painter, the respected judge, or the successful negotiator, has made the tools and techniques his or her own, incorporating them into skilled performance, a smooth engagement with the world.[416]

We should take every opportunity to engage our students in a discussion of what we are trying to accomplish and how it is intended to enhance their professional development.

E.   Choose Teaching Methods That Most Effectively and Efficiently Achieve Desired Outcomes.

Principle: The teachers use the most efficient and effective methods available for accomplishing desired outcomes.

Comments:

Student learning is enhanced when we have clear educational objectives and use the most effective means to make learning possible. In legal education in the United States, most law teachers use a limited range of teaching methods that are not always carefully chosen for their effectiveness.

The selection of the most appropriate instructional tools depends largely on having clearly articulated educational goals. The best method for imparting information is not likely to be the best method for teaching analytical skills. Some tools may be better for developing basic understanding and abilities, whereas others would be better for developing in depth mastery of subjects. Although a particular technique may be unquestionably more effective, it may not be sufficiently efficient to warrant its use.

---

[416] SULLIVAN ET AL., *supra* note 7, at 137.

Determining what constitutes the 'best' teaching method requires two steps. The first step is to determine which method . . . best meets the instructional objectives of the course . . . defined as the method that would contribute most to student achievement in mastering the professor's objectives as measured by performance on [the assessment method]. The second step involves a cost-benefit analysis to determine whether the benefits of the method are sufficiently great to warrant the associated costs – [for example] the time demands on students and on the institution. From a cost-benefit perspective, a method that produces a modest grade enhancement at nominal costs might be a better method than one that provides greater grade enhancement but at substantial cost.[417]

Law teachers should thoughtfully reexamine our assumptions about teaching and learning. We should especially consider the benefits of making our classrooms student-oriented instead of faculty-oriented, that is, we should keep in mind the guiding principle of education: "[t]he aim of teaching is simple: it is to make student learning possible."[418] Judith Wegner made the following observations about the differences between traditional law school instruction and instruction that frequently occurs in legal writing programs.

Some discomfort may stem from hitherto unrecognized assumptions about teaching and the educational process, perhaps reflecting the legal academy's love affair with the case-dialogue method and its powerful success in the first-year core. This prototype places emphasis on the teacher, in a heavily populated, theatrical classroom, where the dynamic is often imperial as the teacher drives the conversation, and the focus is on deconstruction of arguments and text. Effective instruction in legal writing arena is different in virtually every respect from that model. It focuses more on *learning* than teaching, attends very closely to the *individual* student in a sustained fashion that large classes tend to ignore. Students are required to take responsibility rather than allowed to be *passive* observers. They must *collaborate* and work in teams with their classmates and their teachers, rather than benefitting by keeping to themselves and going it alone. They are asked to *construct* written products through an ongoing *process* with a *social* dimension, rather than dismember others' statements that lie dead on the page. Good teaching in such a setting is often *invisible*, conducted through one-on-one conversations or small group caucuses, rather than captured by rave reviews for the "sage on the stage." None of this is to say that the case-dialogue method and its enshrined place in the first-year pantheon is unwarranted, but only to suggest that it may influence faculty imaginations about what is educationally important and how other sorts of instructional goals might best be achieved.[419]

---

[417] Steven Hartwell & Sherry L. Hartwell, *Teaching Law: Some Things Socrates Did Not Try*, 40 J. Legal Educ. 509, 510 (1990)

[418] Diana Laurillard, Rethinking University Teaching: A Framework for the Effective Use of Educational Technology 13 (1993) (quoting Paul Ramsden, Learning to Teach in Higher Education 5 (1992)).

[419] Wegner, Theory and Practice, *supra* note 48, at 31-32.

We encourage law teachers to reassess their reliance on the Socratic dialogue and case method, reexamine assumptions about all teaching methods, and employ instructional techniques that are best suited for achieving the educational objectives of our programs of instruction. Best practices for using a variety of teaching methods are discussed later in this document.

Members of a law school faculty should base their teaching decisions on research about effective teaching, or at least hypotheses grounded in research. Faculty members should apply to their teaching the same standards they apply to their scholarship. For example, a professor who wishes to use certain materials or methods of instruction in a course should base the decision on evidence (for example, studies of student learning) that the material or method is likely to achieve the educational goals of the course more effectively and efficiently than other methods of instruction. Curriculum committees should request this evidence before approving new courses.

F.   Use Multiple Methods of Instruction and Reduce Reliance on the Socratic Dialogue and Case Method.

Principle: **The teachers employ multiple methods of instruction and do not overly rely on the Socratic dialogue and case method.**

Comments:

Law teachers need to be multi-modal in our teaching and reduce our reliance on the Socratic dialogue and case method. There are many more tools for reaching students than one finds in the typical law school classroom. In a seminal work on teaching methodologies,[420] Donald Bligh summarized the reasons why excellent teachers vary their teaching techniques in every class session. These include encouraging deep processing, maintaining high levels of attention, fostering motivation, matching the mix of student learning styles within the classroom, and providing students with opportunities for feedback.[421]

Best practices for utilizing the most common methods of law teaching, including the Socratic dialogue and case method, are discussed later in this document, but law teachers should be conversant with a much wider range of techniques such as those on the following list taken from Bligh's book:[422]
- *brain-storming*. An intensive discussion situation in which spontaneous suggestions as solutions to a problem are received uncritically.
- *buzz groups*. Groups of 2-6 students who discuss issues or problems for a short period, or periods, during a class.
- *demonstrations*. The teacher performs some operation exemplifying a phenomenon or skill while the students watch.
- *free group discussion*. A learning situation in which the topic and direction are controlled by the student group; the teacher observes.
- *group tutorial*. The topic and general direction is given by the tutor, but the organization (or lack of it), content and direction of the discussion depends on the student group of up to 14 students.
- *individual tutorial or "tutorial."* A period of teaching devoted to a single

---

[420] BLIGH, *supra* note 389.
[421] *Id.* at 252-57.
[422] *Id.* at 150-54.

student.
• *problem-centered groups.* Groups of 4-12 students discussing a specific task.
• *programmed learning.* Usually a text or computer program containing questions each of which must be answered correctly before proceeding.
• *syndicate method.* Teaching where the class is divided into groups of about 6 members who work on the same or related problems with intermittent teacher contact and who write a joint report for the critical appraisal of the whole class.
• *synectics.* A development of brain-storming in which special techniques, such as choosing group members from diverse backgrounds, are used to produce a creative solution to a problem.
• *T-group method.* A method of teaching self-awareness and interpersonal relations based on therapeutic group techniques in which individual group members discuss their relationships with each other.

We owe it to our students to try to be excellent teachers who skillfully employ a wide range of teaching methods. While poor instructional techniques may not particularly affect the very best students, the average and below average students depend on the quality and effectiveness of our instruction to succeed in law school, on the bar exam, and in practice. Law teachers should expertly employ a wide variety of teaching methods. Unfortunately, many of us do not.

The main impediment to improving law school teaching is the enduring over reliance on the Socratic dialogue and case method. Typical classroom instruction at most law schools today would be familiar to any lawyer who attended law school during the past hundred thirty years. Certainly, there have been some innovations,[423] but the basic method of instruction is for the instructor to engage in one-on-one dialogues with individual students in which the instructor questions students about the facts and legal principles involved in appellate court decisions. This is the Socratic dialogue and case method.

The Socratic dialogue and case method was introduced into the law school curriculum by Christopher Columbus Langdell in the 1870s. Langdell's goal in using the method was not primarily to prepare his students for practice, because law schools of the time were intended to complement apprenticeships, not replace them. Langdell's objective was to engage in the "scientific" study of law by distilling its principles from the study of cases. In his mind, "cases, that is to say, the opinions of judges comprise the matter of the science of law."[424] Langdell articulated a vision of the law as an organic science with several guiding principles rather than as a series of facts and rules to be memorized. It was the law professor's job to mine the language of appellate cases for general principles of law.[425]

As it turned out, Langdell was wrong both about the usefulness of the case

---

[423] More doctrinal teachers are using problem-solving techniques, clinical education is expanding and becoming more diverse, more specialty tracks are being developed, and some schools are introducing students to the history and values of the legal profession in the first year and even allowing first year students to participate in simulated lawyering activities.

[424] MARTHA RICE MARTINI, MARX NOT MADISON: THE CRISIS OF AMERICAN LEGAL EDUCATION 58 (1997).

[425] Mark Bartholomew, *Legal Separation: The Relationship Between the Law School and the Central University in the Late Nineteenth Century,* 57 J. LEGAL EDUC. 368, 378 (2003).

method for discovering the basic principles of law and about the similarities of his approach to German scientific inquiry. "Later academics, like William Keener, were more sophisticated and saw the law as more complex, with an infinite variety of principles."[426] It became "clear to a rising generation of young academics that the Langdellian claims that all law could be found in the books and that law was a series of logically interwoven objective principles were, at most, useful myths."[427]

> This led Keener and others to place less emphasis on the genius of the case method as a means of teaching the substantive principles of law, but to stress more strongly the case method's unique ability to instill a sense of legal process in the student's mind. In other words, the main claim for the case method increasingly became its ability to teach the skill of thinking like a lawyer. Methodology rather than substance became the nub of the system.[428]

The avowed primary purpose of law school in the United States henceforth was not to teach the law but to teach how to think like a lawyer.[429]

When properly used, the Socratic dialogue and case method is a good tool for developing some skills and understanding in law students.

> The case-dialogue method is a potent form of learning by doing. As such, it necessarily shapes the minds and dispositions of those who apprentice through it. The strength of the method lies, in part, in how well it results in learning legal analysis, and in part in its significant flexibility in application. As our examples suggest, it is a highly malleable instructional practice. It encourages, at least for skillful teachers, the use of all the basic features of cognitive apprenticeship. It seems well suited to train students in the analytic thinking required for success in law school and legal practice. In legal education, analysis is often closely integrated with application to cases. The derivation of legal principles, such as we witnessed in our classroom examples, generally occurs through a process of continuously testing, using hypothetical fact patterns or contrasting examples to clarify the scope of rules and reasoning being distilled. This central role of analysis and application, then, is well served by the method.[430]

The potential value of the Socratic dialogue and case method is diminished, however, because we use it in large classroom settings, over rely on it in the first year, continue using it long after students "get it," and sometimes harm students by abusing the method.

The Socratic dialogue and case method has significant defects as an instructional tool. Its impact on individual students is sporadic, it emphasizes certain steps of the cognitive process while ignoring others, and it does not provide a

---

[426] STEVENS, *supra* note 2, at 55.

[427] *Id.* at 134.

[428] *Id.* at 55.

[429] MARTINI, *supra* note 424, at 59.

[430] SULLIVAN ET AL., *supra* note 7, at 77.

feedback mechanism to address and correct skills deficiencies.[431]

Let us briefly examine a typical first year torts class taught Socratically using the case method. The student must read each case and become familiar with its facts (knowledge). When called upon, he or she may be asked to summarize these facts (comprehension), to comment on the issues, arguments and *ratio decidendi* (analysis), and, occasionally, to discuss the case critically (evaluation). Although application is to some extent involved within both analysis and evaluation, and although synthesis is involved within the latter, it is significant that neither application nor synthesis are often dealt with independently in the course of a Socratic dialogue; yet these are probably the two most crucial skills required for exam writing and, indeed, for lawyering.

Furthermore, when a skill deficiency is revealed through a student's response, the Socratic technique does not lend itself to focusing on that student in order to explore and identify the source of his or her problem. Rather, in order to continue the dialogue, the instructor is more likely to provide the correct response or move on to another student. And given the sporadic involvement of students within the dialogue, there is no telling when that student will get another chance to participate at that skill level.

There are those who defend the Socratic dialogue by claiming that it teaches intellectual skills by example as well as by direct involvement of the student, but we have already seen why that is not the case. The responses of a classmate who is engaged in the dialogue can provide the listening student with knowledge of that classmate's comprehension, analysis, and evaluation, and may indicate to the listening student whether his or her answer would have been right or wrong, but what they cannot do is to show the listening student where his or her intellectual deficiencies lie nor can they give him or her the feedback required to correct those deficiencies.[432]

Michael Schwarz refers to the Socratic dialogue and case method as the Vicarious Learning/Self-Teaching Model.[433] It involves vicarious learning because most students in the class are not engaged in the professor-on-student dialogue and must experience vicariously what the speaking student actually experiences. It involves self-teaching because law professors expect students to figure out on their own, or through study groups, what they need to know and be able to do to succeed in the class.

Moreover, while most professors critique the selected students' classroom attempts to perform legal analysis, law professors fail to state explicitly what students need to know, or to explain how to spot legal issues or to perform legal analysis. In fact, law professors devote considerable time to critiquing students'

---

[431] Andrew Petter, *A Closet Within the House; Learning Objectives and the Law School Curriculum, in* ESSAYS ON LEGAL EDUCATION, *supra* note 225, at 76, 86.

[432] *Id.* at 86-87.

[433] Schwartz, *Teaching Law by Design, supra* note 396, at 351-53.

case reading and case evaluation skills even though, ironically (or, perhaps, perversely), law professors seldom test case reading skills explicitly.[434]

Schwartz concludes that "law teaching is neither effective, efficient, nor appealing" and that it is out of step with "the explosive evolution of learning theory throughout the twentieth century and the rise, in the second half of the century, of the field of instructional design, a field devoted to the systematic and reflective creation of instruction."[435]

The Socratic dialogue and case method has been criticized on many levels by many people. John Elson summarized five criticisms.

(1) Appellate opinions' reduction of the real world of factual complexity and indeterminacy into a set of seemingly clear-cut, independent variables which appear to foreordain the outcome of cases conveys an inaccurate sense of the indeterminacy and manipulability of the factual reality that lawyers must organize and create. The case method's formal criteria for analyzing and distinguishing cases are necessary elements of lawyering that students must master to become effective practitioners. Nevertheless, when that methodology is applied outside the context of a problem situation, it distorts students' understanding of how lawyers actually analyze cases in order to solve a specific problem. By repeatedly leading students through a highly routinized set of analytical rules and distinctions, the traditional case method tends to dampen creative problem-solving by instilling an essentially passive thought process, one that is inflexible and ill-suited to the inchoate factual world lawyers must actively try to manipulate.

(2) The case method is an inefficient and, often haphazard, way to convey to students the doctrinal knowledge that is necessary for effective problem-solving and the ways lawyers must identify and acquire the doctrinal knowledge they will need to solve problems in unfamiliar areas.

(3) The case method is also an ineffective, and likely misleading, approach toward helping students understand the underlying social forces that are interacting to determine the outcome of events in a field of law. This misplaced focus on case law as the primary medium for understanding the dynamic of an area of practice retards students' ability to develop an effective approach toward practice.

(4) The teachers who rely principally on case books to develop an understanding of, and a pedagogical approach to, a field of law are being distracted from engaging in readings and experiences that will give them a more coherent and penetrating vision of the social and legal processes that are governing the field.

---

[434] *Id.* at 352.

[435] *Id.* at 358. Schwartz is joined by many others in criticizing current law school instructional approaches. *See id.* at 357 n.36.

(5) The case method's exclusive focus on the outcomes of litigation diverts students' attention from the many other arenas of lawyering with which competent practitioners should be familiar, such as alternative dispute resolution, administrative practice, legislative advocacy and client counseling.[436]

Deborah Rhode points out the shortcomings of using appellate casebooks as the vehicle for teaching students about law and the legal profession.

The dominant texts are appellate cases, which present disputes in highly selective and neatly digested formats. Under this approach, students never encounter a "fact in the wild," buried in documents or obscured by conflicting recollections. The standard casebook approach offers no sense of how problems unfolded for the lawyers or ultimately affected the parties. Nor does it adequately situate formal doctrine in social, historical, and political context. Much classroom discussion is both too theoretical and not theoretical enough; it neither probes the social context of legal doctrine nor offers practical skills for using that doctrine in particular cases. Students get what Stanford professor Lawrence Friedman aptly characterizes as the legal equivalent of "geology without the rocks . . . dry arid logic, divorced from society." Missing from this picture is the background needed to understand how law interacts with life.[437]

Some scholars believe that claims about the effectiveness of the Socratic dialogue and case method are overstated and that problem-based instruction would be more effective.

[I]nflated claims for the effectiveness of the case method are based on flawed premises, and are demonstrably false. It is time for law school teaching to relegate the case method to its appropriate position - as only one analytical tool among many which can be employed in the resolution of a client's problems. The skills developed by the case method are at best rudimentary; the much touted "legal analysis" of the case method is little more than a narrow articulation of rather obvious adversarial positions, accompanied by the selective matching of factual data with so-called legal elements to justify the positions advanced. Compared to more sophisticated methods of problem-solving, case analysis is a blunt instrument. Even worse, as a methodology it is antithetical to the effective

---

[436] John Elson, *The Regulation of Legal Education: The Potential for Implementing the MacCrate Report's Recommendation for Curricular Reform,* 1 CLINICAL L. REV. 363, 384-85 (1994). Other critics include SULLIVAN ET AL., *supra* note 7, at 80-81 (concluding that the case-dialogue method can have a corrosive effect on the development of the full range of understanding necessary for a competent and responsible legal profession and can lead to lawyers who are more technicians than professionals invested with a sense of loyalty and purpose); Aaronson, *supra* note 33, at 6-7 (pointing out that the method narrows students frame of reference to legal issues alone and creates a cognitive bias that recurringly under-emphasizes the nonlegal, intellectual, or emotive dimensions of a problem situation); Moskovitz, *supra* note 160, at 244 (suggesting that "[i]t might be time to go back to the drawing board").

[437] RHODE, *supra* note 109, at 197-98. Paul Brest also noted that appellate cases embody static situations with determinate facts. Paul Brest, *The Responsibility of Law Schools: Educating Lawyers as Counselors and Problem Solvers,* 58 LAW & CONT. PROBS. 5, 7 (1995).

resolution of most clients' problems.[438]

Other critics question whether the adversarial skills developed by Socratic dialogue are even the skills that most students will need for modern law practice, echoing concerns raised by lawyers since the late 1800s.

> Conservative pedagogical theory prevails in the law school classroom. This is most evident in the reluctance to depart from the Socratic method, which, as traditionally practiced in law schools, is meant to groom students for an adversarial role. Arguably, however, the lawyer-as-adversary model better reflects the notions of popular culture than the reality of law practice today. According to a 1991 publication by the ABA Young Lawyers Division, most lawyers spend more time in client contact, research and memo writing, and negotiation than they do in courtroom activities. Supplementing classroom teaching with more discussion and collaborative work could better include students whose natural learning styles are undervalued by traditional legal pedagogy and promote the development of practical team-oriented skills.[439]

Practicing lawyers seem to agree that the Socratic dialogue and case method is not a particularly effective tool for preparing lawyers for practice. "[D]ata suggest that case-dialogue teaching is not seen by recent law graduates as particularly helpful in enabling them to move from school to professional practice."[440]

The bottom line is that whatever one believes about the utility of the Socratic dialogue and case method, it can only partially prepare most students for the jobs that await them. The skills and knowledge that can be acquired through the Socratic dialogue and case method are only a small part of the skills and knowledge needed to practice law effectively and responsibly. Judith Wegner concluded that the Socratic dialogue and case method has some positive effects in teaching students to "think like lawyers," but "key intellectual tasks receive much less attention, so that students receive more limited instruction in application of the law to complex fact patterns, synthesis of ideas, and evaluation against criteria relating to fairness or justice."[441]

> While well-adapted to instruction that focuses on knowledge, comprehension, analysis and simple application, the case-dialogue method does not, in itself, provide ready means for developing the capacity for applying the law to more complex problems, synthesizing ideas broadly, or engaging in evaluation that involves external rather than internal critique. Neither does it, in its traditional form, meet

---

[438] Janeen Kerper, *Creative Problem Solving vs. The Case Method: A Marvelous Adventure in Which Winnie the Pooh Meets Mrs. Palsgraf*, 34 CAL. WEST. L. REV. 351, 352 (1998). Similar conclusions are reached by Peggy Cooper Davis and Elizabeth Ehrenfest Steinglass in Davis & Steinglass, *supra* note 281.

[439] Cruz Reynoso & Cory Amron, *Diversity in Legal Education: A Broader View, A Deeper Commitment*, 52 J. LEGAL EDUC. 491, 503 (2002) (citation omitted). Additional critics of Socratic dialogue include, *inter alia*, MARTINI, *supra* note 424, at 2 (criticizing the method, particularly for its proclivity for humiliating students); Fernand N. Dutile, *Excerpt from Introduction: The Problem of Teaching Legal Competency*, in LEGAL EDUC. AND LAW. COMPETENCY 1-6 (1981) (discussing the weaknesses of traditional case method of teaching law).

[440] SULLIVAN ET AL., *supra* note 7, at 79.

[441] Wegner, Theory and Practice, *supra* note 46, at 33.

the needs of diverse learners or provide the opportunity to tap into the heightened level of engagement that is found when learning in context is explored.[442]

The Socratic dialogue and case method "implicitly asks the student to assume a perspective outside, or above, the controversy in the cases – the perspective of the judge (or judicial clerk, or law professor) rather than that of the lawyer."[443] The result of our over reliance on the Socratic dialogue and case method is that "[w]e have a system quite well designed to produce judicial clerks and appellate advocates, notwithstanding that very few law graduates ever play those roles."[444] "For example, of the more than 100,000 California lawyers, 'no more than 200 . . . practice more than 50 per cent of the time in the appellate courts.'"[445] Janeen Kerper expands on this theme:

> [W]e should recognize the truth about the case method: it does not teach law students to think like lawyers; it teaches them to think like judges – with all of the constraints that role implies. This is not a bad thing. In order to be competent advisors, lawyers must understand how judges think. But they also need to understand that, as lawyers, their available options are greater, and therefore their own thought processes can be much broader. They will be much more effective in representing their clients if they think more as creative problem-solvers, and less like the ultimate decision maker.[446]

The most important reason to reconsider our use of the Socratic dialogue and case method, however, is not because of its limitations as a teaching tool. The main reason is that too many law teachers abuse it and contribute to the damage that the law school experience unnecessarily inflicts on many students. Traditional teaching methods and beliefs that underlie them undermine the sense of self-worth, security, authenticity, and competence among students.

Law students get the message, early and often, that what they believe, or believed, at their core, is unimportant – in fact "irrelevant" and inappropriate in the context of legal discourse – and their traditional ways of thinking and feeling are wholly unequal to the task before them."[447]

> [T]he traditional law school pseudo-Socratic method of instruction, [emphasizes] "hard" cases and supposedly rigorous and rational cognitive processes at the expense of students' emotions, feelings, and values. These traditional techniques desensitize students to the critical role of interpersonal skills in all aspects of a professionally proper attorney-client relationship and, for that matter, in all aspects of an ethical law practice. They also set students' moral compasses adrift on a sea of relativism, in which all positions are viewed as "defensible" or "arguable" and none as "right"

---

[442] *Id.* at 44.

[443] Blasi, *supra* note 15, at 359-60.

[444] *Id.* at 386-87 (citation omitted).

[445] *Id.* at n.211 (citing Gerald F. Uelmen, *Brief Encounters: The New Demands of Appellate Practice*, 14 CAL. LAW. 57, 60 (1994)).

[446] Kerper, *supra* note 438, at 371.

[447] Krieger, *Institutional Denial*, *supra* note 76, at 125.

or "just," and they train students who recognize and regret these developments in themselves to put those feelings aside as nothing more than counter-productive relics from their pre-law lives.[448]

The Carnegie Foundation's report on legal education concluded that the devaluing and demoralization of individual students contribute to the demoralization of the legal profession. "In so far as law schools choose not to place ethical-social values within the inner circle of their highest esteem and most central preoccupation, and in so far as they fail to make systematic efforts to educate toward a central moral tradition of lawyering, legal education may inadvertently contribute to the demoralization of the legal profession and its loss of a moral compass, as many observers have charged."[449]

> In law school, students learn from both what is said and what is left unsaid. There is a message in what the faculty addresses and what it does not. When faculty routinely ignore – or even explicitly rule out of bounds – the ethical-social issues embedded in the cases under discussion, whether they mean to or not, they are teaching students that ethical-social issues are not important to the way one ought to think about legal practice. This message shapes students' habits of mind, with important long term-effects on how they approach their work. Conversely, when faculty discuss ethical-social issues routinely in courses, clinics, and other settings, they sensitize students to the moral dimensions of legal cases.[450]

The authors of the Carnegie Foundation's report acknowledged that there is a possible pedagogical justification for flipping off the switch of ethical and human concern to focus on helping students master the central intellectual skill of thinking like a lawyer. They concluded, however, that the failure of law schools to explain what was happening and why, coupled with the fact that substantive and moral concerns were seldom reintroduced in advanced courses, created a "danger for second and third year students that the analytic binders they have laboriously developed may never come off when they deal with the law – or with clients."[451] "A more effective way to teach is to keep the analytical and the moral, the procedural and the substantive in dialogue throughout the process or learning the law. This approach is not new to legal education. It is just too infrequently practiced, perhaps because the issues are too rarely thought through rigorously."[452]

Unfortunately, many law teachers continue to rely exclusively on the Socratic dialogue and case method, not just in the first year, but also in second and third year courses long after students become competent in case analysis and "thinking like a lawyer." This contributes to student boredom and loss of interest in learning. Deborah Maranville described the situation at many law schools when she wrote:

> Many law students are so bored by the second year that their attendance, preparation, and participation decline precipitously; by graduation they have lost much of the passion for justice and

---

[448] *Id.*
[449] SULLIVAN ET AL., *supra* note 7, at 170.
[450] *Id.* at 171.
[451] *Id.* at 173.
[452] *Id.* at 174.

enthusiasm for helping other people that were their strongest initial motivations for wanting to become lawyers. And even in the first year, when most students remain engaged, many fail to learn even the black-letter law at a level that faculty consider satisfactory.[453]

Judith Wegner's field research for the Carnegie Foundation verified Maranville's conclusions. She found that by the end of the first year most students have "got it," that is, they have mastered the ability to "think like a lawyer" and they are bored by continued use of the method. Even students who are still struggling to master the skill tend to tune out.

> The first year of law school derives its power in large part from the development of advanced levels of cognitive skill rather than from the introduction to new subject matter. As discussed earlier, most students experience a wrenching and largely unrecognized shift from an epistemology that relies on receiving and internalizing information from outside experts to one that emphasizes construction of knowledge for oneself. By the end of the year, they have come to expect much more than the transmittal and reception of knowledge that may have characterized many prior academic experiences, and instead assume that law school courses will incorporate some additional mental stretch to higher levels of cognitive functioning or other modalities of learning and knowing. Absent such progression in the nature of learning or knowing, students who have mastered introductory "thinking" are apt to be bored, while those who are still struggling are apt to tune out and relinquish expectations of becoming engaged.[454]

If law schools are to become dynamic, effective educational institutions, law teachers need to diversify their teaching methods, improve their teaching skills, and reduce their reliance on the Socratic dialogue and case method.

G.   Employ Context-Based Education Throughout the Program of Instruction.

Principle: The teachers use context-based education throughout the program of instruction.

Comments:
Legal education would be more effective if law teachers used context-based education throughout the curriculum. As explained more fully in the following sections, law teachers should use context-based education to teach theory, doctrine, and analytical skills; how to produce law-related documents; and how to resolve human problems and cultivate practical wisdom.

"Context helps students understand what they are learning, provides anchor points so they can recall what they learn, and shows them how to transfer what they learn in the classroom to lawyers' tasks in practice."[455]

---

[453] Maranville, *supra* note 404, at 51.
[454] Wegner, Theory and Practice, *supra* note 46, at 6-7.
[455] Maranville, *supra* note 404, at 52.

Adult learning theory suggests that our students will learn best if they have a context for what they are learning. Context is arguably important for three reasons. First, students are more interested in learning when the information they are studying is placed in a context they care about. Second, when teachers provide context for their students, they increase the likelihood that students will understand the information. Third, and especially significant for the law school context, in learning information, we may organize and store it in memory differently for the purpose of studying for a test than we do in order to retrieve it for legal practice.[456]

Judith Wegner believes that "greater openness to the modalities of knowledge and the potential differences in thinking and problem-solving within specific content-oriented contexts could foster a deeper level of engagement among faculty and students and significant new dimensions that could add a sense of momentum and progression beyond the first year."[457]

As discussed in Chapter Two, the core educational goal of law schools should be to help students develop competence, which is the ability to resolve legal problems effectively and responsibly.

It takes time to develop expertise in legal problem-solving. Problem-solving skills can be developed only by actually working through the process of resolving problems.[458] Developing problem-solving expertise requires "repetitions of 'training' as against the hard world of consequences, of repeated success and failure, and some inductive efforts at understanding what works and what does not, what seems important and what does not."[459]

[I]f one conceives of lawyering as problem-solving in a much broader range of activities [than expertise in learning to "read cases" and extract and apply legal rules by analogy to new situations], more is required [than teaching students how to analyze appellate cases]. In every other human endeavor, expertise in problem-solving is acquired by solving problems. There may be better and worse ways to learn to solve problems, but there appears to be no substitute for context. Legal education has completely internalized the lesson that in order to learn to solve problems of doctrinal analysis, one must actually engage in solving doctrinal problems. But the lesson has not been everywhere extended to the other areas of lawyering. We often teach civil procedure as if one can learn about making decisions in litigation by reading about how a few such decisions were made. This seems no more likely a possibility than that we could learn how to

---

[456] *Id.* at 56.

[457] Wegner, Theory and Practice, *supra* note 46, at 29.

[458] Of course, giving students opportunities to practice solving problems is not all that needs to be done. As noted earlier in the section encouraging law schools to make teaching problem-solving the primary goal of legal education, in addition to experience, students can more rapidly develop problem-solving expertise by studying problem-solving theory, observing how experts solve problems and drawing on their expertise by analogy, and receiving mentoring as to which aspects of their problem-solving experience should be most closely attended.

[459] Blasi, *supra* note 15, at 378.

solve doctrinal problems by reading The Paper Chase.[460]

Simply providing opportunities to engage in problem-solving activities is not enough. The development of problem-solving expertise is enhanced by studying theories related to problem-solving and by receiving assistance from teachers. Gary Blasi explained that "to some extent each lawyer must construct from experience the schemas and mental models employed in lawyerly problem-solving. But research in other domains suggests that the structured knowledge of experts is made of more than experience."[461] In addition to experience, students can more rapidly develop problem-solving expertise by studying the theory of problem-solving, observing how experts solve problems and drawing on their expertise by analogy, and receiving mentoring as to which aspects of their problem-solving experience should be most closely attended.[462] In other words, "students do not get better through practice alone. If their performance is to improve, they need practice accompanied by informative feedback and reflection on their own performance. And their learning will be strengthened further if they develop the habit of ongoing self-assessment."[463]

Even if everyone can agree that law schools should try to give students opportunities to practice and refine their legal problem-solving skills as early as possible in their legal education and throughout all three years of law school, the challenge is to figure out how to accomplish this.

Law schools can provide opportunities for students to engage in context-based learning in hypothetical as well as real life contexts. Ideally, law schools should present students with progressively more challenging problems as their self-efficacy, lifelong learning skills, and practical judgment develop.

One way to create contexts for teaching is to present students with specific legal problems and have them discuss how they would try to resolve them. Many legal scholars have encouraged law schools to use the problem method more extensively, including former AALS President Judith Areen who wrote, "[o]ne of the best changes to legal pedagogy in recent years is that more of us are moving beyond the case method to problem-based teaching. Bain[464] strongly supports this development by noting that people learn best when they are trying to solve problems that they find intriguing or important, something clinical faculty have long understood."[465] "[A] person with an engaged, active stance and the perspective of a problem-solver inside the problem situation acquires an understanding quite different from that of a person with a passive stance and the perspective of an observer. It is not only that an engaged problem-solver learns more from both instruction and experience, but also that she learns something quite different."[466]

---

[460] *Id.* at 386-87 (referring to JOHN J. OSBORN, JR., THE PAPER CHASE (1971)) (citations omitted). In one of the omitted footnotes, Blasi wrote, "[t]here is a growing body of evidence that all learning is highly situated and context-dependent. JEAN LAVE & ETIENNE WENGER, SITUATED LEARNING: LEGITIMATE PERIPHERAL PARTICIPATION (1991); D. N. Perkins & Gavriel Salomon, *Are Cognitive Skills Context-Bound?*, 18 EDUC. RESEARCHER 16 (1989)." *Id.* at n.213.

[461] *Id.* at 355.

[462] *Id.* at 355-59 and 378.

[463] SULLIVAN ET AL., *supra* note 7, at 178.

[464] BAIN, *supra* note 299, at 18.

[465] Judith Areen, *President's Message: Reflections on Teaching*, AALS NEWS 1 (April 2006).

[466] Blasi, *supra* note 15, at 359.

Another way to provide context for teaching students how to resolve legal problems is to present them with actual cases. In every law school in the United States, students study appellate case decisions. Appellate cases help students distill principles of law and give insights into judicial decision-making. They do not help students understand why litigation was necessary to resolve a dispute, the decision-making processes of lawyers and clients, why settlement efforts failed, or why the judicial process failed to resolve the dispute before the appellate level.

Other than having students read appellate case decisions, law teachers do not frequently use actual cases for instructional purposes, for example, by presenting students with case histories. In recent years, some law teachers have begun using books and movies about actual cases to engage students, especially first year students, in discussions about various aspects of the judicial system, law practice, and other issues. Two of the books that are most frequently used for this purpose are A Civil Action,[467] and The Buffalo Creek Disaster.[468] We encourage law teachers to expand their use of actual cases and case histories, including transactional as well as dispute resolution cases.

Some law students become involved in ongoing actual cases by enrolling in in-house clinics and externship courses where they represent clients or observe lawyers and judges at work.

Whether the case is historical or ongoing, the use of actual cases can enhance students' understanding of law and law practice.

> When legal educators set out to introduce students to the intricacies of legal analysis, they turn to cases. When clinical professors lead students toward addressing clients' needs they are perforce dealing with cases, though in coaching students struggling to develop a "theory of the case" they are also helping to shape the case as well as analyze it. When law school faculty take up issues of jurisprudence and professionalism, they are again very likely to approach these themes through the medium of case discussion. Clearly this is deeply related to the nature of the law itself; that legal thinking, even the creation and application of doctrinal principles, proceed by cases. But could it also reflect more than that? Case teaching may be powerful pedagogy because it distills into a method the distinctive intellectual formation of professionals.[469]

We encourage law schools to follow the lead of other professional schools and transform their programs of instruction so that the entire educational experience is focused on providing opportunities to practice solving problems under supervision in an academic environment. This is the most effective and efficient way to develop professional competence.

> Demonstrations of appropriate problem-solving processes are not very effective in bringing about actual problem-solving competence. [Educational researchers] show that only small gains are attained in critical thinking when merely a single course in a

---

[467] JONATHAN HARR, A CIVIL ACTION (1995).

[468] GERALD STERN, THE BUFFALO CREEK DISASTER (1977).

[469] SULLIVAN ET AL., *supra* note 7, at 255.

college program aims to develop this type of competence. On the other hand, when the entire curriculum is devoted to this same purpose (i.e., when these objectives become the theme that plays through a large number of courses) the students' gains in critical thinking become very large. In effect, the entire educational environment must be turned toward the achievement of complex objectives if they are to be attained in any significant way.[470]

Problem-based education is consistent with pedagogical trends in undergraduate education as well as in professional education. Problem-based education has been the norm in graduate schools of business for many years (at Harvard since 1911), and more recently it has become the norm in medical and other professional schools.[471] In medical schools, the adoption of problem-based instruction required overcoming some of the same hurdles that impede its adoption by law schools.[472]

> Medical schools too have been staffed by people who had no training in teaching and simply adopted the teaching methods (mainly lectures) used on them as students. Many medical professors have viewed problem-solving as a vocational skill, inappropriate for academic study. Others have imagined the problem method to be more expensive and time-consuming than conventional medical education.

> But the realities of what medical students need to learn overcame these obstacles. Doctors (like lawyers) spend their careers trying to solve problems, and to do so they must "learn how to learn." . . . [The problem method] helps students retain knowledge: knowledge acquired to help solve a problem is remembered better than knowledge acquired without such a motivation. "Knowledge used is better remembered." And the problem method motivates medical students to work harder, for it "challenges them with the very situations they will face in their elected professional field."[473]

Creating a curriculum that focuses on developing professional problem-solving expertise will take some reconceptualizing of the law curriculum and the faculty's roles in it.

> A problem-solving curriculum is different from a traditional knowledge-based curriculum. In the knowledge-based approach,

---

[470] BENJAMIN BLOOM, TAXONOMY OF EDUCATIONAL OBJECTIVES: COGNITIVE AND AFFECTIVE DOMAINS 77-78 (1956).

[471] "The most notable example is the evolution of problem-based instruction in medicine. For two recent surveys, see Mark A. Albanese & Susan Mitchell, *Problem-Based Learning: A Review of the Literature on Its Outcomes and Implementation Issues*, 68 ACAD. MED. 52 (1993); Geoffrey R. Norman & Henk G. Schmidt, *The Psychological Basis of Problem-Based Learning: A Review of the Evidence*, 67 ACAD. MED. 557 (1992). For a survey of efforts to introduce problem-based instruction into other professions (in Australia), including mechanical engineering, social work, optometry, architecture, informatics, management, and law, see THE CHALLENGE OF PROBLEM BASED LEARNING (David Boud & Grahame Feletti eds., 1991)." Blasi, *supra* note 15, at 387 n.215.

[472] Moskovitz, *supra* note 160, at 247.

[473] *Id.* at 247-248 (citations omitted).

the curriculum is organized into subjects and teachers are regarded as experts in their subject. They impart their subject knowledge to learners who are expected to remember, understand, and apply it.

In the problem-centered approach, the curriculum is organized around problems; students are active learners who work on problems, or simulate problem solving [or solve real life problems]. Teachers are facilitators who guide students in the process of learning by doing. During this process students work, usually in small groups, discovering solutions on their own, gaining insights into their own performance, and acquiring skills and knowledge as they solve problems.[474]

Although it will require some adjustments to our attitudes and practices, the proven benefits of context-based education compel our attention. We encourage law schools to explore as many ways as possible to expand their use of context-based education throughout the curriculum.

1.   **Use Context-Based Instruction to Teach Theory, Doctrine, and Analytical Skills (problem and case-based learning).**

Principle: The school uses context-based instruction to teach theory, doctrine, and analytical skills.

Comments:

Aristotle described three forms of knowledge. One is theory.

Theory ("theoria") derived from contemplation, and involved the search for truth through contemplation in order to attain knowledge for its own sake. Theory generally took the form of abstract, general rules, guided by pure reason and particular forms of intellectual activity (episteme). Certain disciplines were associated with theory (such as philosophy and pure mathematics). A life devoted to theory was regarded as the best and the intellectual virtues as the most valued. Educators, who impart theoretical knowledge and inculcate intellectual virtues, are thus engaged in the highest and most "God-like" of callings ("theo," the root of "theory" referring to God). Theory is often associated with declarative knowledge that can be readily transferred from teacher to student. It has also increasingly been associated with the written word.[475]

Hypothetical problems can provide contexts for helping students develop their analytical skills and attain knowledge and understanding of theory and doctrine. They can also be used as springboards for discussing justice, professional roles, and other important concepts.

---

[474] Stephen Nathanson, *Designing Problems to Teach Problem-Solving,* 34 CAL. W. L. REV. 325 (1998).

[475] Wegner, Theory and Practice, *supra* note 46 at 7 (citing Aristotle, Nichomecean Ethics).

Judith Wegner and other scholars[476] encourage law teachers to make greater use of hypothetical problems, even in first year courses.

> Although the traditional unit of analysis under the case-dialogue method is the case itself or a series of cases, an important alternative exists – to concentrate on a presenting problem, in much the way that alternative forms of "case method" such as those used in business schools commonly do. This approach assumes (or expressly states) that the relevant conceptual unit for analysis is a "problem," even though it may continue to use a case or cases as illustrations or as resources for reaching a solution. In effect, this form of "problem/case" method embeds cases in the problem – rather than treating a judicial decision as itself the problem to be solved, or pondering problems embedded in such a decision – performing what amounts to a figure-ground shift.[477]

Wegner observed first year law teachers using the problem and case approach successfully at very different schools located far apart. She found that the method "resonates quite powerfully with aspects of the theory of 'cognitive apprenticeship'" that is one of the strengths of the Socratic dialogue and case method.[478]

> The professors each asked questions that were clearly genuine, not rhetorical. They functioned in unison with their students as they approached a shared task, and modeled the role of "senior partner" working with more junior associates. They involved students in the performance of analytical routines, but these routines were not solely critical, designed to take apart someone else's argument or a judicial text. Instead, they presented lucid examples of constructive thinking, that is, how to foresee and avoid problems, how to understand the potential views of a range of real or potential disputants, and how to look behind positions to interests and search for common ground. Both professors also created space for and demanded discussion of client viewpoints, as they gave their students an opportunity to picture the people whose lives and livelihoods were in truth at stake.[479]

Wegner concluded that the classes she observed using the problem and case method "illustrate what a full-blown effort to implement the theory of 'situated' learning and cognitive apprenticeship might look like. By introducing more challenging intellectual tasks and building a collaborative culture, they fueled a heightened sense of engagement and motivation by helping students see how their 'thinking' could benefit people who might actually exist. A tangible sense of

---

[476] *See, e. g.,* Davis & Steinglass, *supra* note 281, which is discussed at length in Chapter Six in the section on best practices for using the Socratic dialogue and case method; Moskovitz, *supra* note 160, at 247 (describing how he uses problems to stimulate discussion of cases and lead into Socratic dialogue); William Shepard McAninch, *Experiential Learning in a Traditional Classroom,* 36 J. LEGAL EDUC. 420 (1986) (explaining how experiential education can be employed as an adjunct to traditional methodologies regardless of class size).

[477] Wegner, Experience, *supra* note 50, at 39.

[478] Wegner's description of "cognitive apprenticeship" is in Chapter Six in the section on best practices for using the Socratic dialogue and case method, use the Socratic dialogue and case method for appropriate purposes.

[479] Wegner, Experience, *supra* note 50, at 39-40.

professional pleasure was evident as students and professors worked together to construct critical knowledge and imagine problem resolutions that addressed not only the needs of clients but also broader values of fairness and the collective good."[480]

The problem and case approach may provide a good vehicle to "engage issues of professional identity (roles, obligations, clients) that may prove stumbling blocks to learning if continually ignored. This 'problem/case' method may also legitimate and build upon a range of insights in a collaborative manner, reducing the sense of risk in speaking out in front of strangers. Even for faculty who do not select this type of teaching option, there is food for thought that should not be ignored."[481]

The problem and case approach also more closely approximates the structure of most law school and bar examination essay exams than the Socratic dialogue and case method. Thus, teachers who use this approach in the classroom are improving their students' odds of success on bar examinations as well as in law school.

2.   Use Context-Based Instruction to Teach How to Produce Law-Related Documents (legal writing and drafting).

Principle: The school uses context-based instruction to teach how to produce law-related documents.

Comments:
A second form of knowledge described by Aristotle is "productive action."

Productive action ("poiesis") has a distinctive purpose – the creation of a product through the process of "making" something, be it poetry, art, or "products" of other sorts (sometimes referred to as "artifacts"). Such action was thought to be guided by an underlying idea or plan regarding the desired outcome, and was executed through technical skill ("techne") associated with the particular craft. This form of knowing or reasoning has been described as instrumental, since it involves the interplay between idea and capability. It inevitably has three components, however – the idea, the techniques used in the "making" and the "product" or performance that results. Technique improves through repeated production, and production is in turn improved by enhanced technique. Productive action is sometimes associated with disciplines such as engineering.[482]

Law students are initially introduced to productive action in legal contexts in legal writing courses where they are required to write legal memoranda, briefs, motions, and other documents. In the upper class curriculum, all students produce at least one research paper, and students may choose to enroll in drafting, clinical, and other practice-oriented courses that help them learn how to produce various legal documents.

In each of these settings, the educational objectives are much broader than developing students' technical skills. They also aid the students' understanding of theory and doctrine, sharpen their analytical skills, improve their understanding of

---

[480] *Id.* at 40.
[481] *Id.* at 41.
[482] Wegner, *Theory and Practice, supra* note 46, at 8.

the legal profession, and in some instances cultivate their practical wisdom.

Unfortunately, law schools have not created comprehensive programs for teaching students how to produce the documents that lawyers typically use in practice. Law schools should determine what types of legal documents their graduates will be expected to produce when they begin law practice and provide instruction in how to produce such documents. After all, it does no good to teach a student to think like a lawyer if the student cannot convey that thinking in writing.

> **3.   Use Context-Based Instruction to Teach How to Resolve Human Problems and to Cultivate "Practical Wisdom" (role assumption and practice experience).**

Principle: The school uses context-based instruction to teach how to resolve human problems and to cultivate "practical wisdom."

Comments:
> The third form of knowledge described by Aristotle is "practice."

> *Practice* ("praxis") has as its goal the resolution of human problems and the cultivation of "practical wisdom" or "judgment." This way of knowing was associated by Aristotle with ethical and political life (such as the exercise of governmental leadership) – the life of action. It quintessentially concerns an individual's encounter with a question or problem rooted in a specific context, for which no known answer is readily apparent. Instead, the individual needed to be guided by a moral disposition and a capability to interpret the unclear and fluid setting ("phronesis"), while engaging in detached analysis and observation. The ultimate outcome was guided by a complex interplay of detachment and action – understanding, interpretation, reflection, application and skill. At one time, "practice" was thought to entail mere application of previously encountered theories in a relatively passive sense. Over time, it was reinterpreted, however, and its relation to theory has commonly been seen in different terms. In many arenas, theory can only be derived from information and experience with real-life problems encountered in the "practical" realm, just as "practice" should be guided by the continuing evolution of cutting-edge theory.[483]

Law schools cannot help students cultivate practical wisdom or judgment unless they give students opportunities to engage in legal problem-solving activities. "'[P]ractical judgment' in the useful sense described by Aristotle, is context-dependent, linked to intensive interplay between theory and a human problem, as relevant knowledge is developed through reflection in light of the surrounding circumstances and brought to fruition through action."[484]

---

[483] *Id.*
[484] *Id.* at 29.

The authors of the Carnegie Foundation's report concluded that law students should have significant involvement in the experience of performing the tasks of practicing lawyers throughout law school.

> The essential dynamic of professional practice, especially in fields such as law, in which face-to-face relationships with clients are typical, proceeds in the opposite direction from the logic of academic specialization. Practice requires not the distanced stance of the observer and critic but engagement with situations. The sort of thinking required to meet the challenges of practice blends and mixes functions, so that knowledge, skill, and judgment become literally interdependent: one cannot employ one without the others, while each influences the nature of the others in ways that vary from case to case. In counseling or advising a client, it is difficult to know what and how much legal knowledge to apply without also gaining a sure grasp of the complexities of the client's situation and outlook and coming to some determination about the appropriate professional response. For this reason, we believe laying a foundation for the development of practitioners requires that legal education expand along the continuum to include significant involvement in the experience of performing the tasks of practicing lawyers. Beginning students' legal education almost entirely at one end of the pedagogical continuum is simply not the best start for introducing students to the full scope and demands of the world of the law.[485]

While lawyers certainly need to be skilled at analytic thinking, they also need to be skilled at narrative thinking, and this can only be developed by teaching in context. Law schools are familiar with the task of helping students develop analytic thinking skills. "Analytic thinking detaches things and events from the situations of everyday life and represents them in more abstract and systematic ways."[486] The other mode of thinking is based on narrative. "Here, things and events acquire significance by being placed within a story, an ongoing context of meaningful interaction. This mode of thinking integrates experience through metaphor and analogy."[487]

> Actual legal practice is heavily dependent upon expertise in narrative modes of reasoning. Indeed, in all legal reasoning, as Bruner points out, the analytic and paradigmatic models depend upon narrative and metaphor for their sense. Hence, both judicial decisions and law teaching must invoke cases in order to give intelligibility to abstract legal principles. It follows that the formation of the habits of mind needed for legal practice also demand fluency in both the engaged mode of narrative thinking characteristic of everyday practice and the detached mode of analytical thinking emphasized in case-dialogue teaching.

> This twofold aspect of professional expertise is captured by Eliot Freidson when he describes medical education's aim as forming a "clinical" habit of mind so that physicians could "work

---

[485] SULLIVAN ET AL., *supra* note 7, at 87-88.
[486] *Id.* at 108.
[487] *Id.* at 107.

as consultants who must intervene [with specialized, esoteric knowledge] in everyday, practical affairs." In order to treat the patient, the clinician must be able to move back and forth between detached analysis of the medical condition and emphatic engagement with the distressed patient. Medical education clearly demonstrates that this clinical habit of mind can, like analytic thinking, also be developed within a formal education program.[488]

Law schools provide students opportunities to learn how lawyers resolve human problems to some extent in many law school courses, particularly those that emphasize problem-based instruction. But students actually perform as lawyers in resolving problems in simulation-based courses where students perform lawyering tasks in hypothetical situations and in externships and in-house clinics where students represent clients or observe lawyers and judges performing in their professional roles.

Simulation-based courses can help cultivate students' practical wisdom and professional values. For example, students who conduct initial client interviews will consider how to develop rapport with clients and whether and how to obtain personal information from clients. Students who counsel clients will gain insights into how clients' cultural backgrounds and personal values affect their decisions. And students who negotiate with each other must decide whether to lie to gain an advantage. Thus, simulated experience can give students experiences where they can be guided by their personal values and their capability to react to fluid situations, while engaging in a detached anaylsis of the legal problem embedded in the simulation.

Even the best simulation-based courses, however, provide make believe experiences with no real consequences on the line.

As early as possible in law school, preferably in the first semester, law students should be exposed to the actual practice of law. Exposure to law practice may be the only way through which students can really begin to understand the written and unwritten standards of law practice and the degree to which those standards are followed. Students need to observe and experience the demands, constraints, and methods of analyzing and dealing with unstructured situations in which the issues have not been identified in advance. Otherwise, their problem-solving skills and judgment cannot mature.

Experience exerts a powerful influence over the exercise of discretion. Experiential learning is critically important to moral development. Aristotle stated that one had to practice virtuous behavior, modeling oneself on the good, and then reflect on it for such behavior to become a part of one's character. As Justice Holmes said: "We learn how to behave as lawyers, soldiers, merchants or what not by being them. Life, not the parson, teaches conduct."

. . . .

In other words, it is not until students actually experience the reality of practice that they begin to internalize and make their own

---

[488] *Id.* at 109.

moral and ethical judgments that are at the core of practice.[489]

Providing some exposure to actual law practice throughout law school is not only important for helping students develop well-rounded and more realistic perspectives about the legal profession, it also helps students appreciate the importance of other subjects taught in law schools.

Providing exposure to law practice, even in the first semester, does not have to be expensive or time-consuming. Deborah Maranville and others believe that instruction even during the first year "ideally should include some real-life experiences, preferably experiences involving contact with clients."[490] The education of first year students would be enhanced by having each student participate in some straightforward, easy-to-arrange activities during the academic year such as the following.

- take a jail tour or participate in a police ride-along while taking Criminal Law, and engage in a plea bargaining exercise in class.
- observe two hours of the local court motion calendar while taking Civil Procedure (perhaps with an opportunity to see the papers filed by the attorneys in one or more of the cases), and draft a complaint and answer for class.
- negotiate a personal injury claim while taking Torts and collect, compare, and analyze release of liability forms from a range of organizations sponsoring sporting activities.
- interview a client about a contract for a business transaction while taking Contracts and analyze the same release of liability forms as in Torts.
- take pictures of easements, and spend four hours helping interview unrepresented litigants in connection with a bar association project to provide legal advice to pro se litigants in landlord-tenant cases while taking Property.[491]

Students who have opportunities to work on cases as law clerks or to observe lawyers and judges at work learn valuable lessons that are difficult to replicate in the classroom or in simulated environments

Increasing law students' exposure to law practice was the primary anecdote proposed for law student lethargy by Mitu Gulati, Richard Sander, and Robert Sockloskie.[492] They collected data about law students' opinions of legal education and the reasons why they existed. They determined that most law students find the substance of the third year remote and largely irrelevant, and that a surprising percentage of third year students are profoundly disengaged from the educational experience. Among their specific recommendations for reform are for schools to invest more in the depth, evaluation, and comparison of clinical programs, including the expanded use of externships. They also propose that law schools should consider establishing community law practices to provide vehicles for students to practice and study in real-world situations along the lines of upper level medical education.

Law students in the United States became isolated from the legal profession

---

[489] Eleanor Myers, *"Simple Truths" About Moral Education,* 45 Am. U. L. Rev. 823, 835-36 (1996) (citations omitted).

[490] Maranville, *supra* note 404, at 61.

[491] *Id.* at 64.

[492] Gulati et al., *supra* note 3, at 234 n.4.

when law schools adopted the case method and hired recent graduates as teachers, and when admitting authorities dropped apprenticeship requirements.[493] The emergence and growth of clinical education has removed some of the isolation, and many students work in law firms while attending law school. Legal educators in the United States, however, have not yet fully considered and embraced the roles that supervised practice experience should play in the pre-admission education of lawyers.

Law schools can provide exposure to law practice through externships,[494] in-house clinics, or even co-curricular activities. Externships and in-house clinics can provide significant opportunities to experience practice supported by faculty oversight. In externships, the students' direct mentors and supervisors are practicing lawyers and judges, and the practice settings are in established legal offices and judicial chambers, providing opportunities for understanding and critique of those institutions. In campus-based clinics, the students' direct mentors and supervisors are members of the law faculty, and students have opportunities to undertake primary responsibility for the representation of clients, team with other students, and help manage an independent law office. In any format, clinical education can provide individualized feedback on each student's professional behavior and development.

Within clinical legal education, the principal theoretical objectives are to describe and explain the dynamics of legal practice. Sometimes these theories embrace a critical perspective. They point out the limitations, shortcomings, contingencies, and contradictions inherent in the practice of law and in theories about the practice of law. At other times, their function is principally prescriptive. Their purpose is to highlight conceptually what ought to be considered and weighed before lawyers act or proceed. Prescriptive theories about legal practice provide a perspective on what needs to be done but not a mechanical how-to-do-it approach. The details and choices have to be worked out in the particular context.

Pedagogically, clinical legal education seeks not just to impart legal skills, but to encourage students to be responsible and thoughtful practitioners. There is considerable emphasis on problem-solving approaches, such as ends-means thinking; on skills training in addition to legal reasoning; on making ethically responsible decisions, particularly when obligations are in conflict; and on being continually self reflective and critically analytical about one's own experiences.[495]

---

[493] According to a person who lived in those times, apprenticeships went out of favor because modern inventions rendered the services of law students of no value to law firms. "The general introduction, since 1880, of telephones, stenographers, typewriters, dictating and copying devices, and improvements in printing, in connection with changes in practice already noted, has made *students* not only unnecessary but actually undesirable in most of the active law offices. Plainly speaking, they are considered to be a nuisance." Rowe, *supra* note 2, at 600.

[494] *See* James H. Backman, *Where Do Externships Fit? A New Paradigm is Needed: Marshaling Law School Resources to Provide an Educational Externship for Every Student*, 56 J. Legal Educ. (forthcoming Spring 2007) (arguing that externships providing valuable educational benefits can and should be provided to all law students).

[495] Aaronson, *supra* note 176, at 249.

In the United Kingdom and other places, supervised real life experience is considered an essential part of legal education, though it takes place after graduation from undergraduate law school and completion of a professional training course. The Law Society of England and Wales discussed the importance of real life experience in its statement of proposed educational outcomes:

> It is suggested that it would not be possible for an individual to develop and demonstrate effectively all of the required outcomes, e.g., that they could work with clients, organise work effectively, or maintain files, unless they had actually worked within a legal practice environment. The review group also considers it essential that all new entrants to the profession have had an opportunity to experience the culture of the profession before they become full members of it, and to have had some exposure to the economic, social and business context in which law is practised. This requires that individuals should have worked alongside other solicitors, learned how the values, behaviours and attitudes required of the profession apply (and are sometimes challenged) in practice and how risks should be managed.[496]

Supervised law practice plays important symbolic and functional roles in the preparation of lawyers that are quite different from any role played by the Socratic dialogue and case method, problem discussion, or simulated role-playing. While supervised practice is not the most effective method for imparting information about the law or legal processes, supervised practice is more effective than classroom instruction for teaching the standards and values of the legal profession and instilling in students a commitment to professionalism.

"Clinical teaching resonates well against the well-documented importance of active learning in role. Its most striking feature, however, is perhaps the power of clinical experiences to engage and expand students' expertise and professional identity through supervised responsibility for clients."[497]

The positive impact of supervised practice experience on professional identity is why most countries in the world, including those in the United Kingdom, require lawyers to engage in a period of supervised practice before allowing them to be fully licensed. In explaining why English solicitors and barristers have always highly valued articles and pupillage, Michael Burrage wrote:

> By forcing clerks and pupils to submit to a period of hardship, drudgery and semi-servitude, it necessarily conveyed a due appreciation of the value of membership in the profession. It also instilled respect for one's elders, for their experience, for their manners, conventions and ethics and for their sense of corporate honour. Articles and pupillage could, therefore, provide cast iron guarantees about the attitudes, demeanor and commitment of those who were to enter the profession. A university degree, by contrast, guaranteed only the acquisition of legal knowledge of uncertain relevance to the actual practice of law.

---

[496] Law Society Second Consultation, *supra* note 138, at § 4, ¶ 68.

[497] SULLIVAN ET AL., *supra* note 7, at 142.

. . . They were forms of moral training, of initiation into networks that linked every past and present member of the profession, by ties of obligation, loyalty, and possibly affection, that enabled the newcomer to belong, to empathize with its aspirations and concerns and to share its sense of honour.[498]

In the United States, it is only in the in-house clinics and some externships where students' decisions and actions can have real consequences and where students' values and practical wisdom can be tested and shaped before they begin law practice.

Responsibility for clients and accountability for one's own actions are at the center of clinical experiences. Assuming responsibility for outcomes that affect clients with whom the student has established a relationship enables the learner to go beyond concepts, to actually become a professional in practice.[499]

It is especially important for students to have opportunities to engage in supervised client representation during law school because most law school graduates will become fully licensed to practice law as soon as they pass a bar examination without any requirement that their work be supervised until they demonstrate competence.[500]

In 1917, William Rowe argued that clinical education during law school was necessary to instill professional values in law students.

The real need . . . is education, training and discipline in the conduct of professional life – the development of what may be called the professional character, spirit and savoir faire, in the only possible way, that is to say, by placing the student in a proper law office, which we will call *a clinic, under systematic instruction and training,* and in constant touch with reputable practitioners of high character, who, in a *general practice,* are applying the law in the concrete, as a living force, to the living problems of our people. The student thus *lives* in an atmosphere of the law, and absorbs the spirit of its practice, day by day, in the course of actual dealings between the lawyer and client.

As in the case of the Inns of Court and the English barristers' and solicitors' offices, the student unconsciously develops in such an atmosphere, under the influence and contact of character and personality working in the harness of the law, the trained professional conscience and practical sense – the instinct for right and the consciousness of wrong, which constitute the true spirit of the profession, and lead, regardless of rewards, to that necessary self-sacrificing devotion to the vindication of the good and true and the

---

[498] Michael Burrage, *From a Gentleman's to a Public Profession: Status and Politics in the History of English Solicitors,* 3 INT'L J. LEG. PROF. 45, 54 (1996).

[499] SULLIVAN ET AL., *supra* note 7, at 143.

[500] As mentioned at the beginning of the document, we consider the failure to require supervised practice before full licensure to be the biggest shortcoming of the United States' method of producing lawyers.

punishment of evil and the false, upon which, with us, must largely rest the welfare of our profession and much of our advancement in social development and organized government. This is the spirit of the real law office which the law schools must now supply.[501]

Unfortunately, Rowe's arguments for making clinical education a significant component of legal education went unheeded. One can only speculate as to whether law practice in the United States would be conducted more professionally today if clinical education had been embraced in 1917.

Much more recently, the authors of the Carnegie Foundation's report also recognized the critical importance of supervised practice experience to the preparation of law students for entry into the legal profession.

The development of competence in novice lawyers requires more than teaching knowledge, skills, and values. It also requires helping students form habits of ethical practice and a commitment to self development. This requires giving students opportunities to experience practice under supervision.

In actual professional practice, it is often not the particular knowledge or special skill of the lawyer or physician that is critical, important as these are. At moments when judgment is at a premium, when the practitioner is called upon to intervene or to react with integrity for the values of the profession, it is the quality of the individual's formation that is at issue. The holistic qualities count: the sense of intuitive engagement, of habitual disposition that enable the practitioner to perform reliably and artfully. Thinking about how to train these capacities inevitably calls up words such as "integration" and "focus" to describe deep engagement with knowledge, skills, and defining loyalties of the profession.

Ultimately, the goal of formative education must be more than socialization seen as molding human clay from without. Rather, formative education must enable students to become self-reflective about and self-directing in their own development. Seen from a formative perspective, law school ought to provide the richest context possible for students to explore and make their own the profession's possibilities for a useful and fulfilling life. The school contributes to this process by opening apprenticeship to its students as effectively as its faculty is able. Concretely, this means enabling students to grasp what the law is as well as how to think within it, just as it means giving students the experience of practicing the varied roles lawyers play while coming to appreciate the engagements of self and the world that these entail.[502]

The authors of the Carnegie Foundation's report believe that actual experience with clients is "an essential catalyst for the full development of ethical engagement,"[503] and "there is much to suggest that ethical engagement provides a

---

[501] Rowe, *supra* note 2, at 597-98.

[502] SULLIVAN ET AL., *supra* note 7, at 92-93.

[503] *Id.* at 198.

pivotal aspect in the formation of lawyers."[504]

Perhaps this time the legal academy will give supervised client representation the place it deserves in legal education. There are signs that the accrediting body for law schools is beginning to recognize the value of supervised client representation experience during law school. The ABA accreditation standards now provide that "[a] law school shall offer substantial opportunities for live-client or other real-life practice experiences, appropriately supervised and designed to encourage reflection by students on their experiences and on the values and responsibilities of the legal profession, and the development of one's ability to assess his or her performance and level of competence."[505] It is not yet clear what impact this will have on legal education, but it is a positive development.

It is not difficult to recognize the value of real life experience. The difficult part is defining the type and extent of practice experience that law schools should provide to achieve educational goals that cannot be achieved more efficiently and effectively through other means. It is also difficult to determine how much and what types of practice experience are necessary to protect future clients' interests. These issues warrant careful study. It may be that some aspects of becoming a competent lawyer can only be learned and evaluated in the actual practice of law after graduation.

Although it is unlikely that any law school can provide students sufficient practice experiences to develop fully their practical wisdom, self-understanding, and professional values, law schools should develop as many opportunities as possible for students to practice resolving human problems and cultivating practical wisdom and judgment.

H.   Integrate Practicing Lawyers and Judges Into the Program of Instruction.[506]

Principle: The school properly integrates practicing lawyers and judges into the program of instruction.[507]

Comments:
The accreditation standards of the American Bar Association encourage law schools to include experienced lawyers and judges as teaching resources.

A law school should include experienced practicing lawyers and judges as teaching resources to enrich the educational program. Appropriate use of practicing lawyers and judges as faculty requires that a law school shall provide them with orientation, guidance,

---

[504] *Id.*

[505] Standard 302(b)(1), ABA STANDARDS, *supra* note 28, at 18.

[506] University of South Carolina law student Jodi Ramsey, class of 2006, researched and drafted this section.

[507] In 2005, the ABA Section of Legal Education and Admissions to the Bar published a comprehensive handbook on adjunct faculty. AMERICAN BAR ASSOCIATION, SECTION OF LEGAL EDUCATION AND ADMISSIONS TO THE BAR, ADJUNCT FACULTY HANDBOOK (2005) [hereinafter ADJUNCT FACULTY HANDBOOK], *available at* http://www.abanet.org/legaled/publications/adjuncthandbook/ adjuncthandbook.pdf. The book includes guidelines for everything from hiring to firing adjunct faculty. The handbook can be downloaded for free.

monitoring, and evaluation.[508]

Practicing lawyers and judges can be valuable assets to the faculty and students of law schools. They can give students a realistic view of the practice of law that they may not get from the full-time faculty, and they can bring diversity to the faculty.[509] In most law schools, practicing lawyers and judges currently play formal and informal roles in the educational process. Many visit law schools to speak to student organizations or to participate in formal co-curricular speaker programs. Some schools are integrating them into the orientation process as participants in small groups to discuss the legal profession, the roles that law schools play in preparing students for practice, and the importance of living a balanced life during and after law school. It is becoming frequent practice for schools to pair up incoming students with practitioners who agree to serve as informal mentors.

Practicing lawyers and judges also participate in legal education as adjunct faculty with full responsibility for teaching courses. This creates some special challenges and obligations for law schools, however, since adjuncts usually carry full caseloads in addition to their teaching responsibilities. This means their time in the school will be limited, court schedules will sometimes conflict with class, and their professional obligations to clients may conflict with class preparation.

Law schools have not done a good job, generally, in nurturing adjunct faculty. Adjuncts are not always included in law school events, and full-time faculty do not seek opportunities to interact with adjuncts regarding course design, teaching techniques, or other important matters.[510]

Most adjuncts are not "professional" teachers, and new adjuncts especially need some guidance about where and how to begin. Law schools should organize orientation programs for new adjuncts that cover such topics as the different methods of teaching (for example, problem method, case method, Socratic dialogue, discussion, lecturing), how exams should be structured and graded, how to prepare a syllabus, and how to evaluate themselves.[511] It is helpful for the school to prepare an adjunct handbook that covers such topics as how to cancel or re-schedule classes, when grades are due, and people to contact for help.[512] Schools should consider providing each adjunct with a full-time faculty mentor, but at the least, adjuncts should be informed of which full-time faculty members teach classes in similar subjects.[513]

In addition to providing orientation or workshops before school starts, the school should have an ongoing system for facilitating communication between the adjuncts and the law school.[514] An administrator or faculty committee can

---

[508] Standard 403(c), ABA Standards, *supra* note 28, at 30.

[509] Marcia Gelpe, *Professional Training, Diversity in Legal Education, and Cost Control: Selection, Training and Peer Review for Adjunct Professors*, 25 Wm. Mitchell L. Rev. 193, 194 (1999).

[510] Karen Tokarz, *A Manual for Law Schools on Adjunct Faculty*, 76 Wash. U. L. Q. 293, 298 (1998).

[511] *Id.* at 297. Specific suggestions for adjunct orientation are included in Adjunct Faculty Handbook, *supra* note 507.

[512] Gelpe, *supra* note 509, at 213. Specific suggestions for handbooks are included in Adjunct Faculty Handbook, *supra* note 507.

[513] Tokarz, *supra* note 510, at 298.

[514] *Id.* at 297. Specific suggestions for communicating with adjunct faculty are included in Adjunct Faculty Handbook, *supra* note 507.

be designated to keep adjuncts informed about law school events, facilitate their integration into the law school community, and encourage full-time faculty to get to know their adjunct peers.[515]

It is important to provide adjuncts with feedback[516] and to evaluate and reward them when appropriate.[517] "Especially because the financial remuneration is so meager, the gratitude of the faculty and administration should be loud and clear, and repeated often."[518] The evaluation of adjuncts should include clearly identifying standards for teaching, assisting adjuncts in meeting the standards, and dismissing adjuncts who do not meet the standards.[519]

> The full time faculty should adopt a statement of standards for adjunct teaching that should be furnished to all adjuncts. Full-time faculty should then sit in on classes taught by adjuncts. This can be done in the same way as full-time faculty sit in on classes of untenured faculty. Class visits should be followed by detailed feedback, based on the stated standards, with specific suggestions on what to keep, what to change, and how to make needed changes.[520]

To maximize the benefits of using adjunct professors, full-time faculty need to participate every step of the way, from the hiring process to the evaluation of adjuncts' performance, and hopefully to a continuing relationship that benefits the adjunct, the school, and the students.[521]

I.   Enhance Learning With Technology.

Principle: The teachers effectively use technology to enhance learning.

Comments:
If technology is not the future of legal education, it is at least part of the future.[522] Proven and experimental uses of technology will continue to grow, and some components of legal education will be transformed by it.[523] Distance learning

---

[515] *Id.* at 298.

[516] Gelpe, *supra* note 509, at 220.

[517] Tokarz, *supra* note 510, at 303-04.

[518] *Id.* at 304.

[519] Gelpe, *supra* note 509, at 220.

[520] *Id.* at 221. Specific suggestions for evaluating adjunct faculty are included in AD-JUNCT FACULTY HANDBOOK, *supra* note 509.

[521] *Id.* at 221.

[522] Articles that delve into the merits and specific details of using technology in law schools include Kristin B. Gerdy, Jane H. Wise & Alison Craig, *Expanding Our Classroom Walls: Enhancing Teaching and Learning Through Technology*, 11 LEGAL WRITING 263, 263-66 (2005); Caron & Gely, *supra* note 392, at 552; Craig T. Smith, *Technology and Legal Education: Negotiating the Shoals of Technocentrism, Technophobia,* and *Indifference, in* ERASING LINES, *supra* note 38, at 247; Lasso, *supra* note 133. An article that raises concerns about overusing technology in legal education is David M. Becker, *Some Concerns About the Future of Legal Education*, 51 J. LEGAL EDUC. 469, 477-85 (2001).

[523] For a growing collection of articles and reports on technology in legal education, including information and communications technology, virtual learning environments, curriculum design, and more, visit the blog site of Sefton Bloxham, Patricia McKellar, Karen Barton, and Paul Maharg, http://zeugma.typepad.com (last visited August 29, 2006).

is already becoming an accepted part of the landscape of legal education, and interactive computer programs are allowing students to acquire knowledge and skills outside of the classroom setting.[524]

Technology can make instruction and evaluation more efficient and effective, but technology is no more and no less than a tool for implementing best teaching practices. Current technologies allow law professors to implement many of the best practices described in this document. For example, course web pages can be used to disseminate instructional objectives; to encourage and reward reflection on students' learning processes; require students to adopt active learning practices, such as by posting graphic organizers or original mnemonics; create cooperative learning projects, such as analyses of hypotheticals or development of student-authored practice exams; increase student opportunities for practice and feedback, such as online multiple choice and short answer quizzes; and encourage student adoption of active learning practices. Likewise, PowerPoint can be a tool for responding to students' diverse ways of learning by integrating visual movement and imagery.

Other forms of technology being used in law schools include television, videotapes and DVDs, overhead projectors, digital recorders, electronic visual presentation cameras,[525] and classroom performance systems[526] to name a few.[527] Classroom performance systems use "clickers," in which each student is given a keypad to respond to in-class multiple choice questions. The software records and reports on the results as a tool for responding to students' diverse ways of learning and serves as a classroom assessment technique that informs the teachers whether the students are learning and informs the students whether their learning strategies are working productively. Another technological innovation is the use of recording systems that automatically make video and sound records of students' classroom answers and performances for subsequent review.

Digital technology is making it possible to record and broadcast classroom instruction over the internet, "podcasting." After running a pilot project, CALI announced on August 23, 2006, that it is offering free digital recorders and blog accounts for faculty who want to use podcasting in their courses.[528] In phase one of its legal education podcasting project, CALI found that "students will re-listen to classroom lectures or weekly summaries created by the instructor and because of the anytime, anywhere nature of podcasts, they do this at times that are not necessarily

---

[524] The Center for Computer Assisted Legal Instruction (CALI) offers many programs. The CALI website at http://www2.cali.org is organized into three sections – learning the law, teaching the law, and technology in law schools – and includes tools to help faculty evaluate CALI lessons.

[525] Electronic visual presentation cameras (sometimes referred to as document cameras) are devices that capture visual images by using a video camera mounted vertically on a base. Images of just about anything that can be placed on the base (objects, book pages, documents, etc.) are converted to an electronic signal that can be transmitted to an LCD projector, a video monitor, or a computer. *See, e.g.,* Elmo Electronic Imaging, *available at* http://www.pharmnet2000.com/ELMO/index.html (last visited November 28, 2006).

[526] Classroom Performance System (CPS) is an electronic application that permits instant assessment of classroom performance. More information on CPS can be found at http://www.einstruction.com (last visited November 28, 2006). A good discussion of CPS is included in Caron & Gely, *supra* note 392, at 560-69.

[527] Lasso, *supra* note 133, at 46-47.

[528] E-mail from John Mayer, jmayer@cali.org, to the LawProf list serve, lawprof@chicagokent.kentlaw.edu, August 23, 2006 at 6:30 p.m.

dedicated to studying (for example, driving in the car during commutes, working out at the gym, and making dinner)."[529]

Technology exists to help prepare and deliver teaching materials and assessment tools. For example, there is a web-based platform called "Cyber Workbooks" that allows faculty to publish their course materials by integrating learning outcomes such as critical thinking, applied reasoning, and creative problem-solving. The platform consists of an authoring tool for developing course modules with lessons, questions, and answers; a user website accessible by students with a user name and password; and an administrative site for generating reports and allowing faculty to evaluate course modules. The platform has built-in assessment features that will identify, measure, validate, and report on learning outcomes and identify student weaknesses, without any special training. The program will time, grade, and record student responses to minimize faculty time and burden.[530]

Perhaps technology's greatest unused role in achieving learning outcomes is in helping students acquire core legal knowledge and understanding. Software programs exist that can generate a myriad of formative assessments, quizzing students on substantive law principles and other subjects using multi-state-type questions. The process of drill and practice enables students to know immediately if they are learning the assigned materials. "Behavioral adult educational philosophy from which the drill and practice technique emanates is highly regarded for its ability to develop competencies in areas where there are well established norms to which to teach."[531] Utilizing a variety of learning processes and providing feedback and reinforcement from such drills are often motivational for adult learners.[532]

J.　　Establish a Learning Center.

Principle:　　The school has a learning center.

Comments:[533]

We agree with Judith Wegner that it would be a very positive development for law schools to establish learning centers.

The creation of learning centers is a logical step that would build upon the academic support and other special needs programs that many law schools developed during the past decade. Each of these developments suggests that students can benefit from individualized help, yet law schools and universities remain fragmented in how that help is provided and how broadly it is dispersed. Moreover, law schools have not yet grappled with potential organizational strategies that could enhance

---

[529] *Id.*

[530] For more information about "Cyber Workbooks" go to http://www.cyberworkbooks.com.

[531] E-mail from Jack R. Goetz, Dean Emeritus, Concord Law School, to Professor Roy Stuckey (Jan. 13, 2005) (on file with Roy Stuckey) (referencing J. L. Elias & S. B. Merriam, Philosophical Foundations of Adult Education (2d ed. 1995); L. M. Zinn, *Identifying Your Philosophical Orientation, in* Adult Learning Methods 37-72 (M. W. Galbraith ed., 2d ed. 1998)).

[532] *Id.*

[533] Except for the first paragraph, the comments in this section were copied verbatim from Judith Wegner's preliminary conclusions from her study of legal education with the Carnegie Foundation for the Advancement of Teaching. Wegner, Assessment, *supra* note 24, at 73-75.

student learning, faculty teaching, and program improvement in fresh and useful ways.

Law schools could create model "learning centers" that could address such needs in innovative, cost-efficient ways. Law school learning centers could have the following characteristics:

1. A law school learning center would be directed by a faculty member with significant expertise in both law and educational issues, assisted by a student-faculty-administrative advisory committee, and appropriate additional personnel. Schools with a particular commitment to exploring the full potential of the model might appoint a faculty director who could function at the level of a specialized associate dean, working with a full-time director of academic support services, the director of legal writing, and requisite support personnel.

2. Learning centers could be charged with a number of functions. Most significantly, they would provide a range of "educational" (rather than "evaluative") assessment services – intensive academic support programming for students who may face special challenges, broader diagnostic testing and informal programming to benefit all students interested in becoming more effective learners, tutorial programming especially geared to first year, training for teaching assistants and volunteer tutors, training for students interested in incorporating better approaches to self-assessment and peer-assessment as part of individual or study-group techniques; and optional formative assessment activities that allow students to get feedback on simple problems or other exercises that evidence their proficiency in legal reasoning. They would also be responsible for coordination of student advising, information and logistics related to development of student educational portfolios,

3. In addition, "learning centers" could serve as "assessment centers" that provide assistance to faculty members wishing to use innovative approaches to "evaluative" assessment, for example by scheduling and administering timed and proctored assignments using a law school computer lab, videotaping performance-based assignments associated with certain kinds of "lawyering skills" or team-based tasks, or a variety of other sorts of "performance-based" tests.

4. Learning centers could also serve as a resource for faculty interested in innovations in teaching and learning (perhaps in cooperation with campus teaching and learning centers and legal educators elsewhere), and might coordinate faculty professional development workshops on topics such as use of advanced technology or collaborative learning

techniques. In addition, learning centers could be charged with institutional research regarding educational innovations or student performance. . . .[534]

"Learning centers" of the sort imagined here would represent an important innovation in American legal education, although they build upon recent efforts to create effective academic support programs as discussed above. They could draw upon lessons learned by innovative programs such as that of Alverno College (which uses performance-based student assessments quite extensively), and the use of performance-based assessment strategies in an increasing number of medical and business schools.[535]

Law school learning centers could also gain insight from more than forty years' experience with "assessment centers" in industrial, educational, military, government, and professional contexts, as they have been used as an aid in recruiting and placing managerial level employees, diagnosing strengths and limitations to develop individual or corporate training plans, and certifying teachers.[536] Notwithstanding these useful analogues, learning centers would represent an important breakthrough for both law schools and their host universities, since they would address law schools' own significant needs relating to student learning, advising, assessment, and related research, while serving as a useful prototype for initiatives that could prove useful in other programs or on larger scales.

Learning centers would provide a clear and readily accessible source for education about learning for all students, making learning a visible part of the law school landscape in a personalized way that effectively supplements the instructional design of traditional large classes and provides advising services that most schools seem to lack. They would assist all learners, as individuals, to make demonstrable progress at their own pace, taking their own learning styles and goals into account without stigma, while empowering them to take personal responsibility for their professional development from the outset of their careers. They would serve as a flexible means of introducing new forms of "educational" (formative) assessment with minimal burden upon faculty, assisting first-year students and others who have difficulty mastering fundamental "thinking" skills. Finally, they would help law schools attend to their special institutional context and its implications for instruction and assessment, by providing a capacity for informed institutional research on important issues that most schools currently lack.

---

[534] *Id.* at 73-74.

[535] Ronald Riggio & Monica Aguirre, *The Use of Assessment Center Methods for Student Outcome Assessment,* 12 J. SOC. BEHAV. & PERSONALITY 273-89 (1997); Lynn K. Bartells, William H. Bonner & Robert S. Rusbin, *Student Performance: Assessment Centers Versus Traditional Classroom Evaluation Techniques,* 75 J. EDUC. FOR BUS. 198-201 (2000).

[536] *See, e.g.,* Ann Howard, *A Reassessment of Assessment Centers: Challenges for the 21st Century,* 12 J. SOC. BEHAV. & PERSONALITY 13 (1997).

Chapter Five
Best Practices for Experiential Courses

A.   **Experiential Courses, Generally.**[537]

1.   **Introduction to Experiential Courses.**[538]

Experiential courses are those courses that rely on experiential education as a significant or primary method of instruction. In law schools, this involves using students' experiences in the roles of lawyers or their observations of practicing lawyers and judges to guide their learning.

Experiential education integrates theory and practice by combining academic inquiry with actual experience. "Learning is not education, and experiential learning differs from experiential education. Learning happens with or without teachers and institutions. For example, eavesdroppers learn about the things they hear, yet they are not educated simply by the fact of eavesdropping because the activity is not accompanied by a teacher's or institution's participation in the learning process. Education, in contrast to a learning opportunity, consists of a designed, managed, and guided experience."[539] Thus, while part-time work experiences of law students in legal settings can be valuable learning experiences, they are not considered experiential education because the learning in such environments is not necessarily accompanied by academic inquiry.

Our discussion of experiential education is primarily concerned with those courses in which experience is a significant or primary method of instruction, as opposed to courses in which experiential education is a valuable but secondary method of instruction. In some subject matter courses, law teachers encourage or require students to spend time in legal settings that illuminate issues considered in the course. For example, a course on judicial management of litigation may arrange for students to observe pretrial or settlement conferences in judges' chambers. A family law professor teaching a seminar on "the child and state" may have students visit family court, the child advocate, or a law guardian. Courses that use Socratic dialogue or discussion as the principal pedagogical methodology also may employ simulation exercises or role-playing from time to time.[540] For example, in an

---

[537] This section and the sections on simulations, in-house clinics, and externships combine materials prepared for the Best Practices Project by J.P. (Sandy) Ogilvy, Catholic (best practices for simulation-based courses); Mike Norwood, New Mexico (best practices for in-house clinics); and Harriet Katz, Rutgers, Camden, incorporating edits by Alex Scherr, Georgia; Cynthia Barr, Temple; Francis Catania, Jr., Widener; Mary Jo Eyster, Brooklyn; and Liz Ryan Cole, Vermont (best practices for externships). Roy Stuckey is primarily responsible for the subsections on setting clear, explicit learning objectives. To learn more about best practices in clinical legal education, see J. P. Ogilvy with Karen Czapanskiy, *Clinical Legal Education: An Annotated Bibliography* (3d ed.): *Part Three: Synopses of Articles, Essays, Books and Book Chapters,* 12 Clinical L. Rev. 101 (2005), *available at* http://faculty.cua.edu/ogilvy/Index1. htm.

[538] This section should be read in conjunction with the earlier section, "Employ context-based instruction throughout the program of instruction."

[539] James E. Moliterno, *Legal Education, Experiential Education, and Professional Responsibility,* 38 Wm. & Mary L. Rev. 71, 78 (1996) (citations omitted).

[540] *See* Hess & Friedland, *supra* note 304, at 108-09.

Evidence class, the instructor may create an on-the-spot role play to teach a concept by designating one student in the class as a prosecutor in a criminal case who is seeking to admit a piece of evidence, another student as defense counsel who is to resist admission, and a third student as the judge who is to rule on the proffer.[541] Although we are not focusing on such uses of experiential education, many of the principles set forth in this section are applicable to them.

Experiential education is the primary mode of instruction in various law school courses, especially courses that are generally described as "clinical:" simulation-based courses, in-house clinics, and externships.[542] These courses in law schools differ from each other in the following ways:
- in **simulation-based courses**, students assume professional roles and perform law-related tasks in hypothetical situations,
- in **in-house clinics**, students represent clients or perform other professional roles[543] under the supervision of members of the faculty, and
- in **externships**, students represent clients or perform other professional roles under the supervision of practicing lawyers or they observe or assist practicing lawyers or judges in their work.

All of these pedagogies are based in an understanding that students must perform complex skills in order to gain expertise. They also recognize that students do not get better through practice alone. If their performance is to improve, they need practice accompanied by informative feedback and reflection on their own performance. And their learning will be strengthened further if they develop a habit of ongoing self-assessment.[544]

Optimal learning from experience involves a continuous, circular four stage sequence of experience, reflection, theory, and application.

Experience is the immersing of one's self in a task or similar event – the doing. Reflection involves stepping back and reflecting on both the cognitive and affective aspects of what happened or was done. Theory entails interpreting the task or event, making generalizations, or seeing the experience in a larger context. Application enables one to plan for or make predictions about encountering the event or task a second time.[545]

---

[541] See Maranville, *supra* note 404, at 63-65 (providing examples from courses in Criminal Law and Civil Procedure and a chart that suggests several types of integrated simulation exercises and add-on simulation-based lab courses); *id.* at 66; Jay M. Feinman, *Simulations: An Introduction,* 45 J. LEGAL EDUC. 469, 470 (1995) (explaining that a continuum of simulations includes doctrinal problems, single-experience exercises, extended exercises, continuing exercises, and simulation courses); McAninch, *supra* note 476 (explaining how experiential education can be employed as an adjunct to traditional methodologies regardless of class size).

[542] We acknowledge that some people define experiential education as involving "real life," not simulated, experience. *See, e.g.,* HESS & FRIEDLAND, *supra* note 304, at 105. We include simulated as well as real life experience. Although law students certainly learn from their experiences while working for legal employers, such learning does not fit within our concept of experiential education because it is not accompanied by academic inquiry.

[543] Two examples of "other professional roles" are serving as mediators or teaching street law.

[544] SULLIVAN ET AL., *supra* note 7, at 178.

[545] Steven Hartwell, *Six Easy Pieces: Teaching Experientially,* 41 SAN DIEGO L. REV.

There are three domains of learning, and students who are being educated experientially are involved in all three:
- the cognitive domain (increasingly complex sorts of understandings and analytical processes),
- the psychomotor or performance domain (complex patterns of physical or motor activity such as lawyering activities), and
- the affective or feeling domain (values, attitudes, and beliefs).[546]

Jay Feinman further described the cognitive, performative, and affective skills that law students need to develop.
- *Cognitive skills* range from simple recall of facts, through the ability to apply prior knowledge to solve new problems, up to the ability to evaluate the use and implications of one's knowledge. In law school, these skills involve the understanding of substantive law, legal process, and related matters such as professional responsibility.
- *Performative skills* in law are increasingly defined by the MacCrate Report's catalog of skills beyond legal analysis and reasoning, including legal research, factual investigation, counseling and the management of legal work.
- *Affective skills* include personal and professional issues: how students feel about their competency as lawyers, how they relate to the client, how they respond to problems of professional responsibility, and how their values inform their role.[547]

Experiential education gives students opportunities to be actively involved in their own education, and it has positive effects on their motivation, attitudes toward the course, willingness to participate in class, ability to ask insightful questions, and acquisition of knowledge and skills.

> When seen as parts of a connected whole, the practical courses in lawyering and clinical-legal education make an essential contribution to responsible professional training. These courses are built around simulations of practice or law clinics involving actual clients. But they can do more than expand the apprentice's repertoire of knowledge and skill. Critically, they are the law school's primary means of teaching students how to connect the abstract thinking formed by legal categories and procedures with fuller human contexts.[548]

Experiential education is a powerful tool for forming professional habits and understandings. We encourage law schools to expand its use.

1011, 1013 (2004).

[546] Kenneth R. Kreiling, *Clinical Education and Lawyer Competency: The Process of Learning to Learn From Experience Through Properly Structured Clinical Supervision,* 40 MD. L. REV. 284, 287 n.10 (1981).

[547] Feinman, *supra* note 541, at 472.

[548] SULLIVAN ET AL., *supra* note 7, at 52-53.

2. **Best Practices for Experiential Courses, Generally.**

a. **Provide students with clear and explicit statements about learning objectives and assessment criteria.**

Principle: **Experiential teachers provide students with clear and explicit statements about the learning objectives of their courses and assessment criteria.**

Comments:

In order to maximize the effectiveness of instruction, both faculty and students must be aware of and share a common set of instructional goals and objectives, which should be explicit, published, and widely disseminated.

To the extent that the teacher has defined the goals of an exercise, it is important to communicate those goals clearly to the students. People generally learn better when they know what they are supposed to be learning. And explicitly specifying the goals helps avoid two common, conflicting reactions. Students are wont to regard a lawyering simulation as something added on the periphery of a traditional course – more work, not central to the experience, not as important as the substantive material that will be on the exam. Conversely, students can view an exercise as the best thing in the course for the wrong reason: that it is the only practical or meaningful part of the course. If the objectives of the exercise are made clear and explicit, either reaction is less likely.[549]

Faculty who teach experiential courses should cover in depth their learning objectives and assessment processes with students at the beginning of their enrollment. These matters are important enough to the success of the course and students' goals to be put in writing.

b. **Focus on educational objectives that can be achieved most effectively and efficiently through experiential education.**

Principle: **The teachers focus on educational objectives that can be achieved most effectively and efficiently through experiential education.**

Comments:

Any subject can be taught using experiential education. The challenge is to determine what lessons can be taught more effectively and efficiently using experiential education than through other methods of instruction and to focus our time and energy on accomplishing those educational objectives.

In the early years of clinical legal education when the survival of clinical education was uncertain, there were many efforts to describe the educational goals of clinical courses and, thereby, justify their existence in law schools.[550] As one

---

[549] *See* Feinman, *supra* note 541, at 471-72.

[550] *See, e.g.,* Carrie Menkel-Meadow, *Two Contradictory Criticisms of Clinical Education: Dilemmas and Directions in Lawyering Education,* 4 ANTIOCH LAW REV. 287 (1986); Jane Aiken, David A. Koplow, Lisa G. Lerman, J.P. Ogilvy & Philip G. Schrag, *The Learning Con-*

might imagine, the proposals were diverse and wide-ranging. One of the more insightful statements about the general goals of clinical education was made by Tony Amsterdam in 1982.[551] Amsterdam presented the following list of the objectives and potential uses of clinical techniques.

- to expose students to the demands, constraints, and methods of thinking in role, and to explore the impact of role on thinking.
- to expose students to the demands, constraints, and methods of analyzing and dealing with unstructured situations, in which the "issues" have not been pre-identified.
- to give students a basis for examining the interaction of legal analysis and human behavior, including interpersonal dynamics and communication.
- to give the students an opportunity to learn how to learn from experience.
- to provide professional skills instruction.
- to provide the basis for insights into the functioning of the legal system and to raise questions about its capacities and limitations.[552]
- in general, to provide students with the opportunity to develop and to guide them in developing – a breadth of perspective, a depth of insight, and a rigorously systematic set of analytic and behavioral techniques, which they can train on the varied problems that confront lawyers and the law.

While one may be struck by how often Amsterdam described these objectives in terms of "exposing" and "providing opportunities" rather than "teaching" or "learning," we can see that he was emphasizing the value of clinical education for helping students:

- adjust to their roles as professionals,
- become better legal problem-solvers,
- develop interpersonal and professional skills, and
- learn how to learn from experience.

We will discuss each of these objectives in order.

---

tract in Legal Education, 44 MD. L. REV. 1047 (1985); Peter Hoffman, *Clinical Course Design and the Supervisory Process,* 2 ARIZ. ST. L. J. 277 (1982); Frank Bloch, *The Andragogical Basis of Clinical Legal Education,* 35 VAND. L. REV. 321 (1982); Kreiling, *supra* note 546; AALS/ABA GUIDELINES FOR CLINICAL LEGAL EDUCATION (1980) [hereinafter, AALS/ABA GUIDELINES]; Gordon Gee & Donald Jackson, *Bridging The Gap: Legal Education and Lawyer Competency,* 4 BYU L. REV. 689 (1977); David Barnhizer, *Clinical Education at the Crossroads: The Need for Direction,* 4 BYU L. REV. 1025 (1977).

[551] Anthony G. Amsterdam, Remarks at Deans' Workshop, ABA Section of Legal Education and Admissions to the Bar, Jan. 23, 1982 (unpublished) (copy on file with Roy Stuckey).

[552] This objective and the next one were not included in Amsterdam's remarks at the Dean's Workshop but were added to the preceding goals in an internal NYU memo dated Mar. 23, 1983, from the Clinical Faculty Group to the Personnel Committee on the Status of Clinical Faculty, "Background Paper on 'Objectives and Methods of Clinical Legal Education, As Relevant to Issues Regarding the Status of Clinical Faculty'" (copy on file with Roy Stuckey).

(1)   Help students adust to their roles as professionals.

Principle: The course helps students adjust to their roles as professionals.

Comments:
        Gary Bellow explained the important role that experiential courses play in helping students learn about and adjust to their future roles as professionals.

>   The central feature of the clinical method is its conscious use, both conceptually and operationally, of the dynamics of role adjustment in social life. . . . As used in this essay, a person's role refers to the set of actions and qualities which are expected in a given social position or status. To perform in a role – that is to "validate one's occupation of the position" – the actor must learn: 1) the duties, rights, obligations, and privileges that are the defining characteristics of the position; 2) the cues, signs, behaviors, and demands which enable the actor to choose the appropriate role manifestation in a particular situation, i.e., "he must locate others and himself in social space;" 3) the aptitudes (cognitive, perceptual, verbal, gestural) needed to perform in the position.[553]

        There is no more effective way to help students understand what it is like to be a lawyer than to have them to perform the tasks that lawyers perform or observe practicing lawyers at work.

(2)   Help students become better legal problem-solvers.

Principle: The course helps students become better legal problem-solvers.

Comments:
        As explained earlier a primary goal of legal education is to help students begin developing expertise in solving legal problems. All forms of experiential education involve problem-based learning, so one of the strengths of experiential education is that it gives students opportunities to practice solving problems and to receive feedback on the quality of their efforts.

(3)   Help students develop interpersonal and professional skills.

Principle: The course helps students develop interpersonal and professional skills.

Comments:
        Experiential education is an effective way to help students develop interpersonal and professional skills. One cannot become skilled simply by reading

---

        [553] Gary Bellow, *On Teaching the Teachers: Some Preliminary Reflections on Clinical Education as Methodology, in* CLINICAL EDUCATION FOR THE LAW STUDENT: LEGAL EDUCATION IN A SERVICE SETTING: WORKING PAPERS PREPARED FOR CLEPR NATIONAL CONFERENCE, BUCK HILL FALLS, PENNSYLVANIA, JUNE 1-9, 1973, at 374, 381 (1973).

about skills or watching others perform lawyering tasks. One must perform the skills repeatedly, preferably receiving expert feedback.

Unfortunately, a common misunderstanding about the educational potential of experiential education in law schools is that clinical courses are primarily vehicles for instruction in the mechanical techniques of lawyering skills. Instruction in interpersonal and professional skills is an important part of clinical education, but skills instruction is seldom, if ever, limited to technique alone. Such matters as the theoretical underpinnings of skills, strategic considerations, preparation for performance, the values and ethical constraints inherent in the performance of the skills, the assumptions of the adversary system underlying the application of the skills, and the efficacy of skills being taught are all part of the educational objectives of "skills instruction" in clinical courses.

Instruction about skills also includes consideration of when and why lawyering skills are employed including the role of personal and professional values. Just teaching technique is not sufficient; "[o]ur additional obligation to law students is to teach the norms and values in support of which those skills will be applied."[554] Among the values that we should include in our instructional design are the lawyer's obligations to truth, honesty, and fair dealing; the responsibility to improve the integrity of the legal system within which the lawyer exercises the skills that are taught; the obligation to promote justice; and the obligation to provide competent representation.[555]

> Within clinical legal education, the principal theoretical objectives are to describe and explain the dynamics of legal practice. Sometimes these theories embrace a critical perspective. They point out the limitations, shortcomings, contingencies, and contradictions inherent in the practice of law and in theories about the practice of law. At other times, their function is principally prescriptive. Their purpose is to highlight conceptually what ought to be considered and weighed before lawyers act or proceed. Prescriptive theories about legal practice provide a perspective on what needs to be done but not a mechanical how-to-do-it approach. The details and choices have to be worked out in the particular context.

> Pedagogically, clinical legal education seeks not just to impart legal skills, but to encourage students to be responsible and thoughtful practitioners. There is considerable emphasis on problem-solving approaches, such as ends-means thinking; on skills training in addition to legal reasoning; on making ethically responsible decisions, particularly when obligations are in conflict; and on being continually self reflective and critically analytical about one's own experiences.[556]

The truth of the matter is that few, if any law schools, have programs or resources to develop the full range of the skills needed for law practice to the degree of proficiency expected of practicing lawyers. This reality makes it all the more

---

[554] Steven Lubet, *What We Should Teach (But Don't) When We Teach Trial Advocacy,* 37 J. LEGAL EDUC. 123, 126 (1987).

[555] *Id.* at 139-41.

[556] Aaronson, *supra* note 176, at 249 (citations omitted).

important to help students learn how to learn from experience.

(4)   Help students learn how to learn from experience.

Principle: The course helps students learn how to learn from experience.

Comments:
Developing lifelong learning skills may be the most important goal of legal education. In his 1982 remarks, Amsterdam stressed that "the most significant contribution of the clinical method to legal education" is giving students an opportunity to learn how to learn from experience.

> The students who spend three years in law school will next spend 30 or 50 years in practice. These 30 or 50 years will be a learning experience whether we like it or not. It can be, as conventional wisdom has it, merely a hit-or-miss learning experience in the school of hard knocks. Or it can be a mediated and systematic learning experience if the law schools undertake as part of their curricula to teach students techniques of learning from experience. Clinical courses can do this – and should focus on doing it – because their very method is to make the student's experience the subject of critical review and reflection.[557]

One of the reasons why helping students develop their ability to learn from experience should be a core goal of clinical courses is that students are unlikely to develop their problem-solving expertise fully before beginning law practice, particularly in systems of legal education such as the United States' where legal education only lasts three years before a person can obtain an unrestricted license to practice law. No matter how long it takes to become a lawyer, however, lawyers continue to develop problem-solving expertise throughout their careers. Lifelong learning skills are, therefore, important for all lawyers to acquire.

Ken Kreiling pointed out that an effective way to learn from experience is to use "theories of practice" to develop and articulate "espoused theories of action."[558] "Theories of practice" provide a basis upon which students can evaluate behaviors they observe and their own performances. These theories may involve information about how lawyers should conduct themselves, how certain aspects of the judicial system should work, or whatever else is relevant to understanding the legal profession and the roles of lawyers.

"Theories of action" explain how a student hopes to perform in a lawyering situation, for example, to build a close and trusting relationship in an initial client interview, to use only leading questions during a cross examination, or to be flexible about means and rigid about goals in negotiation. Following a performance, the espoused theory of action can be compared to the behavior actually exhibited, the "theory in use."[559] If the comparison discloses that the student was ineffective in applying the espoused theory of action, the student and the teacher can analyze what caused the ineffectiveness – the quality of the espoused theory; the student's skills,

---

[557] Amsterdam, *supra* note 551.
[558] Kreiling, *supra* note 546, at 286.
[559] *Id.* at 291-97.

values, or knowledge; or some other factor.

It is therefore important for clinical teachers to:

> • teach students theories of practice and provide them with information, models, and frameworks that will enable them to develop espoused theories of action against which their performances can be compared. "Without theory and the ability to theorize, one muddles through, is often ineffective, and cannot generalize from experience."[560]
> • help students learn how to analyze their performances and generalize from those experiences.

Experiential education is the best tool for helping students develop self-directed learning skills, if it is done properly.

We should also keep in mind that a significant part of student learning in experiential courses depends on the individual experiences of each student. Each student's experience is unique, and each student's perceptions of his or her experiences is unique. Thus, it is impossible to determine in advance everything that a student will have an opportunity to learn in a clinical course, to control its delivery, or to evaluate how well students understand what they have learned. We can, however, assist individualized student learning by seizing "teaching opportunities" when they arise or by working with students to help them select and achieve student-specific learning objectives.[561]

We can also assist students' self-learning by creating structures and protocols that will help them reflect on and understand better what they are learning from experience, whether or not it is something we intend for them to learn. For example, teachers can give students materials on the value of reflective thinking, require students to write reflective journals, and have students perform self-evaluations at one or more points during the semester and at the end of the term.

c.   Meet the needs and interests of students.

Principle: The program of instruction includes enough experiential education courses to meet the needs and interests of its students.

Comments:

If experiential education courses are essential for preparing students for practice, law schools cannot meet their obligation to prepare students for practice unless they offer enough experiential education courses to meet the needs of their students. The types and number of experiential education courses that a school should offer will vary from school to school depending on the mission of the law school, the law practice settings in which the school's students are likely to find their first professional jobs, and post graduation bridge-the-gap or other educational requirements and opportunities.

---

[560] *Id.* at 306 n.73.

[561] *See, e.g.,* Aiken et al., *supra* note 550, at 1064 n.66 (describing learning contracts in which students select three learning objectives from a list of thirty seven potential learning objectives to pursue during a client representation course).

d.   Grant appropriate credit.

Principle: The school grants appropriate credit to students enrolled in experiential education courses.

Comments:

Experiential education courses should be structured so that students spend approximately the same amount of time per credit hour as they spend in non-experiential courses.[562] Credit should be awarded commensurate to the credit given in the rest of the curriculum for comparable expenditures of student time. A typical calculation is 1 credit for every 3.5 hours a week that students are expected to spend, on average.

Credit should be given for all the time that the course requires of students. For example, in-house clinical and externship students expend time and effort completing the tasks necessary to represent clients or perform other assigned tasks, attending supervision sessions with their instructors, preparing for and attending classroom components, adhering to case management protocols, and reflecting on their experiences. Workloads, frequency of classes, requirements for supervision sessions, and expectations of time on task should all be part of the calculus of determining appropriate credit for in-house clinics and externships.

e.   Record student performances.

Principle: Student performances are recorded and used for providing feedback or self evaluation.

Comments:

Students' performances in the roles of lawyers should be digitally recorded or videotaped as often as possible. Digitally recorded performances can be stored indefinitely at no cost. This facilitates student and faculty review and enables students to include performances in their portfolios.

Even when a performance is observed by a member of the faculty or field supervisor, the quality of the learning experience is enhanced if the teachers use recordings to point out specific behaviors to reinforce or to suggest changes.[563] The recordings can be used by the students for self-evaluation and by the faculty for giving further out-of-class critique and feedback to students. Inexpensive web cameras can be used to record performances directly into students' laptop computers.

f.   Train those who give feedback to employ best practices.

Principle: Individuals who give feedback are trained to do so and employ best practices for providing feedback.

---

[562] *See Report of the Committee on the Future of the In-House Clinic*, 42 J. LEGAL EDUC. 508, 561 (1992) [hereinafter *Future of the In-House Clinic*], and AALS/ABA GUIDELINES, *supra* note 550, at 27.

[563] "The Committee concluded that the capacity to evaluate student performances and examine the dynamics of the lawyering process is greatly enhanced by recording and replaying simulations." AALS/ABA GUIDELINES, *supra* note 550, at 75.

Comments:

The guidance and feedback that students receive in experiential education courses influences the quality of the experience more than any other component. A positive relationship between student and supervisor is of paramount importance. Teachers of simulation courses must be knowledgeable about lawyering theories and actual practices. Supervising attorneys in in-house clinics and externships must be knowledgeable about law practice and competent practitioners. They all must be effective teachers to provide positive learning experiences for their students.

Faculty members and field supervisors must decide what information to provide and under what circumstances. In making these decisions, they need to evaluate not only the student's learning experience, and possibly a client's needs, but also how her decision may affect the relationship with the student. If a student does not get the information she seeks, she may feel the supervisor is playing a game of "hide the ball" that is unnecessary. An effective supervisor will explain the reasons behind her teaching methods so that the student will understand and may be more accepting.[564]

Teachers should give students candid constructive views of their development. Students should be encouraged to seek such evaluations. Clinical faculty who are in charge of externship courses should teach externship supervisors how to provide such feedback, take steps to assure that the process takes place, and prepare students to use this information effectively.

Feedback about their performances should help students understand what conduct is inappropriate (and requires avoidance) and what conduct is acceptable (and deserves repeating). It may be more important to praise the positive aspects of students' performances than to point out the negative aspects. "[L]earning exercises are almost meaningless unless the learner is evaluated and good habits rewarded."[565] "There is 'conclusive evidence that nonreward (when reward is expected) has an adverse effect much like punishment.' This theory of 'frustrated nonreward' places a heavy burden on the clinical teacher to give effective feedback and to reinforce good performance."[566]

The way a person approaches feedback has a substantial impact on the quality of the learning experience for the student. The success of the feedback process depends on both the quality of the feedback and the receptiveness of the student. To be useful to the student, feedback should be relevant and focused on learning dilemmas. Feedback must also be acceptable to the student, who may become defensive and reject criticism. By providing feedback in a way that is constructive, but also readily acceptable to the student, the person providing feedback helps facilitate growth rather than frustration, self-criticism, or complete disconnect on the part of the student.

---

[564] *See, e.g.,* Ann Shalleck, *Clinical Contexts: Theory and Practice in Law and Supervision,* 21 N.Y.U. REV. L. & SOC. CHANGE 109, 146-48 (1993-1994); David F. Chavkin, *Am I My Client's Lawyer?: Role Definition and the Clinical Supervisor,* 51 S.M.U. L. REV. 1507, 1539 (1998).

[565] Joseph D. Harbaugh, *Simulation and Gaming: A Teaching/Learning Strategy for Clinical Legal Education, in* AALS/ABA GUIDELINES, *supra* note 550, at 208.

[566] *Id.* at 210 (quoting E. HILGARD & G. BOWER, THEORIES OF LEARNING (4th ed. 1975) (citing the studies of Amsel and Wagner)).

The ideal is for all student activities to be observed by faculty or field supervisors who have been trained to provide feedback and critique. However, students can also benefit by receiving feedback from properly trained peers. In some instances, students' self-critiques may provide adequate feedback if they are given information and guidance for self-critiquing.

These are some guidelines for performing effective critiques:
- *Be prepared to critique.* Take [time] to organize your critique before delivering it.
- *Be selective.* Select one or two points on which to critique and fully develop these points.
- *Start with a positive comment.* People tend to be more open to constructive criticism if they hear it after being reassured of their "worth." In every performance, there is something that can be praised.
- *Be specific.* Relate your critique to specific events in the student's performance . . . . To do this well, you need to take accurate, detailed notes during the [performance].
- *Be constructive.* If you offer negative feedback, don't just criticize but suggest alternatives of what the person could have done differently. Focus your critique on an area you think the student will be able to improve.
- *Be succinct.* Get to the point of your critique. Don't ramble on.
- *Be honest.* Your job is not to be popular, but to help the student improve. Tell it like it is, but be supportive. Note what was done well, but only if it was done well.
- *Take responsibility for your critique.* Present the critique in the first person ("I think..."; "In my experience..."; "I think the better practice is..."). Avoid presenting points of critique as universal principles unless, of course, they are (i.e., "Never address the court as "Hey, dude!"").
- *Critique the performance, not the person.* Do not be judgmental or sarcastic. Tell the person what you saw or heard and the effect it had on you. Don't just label it as "good" or "bad."
- *Make the student a partner in the critique.* Ask questions: "What were you trying to achieve?"; "What do you think went wrong?"; "What alternative approaches might you have tried?"
- *Teach by example.* A critique is a performance unto itself. People learn as much or more from how we say things as from what we say. Incorporate good communication skills into your critique. Use eye contact. Listen intently. Use gestures. Put emphasis in your voice. Be adaptable. Speak in plain English.[567]

g.   Train students to receive feedback.

Principle: Students are trained to maximize the learning potential from feedback.

Comments:
Feedback to students is more effective if the students are receptive to

---

[567] Ralph M. Cagle, *Guide for Evaluators, in* Hess & Friedland, *supra* note 304, at 311-12 (modified here to fit all forms of experiential education, not just simulations).

feedback and understand how to maximize its value to them. Some guidelines for students are:

> To maximize the learning opportunities . . . you need your own "critique skills," – that is, the techniques of how best to receive and implement critique. The following guidelines should be helpful to you:
>
> • *Listen to the critique with care and an open mind.* Try not to take the critique as personal criticism. Don't get defensive or immediately argue with or reject the critique.
>
> • *Be sure you are clear about what has been said.* If you are not clear or don't understand, ask.
>
> • *Focus on specifics.* Try to learn as specifically as possible things you might do to improve your performance in the future.
>
> • *Keep your perspective.* See the critique as offering you new choices, rather than dictating the one right way to do something.
>
> • *Clarify.* If you disagree with the critique, respectfully – but directly – raise the issue and ask for comment (but only after the instructors have completed their critique).
>
> • *Ask questions.* If you want feedback on a specific matter and didn't receive it, ask (time permitting).
>
> • *Don't overly rely on anyone person's critique.* Compare it, to the extent possible, with others' . . . . Ask others who may know you and whom you trust about the substance of the critique.
>
> • *Pay careful attention to the critique of other [students].* This is an opportunity to learn additional aspects of the [lessons] involved. It also is a more objective perspective from which to observe the dynamics of the critique method.
>
> • *Look for ways to use the information.* At the end of the critique session, ask yourself: "What do I know now (or know better than before)?" Write it down. That is the standard of success of a . . . critique . . . .
>
> • *Say "thank you."*
>
> • *Look for opportunities to implement what you learned from the critique.*
>
> • *Save your evaluation forms (self and faculty) or any notes of what you learned.* Review them the next time you are about to perform the activity that was the subject of the critique. Learning [about law practice] is an incremental process.[568]

h. Help students identify and plan how to achieve individually important learning goals.

Principle: **Each student has opportunities to achieve individually important learning goals.**

Comments:

Each student has a unique set of strengths and weaknesses, and experiential courses not only provide instruction that is tailored to the student's personal needs, they also give the student opportunities to pursue individually important learning goals.

---

[568] *Id.* at 312-13.

In some in-house clinics and externship courses, students and teachers enter into "learning contracts" that describe individualized learning objectives for the student and how they are to be achieved. Regardless of whether a learning contract is used, students in such courses should be encouraged to articulate their own goals so the instructor can advance these goals to the extent possible in the course.[569] Simulation-based courses also allow students to pursue learning goals in addition to those selected by the instructor.

i.   Give students repeated opportunities to perform tasks, if achieving proficiency is an objective.

Principle: If proficiency in the performance of specific lawyering tasks is an educational objective, students have repeated opportunities to perform the tasks to be learned or improved upon until they achieve the desired level of proficiency.

Comments:

"Virtually all learning theorists agree that most learning is enhanced by repetition."[570] This is certainly the case with respect to the development of professional skills. Repetition is not necessary, however, if the goal of a course or an exercise is to enhance students' knowledge and understanding of law, law practice, or professional skills rather than to develop proficiency.

It is not necessary to develop skills proficiency in a single course. Law schools already spread development of analytical, research, and writing skills through all three years of the curriculum. The development of proficiency in other skills should likewise occur in multiple courses throughout all three years of law school.

A shortcoming of skills instruction in law schools in the United States, including the development of analytical, research, and writing skills, is that we have not established benchmarks that describe desired levels of proficiency at various stages of a student's law school career or upon graduation. Nor have we required students to demonstrate a desired level of proficiency before they advance to the next level of instruction. This is an issue that warrants our attention.

j.   Enhance the effectiveness of faculty in experiential courses.

Principle: The school uses qualified faculty, provides professional development opportunities, and assigns reasonable workloads in its experiential education courses.

Comments:

The effectiveness of full-time and part-time faculty in experiential courses is enhanced by hiring qualified faculty, providing professional development opportunities, and assigning reasonable workloads.

Effective experiential teachers must have the skills, knowledge, and

---

[569] *See Future of the In-House Clinic, supra* note 562, at 562.

[570] Don Peters, *Mapping, Modeling, and Critiquing: Facilitating Learning Negotiation, Mediation, Interviewing, and Counseling,* 48 Fla. L. Rev. 875, 885 (1996).

commitment to teach students using experiential education and other techniques. In-house clinical teachers and externship supervisors must have adequate and appropriate experience, skills, knowledge, and values to represent clients and perform any other professional roles required by the job.

Encouraging and providing resources for regular attendance and participation in professional meetings promotes the professional development of experiential teachers. Participation in internal and external teacher training programs is beneficial, especially for new teachers.[571] Developing supervision skills and classroom teaching skills are both important. Simulation-based courses, in-house clinics, and most externships include classroom components.

The opportunity to engage in scholarship is one of the main attractions of an academic career for many experiential teachers. Publication is essential for those on a tenure track or who have similar publication expectations from their institutions. Law school support for publication should include reduced course loads, research assistance, funds for travel, staff support, and computer equipment. An in-house clinician may need relief from responsibility for clinical supervision in order to pursue writing projects. When that is required, the law school should provide for clinical coverage in the instructor's absence through a visitor or other workable arrangement that will not harm clients, students, or the clinic's relationships with the community.[572]

The demands of experiential teaching are different from non-experiential teaching, and schools should take care to ensure that student-faculty ratios, caseloads in in-house clinics, and the overall obligations of experiential teachers are conducive to achieving the educational and programmatic goals of their courses. One must balance the need to give students meaningful experiences against the risk of overloading students or teachers and interfering with their abilities to achieve the educational goals of their courses.[573]

B.   Simulation-Based Courses.[574]

1.   Introduction to Simulation-Based Courses.

Simulation-based courses are courses in which a significant part of the learning relies on students assuming the roles of lawyers and performing law-related tasks in hypothetical situations under supervision and with opportunities for feedback and reflection.

Simulations, role plays, and games have an important place in legal pedagogy.[575] Some courses commonly denominated as skills courses are taught

---

[571] *See* Justine A. Dunlap & Peter A. Joy, *Reflection-In-Action: Designing New Clinical Teacher Training by Using Lessons Learned From New Clinicians,* 11 CLINICAL L. REV. 49 (2004).

[572] *See Future of the In-House Clinic, supra* note 562, at 557.

[573] *See* Guidelines VII (E) & (F), AALS/ABA GUIDELINES, *supra* note 550, at 24-25. Caseload is also identified as an important consideration at 552.

[574] This section was originally prepared by J.P. (Sandy) Ogilvy, Catholic. Roy Stuckey is primarily responsible for the subsection on setting clear, explicit learning objectives.

[575] Steven I. Friedland, *How We Teach: A Survey of Teaching Techniques in American Law Schools,* 20 SEATTLE L. REV. 1, 30-31 (1996); MICHAEL MELTSNER & PHILIP G. SCHRAG, TOWARD

principally through simulated lawyering tasks,[576] for example, Interviewing, Counseling, Negotiating, Fact Investigation, Law Office Management, Trial Practice,[577] and Appellate Practice, as well as specialized courses denoted as practicums such as Education Law Practice. Most instructors of these courses utilize a series of discrete, role playing exercises that mimic some aspect of law practice. Other courses use a single, comprehensive simulated scenario that is developed throughout the course. In this category, for example, are courses where students represent a simulated client from an initial interview through post-trial motions over the course of a semester or full academic year.

In client-based clinics and some traditional classroom courses, simulations and role plays are used as an adjunct or supplemental pedagogy to the principal pedagogical methodology.[578] For instance, clinical pedagogy principally involves close supervision of student representation of clients by a faculty attorney. However, clinic students often will simulate lawyering tasks in a classroom setting before attempting the same tasks with clients or on their behalf.

This section is concerned principally with best practices for the design and implementation of simulation-based courses. Many of the principles, however, are applicable in other courses in which simulated lawyering exercises or role plays are used as a supplemental pedagogy.

2.   Best Practices for Simulation-Based Courses.
Remember that the best practices described below are in addition to the best practices for experiential courses discussed earlier.

> **a. Use simulation-based courses to achieve educational goals more effectively and efficiently than other methods of instruction could achieve.**

Principle: **The school uses simulation-based courses to achieve clearly articulated educational goals more effectively and efficiently than other methods of instruction could achieve.**

SIMULATION IN LEGAL EDUCATION: AN EXPERIMENTAL COURSE IN PRETRIAL LITIGATION 10-20 (1975); HESS & FRIEDLAND, *supra* note 308, at 193-22 (simulations & role plays). Simulation is used extensively in other disciplines, notably medicine. *See* J. Lindsey Lane, Stuart Slavin & Amitai Ziv, *Simulation in Medical Education: A Review,* 32 SIMULATION & GAMING 297 (2001); CLARK C. ABT, SERIOUS GAMES 13 (1970) ("Games are effective teaching and training devices for students . . . because they are highly motivating, and because they communicate very efficiently the concepts and facts of many subjects. They create dramatic representations of the real problem being studied. The players assume realistic roles, face problems, formulate strategies, make decisions and get fast feedback on the consequences of their actions. Also, with games, one can evaluate the students' performances without risking the costs of having errors made in "real-world" tryouts . . . ").

[576] Friedland, *supra* note 575, at 30.

[577] Lubet, *supra* note 554, at 125.

[578] *See* Paul Bateman, *Toward Diversity in Teaching Methods in Law Schools: Five Suggestions From the Back Row,* 17 QUINNIPIAC L. REV. 397, 420 (1997) ("[S]ound educational theory supports the use of games at least as a supplement to a law school class. Perhaps most surprising, educational theory actually suggests that games as a supplement to the traditional class setting are particularly effective when that traditional setting employs the Socratic method as its main teaching method").

Comments:

There is general agreement that simulation-based courses can be an important site for developing the professional skills and understandings essential for practice, including self-directed learning skills. They "can also provide the setting for teaching the ethical demands of practice,"[579] when they require students to resolve ethical as well as technical problems and work through professionalism issues in contexts that replicate actual practice.

> Decades of pedagogical experimentation in clinical-legal teaching, the example of other professional schools, and contemporary learning theory all point toward the value of clinical education as a site for developing not only intellectual understanding and complex skills of practice, but also the dispositions crucial for legal professionalism. In their modeling of and coaching for high levels of professionalism, clinics and some simulations exemplify the integration of ethical engagement along with knowledge and skill.[580]

Simulation-based courses can also help students improve their practical reasoning and judgment.

> Other professional fields provide some well-tested instances of pedagogies that teach complex practical reasoning and judgment, blending the cognitive and practical apprenticeships. For example, medical schools use various simulation devices, even professional actors, as "simulated patients," in order to train clinical skills. In such simulations, performance can be rehearsed, criticized, and improved "off-line." This removal from the exigencies of actual practice permits the instructors to focus on particular aspects of the complex ensemble of skills they are trying to teach. The elements and sequence of skills can then be modeled and rehearsed in safety – without real-world consequences or immediate responsibility for the welfare of others. This kind of teaching makes it more likely that students will reach a basic level of competent practice from which expertise can be subsequently developed.[581]

Once an institution decides which skills and understandings it wants to achieve with simulation courses, it should then decide where in the program of instruction students will be introduced to each subject of study and how instruction should progress until students achieve the desired level of proficiency. In the ideal world the targeted level of proficiency would be the level of proficiency that a new lawyer needs to provide competent legal services.

Professional skills instruction in most United States law schools does not produce sufficiently proficient graduates. The fact of the matter is that very few, if any, simulation courses develop proficiency in any professional skill to the level that a new lawyer needs. Some skills instruction is better than none at all, but law students will not develop adequate entry level lawyering skills as long as professional skills instruction for most law students is relegated to one course in the second or third year of law school.

---

[579] SULLIVAN ET AL., *supra* note 7, at 196.

[580] *Id.* at 141.

[581] *Id.* at 112-13.

Consider, for example, the current approach to teaching professional skills in simulation courses, using as an example the approach that many teachers use to teach students how to conduct an initial client interview. The teacher begins by giving students information about the goals of client interviewing and techniques for conducting one and then provides demonstrations of interviewing techniques to help illustrate key points. The teacher tries to persuade students to employ client friendly philosophies of lawyering. Students are given one or more opportunities to practice applying what the teacher tried to teach, and receive feedback about how well they performed. Sometimes teachers grade the students' performances. What teachers usually do not do is to require them to continue practicing with feedback until they demonstrate an acceptable level of proficiency. In many lawerying skills courses, for example, students may conduct only one simulated client interview before moving on to another skill where they once again may have only one opportunity to perform the skill and receive feedback. Students in such courses do not develop proficiency.

This criticism is not to demean the value of what simulation-based courses are accomplishing. The current approach gives students a better understanding of the complexities of interviewing, information about how to conduct interviews, and some insights into their level of competence. As Tony Amsterdam explained,

> It is not necessary or possible for the law school to turn out accomplished trial lawyers, counselors, negotiators, etc. But it is possible and desirable to get the students past the kind of first-level errors that are so disruptive of performance and so unnerving to the performer that they cannot even serve as a valuable learning experience in the school of hard knocks. By giving students the opportunity to commit these first-level errors in law school, and by giving them the opportunity and assistance which only an educational institution can provide to reflect upon the errors and develop some initial insight into their causes and probable cures, clinical courses can aim to graduate lawyers capable of making educationally productive second-level errors and learning from them in practice.[582]

Jay Feinman observed that "[i]n a large basic course, a reasonable performance objective is to make students aware of the importance of skills in the lawyering process and of the possibility of treating skills learning as a subject requiring the same kind of conceptual generalization that helps one understand other subjects in law school. With this introduction, students can proceed to advanced courses that are more appropriately skills-focused."[583]

Introductory courses are important for developing important skills and understandings, but they are only the first step toward professional competence.

> In learning lawyering skills, rules and procedures are essential scaffolds that enable beginners to gain a grasp on how to function in a variety of practice situations. Law students at this

---

[582] Amsterdam made his remarks during a Dean's Workshop conducted by the ABA Section of Legal Education and Admissions to the Bar on Jan. 23, 1982. Amsterdam, *supra* note 555. Although we agree with the sentiment that some instruction is better than none, we believe (and we think Amsterdam likely agrees with us) that law schools can accomplish more ambitious skills development goals than were thought possible in 1982.

[583] Feinman, *supra* note 541, at 473.

stage are what the Dreyfuses call the novice. The prime learning task of the novice in the law is to achieve a basic acquaintance with the common techniques of the lawyer's craft. The novice should not be asked to exercise judgment or interpret a situation as a whole. Instead, the novice must learn to recognize certain well-defined elements of the situation and apply precise and formal rules to these elements, regardless of what else is happening. Following the rules allows for a gradual accumulation of experience. But in order to progress, the student has to attend to the features of the context, events that occur even outside the rules.

With proper coaching and sufficient experience, the novice can progress toward competence.[584]

Unfortunately, most law schools do not yet provide all students with an introduction to professional skills, much less opportunities to develop proficiency. Our current failure to help students develop skills proficiency during law school is a shortcoming to keep in mind. It also highlights the need for us to be careful in articulating the educational objectives of simulation courses, both to keep from misleading students and ourselves about what we can accomplish and also to make us more thoughtful about which skills we choose to teach and to what level of proficiency. If we assert that "students who complete this course will be able to conduct an initial client interview at an appropriate level of competence for a new lawyer," then we would have an obligation to work with each student until that level of proficiency is achieved. On the other hand, if our goal is that "students who complete this course will be able to describe the goals and components of an effective client interview," our educational obligations would be quite different, as would our assessment efforts.

Simulation courses are well-suited for achieving additional educational goals beyond providing an introduction to professional skills, but one must make a decision to pursue them and then design the course accordingly. Without suggesting that they are the only or even the most appropriate goals, many simulation courses can achieve the following objectives that were identified as desirable goals in Chapter Two, Section F:
- to begin developing a student's "capacity to recognize personal and professional strengths and weaknesses, to identify the limits of personal knowledge and skill and to develop strategies that will enhance professional performance."
- to develop a student's "ability to recognize and resolve ethical dilemmas" and "employ risk management skills."
- to give students "a practical understanding of and commitment to the values, behaviors, attitudes, and ethical requirements of a lawyer (professionalism)," at least partially. For example, one cannot teach negotiation without discussing the conventions about lying during negotiation and their potential implications, and students participating in simulated negotiations must decide whether to misrepresent relevant facts or otherwise engage in deceitful conduct.

In order to achieve these or any other educational goals, however, it is important that we provide students with relevant instructional materials and lessons

---

[584] Sullivan et al., *supra* note 7, at 137.

to enable them develop "espoused theories of action" and deliberately design our simulations and feedback mechanisms to help achieve the desired educational goals.

We also need to improve our methods for determining whether simulation courses are achieving their goals. A serious question is whether we are approaching evaluation correctly in simulation courses. Typically, a teacher will observe a student's performance, provide feedback, and assign a grade (or determine whether to pass or fail the student). It may not be fair, or educationally effective, to grade students on performances without first giving them opportunities to practice and receive feedback before being graded. Perhaps in courses that can only provide limited opportunities to perform, we should use those practice opportunities to help students better understand the information being delivered in the course but not assign grades to their performances. We should also consider how accurately we can evaluate student performances without first establishing performance benchmarks. It may be a fairer and more accurate measure of student learning to test students' understanding of the materials and lessons, that is, to test their knowledge and understanding of lawyering rather than their skills. Issues related to assessing student learning are discussed more fully in Chapter Seven.

> **b.   Ensure that each simulation is appropriate for the participants and its purposes and instructions are clear.**

Principle: The simulations are appropriate for the participants and their purposes and instructions are clear.

Comments:
The appropriateness of an exercise for the intended participants should be measured by several criteria, including the likelihood that the exercise will achieve one or more of the instructor's course goals in a cost effective manner and serve the learning needs of the intended participants.

> [A]t the outset of simulation building, the teacher must decide what students do not know (e.g., "law students are unaware of the dynamics of multiple-party negotiations;" "telephone interviewing skills are underdeveloped in students;" "students understand the law surrounding motion practice, but are unaware of the lawyering tactics involved"). This is necessary in order to isolate the learning problem to be addressed by the simulation. Other considerations include whether the environment is right for gaming? (time, space, furnishings, tolerance); whether the learners are open to gaming? (fear of looking foolish, distrust, flexibility); and whether the content lends itself to gaming? (some content is inherently too serious).[585]

"[T]he teacher introducing the simulation should initially choose a task that correlates well with students' prior experiences (e.g., virtually all students have successfully interviewed in other contexts) and explicitly call attention to the correlation."[586] The time available for the exercise and the size of the participant

---

[585] Harbaugh, *supra* note 565, at 211-12.
[586] *Id.* at 204.

group also must be considered.[587]

Student learning is enhanced when students understand why they are performing an activity and the rules and procedures are clear. "The clinical teacher who creates a simulation must establish the rules and communicate them in advance to the student participants."[588] "An important role of the instructor . . . is to ensure that students have actual notice of what is entailed . . . the instructor should seize every available opportunity to inform potential students that the simulation is difficult and time-consuming, that it may be stressful, and that it involves teaching methods and subject matter which are radically different from those found in other courses . . . . The opening class should include an overview of the simulation and some explanation of the instructor's goals and methods . . . ."[589]

Of course, this principle does not apply if the educational objectives are served better by not informing students of the goals, rules, or procedures in advance, as when it is designed explicitly to be performed prior to instruction to provide context for instruction subsequent to the exercise.[590] Even here the students will need information about the rules and procedures for the exercise. Typically, this will include assigned readings, classroom discussion, live or recorded demonstrations of similar performances, and perhaps in-class opportunities to practice some or all of the skills to be developed.[591]

c. Base simulations on articulated theories of practice.

Principle: **Simulations are based on articulated theories of practice.**

Comments:
"[I]n order to create a teaching simulation in law, the legal educator must build a *dynamic model* of a portion of the *legal process* by *abstracting, simplifying,* and *substituting* parts of the *actual legal system* so that the model presents the underlying *theories* to the learner in a clearer fashion than would another teaching model."[592]

> The theories of lawyer advocacy are at best tentative and underlying data . . . virtually nonexistent . . . [but] the weakness of the theory and the absence of the data . . . should not preclude clinical legal educators from constructing simulations that test . . . theories of advocacy. Such exercises will aid students in developing litigation

---

[587] *See* Donald B. King, *Simulated Game Playing in Law School: An Experiment,* 26 J. Legal Educ. 580, 581 (1974) (noting that more complex games take longer to play and that large groups are not workable for some complex simulations).

[588] Harbaugh, *supra* note 565, at 213.

[589] Meltsner & Schrag, *supra* note 575, at 64-65.

[590] For example, a teacher may have students participate in a simple negotiation exercise with a wide settlement range, such as Sally Swansong and the Lyric Theater, before providing any instruction about negotiation. Most students accept the first offer put on the table. The teacher would not want to explain before the exercise that the goals of the exercise are to help students understand the difference between making a deal and negotiating a deal and to begin considering the lawyer's obligation to seek the best possible result for the lawyer's client and how a client's view of the best result may differ from the lawyer's.

[591] Peters, *supra* note 570, at 904 (recommending using video vignettes as demonstrations of skills to be learned preceding student performances).

[592] Harbaugh, *supra* note 565, at 195-96.

skills and provide a laboratory for clinical teachers to examine the theory. . . . In designing the problem the teacher *must* have a theory or a set of theories about the real world capable of being isolated, manipulated, and examined in the simplified environment of the simulation. Without an articulated theory about the real legal world, the simulation model cannot guarantee that either the clinical teacher will teach or the student will learn anything about lawyering.[593]

"The clinical teacher must take the time to sort out the theories he or she has about the lawyering process in order to build the simulated circumstances that will allow the theories to be tested."[594]

d.   Balance detail, complexity, and usefulness.

Principle: Each simulation appropriately balances detail (faithfulness to reality), complexity, and usefulness.

Comments:

In designing simulation exercises, the instructor must balance the desire and need for congruity between the exercise and the referent system (some aspect of the legal system) and the usefulness of the exercise.

Fidelity of the simulation to the real world analog is a critical aspect of design, because it fosters transference of learning from the exercise to the real world and motivates students to engage in the exercise and to suspend disbelief. Yet too much detail can increase the complexity of the exercise. If the exercise is too complex, there may be insufficient time available for it, the students may become focused on trying to learn the rules and procedures, and the exercise founders because students are too discouraged to participate fully in the exercise.[595]

The degree of uncertainty in a problem is usually a major source of challenge and interest for students. First, there is uncertainty about the facts themselves, particularly in a simulation in which students must do some fact investigation (as through interviewing). Second, there is the uncertainty about which doctrines apply to a problem, or which doctrines should apply. A business dispute can be viewed as the basis for either an antitrust claim or an unfair competition action; in a transactional setting, students can choose partnership, corporation, limited liability company, or S corporation as the form of business organization. Third, the law and facts can give rise to uncertainty about how to apply a doctrine once it is identified;

---

[593] *Id.* at 197.

[594] *Id.* at 212.

[595] *See* Maranville, *supra* note 404, at 68 ("Simulation exercises . . . can be designed to achieve differing levels of detail. Typically there is a tradeoff between detail and manageability, in the form of narrowing the issues and the complexity of the simulation. Detail can play an important role in creating a sense of reality that will engage the students and provide a useful level of lawyering-task context."); MELTSNER & SCHRAG, *supra* note 575, at 67-68 (describing the choice between complexity and simplicity the authors made in light of their teaching goals and time frame for the simulation they designed to teach pretrial litigation); JOHN R. RASER, SIMULATION AND SOCIETY: AN EXPLORATION OF SCIENTIFIC GAMING 12 (1969) ("It is not possible, however, to judge the merits of a simulation on the basis of its simplicity or complexity except in terms of its purpose").

this is a richer version of the typical classroom situation in which students argue different sides of a question. The difference here is that they must make a judgment about the relative merits and take action based on their judgment. All three types of uncertainty are beneficial, at least in moderate amounts. Some uncertainty teaches important lessons about doctrine, lawyering, and legal process, and it forces students to exercise judgment – usually a primary objective of the simulation. But students must have a reasonable basis for exercising judgment. When facts become so uncertain that students have no rationale for choosing among them or using them as a basis for applying the law, frustration and paralysis will inhibit learning.[596]

Ideally, students should participate in increasingly complex simulations throughout their law school careers as their knowledge, self-efficacy, and problem-solving skills progress.

e. Debrief simulations with all students in the course.

Principle: **Simulations are debriefed and evaluated with all students in the course.**

Comments:
It is valuable for students and faculty to debrief each simulation. The goals of debriefing are different from providing feedback to individual students on their performances. The goals of debriefing are to explore issues that were encountered by multiple members of the group, consider how they should have been resolved, and evaluate the effectiveness of the exercise.

"[D]ebriefing is perhaps the most important part of a simulation/game. . . ."[597] "An important element of any simulation is an opportunity for students to reflect on the cognitive, performative, and affective elements of their experience" through class discussion, journals, and response to questions.[598]

> When attempting to teach certain skills by means of gaming simulation, a reflection phase is necessary to evaluate the experiences gathered during the game session. During this process, the experiences of the participants are consolidated by means of reflection, evaluation, and open feedback, which are key social skills in carrying out cooperative actions. The reflection phase allows participants to apply the knowledge acquired during the gaming simulation to the real world . . . . Debriefing offers . . . an opportunity wherein participants can compare their view of reality with the simulated reality, find differences and commonalities, and achieve a transfer of the acquired knowledge for reality.[599]

---

[596] Feinman, *supra* note 541, at 473-74.

[597] David Crookall, *Debriefing*, 23 SIMULATION & GAMING 141 (1992).

[598] Feinman, *supra* note 541, at 477-78.

[599] Willy C. Kriz, *Creating Effective Learning Environments and Learning Organizations Through Gaming Simulation Design*, 34 SIMULATION & GAMING 495, 497 (2003). *See also* Vincent A. M. Peters & Geert A. N. Vissers, *A Simple Classification Model for Debriefing Simulation Games*, 35 SIMULATION & GAMING 70, 71-74 (2004) (discussing the origins of debriefing and presenting a model for debriefing); Charles F. Petranek, *Written Debriefing: The Next Vital Step in Learning With Simulations*, 31 SIMULATION & GAMING 108 (2000) (arguing for the use of private, written debriefing in addition to oral, public debriefing of exercises).

"Following the use of a simulation, the teacher should reflect on the operation, seek out the evaluations of those who participated in the game and use that information to modify the problem for future use."[600]

Students should also be given an opportunity to evaluate each exercise.[601]

f.   Provide adequate facilities, equipment, and staffing.

Principle: The school has sufficient facilities, equipment, and staffing to achieve the educational goals of its simulation-based courses.

Comments:
        Ideally, the settings in which simulated lawyering performances occur should resemble the real world settings where such activities take place, most commonly law offices and courtrooms. If student performances are recorded, adequate provision for playback and viewing of the recordings is important. Students should be afforded the opportunity to review their performances privately or with other students. In addition, facilities should be available to enable review by the student and faculty member as well as the entire class, when appropriate. "The enactment of simulations and the use of video equipment requires appropriate space to conduct the simulations, as well as classrooms and offices to view the tapes."[602] The availability of inexpensive web cameras that record performances onto students' laptops reduces the need for schools to provide extensive equipment or facilities.

        Support staff should handle administrative tasks such as scheduling the recording facilities for out-of-class simulations, preparing and distributing simulation packets, engaging and scheduling actors (if used), providing videotapes, recordable DVDs, or web cameras, maintaining the equipment and space, and either instructing students in the operation of the recording equipment or operating it for them.[603]

C.   In-House Clinical Courses.[604]

1.   Introduction to In-House Clinical Courses.

        In-house clinics are courses in which a significant part of the learning relies on students representing clients or performing other professional roles under the supervision of members of the faculty.

        In-house clinics offer a wide variety of experiences to students in assuming personal professional responsibility for cases assigned to them. Some clinics expect students to serve as "lead counsel" for clients on matters within their level of competence, while others expect students to be responsible for more narrowly defined tasks on complex matters that remain the primary responsibility of the clinical

---

        [600] Harbaugh, *supra* note 565, at 215.

        [601] MELTSNER & SCHRAG, *supra* note 575, at 65.

        [602] AALS/ABA GUIDELINES, *supra* note 550, at 75.

        [603] *See id.* ("The video specialist is becoming a crucial member of the clinical legal studies staff.")

        [604] This section was drafted by Mike Norwood, New Mexico. Roy Stuckey is primarily responsible for the subsection on setting clear, explicit learning objectives.

faculty. The design and operation of the in-house clinic considers the nature and the quantity of the cases it undertakes in awarding credit and assigning professional responsibility to students.[605]

2.   Best Practices for In-House Clinical Courses.

Remember that the best practices described below are in addition to the best practices for experiential courses, in general, discussed earlier.

> **a.   Use in-house clinical courses to achieve clearly articulated educational goals more effectively and efficiently than other methods of instruction could achieve.**

Principle: **The school offers in-house clinical courses to achieve clearly articulated educational goals more effectively and efficiently than other methods of instruction could achieve.[606]**

Comments:

It is impossible to describe fully what a student might learn by participating as a lawyer in the representation of real clients. Potentially it encompasses everything about being a lawyer. The almost infinite opportunities for teaching and learning in client representation courses makes it particularly important to have clear understandings about what we want students to learn, especially in light of the high cost of in-house clinics.

Some of the educational goals of client representation courses are predetermined and unavoidable. We must teach students about office procedures, including the central importance of avoiding conflicts of interests and maintaining confidences. We also have to teach students about the law, procedures, systems, and protocols of the types of practice settings in which they will be engaging. We have to teach students about their relationships with us and the restrictions we are placing on their freedom to act as lawyers. Sometimes we have to teach things students should have learned before enrolling in client representation courses such as the rules of evidence and professional conduct and basic lessons about lawyering skills.

While these are important topics, we should dispatch with these matters as efficiently as we can by giving students manuals and by setting up our office systems to make it as easy as possible for them to process the legal work. If we can help students process the legal work efficiently, we will have more time to help them learn the really important lessons that supervised practice can teach.

The most important lessons that can be learned in client representation

---

[605] *See Future of the In-House Clinic, supra* note 562, at 565.

[606] We acknowledge that there are some sound justifications for having in-house clinics that are unrelated to their educational effectiveness or efficiency. Some schools see in-house clinics as a way to demonstrate their role in providing services to their communities. Others include in-house clinics as part of specialty tracks. Another valid justification is to use clinics as laboratories for studying law practice and how one learns to become a lawyer. And some schools use clinics to provide a place for nurturing their students who are committed to social justice issues. All of these are valid reasons for law schools to house in-house clinics that serve a small percentage of the student body. Schools that are satisfied with these justifications will continue to support the existence of in-house clinics irrespective of their educational effectiveness or efficiency.

courses include many of the same lessons that can be learned through simulations or observation, including the values, behaviors, attitudes, and ethical requirements of a lawyer (professionalism). However, the learning is deeper and more meaningful when a student is participating as a lawyer, rather than as an observer or assistant or in a make believe simulation. This is particularly true of the key values of the profession: the importance of seeking justice and providing access to justice, the reasons for fostering respect for the rule of law, the essentiality of integrity and truthfulness, the need to deal sensitively and effectively with diverse clients and colleagues, and the value of nurturing quality of life in light of the stresses and time commitments of law practice.

> [C]linics can be a key setting in which students learn to integrate not only knowledge and skill but [also] the cognitive, practical, and ethical-social. The experience of clinical-legal education, corroborated by the research of Dreyfuses and Benner on the acquisition of practical expertise, points toward actual experience with clients as an essential catalyst for the full development of ethical engagement. This position is bolstered by analysis of medical training. There, beyond the inculcation of knowledge and the simulation of skills, it proves to be the assumption of responsibility for patient outcomes that enables the student for the first time to fully enter and grasp the disposition of a physician. In legal education, too, there is much to suggest that ethical engagement provides a pivotal aspect in the formation of lawyers.[607]

Many in-house clinical courses and internships give students opportunities to meet and serve people who have few other resources for resolving legal problems and seeking justice. The process of providing services to under-represented segments of society helps develop positive professional characteristics.

> The kind of personal maturity that graduates need in order to practice law with integrity and a sense of purpose requires not only skills but qualities such as compassion, respectfulness, and commitment. Coursework can contribute to the development of moral values, goals, identity and compassion as well as ethical understanding and skills. These outcomes depend even more on pedagogies that actively engage the students than do more traditional dimensions of academic understanding. Compassion and concern about injustice become much more intense when students develop personal connections with those who have experienced hardship or injustice.[608]

Representing clients presents opportunities for students to test for the first time on a personal level a number of abilities that are essential for lawyers and which are included on the list of desirable outcomes for legal education in Chapter Two. These include, for example, such challenges as whether they:
  • can "communicate effectively with clients, colleagues, and members of other professions,"
  • have "effective skills for client relationship management and knowledge of how to act if a client is dissatisfied with the advice or service rendered," and

---

[607] SULLIVAN ET AL., *supra* note 7, at 198 (citations omitted).
[608] *Id.* at 179.

• can "handle personal workload and to manage efficiently, effectively, and concurrently a number of client matters."

More importantly, representing clients tests a student's ability:
• to engage in "appropriate behaviors and integrity in a range of situations," and
• to deal sensitively and effectively with clients, colleagues, and others from a range of social, economic, and ethnic backgrounds, identifying and responding positively and appropriately to issues of culture and disability that might affect communication techniques and influence a client's objectives."[609]

In sum, students in client representation courses are beginning to learn the extent to which they are able to conduct themselves professionally.

Students participating as lawyers also test their intellectual and analytical skills, and they learn how well they are able to apply practical judgment to the situations they encounter.

As we observed clinical instruction, one of its striking features was the pedagogical shift from reliance on the hypothetical questions typical of other phases of legal education (such as "What might you do?") to the more immediately involving and demanding: "What will you do?" or "What did you do?" Responsibility for clients and accountability for one's own actions are at the center of clinical experiences. Assuming responsibility for outcomes that affect clients with whom the student has established a relationship enables the learner to go beyond concepts, to actually become a professional in practice. Taught well, it is through this experience of lived responsibility that the student comes to grasp that legal work is meaningful in the ethical as well as cognitive sense. Or rather, the student comes to understand that the cognitive and the practical are two complimentary dimensions of meaningful professional activity that gets its point and intensity from its moral meaning. Taking the role of the lawyer in real cases makes visible the ways in which the lawyer's decisions and actions contribute to the larger functioning of the legal order. At the same time, it also reveals the value of that activity as part of the larger function of the law in securing justice and right relations for actual persons in society.

Clinics can be a key setting for integrating all the elements of legal education, as students draw upon and develop their doctrinal reasoning, lawyering skills, and ethical engagement, extending to contextual issues such as the policy environment.[610]

Thus clinical courses can go well beyond simply filling gaps in students' legal preparation. If one were to search for a single term to describe the ability they hone best, it is probably "legal judgment." In

---

[609] A similar, but somewhat different list and a brief explanation of appropriate goals of in-house clinics is in *Future of the In-House Clinic, supra* note 562.

[610] SULLIVAN ET AL., *supra* note 7, at 142-43.

a wide sense, of course, this is the end of all legal education.[611]

Watching lawyers and judges in practice helps students understand these things, but students must practice law themselves before they can evaluate how far they have to go before they will be effective, responsible lawyers. Only in real life contexts can students learn how they measure up to the requirements and expectations of the legal profession. Only then can they really test how their "espoused theories of practice" play out in the actual practice of law.

An issue that legal educators should carefully evaluate is the degree to which externships in which students engage in practice under supervision can achieve the educational objectives described above. One of our operating assumptions is that in-house clinical faculty have superior one-on-one teaching skills for helping students learn how they function as lawyers and how they can grow. Perhaps only in in-house clinics are they likely to encounter teachers who will help them learn about their strengths and weaknesses and develop strategies for improving.

In-house clinic teachers may be uniquely situated to help students "recognize personal and professional strengths and weaknesses, to identify the limits of personal knowledge and skill and to develop strategies that will enhance professional performance." Such instruction requires the teacher to be attentive to individual students' attributes and to develop specialized teaching skills that neither externship supervisors or students' first employers in practice are likely to have. At least that is the theory.

We are unaware of any data comparing the teaching effectiveness of externship supervisors with in-house clinic faculty. In theory, the lessons described above could be taught and learned in externships in which students participate as lawyers under the supervision of practicing lawyers. This would be possible, however, only if the externship supervisors embrace their educational functions and work to develop their teaching knowledge and skills. This is not likely to happen unless the law school makes this expectation clear, selects externship supervisors based on their teaching potential, provides training about the educational goals of its externships and methods of instruction, exercises control over the tasks to be assigned to students, establishes protocols for observing student performances and providing feedback, coordinates the fieldwork experience with assigned readings and classroom discussions, and closely monitors the performance of externship supervisors.

Another way in which the potential value of in-house clinics may surpass that of externships is that in-house clinics can afford the time to encourage students "to aim beyond the typical standard of the marketplace, a standard often based on 'theories' that do more to make the lawyer's work easier than to serve the clients, and that include elaborate rationalizations for ineffectiveness so as to make it easier to externalize failure. The law school clinical program must start the student on the road to excellence."[612] Perhaps only in-house clinical courses can give students an "attitudinal and learning model sufficiently strong to insulate the student from external pressures toward mediocre practice."[613]

---

[611] *Id.* at 144.

[612] Kreiling, *supra* note 546, at 305.

[613] *Id.* at 306.

We are unsure how closely this vision of the educational potential of courses involving supervised law practice resembles reality. We worry that too many in-house clinics are overwhelmed with processing cases and with teaching those matters described earlier that we cannot avoid teaching, for example, office procedures and how to process certain kinds of cases. As mentioned earlier, it is important and valuable for students to learn these things. We just do not believe they are the most valuable lessons that students can learn in in-house clinics, and there may be more efficient and effective ways to teach these lessons. If an in-house clinic cannot demonstrate that it is doing more than teaching office procedures and how to process certain types of cases, perhaps it should be replaced with a less expensive simulation-based or externship courses that can achieve the same objectives.

As with every other course in the law school, we would benefit from developing clear statements of the outcomes that each client representation course seeks to achieve. Until we do this, we will be less focused on accomplishing our objectives and less able to evaluate the success of our efforts.

We also need to improve our methods for determining whether supervised practice courses are achieving their goals. The authors do not know if there is a typical way in which students in such courses are graded. We know that some teachers base a student's grade on an evaluation of the student's overall effort and abilities in handling the casework. Some evaluations are linked to written descriptions of lawyering competence that are handed out at the beginning of the semester. We do not know of any in-house clinic or externship that gives written or oral exams, nor do we know of any that evaluate what students know at the end of the semester about the lessons that were the subject of instruction during the semester. The focus is almost always on how the student performed rather than what the student learned except, perhaps, in those situations that also incorporate students' end of the semester self-evaluations. We do not propose an answer, but evaluating student learning in client representation courses is an issue that legal educators have not yet adequately addressed.

b.   Be a model of law office management.

Principle: The in-house clinical courses provide a model of law office management in which appropriate case and office management systems are utilized.

Comments:
The important role in-house clinics perform in assisting students in transitioning from law school to practice cannot be overstated. Many students leave law school to enter solo or small firm practices. Exposure to robust and well-run office management systems is critical for students' professional development as effective, responsible practitioners. Many students in these settings adopt the management practices they experience in their in-house clinics to their own practices upon graduation.

Tracking case status, docketing and calendaring, file maintenance, clearly delineating case responsibilities, conflict checking, and balancing trust and office accounts according to acceptable accountancy and ethical practices are all part of providing ethical and competent legal services. In-house clinics should have management systems that assure their clients receive quality legal services. In low caseload clinics this can be done with manual systems aided by "home grown" computer programs. In higher volume and long-standing clinics, up-to-date computerized law office management systems should be expected.

In-house clinics should have clear, written protocols for monitoring the quality of law practice and for responding effectively if issues arise. Clients' opinions about their satisfaction with the quality of representation should be systematically canvassed, including whether they felt treated with dignity and respect. Surveys about the quality of in-house clinics' law practice, including professionalism, should be conducted periodically and should canvas people who interact with the program's faculty and students, such as judges, hearing officers, judicial and agency staff, and opposing counsel.

There should be clear, written guidelines regarding who has the authority and responsibility for making decisions about case intake and representation, including the role of law school administrators, nonclinical faculty, and the clinical faculty individually and collectively. These written guidelines should comply with applicable ethical rules, and issues such as client confidentiality and client decision-making prerogatives should never be compromised. In-house clinics should have a system for identifying and dealing with possible conflicts of interests between potential clients and the law school and any parent university, preferably before undertaking representation.

c.   **Provide malpractice insurance.**

Principle: The school provides adequate malpractice insurance for students and faculty in the in-house clinical program.

Comments:
        Students and their clients should not be put at risk of financial loss if malpractice is committed by a student or faculty member that results in harm to a client, opposing party, or someone else. Therefore, the school should provide malpractice insurance for students and faculty. Affordable malpractice insurance is available to most clinical programs through the National Legal Aid and Defender Corporation. Also, some state bar associations provide malpractice coverage for attorneys when they handle pro bono cases. Students and faculty may be eligible for this coverage, too.

d.   **Approve student work in advance and observe or record student performances.**

Principle: All student lawyer activities that are client- or outcome-significant are approved in advance by clinical faculty and either directly observed by clinical faculty or recorded for subsequent review. Other activities of students are similarly reviewed if learning to perform those activities and demonstrating skill in performing them are educational objectives of the course.

Comments:
        Clinical faculty have obligations to their clients and their students. In order to protect clients' interests, clinical faculty should approve in advance and monitor student activities that could affect the client's interests or, in the absence

of an individual client, the outcome of the representation. At a minimum, the clinical faculty should review all correspondence and legal documents prepared by students, observe meetings with clients or opposing parties or counsel, monitor students' adherence to office and practice management protocols, and attend all court appearances by students.

Clinical faculty can discharge their responsibilities as teachers only when they observe or review student activities that are related to the educational objectives of the course. At the same time, observation or review of mundane, routine activities is not necessary if they are unrelated to educational objectives or clients' interests. Students may also be given more autonomy as they demonstrate proficiency in specific activities.

> e.   **Balance student autonomy with client protection.**

Principle: The clinical faculty appropriately balances the goal of giving students independence and responsibility with the goal of protecting clients' interests.

Comments:
Every in-house clinical teacher seeks cases that provide students with challenging but manageable learning experiences, cases in which students can have significant responsibility for determining the outcome without unduly risking harm to clients' interests. The goal of most clinical teachers is to allow students to carry complete responsibility for their cases while the teacher serves as a resource when needed. There are times, however, when the clinical teacher should intervene to protect clients from harm.

Deciding when and how to intervene in a student's representation of a client is one of the most difficult decisions faced by clinical teachers. When a supervisor intervenes too early in the process, the student is not afforded the opportunity to learn from approaching the problem by herself. While a supervisor may be committed to particular concepts, she must be careful in attempting to shape a student's experience, as a primary goal is for the student to develop a reflective and critical approach to her own experience. Furthermore, a clinical teacher who is constantly "rescuing" a student is likely to undermine the student's confidence in her ability to become a capable lawyer. At the other extreme, a supervisor who provides little or no intervention when it is apparent the student is beyond his or her capabilities risks real harm to the client.

The highest quality experience comes from a supervisor who can strike the appropriate balance. Every choice a supervisor makes should be a conscious choice with a specific goal in mind. The clinical supervisor leads with respect for the student and with the clinical method's cornerstone of providing opportunities for the student to experience primary professional responsibility for real legal matters. But the supervisor never loses sight of the requirement that no client be subjected to incompetent representation.

In coming to supervisory choices, a great deal of student-specific diagnosis is required. The characteristics and needs of individual students should be a main consideration in all supervisory decisions. Ann Shalleck identified three aspects that should be considered in each decision.[614] First, the supervisor must be aware of the scope of the student's knowledge, including the student's grasp of end-means thinking in planning and the student's mastery of reflective learning. Second, the supervisor must be aware of situations that create difficulties for the student. Finally, the supervisor should be aware of how characteristics such as gender or race affect the student's experience.

In addition to the effect of supervisory choices on the student, the supervisor must also consider the relationship with the client. David Chavkin pointed out that the presence of a supervisor, or "real" attorney, may distort the student-client relationship.[615] The client may look to the "real" lawyer for definitive answers, impeding the student in developing a true lawyer-client relationship. Before intervening in a way visible to the client, the supervisor must evaluate whether the benefits of intervention will outweigh the negative aspects. One way to avoid this issue is to use a closed circuit television system that enables the supervisor to observe and listen to students' meetings with clients without being in the same room. This allows the faculty member to intervene if necessary by telephoning the student during the meeting or to be prepared to answer students' questions either before clients leave the office or immediately afterward. Closed circuit systems are inexpensive and simple to install in most buildings, especially where the students' interview rooms are located near the clinical teachers' offices.

While supervisors should strive to empower students to become their own lawyers, there are elements of clinical practice where a supervisor's direction may be appropriate. For example, one area in which the supervisor's guidance is important is in the planning stages of a case. Translating case theory into action is not a skill easily taught in the traditional law school setting, and it is at times critical to a client's case. Supervisors can provide a forum for discussion as well as help students confront conflicts they might feel while developing a case strategy.

As with almost all areas of the clinical experience, the supervisor must evaluate the need for supervision. Each decision is individually tailored to the student's abilities and needs. The supervisor may consider such factors as whether the student has had previous opportunities to address the lawyering task, whether the student has shown a capacity to learn and reflect without supervision, and how the exercise of responsibility has affected the student's learning. Students often look to supervisors for knowledge and may expect the supervisor to provide a variety of information such as procedural rules, legal arguments and others. The supervisor must decide what information to provide and under what circumstances. In making these decisions, the supervisor not only needs to evaluate the student's learning experience and the client's needs, but also how her decision may affect the teacher's relationship with the student.

f.   Have a classroom component.

Principle: In-house clinical courses include classroom components that help accomplish the educational goals of the courses.

Comments:

A clinical seminar or classroom component reinforces and advances the

---

[614] Shalleck, *supra* note 564.
[615] Chavkin, *supra* note 564, at 1539.

shared learning experience of students enrolled in an in-house clinic. The classroom component can be used to transmit knowledge and information necessary for competent representation of the population of clients served by the clinic, for "grand rounds" sharing of learning experiences, for group case planning exercises, for simulations directly related to the actual case experiences of students, for group discussion on perspectives of lawyering in context, for providing a forum for outside professionals to share their perspectives on legal concerns, and for other matters directly connected to the advancement of students' professional development.[616]

g. Provide adequate facilities, equipment, and staffing.

Principle: **The school provides adequate facilities, equipment, and staffing for in-house clinics.**

Comments:

In-house clinics are responsible for the competent representation of actual clients by law students working under the supervision of qualified instructors. The facilities, equipment, and staffing must be appropriate for providing both competent representation to clients and meaningful instruction to students. This means that clinical offices should include reception areas, confidential client interviewing space, appropriate work areas for students, adequate room for professional staff and faculty, supportive staff services, means for investigation, research resources, classrooms, and multimedia technology.[617]

h. Respond to the legal needs of the community.

Principle: **The school has in-house clinics that respond to the legal services needs of the communities in which they operate.**

Comments:

Providing access to justice and seeking justice are two of the most important values of the legal profession. One way in which a law school can impart these values to students is by establishing and supporting in-house clinics that respond to the legal service needs of the communities in which they operate.

In-house clinics are all too familiar with the tension between providing needed legal services and educating students through the clinical method. Education should be the first priority. Nevertheless, several pedagogical goals available to in-house clinics are best pursued when they are designed and operated mindful of the social justice mission assigned to the legal profession, including "imparting the obligation for service to indigent clients, information about how to engage in such representation, and knowledge concerning the impact of the legal system on poor people."[618] In-house clinics that relate to and respond to the under-served legal needs of the communities in which they operate have the best chance of imparting this knowledge.

---

[616] *See Future of the In-House Clinic, supra* note 562, at 569.

[617] *See id.* at 550 and AALS/ABA GUIDELINES, *supra* note 554, at 25.

[618] *Future of the In-House Clinic, supra* note 562, at 515. A discussion of the history and continuing significance of the social justice dimension of clinical legal education is included in Barry et al., *supra* note 283, at 12-16.

D.   **Externship Courses.**[619]

Principle: The school employs best practices in externship courses.

1.   **Introduction to Externship Courses.**

Externships are courses in which a significant part of the learning relies on students either representing clients or performing other professional roles under the supervision of practicing lawyers or observing or assisting practicing lawyers or judges at work. Note that if students in an externship course are actually engaging in law practice, not just observing or assisting lawyers, many of the principles of best practices for in-house clinics are equally applicable to such externships, in addition to the ones set forth below.

In this section, "faculty" refers to members of the law school faculty who have control over or other responsibilities related to externship courses. "Field supervisors" refers to lawyers or judges who supervise and teach students at the field placement sites where students are working.

2.   **Best Practices for Externship Courses.**
Remember that the best practices described below are in addition to the best practices for experiential education discussed earlier.

      a.   **Use externship courses to achieve clearly articulated educational goals more effectively and efficiently than other methods of instruction could achieve.**

Principle: The school offers externship courses to achieve clearly articulated educational goals more effectively and efficiently than other methods of instruction could achieve.

Law teachers have had a surprisingly difficult time articulating the educational goals of externship courses in which students observe or assist lawyers or judges and figuring out what to do with their classroom components. We understand, of course, that putting students in prosecutors' or defenders' offices will help students learn about criminal law practice, that placing students with judges will help them learn about the workings of the judiciary, and so forth. These are all valid purposes for externships that suggest natural topics for materials and class discussion.

What is surprising is the apparent absence of our collective appreciation of practice observation courses as a forum for studying the values, behaviors, attitudes, and ethical requirements of lawyers (professionalism). Perhaps, this is such an obvious benefit that it is not always articulated.[620] In-house clinics have special strengths, but most do not accurately replicate the atmosphere of law practice in terms of their office settings, workloads, and ivory tower approaches to practice.

---

[619] This section was originally prepared by Harriet Katz, Rutgers, Camden, incorporating edits by Alex Scherr, Georgia; Cynthia Batt, Temple; Francis Catania, Jr., Widener; Mary Jo Eyster, Brooklyn; and Liz Ryan Cole, Vermont. Roy Stuckey is primarily responsible for the subsection on setting clear, explicit learning objectives.

[620] *See* Backman, *supra* note 494 (recounting a discussion of the BYU faculty in which some defended "the value of the externship as a means of providing a crucial practice-oriented opportunity to learn about the legal profession").

Placing students in practicing lawyers' and judges' offices removes this artificiality, and students know they are working in contexts similar to those that await them after graduation. Students' observations and experiences in all types of externships can provide rich fodder for discussing and reflecting on professionalism issues, if protocols are established to avoid jeopardizing confidences.

The problems that supervising lawyers and judges encounter and the environments in which they work are not artificial. When a student sees a lawyer turn away a potential client because of a remote possibility of a conflict of interest arising, it affects the student's opinion of the relationship of the rules of ethics to real life practice. When a student hears a judge describe how a particular lawyer cannot be trusted because he makes up reasons for requesting delays of hearings, the student learns a lesson in a more meaningful way than can be learned from a book or a law professor.

Some externships also provide excellent opportunities to study and learn about the functioning of the legal system and its capacities and limitations. It is especially important for students to study issues of justice in our society and to learn to appreciate the importance of the rule of law for ensuring justice to all members of society. Only in a real world context can students examine the interaction of legal analysis and human behavior, including interpersonal dynamics and communication. They should learn during law school how the law can affect people's lives by bringing fear or hope, sadness or joy, pain or relief, frustration or satisfaction.

Externships in which students primarily observe lawyers and judges at work can also help students develop insights into professional skills and problem-solving expertise.

> Much of the learning in apprenticeship is by observation and imitation because much of what experts know is tacit. It can be passed on by example, but often it cannot be fully articulated. By carefully observing expert performance, however, learning theorists argue, it is possible to render important aspects of practice explicit. As in the case of simulation techniques employed in clinical domains, these articulations of good performance can then become objects of imitation and practice for learners. By making explicit important features of good performance through various conceptual models and representations, teachers can guide the learner in mastering complex knowledge by small steps. These devices of representation serve as "scaffolds," in the language of learning theorists, to support efforts at improved performance. Feedback from more accomplished performers directs the learner's attention, supporting improved attempts at a goal.[621]

Externships would benefit from developing statements of expected outcomes that participants in the course will achieve. It is common for externships to require supervisors to give students opportunities to observe or participate in a range of activities, such as observing an initial interview, drafting interrogatories, and attending a trial. A statement of outcomes would be better. A statement of an outcome would begin "upon completion of the externship, students will be able to _____." The blank would contain a statement of what students would know,

---

[621] SULLIVAN ET AL., *supra* note 7, at 8.

understand, or be able to do, for example, "draft interrogatories in a civil lawsuit," "present the state's case in taking a guilty plea," "draft a motion for continuance," "describe how criminal cases proceed from arrest to conviction," or "explain the value of a lawyer's reputation for integrity." Such statements of outcomes, even if they do not encompass everything a student might learn in the course, would force us to think more carefully about what we believe are the most important purposes of our courses and guide us in designing the delivery of the promised outcomes.

One of the challenges for teachers of externship courses is to demonstrate why the teaching and learning that occurs in placement settings should be learned during law school rather than in the first year of practice. While one can plausibly claim that exposure to law practice during law school is inherently valuable, exposure alone is insufficient to warrant awarding academic credit and charging high tuition for providing that exposure. Students can gain exposure to practice by clerking for a law firm or volunteering to work with an agency or a judge. Thus, it is critical that externships have clear educational objectives that are accomplished through a combination of assigned readings (about professionalism and other topics to be studied), classroom discussions, supervisors who will take time to explain and answer questions, and structured systems that require students to reflect on their experiences.

We also need to improve our methods for determining whether we are achieving our goals. The authors do not know if there is a typical way of evaluating what students learn in externships. Some externships are pass/fail courses, and the results appear to be based primarily on whether students put in the requisite number of hours at the placement site. They involve no evaluation of learning. Other externships require journals and papers, but we are unsure if these ensure a connection between what students are learning and the educational objectives of the course. We do not know of any externship courses that give exams. Perhaps this should be reconsidered. If an externship course has educational objectives, some effort should be made to determine if it is achieving them.

b.   Involve faculty enough to ensure achievement of educational objectives.

Principle: Members of the law faculty control and participate in externship courses to the extent necessary to ensure the achievement of educational objectives.

Comments:

A member of the law faculty who is familiar with experiential education and law practice should have control over each externship course to ensure that the educational objectives are recognized, emphasized, and achieved.

To the extent that it is appropriate to the educational goals set by the school, the faculty member in charge of the externship should:
- communicate expectations and goals to field supervisors,
- periodically review the progress of students with supervisors, offering assistance as necessary,
- periodically review field supervisors' accomplishment of educational and supervision requirements and provide guidance toward improvement, and
- share new ideas and developments about clinical teaching, or collaborate

with supervisors in ongoing conduct of and improvements to the externship course or program.

Externship faculty must establish and maintain appropriate relationships with externship supervisors in order to communicate standards, monitor compliance with program requirements, monitor student progress, and help placements improve their educational practices.

The faculty should engage with the relevant legal community to create and advocate for appropriate opportunities for student practice experience.

c. Establish criteria for approval of sites and supervisors.

Principle: **The school has criteria for approval of field placement sites and supervisors.**

Comments:
Criteria for approval of field placement sites should include suitability of work provided for students and adequacy of supervision provided by mentors at the placement. Law schools should have agreements with field placement sites that clearly describe the roles and responsibilities of the school, placement site, faculty, supervisors, and students.

The range and nature of placements offered in a given externship program should relate to articulated educational goals for that program. Placement sites should be committed to providing students opportunities to observe or engage in activities that are consistent with the educational goals of the program.

Supervisors at field placement sites should have a demonstrated commitment to mentoring law students, consistent with the school's goals for the students. Faculty should consider additional standards for supervision at sites with multiple lawyers to assure the best supervision. For example, senior leadership at the proposed site should be committed to mentoring law students, so that those directly supervising students understand that their work with students is regarded as valuable by their superiors. Where several students are placed at a site, it may be helpful if a coordinator at the site monitors students and their relationships with their mentors and maintains contact with the school.

d. Establish standards to assure that work assigned to students will help achieve educational objectives.

Principle: **The school has standards assuring that work assigned to students is likely to help achieve educational objectives.**

Comments:
Work assigned to students at their externship sites should meet as many of the following criteria as are consistent with the educational goals of the externship. The work:
• is substantial legal work, appropriate for students, including more advanced work for students as they become more capable,
• consists of the authentic work of the placement and does not include work assignments created solely to occupy the student without reference to the

work demands of the office,
• is appropriate to the student and law school educational objectives,
• places students in lawyering roles to the extent possible. This may include:
  • a primary counsel role, subject to relevant student practice rules,
  • a supporting role, in which the student engages in collaborative work with the supervising attorney, and
  • a role in which the student is given opportunities to observe experienced lawyers or judges performing complex tasks and tasks that are beyond the scope of the student's current capabilities and to discuss those observations with mentors,
• provides the student with an understanding of all aspects of the work of the placement, and
• exposes students to decision-making on active cases or problems, whether through staff meetings, conversations with mentors and other attorneys, or other collaborative work processes.

> **e.   Establish standards to assure that field supervision will help achieve educational objectives.**

Principle: **The school has standards which assure that the supervision provided by field supervision attorneys, clerks, and judges is consistent with the educational objectives.**

Comments:

Standards for supervision should communicate to supervisors that they are expected to:
• understand the educational objectives of the externship course or program,
• provide an orientation to the resources and mission of the placement site,
• assist students in developing appropriate individualized educational objectives that are appropriate to the work of the field placement and that take advantage of all of the experiences the placement has to offer to students,
• assign work consistent with the principles stated in this document,
• encourage students to evaluate their field experience critically and regularly engage the student in constructive critical evaluation of the student's field experience,
• observe or review student performances at regular intervals, and provide constructive feedback on student performance designed to improve student skills and understanding,
• provide constructive evaluation to students about their general professional development,
• regularly communicate with the externship faculty about student progress, and
• model the reflective and conscientious practitioner and welcome questioning of aspects and techniques of practice.

f.   Consider students' needs and preferences when placing students.

Principle: **The school considers students' needs and preferences when matching students with field placement sites and supervisors.**

Comments:

The faculty should try to place students in situations that will match their needs and preferences consistent with the educational objectives of the course. The faculty should seek out placements that will challenge the student while fitting the student's goals and abilities. While total flexibility to respond to students' needs is not possible where the externship is tied to a particular type of law practice, students' needs and preferences should be considered to the extent possible.

Approaches to assigning students may include meaningful prerequisites, careful review of applications by externship faculty, individual consultations between students and faculty, interviews between students and prospective placement supervisors, and articulating approval standards to students who seek or propose placements independently.

The student matching process should be responsive to specific issues for various students, such as those who possess advanced knowledge or experience in a specialized area, are pursuing a dual degree or blend of careers, are returning students, commuters, or students with other identifiable skill development concerns or special interests, as may be necessary to assist such students to meet their personal educational objectives.

g.   Provide malpractice insurance.

Principle: **Adequate malpractice insurance is provided for students, supervisors, and faculty.**

Comments:

If students are performing functions that could result in malpractice claims against the students or faculty, the school should ensure that either the school or the offices in which students are working provide adequate malpractice insurance for students and faculty – and ideally for field supervisors. Students and their clients should not be put at risk of financial loss if malpractice is committed by a student, supervisor, or faculty member that results in harm to a client, opposing party, or someone else. Affordable malpractice insurance may be available to externship programs through the National Legal Aid and Defender Corporation. Also, some state bar associations provide malpractice coverage for attorneys when they handle pro bono cases. Students, supervisors, and faculty may be eligible for this coverage.

h.   Approve student work in advance and observe or record student performances.

Principle: **All student lawyer activities that are client- or outcome-significant are approved in advance by field supervisors and either directly observed by field supervisors or recorded for subsequent review. Other activities of students are similarly reviewed if learning to perform those activities and demonstrating skill in performing them are educational objectives of the course.**

Comments:
Field supervisors have obligations to their clients and their students. In order to protect clients' interests, field supervisors should approve in advance and monitor student activities that could affect the client's interests or, in the absence of an individual client, the outcome of the representation. At a minimum, field supervisors should review all correspondence and legal documents prepared by students, observe meetings with clients or opposing parties or counsel, monitor students' adherence to office and practice management protocols, and attend all court appearances by students.

Field supervisors can discharge their responsibilities as teachers only when they observe or review student activities that are related to the educational objectives of the course. At the same time, observation or review of mundane, routine activities is not necessary if it is unrelated to educational objectives or clients' interests. Students may also be given more autonomy as they demonstrate proficiency in specific activities.

i.   Ensure that students are prepared to meet obligations.

Principle: **Students are adequately prepared to meet their obligations.**

Comments:
The question of preparation is not as critical if the students are only observing law practice, but a school should place only students who are competent to perform the tasks that will be assigned to them. Law schools should consider whether prerequisites should be met before students enroll in an externship. For example, Evidence would be a logical prerequisite for any litigation-focused placement, and Professional Responsibility may be an important prerequisite for any placement. In some cases, it may be necessary to provide relevant instruction immediately before students begin working at their placement sites.

Co-requisite courses or instruction that takes place during the externship may enhance the educational value of the externship and make the co-requisite courses or instruction more vivid and meaningful to the students, but they do not prepare students to accomplish any tasks they will be assigned at the beginning of the course.

j.   **Give students opportunities to interact with externship faculty and other students.**

Principle: The externship provides sufficient opportunities for students to interact with externship faculty and other students in the course.

Comments:

The appropriate degree and type of interaction between and among students and faculty will depend on the model of the externship and its educational goals. These contacts should be frequent and substantive enough to achieve the educational purposes of the externship and could include seminars, speakers, presentations, tutorials, individual meetings, and journals involving reflection and dialogue.

In many externship courses, a regularly scheduled on-campus classroom meeting is the best way to provide opportunities for interaction. A classroom component may involve various forms of contact between student and faculty. In some externships, students are placed at sites that are too remote for students to meet regularly throughout the term of the course. In such cases, classroom sessions can be held immediately before and after the students' stints at the placement sites or intermittently during the term. Distance learning technology allows classroom sessions to continue throughout the course no matter how far from the law school students are placed.

Communication among all students or a subset of students in similar placements can help students learn from experiences in other placements and minimize the potential disconnection between the externship faculty member and the realities of a given office (or a given set of offices). These group meetings may include traditional seminar or classroom teachings, staff meetings, Listserv discussions, and video-conferencing.

Regular individual contact between faculty and students helps assure the quality of students' experiences. The faculty should seek out opportunities to engage in discussions with each externship student, whether through informal contact, site visits, written journals with faculty feedback, or formally scheduled interviews.

k.   **Ensure that adequate facilities, equipment, and staffing exist.**

Principle: The school has sufficient facilities, equipment, and staffing to achieve the educational goals of its externship courses.
Comments:

Most externship courses have modest needs in terms of facilities, equipment, and administrative staff support. The school should ensure that the placement sites provide acceptable space, word processing equipment, and supplies to enable students to accomplish their assignments.

In large externship programs, administrative support should be provided to assist the faculty in recruiting, monitoring, and communicating with field supervisors, keeping track of whether students are meeting their obligations, and providing other support as needed.

Chapter Six
Best Practices for Non-experiential Teaching Methods

A.   Socratic Dialogue and Case Method.

1.   Introduction to the Socratic Dialogue and Case Method.

The principal method for teaching legal doctrine and analytical skills in United States' law schools is the Socratic dialogue and case method. Students read appellate courts' decisions in casebooks and answer professors' questions about the holdings and principles of law contained in the cases. This question and answer practice is loosely referred to as "Socratic dialogue."

Although the Socratic dialogue and case method is no longer the exclusive method of instruction in law schools in the United States, it is still frequently used in legal studies beyond the point where its benefits have been achieved, and many teachers use the case method exclusively even when other methods of instruction would accomplish their educational objectives more effectively. In this section, we describe best practices for using the Socratic dialogue and case method, though we recommend that its use be limited.[622]

Before discussing the best practices of contemporary law teachers in using Socratic dialogue, it may be useful to compare Socrates' methods with Langdell's. This description was taken from Peggy Cooper Davis and Elizabeth Ehrenfest Steinglass, *A Dialogue About Socratic Teaching,* 23 N.Y.U. REV. L. & SOC. CHANGE 249 (1997). The authors graciously consented to our adaptation of their work. The language in the text is theirs, except for the segments that are offset with brackets.

a.   Socrates' methods (as described by Davis and Steinglass).

While it is difficult to generalize about Socrates' methods, the literature on the early and middle Platonic dialogues does refer with consistency to a few basic elements. In general, the dialogues are said to begin with elenchus – a process through which Socrates' interlocutor is made to realize that he does not know what he thought he knew. After eliciting his interlocutor's position, Socrates asks a series of leading questions designed to elicit agreement with a series of related propositions. Socrates then reveals what he knew all along – that the statements to which his interlocutor has agreed contradict the interlocutor's original position. One scholar has described the process in this way:

> His tactics seem unfriendly from the start. Instead of trying to pilot you around the rocks, he picks one underwater a long way ahead where you would never suspect it and then makes sure you get all the wind you need to run full-sail into it and smash your keel upon it.

This process engaged Socrates' audiences, if not his interlocutors. As

---

[622] The reasons for limiting the use of the Socratic dialogue and case method are explained in Chapter Four in the section, "Use Multiple Methods of Instruction and Reduce Reliance on the Socratic Dialogue and Case Method."

Socrates tells us in the Apology, people enjoyed spending time in his company because they enjoyed hearing him "examine those who think that they are wise when they are not – an experience which has its amusing side." But Socrates had a purpose beyond entertainment. He believed that learning could begin only with the acknowledgment of ignorance and the experience of perplexity, or aporia. Elenchus generated aporia and thus motivated genuine interest in learning.

The elenchus created the necessary conditions for what some analysts describe as the next stage of the dialogue – the psychagogia. This stage is not always identifiable in Socratic dialogues. The early dialogues – those thought to depict Socrates most accurately – consist primarily of elenchus, while the more Platonic versions of the dialogic method, as illustrated by the middle and later dialogues, place less emphasis on the elenchus and greater emphasis on construction of knowledge. In those dialogues in which the psychagogia does occur, it takes the form of a series of questions by which Socrates supports the construction of new understanding from what has already been agreed upon.

The course of both the elenchus and the psychagogia is fixed by a series of inauthentic questions – questions for which Socrates knows the answers. The inauthentic question has a special discursive impact that often causes offense. According to linguists, a question, or a request for information, is authentic when it fulfills three preconditions (each relating to the state of mind of the person being questioned whom we will call the respondent): the respondent must believe that the questioner believes (1) that the questioner does not already have the information; (2) that the respondent does have the information; and (3) that the respondent will not provide the information without being asked. Situations in which the respondent believes that the questioner already knows the answer constitute other types of speech acts, such as a request for display. Linguists also note that requests presume an obligation of deference on the part of the respondent. Because they carry this presumption, requests can easily cause offense. This potential for offense accounts for the fact that requests are usually softened by mitigating language, such as expressions of politeness. The risk of offense is greatest – and the expectation of mitigation is highest – when requester and respondent are peers or the respondent is superordinate. An adult may not mitigate a request made to a child, but it is likely that s/he will mitigate a request made to a supervisor. Genuine questions are mitigated by the questioner's neediness. Requests for display lack this mitigating element. They therefore seem to presume an even greater discrepancy in power and, as a result, are more likely to cause offense.

Throughout the dialogues, Socrates asks questions to which he appears to know the answers. In dialogue with his equals, these questions sometimes seem offensively arch; in dialogues with subordinates, they seem more routine, but more conspicuously hierarchical. [Davis/Steinglass at 253-55.]

[A central philosophy of Socrates' approach is that] "if the same questions are put to him on many occasions and in different ways, you can see that in the end he will have a knowledge on the subject as accurate as anybody's." Modern educators would put it only slightly differently: through repetition and variation, a student can construct, or internalize, an independent understanding of a problem and its solution, developing a sure and waking knowledge of [the subject]. [Davis/Steinglass at 258.]

[One of the significant problems with Socrates' approach is the harmful effect it could have on Socrates' interlocutors and their ability to learn. As Meno, the slave, said at the end of his dialog with Socrates], "Socrates, even before I met you they told me that in plain truth you are a perplexed man yourself and reduce others to perplexity. At this moment I feel you are exercising magic and witchcraft upon me and positively laying me under your spell until I am just a mass of helplessness. My mind and my lips are literally numb, and I have nothing to reply to you."

Socrates' questions have left Meno perplexed and willing to acknowledge his ignorance, but they have also left him helpless and silent. They have reinforced Meno's subordinated position, shifted his attention from virtue to Socrates' approach to virtue, and, implicitly, suggested that there is only one way to approach such problems. [Davis/Steinglass at 259.]

b.   Langdell's methods (as described by Davis and Steinglass).

Christopher Columbus Langdell brought a version of the Socratic method to law school classrooms when he became Dean of Harvard Law School in 1870.

. . . . .

Langdell immediately implemented a variety of reforms. Diplomas were granted only after examinations were passed. Students were expected to begin their studies at the beginning of the academic calendar, and they were obligated to complete seven required courses and seven electives over two years. But the reform for which Langdell is best known took place in his classroom. Everyone knew that Langdell was up to something when he began compiling cases and distributed them before classes began. A large crowd came on the first day to see what he would do. The Centennial History of the Harvard Law School describes the first few minutes of Langdell's class in this way:

Langdell: "Mr. Fox, will you state the facts in the case of Payne v. Cave?"

Mr. Fox did his best with the facts of the case.

Langdell: "Mr. Rawle, will you give the plaintiff's argument?"

Mr. Rawle gave what he could of the plaintiff's argument.

Langdell: "Mr. Adams do you agree with that?"

Though we are cautious about characterizing Langdell's method from the scant descriptions that we have, it seems certain that Langdell's approach was radically different than that of other professors. While his colleagues read to their students from textbooks outlining the rules of law and made occasional comments on their reading, Langdell questioned his students about cases they were expected to read and study in advance. In other classrooms, students passively received the thinking of others, but in Langdell's classes students were expected to think through the cases for themselves. Describing Langdell's method nearly fifty years later, Eliot took pride in the introduction of active learning techniques at the law school:

Professor Langdell had, I think, no acquaintance with the educational theories or practices of Froebel, Pestalozzi, Seguin, and Montessori; yet his method of teaching was a direct application to intelligent and well-trained adults of some of their methods for children and defectives. He tried to make his students use their own minds logically on given facts, and then to state their reasoning and conclusions directly in the classroom. He led them to exact reasoning and exposition by first setting an example himself, and then giving them abundant opportunities for putting their own minds into vigorous action, in order, first, that they might gain mental power, and secondly, that they might hold firmly the information or knowledge they had acquired. It was a strong case of education by drawing out from each individual student mental activity of a very strenuous and informing kind. The elementary and secondary schools of the United States are only just beginning to adopt on a large scale this method of education – a method which is not passive but intensely active, not mainly an absorption from either book or teacher but primarily a constant giving-forth.

Like Socrates, Langdell used questions to provoke critical thinking. But unlike Socrates, Langdell seemed to believe that he knew, and his students could be expected to discover, the truth of the matters being considered. Langdell held that law was a "science" and that doctrine could be applied to facts consistently and certainly. In the introduction to his casebook on the law of contracts, he wrote:

Law, considered as a science, consists of certain principles or doctrines. To have such a mastery of these as to be able to apply them with constant facility and certainty to the ever-tangled skein of human affairs, is what constitutes a true lawyer; and hence to acquire that mastery should be the business of every earnest student of law.

Believing the law to be a science, Langdell concluded that it should be studied as a science. Just as students of natural science derive the laws of nature from real-world phenomena, so should students of law derive legal doctrine from cases. From his theories of law and legal education, we infer that when Langdell posed questions about cases, he expected students' answers to reference the "correct" underlying doctrine. We also infer that Langdell's questions, like those of Socrates, were inauthentic in that they sought an answer that the questioner knew in advance. Based on these scant descriptions, we believe that Langdell's method was similar to that of Socrates in terms of both its strengths and limitations. While Langdell required his students to construct doctrinal knowledge for themselves, he also constrained the process and the outcome of their learning.

Initial public response to Langdell's method was critical. Unfamiliar with the method and wary of articulating novice opinions, students complained that they weren't learning anything – not nearly what they would from lectures – and even suggested that Langdell didn't lecture because he didn't know anything. Soon only seven or eight students were attending the class. Langdell persisted despite criticism and declining enrollments for three consecutive years. Soon enrollment picked up again. Graduates of Langdell's program were apparently well-prepared for employment and were getting good jobs. Within thirty or forty years, schools all over the country were using Langdell's method. In 1914, the Carnegie Foundation commissioned a report on legal education in the United States. The author, Josef Redlich, concluded that the Socratic method was quite effective, but he added that the context in which the method was used was central to its success. Redlich praised the professors he studied for using, in addition to the Socratic teaching method, textbooks, dictionaries and encyclopedias, being available to answer questions during office hours, and providing introductory lectures (although Redlich thought that they did not do so to the extent that they might have). [Davis/Steinglass at 261-64.]

2.   **Best Practices for Using the Socratic Dialogue and Case Method.**

   a.   **Use the Socratic dialogue and case method for appropriate purposes.**

Principle: **The school uses the Socratic dialogue and case method to achieve clearly articulated educational goals more effectively and efficiently than other methods of instruction could achieve.**

Comments:

Law teachers should only utilize the Socratic dialogue and case method when it will accomplish clearly articulated educational objectives better than other methods of instruction. Judith Wegner found three explanations for the staying power of the Socratic dialogue and case method.

> [T]he case-dialogue method's legitimacy is rooted in at least three sorts of claims – its educational effectiveness, its resonance with professional norms, and its capacity to serve social and institutional agendas. These three sources of legitimacy are mutually reinforcing since they reflect an alignment of interests among three types of institutions (the university, the legal profession, and the social elite) and three corresponding sets of values. It can hardly be surprising that the case-method has continued to dominate legal education and resist fundamental change for more than a century.[623]

Regarding its educational effectiveness, even most of its critics concede that it helps students develop some of the key skills needed by lawyers better than the textbook and lecture method that preceded it. Paul Brest explained that "[c]oupled with the issue-spotting style of examination, this method of active learning turned out to be a superb way of inculcating the analytic skills and the skepticism about easy answers that are requisite to any career in the law."[624] Myron Moskovitz also touted the virtues of the Socratic dialogue and case method over the lecture and textbook method.

> Interaction with a Socratic teacher helped to sharpen students' minds. They learned to think on their feet, to express themselves, and to read cases – skills that a practicing lawyer needs and that the lecture/textbook method had done nothing to enhance. In addition, while the prior method taught students the rules of law, the case method gave them a deeper understanding of the rules: it

---

[623] Wegner, Theory and Practice, *supra* note 46, at 9.

[624] Paul Brest, *The Responsibility of Law Schools: Educating Lawyers as Counselors and Problem Solvers,* 58 LAW & CONT. PROBS. 5, 7 (1995).

delved into policy considerations that persuaded judges to adopt them.[625]

Mark Aaronson described some or the specific competencies that the method helps develop.

> [T]he case method provides students with simulated practice in how appellate courts formally reason, and predicting what courts will do is a core skill central to a lawyer's claim to professional expertise. . . . [F]eatures of the case method are also applicable when confronting problems in other contexts. These features include the grounding of analysis in facts, the comprehensive spotting of relevant issues and concerns, the search for governing rules, principles or standards by which to make decisions, the weighing of competing policy considerations in light of their consequences, the value placed on consistency and deference to past decisions, the utility of reasoning by analogy, the importance of reasoned justification, and the need to reach a conclusion and make a decision even if not perfect. Tailored and applied flexibly, the case method as a method of deliberation can provide a logical, overall methodology for approaching and thinking about all sorts of situations.[626]

Wegner uses the metaphor of "cognitive apprenticeship" to describe what the Socratic dialogue and case method can achieve when properly utilized.

> Modern studies of apprenticeship systems have yielded new theories of "cognitive apprenticeship" with associated insights that shed helpful light upon the classroom dynamics associated with formal instruction in law and other fields. The "cognitive apprenticeship" theory of John Seely Brown, Allan Collins, Paul Duguid and others argues that faculty-student interaction associated with effective learning involves a sort of "apprenticeship" through which intellectual development occurs. Although the process of development parallels that found in traditional craft apprenticeships, it is less obvious because the complex cognitive patterns of teacher-experts are generally not explicit and are thus difficult for their student-novices to observe. Likewise, it proves difficult for teachers to discern errors and misunderstandings that may be occurring in students' minds. These difficulties are especially pronounced in large classroom settings such as those in which the case-dialogue method is often employed.[627]

"The metaphor of 'cognitive apprenticeship' resonates powerfully with classical understandings of the case-dialogue method, which exposes students

---

[625] Moskovitz, *supra* note 160, at 244.

[626] Aaronson, *supra* note 33, at 6.

[627] Wegner, Theory and Practice, *supra* note 46, at 16 (citation omitted) (referring to John Seely Brown, Allan Collins & P. Duguid, *Situated Cognition and the Culture of Learning*, 18 EDUC. RESEARCHER 32-41 (1989); Allan Collins, John Seely Brown & Susan E. Newman, *Cognitive Apprenticeship: Teaching the Crafts of Reading, Writing, and Mathematics, in* KNOWING, LEARNING, AND INSTRUCTION: ESSAYS IN HONOR OF ROBERT GLASER 454, 454-55 (Laureen B. Resnick ed., 1989)).

to primary materials and teaches them to model themselves on the expert forms of thinking that faculty display. Many of the insights about teaching methods associated with this theory are already borne out in the established practices of legal educators, such as routine reliance on modeling, coaching, scaffolding, and fading tactics, and expectations that students articulate their insights explicitly, reflect on what they're learning, and explore related applications of ideas."[628]

Wegner also asks "[i]f these significant parallels are already apparent, might the metaphor of cognitive or intellectual apprenticeship be further exploited to identify further ways of enhancing effective teaching and student learning?"[629]

b.   Be skilled in using Socratic discourse.

Principle: **The teacher is skilled in using all four steps of Socratic discourse.**

Comments:
    Although Socratic dialogue has been the primary means of instruction in law schools in the United States for over a hundred years, there are not many written descriptions of the technique or how one should employ it. This description is adapted from Peggy Cooper Davis & Elizabeth Ehrenfest Steinglass, *A Dialogue About Socratic Teaching,* 23 N.Y.U. REV. L. & SOC. CHANGE 249 (1997). In fact, except for these introductory comments and the form in which the principles are stated, this section was created mostly by quoting directly from the article. The language that is not from their article is offset with brackets.

    Our description omits many of the helpful examples that Davis and Steinglass provide in their article, thus readers will be enlightened by consulting the original source. All but one of the footnotes in the Davis/Steinglass article are omitted.

    We begin with the assumption that a teacher has chosen to use Socratic dialogue because it is the best tool for achieving the teacher's educational objectives. As noted by Davis and Steinglass, and others, this is not always the case in legal education. It is a technique that is overused. Nonetheless, this section describes best practices for using it when appropriate.

(1)   Begin by asking a student to "state the case."

Principle: **The teacher begins Socratic discussions by selecting a student and asking that she "state the case," that is, that she engage in a fact-and-rule-fit analysis.**

Comments:
    ["Stating the case" is to engage in a fact-and-rule-fit (FARF) analysis.] The first step in a FARF analysis is to cull from an appellate opinion (1) the facts of the matter before the court, and (2) the rule of law that has been applied. The rule is parsed into a definitional component (prescribing the circumstances under which the rule attaches) and an outcome component (prescribing the result once the rule attaches). FARFing consists of establishing the fit between the facts of the matter

---

[628] Wegner, Experience, *supra* note 50, at 54.
[629] *Id.*

and the definitional component of the rule, so as to justify the result prescribed by the rule's outcome component. It is understood as a deductive process: The rule says that if X happens, Y will be the consequence. X has happened; therefore, Y.

. . . . .

     This is an exercise in reading and recitation. [The teacher] and her students will learn whether [the student who is called on] has read the case with enough care (or found some other means) to be able to identify and recite its facts, the governing law, and its central holding. They will also learn whether [the student] is flustered or able to recite with poise. If the case is complex, the identification of dispositive facts and law and the court's central holding may require sorting through tangential or subsidiary facts, rules and conclusions, but [the student's] initial task has not been daunting. If he has prepared for class and he is calm, he should find it easy to [give the correct response]. [Davis/Steinglass at 265-66.]

(2)   Use closed hypotheticals to relate the case at hand to prior cases.

Principle: **The teacher uses closed hypotheticals that relate the rules and facts in the case at hand to rules and facts in cases studied earlier.**

Comments:
    Once the case has been FARFed, it is likely that [the teacher] will move on to the more difficult terrain of the closed hypothetical [that is, a hypothetical to which there are correct answers known to the teacher and, perhaps, her students]. . . . Answering the closed hypothetical is a step – albeit a rather close step – from reading and recitation. It requires [the student] to recall and consult more material, and it requires him to replicate the deductive process that governed an earlier case by applying the process to a new set of facts. But these processes are not daunting. If [the student] is able to remember (or quickly find) the earlier case and to think calmly, the question should pose few difficulties. [The teacher] will quickly get a correct answer, either from [the first student] or from some better prepared or more composed student, at which point she will undoubtedly turn to something more challenging.

(3)   Use open hypotheticals to demonstrate complexity and indeterminancy of legal analysis.

Principle: **The teacher uses open hypotheticals to demonstrate that simple fact and rule fit analyses often conceal complexity and indeterminance and that the outcomes of cases are not rigidly determinate.**

Comments:
    Until now, [the teacher's] questions have not been authentic; she has been asking questions for which she already had an answer. [The student's] recitations have served, perhaps, to give him practice at public speaking under some stress, but their more important function has been to set before the class a set of principles that will be the subject of discussion for a while. At this point, [the teacher], who understands that doctrinal analysis involves a great deal more than recall and recitation, is likely to shift from requests for recitation and simple deduction and

demand that [the student] engage in interpretive work. And at this point the development and integration of [the student's] lawyering capacities begins in earnest. [The teacher] has carefully chosen her FARF and closed hypothetical inquiries so as to juxtapose legal rules that she thinks are mutually illuminating. Her choices have facilitated some lines of inquiry and made others less likely. . . . Still, the discussion might take a variety of directions from this point, and its direction will be guided, at least to some extent, by additional choices that [the teacher] must now implement. [Davis/Steinglass at 267.]

[The domains that the teacher may choose to explore include:

• *Textual exegesis:* The teacher may choose to] direct the discussion toward the meaning of the statutory terms that embody the rule or the terms of prior opinions that clarify its meaning. If she does this, she is likely to want the discussion to reveal ways in which a rule is ductile.

[• *Rule choice:* The teacher may choose to] direct discussion to whether the [rule applied by the court to decide a case] was the correct or only rule to apply in [the situation]. If she does this, she is likely to want the discussion to reveal a range of choice in fitting complex life situations into legal categories.

[• *Fact development*: The teacher may choose to] direct her students' attention to facts in the record that were neglected in the majority opinions, to the way in which those opinions interpret the facts, or to how the facts might have been developed before and during trial. If she does this, she is likely to want the discussion to reveal ways in which the facts were ductile.

[• *Contextual and policy analyses:* The teacher may choose] to focus on how the facts and context [of the situation] test the contours and legitimacy of the rule. If she does this, she is likely to want the discussion to reveal relationships between the identified function of a rule and its interpretation; she is also likely to want to discuss ways in which case facts suggest a rule's functions and test its efficacy. Of course, she may also want to have a broader discussion of the functions, wisdom and efficacy of the rule, in which case the discussion will turn to policy analysis.

[• *Narrative development*: The teacher may choose to discuss] cultural and narrative patterns that the rule – or the courts' interpretation of it – seems to follow. If she does this, she may want her students to consider the difference between imagining the case [as the plaintiff's or defendant's, or from the perspectives of others who were involved in the case or may be affected by the court's decision]. She might ask students what associations they have with the idea of [legal concepts related to the case]. She will want them to see that proverbial stories and cultural expectations can shape the interpretation of a rule.

A well-rounded legal education requires exploration of all of these domains, for textual exegesis, rule choice, fact development, contextual analysis, narrative development and policy analysis are all integral to sophisticated lawyering. Any of these domains can be explored in the format that is described by the term Socratic teaching, as that term is used in law schools.

[If the teacher's] approach to case analysis acknowledges indeterminacy, her questions will soon become genuine. She will move from establishing the shared premises for discussion to exploring matters as to which reasonable minds in her classroom might well differ. The structure of the exchange between [the teacher and the student] may convey the impression that there are right and wrong answers to all of [the teacher's] questions, but in truth the demand on [the student] at this stage of the class moves from recitation to analysis. [Davis/Steinglass at 267-68.]

(4)   Draw lessons about the nature and processes of lawyering and judging.

Principle: The teacher draws from the discussion lessons about the nature and processes of lawyering and judging.

Comments:
When [a teacher] has explored as many aspects of the presumption of legitimacy as pedagogic judgment counsels her to explore, she may draw from the discussion lessons about the processes of lawyering and judging. [Depending on the situation,] she might say: "So it seems, Mr. [Student], that the interpretation of the . . . statute has depended on a particular understanding of [a person's] needs and circumstances;" or, "So it seems, Mr. [Student], that the outcome of the litigation may have depended on whether it was conceived as a constitutional challenge of the [statute] or as a constitutional challenge of the . . . rule as interpreted by the California courts;" or, "So it seems, Mr. [Student], that the rule responds to different sets of cultural assumptions about [such matters]." However, recognizing the value of active learning, [the teacher] might also, over time, shift responsibility for drawing such conclusions to her students, by asking authentic questions, such as, "Mr. [Student], how might you explain the different outcomes in the cases [we just studied]?" [Davis/Steinglass at 270.]

c.   Do not intentionally humiliate or embarrass students.[630]

Principle: The teacher does not intentionally use Socratic dialogue as a tool for humiliating or embarrassing students.

Comments:
[We understand, as do Davis and Steinglass, that some thoughtful people believe that a Kingsfieldian approach to using Socratic dialogue is an effective way to prepare students for the rigors of law practice. While we agree that calling on students randomly encourages effective preparation, we disagree with the notion that intentionally embarrassing and humiliating students is, on balance, a tactic that should be endorsed or employed by law teachers. Our position is consistent with modern trends in legal education and learning theory.

The following excerpts from the colloquy in Davis and Steinglass' conclusion reveal their thoughts about this issue.]

Liz: But suppose, Peggy, that every student was required to read a proscribed sequence of cases and to attend large classes in which at any moment s/he might be

---

[630] This section appears here because it was in the Davis/Steinglass article about Socratic dialogue and because many of the complaints about classroom abuse of students involve the misuse of Socratic dialogue. Obviously, a teacher could embarrass or humiliate students using any method of instruction.

interrogated about the lessons to be found in those cases. Don't we have to assume, Peggy, that it would be humiliating to be called upon in such a class and shown to be unprepared or uncomprehending?

Peggy: Yes.

Liz: And since you have already told me, my friend, that every person prefers admiration to humiliation, we are left with no alternative but to conclude that under this method students will learn the lessons of their assigned cases. For it is only by doing so that they can avoid humiliation and hold some hope of earning admiration.

Peggy: It seems that you are right, Liz.

. . . . .

Peggy: Well, there are lots of things that I like about Socratic method. But it's a mixed bag. Students tell me that if I call on them without warning and rough them up a bit when they are unprepared, they read more and are more alert in class. But others tell me that constant fear of humiliation interferes with their ability to concentrate.

Liz: I see what you mean. Every study I've seen shows that calling on people is better than taking volunteers from the standpoint of ensuring the participation of women, or of any other group that tends to be less impetuous in conversation. On the other hand, if you call on people only to rough them up, they may feel inclined to retreat. Still, if uninterrupted lecture is the only alternative, then maybe it does make sense to use questioning to force students to be more active. But break out groups would make more students active, and simulations can make them all active.

Peggy: I confess that sometimes I enjoy testing students by coming up with a counter argument for their every argument. But those are cheap shots; I've been thinking about my fields for nearly thirty years.

Liz: Maybe students would feel better if they knew the rules of the game – knew that you refute their arguments not because they are wrong, but to push them to develop their skills in the realm beyond recitation where open and genuine questions are debated.

Peggy: Could be. I do agree that Socratic teaching can be broad ranging enough to address a variety of lawyering contexts and to develop intellectual versatility. Open questions about a case can lead students to reconstruct and critique the processes of fact development and counseling, for example. Or to explore an advocate's or a judge's narrative choices.

Liz: I suppose, but there must be better contexts for getting students to appreciate the complexities of fact development. I would think that always working from appellate opinions down would be limiting; why not do some bottom up work?

Peggy: This may sound stuffy, but tradition is important. Students expect a little One L action.

Liz: I think it was Socrates who said that ideas are apt to run from the mind unless you tether them by working out the reason. I don't feel that I'm working out reasons when I'm being marched through deduction games. You didn't either.

Peggy: I understand. But sometimes Socratic discussion nicely explores the reasons for a result or a rule. It can also foster the development of professional consciousness by modeling a process of thinking through the multiple dimensions of a problem and the consequences of alternative decisions.

Liz: I think students might find it hard to think things through for themselves in a discourse structure designed to demolish rather than weigh their arguments. And in a structure that is so controlled and dominated by the teacher.

Peggy: But you had a good idea for addressing these problems: I think it makes sense to demystify the process for students by making it clear that questions are open and genuine and that it's in the nature of the game that even the best argument will be refuted. You know, there's truth to the notion that Socratic teaching models a style of argumentation that is often used in practice.

Liz: My guess is that it's used because you law professors keep modeling it.

Peggy: Not because it's good?

Liz: In this I really am Socrates: I do not know what goodness is.

[Davis/Steinglass at 277-79.]

(1)   Explain why Socratic dialogue is used.

Principle: **The teacher explains why she uses Socratic dialogue.**

Comments:

It is difficult for students to learn from questioning when teachers don't talk about why they do it. In the absence of explanations, students imagine for themselves. Not knowing, in combination with being anxious about performance, makes it easy for students to accept the worst that they have heard or to conclude that their professors' motives are self- aggrandizing or malevolent. As Redlich pointed out eighty years ago, the success of the Socratic method depends on the social context in which it is used. In a community of homogenous fellowship and privilege, a sequence of questions that moves past one's understanding may be experienced as a playful rite of passage. But in a large, relatively competitive and impersonal class, students may feel (and be) more vulnerable. Moreover, in a heterogeneous context in which race, gender, ethnicity, social class, sexual preference and other categories of difference play a role in shaping interpersonal dynamics and the realities of people's lives, Socratic testing will carry different, and sometimes unfortunate, meanings for different students. For example, a student socialized to expect and prefer what Deborah Tannen refers to as "report talk,"[631] may delight in inauthentic questions,

---

[631] Tannen distinguishes "report talk," which serves the function of asserting independence and achieving status by displaying knowledge, and "rapport talk," which serves the function of establishing connections and negotiating relationships. She observes that in many settings men are more prone to engage in report talk, women to engage in rapport talk. DEBORAH TANNEN, YOU JUST DON'T UNDERSTAND 76-77 (1990).

seeing them as an opportunity to display knowledge, but a student socialized to expect and prefer "rapport talk" may think inauthentic questions rude. [Davis/ Steinglass at 272-73.]

(2) Reassure flustered students and move to another student if a student is unprepared.

Principle: **If a student becomes flustered, the teacher reassures the student without trying to harass or embarrass the flustered student. If a student is unprepared, the teacher moves on to another student without trying to harass or embarrass the unprepared student.**

Comments:

If [a student] is unable to FARF a case, he may be in for the kind of hazing that the general public has come to associate with law school applications of the Socratic method. [The teacher] may respond to a wrong answer with a Kingsfieldian comment like, "Well, [Mr. Student], there's always medical school." But most contemporary law teachers think this sort of hazing rude and pointless. A wrong answer is likely to lead [the teacher] to reassure [the student] if he is flustered or move on to another student if he is unprepared. [Davis/Steinglass at 266.]

(3) Do not use successive questions and answers that leave students feeling passive, powerless, and unknowing.

Principle: **The teacher does not use successive questions and answers to the extent that they leave students feeling passive, powerless, and unknowing.**

Comments:

Steps three and four in [contemporary Socratic discourse] allow [the teacher] to avoid many of the risks associated with the Socratic method. By asking authentic questions about the law, [the teacher] suggests that there are multiple ways of thinking about legal problems and that her students are capable of such analyses. However, each step in the dialogue, including steps three and four, presumes that "question and answer" is a valuable method of teaching. This presumption becomes problematic in light of literature that suggests that successive questions can leave a respondent feeling passive, powerless, and unknowing.

As the linguist's distinction between genuine and inauthentic questions suggests, question and answer interactions presume or attempt to enact a power differential. Only if a questioner has higher status will the respondent tolerate successive questions and not attempt either to resist answering or to turn the tables by asking a question in return. The questioner enacts his or her higher status by presuming authority to command information or display and by determining the topic and direction of the conversation. The respondent enacts his or her lower status by submitting to the question and by allowing the questioner to ask the next question and to determine the direction of the conversation. With successive questions the respondent takes less and less responsibility for the conversation and grows increasingly passive. Some research suggests that with each successive question a respondent's answers will grow shorter and shorter. A sequence of similar questions, which implicitly suggests that the answers given have been inadequate, may have the additional effect of making the respondent defensive about his or her previous answers and/or hopeless about providing the right answer.

In his interdisciplinary review of the literature on questioning, Dillon shows that teachers' presumptions about the value of questioning are the opposite of those of scholars and practitioners in other disciplines. Whereas teachers ask questions to elicit critical thinking, survey researchers and litigating attorneys typically use questions to curtail respondents' answers. Personnel interviewers and psychotherapists avoid questions because they can be silencing; instead, they make statements and remain silent to promote thoughtful discussion. By asking students questions, the teacher may in fact make it more difficult for them to answer and to do the critical thinking she wants them to do. [Davis/Steinglass at 270-71.]

(4)   Use Socratic dialogue to illuminate lessons, not to expose students' lack of understanding.

Principle: The teacher uses Socratic dialogue to illuminate lessons, not to expose students' lack of understanding.

Comments:
        Each step in the dialogue is also colored by the social context in which it takes place. Students' experiences of their professors' questions are inevitably influenced by the classroom setting.

As he explains in the Apology, Socrates used the dialogues to test the wisdom of his interlocutors. Often Socrates engaged Sophists who were certain about the answers to his questions and sometimes even said that his questions were too easy. Believing that intellectual humility was a necessary first step to serious philosophical inquiry, Socrates considered it a duty to demonstrate the limitations of his interlocutors' understanding. Before [a teacher] applies Socrates' method, she might ask herself to what extent her context is similar or different. Are law students so confident of their answers or their knowledge that their lack of understanding must be demonstrated? Depending upon their previous experience and learning, some students may come to law school believing that they understand some areas of the law. However, given the age and limited professional experience of many students, it seems likely that many arrive aware of their ignorance and anxious about their capacity to learn what is expected. Already uncertain, students may experience sequences of Socratic questions as an indication that they have not answered adequately and do not have the necessary capacities.

The one-shot system of evaluation used in many law school classes may make students especially likely to react badly to Socratic testing. Because most law students are formally evaluated only at the end of each semester, students are prone to seek out other opportunities to assess their learning. In effect, every classroom exchange becomes an opportunity for self-assessment. Aware, or simply imagining, that she is being evaluated (by the professor, her classmates, and herself), the student naturally wants to use each interchange to demonstrate knowledge and understanding. For a student working in a self-evaluative mode, it may be particularly difficult to tolerate sequences of questions designed to move past what the student has already thought through. Moreover, in a public forum, before professor and peers, it is easy to imagine that the experience of not knowing would be humiliating. Yet, because Socratic teaching depends heavily on public

questioning that displays the limits of students' understanding, [some] teachers
. . . tend to challenge students no matter what they say, and to extend their very
public questioning beyond issues the responding student has considered in advance.
While some students might respond to this experience determined to return to fight
another day, others will be equally determined to avoid a repetition by avoiding class
participation. All of this may make it very difficult for students to focus on learning
rather than performing. [Davis/Steinglass at 271-72.]

d.   Do not rely exclusively on Socratic dialogue.

Principle: **The teacher does not rely exclusively on Socratic dialogue.**

Comments:

[T]he Socratic method can be used to explore multiple dimensions of
lawyering and to develop a broad range of capacities. Nonetheless, the method may
be less effective than others with regard to some of our goals.

For example, we have found it difficult to compose Socratic questions that
will lead students to adopt critical meta-analytic perspectives on the application
of doctrine. Moreover, Socratic discussion of appellate cases clearly is not the best
context for learning about crucial aspects of lawyering, such as fact development and
problem analysis. Using appellate opinions to organize discussions narrows the focus
of the conversation. Appellate opinions follow, and therefore do not readily expose,
the significant decisions that lawyers and judges make as a matter moves from
problem to resolution.

We have found it easier to foster meta-analysis and to develop capacities
for interpretive and problem-solving work in simulation and clinical contexts. In
these contexts, students can have the experience of managing a matter from the
articulation of a problem in the world to its legal resolution. As a result, they are
positioned to see how interpretations of fact and law evolve as lawyers and other
relevant parties interact. Moreover, they are able to appreciate the significance of
lawyers' choices. For example, if students, in-role, are privy to multiple responses
to the same simulated problem, they naturally compare responses. Additionally, a
negotiating team involved in multiple negotiations can analyze the implications of
key decisions and contextual factors. [Davis/Steinglass at 274-75.]

(1)   Allow students to exercise some control.

Principle: **The teacher allows students to exercise some control over
their learning.**

Comments:

Developmental psychologists have, of course, explored the ways in which
learners construct knowledge. According to Piaget and his followers, children
construct knowledge independently from their experience in the world. Typically,
children make sense of their experience from the perspective of their current
understanding. However, faced with phenomena that call their understanding
into question, children accommodate and develop new perspectives. Alternatively,
Vygotsky and his followers posit that children construct knowledge intersubjectively,
through interactions with teachers who perform such functions as "shielding
the learner from distraction, . . . forefronting crucial features of a problem, . . .

sequencing the steps to understanding, . . . or some other form of 'scaffolding.'" Though significantly divergent, both theoretical perspectives suggest that if it is to be remembered and understood, new knowledge must be connected, in an active, thoughtful process, to old knowledge.

Educational research supports these theories. Whether engaged in independent exploration or in social interactions, learners benefit from active learning experiences in which they maintain a measure of control over their work. For example, third and fourth grade writers learned more from collaborative interactions when they were able to exercise control and ensure that the interactions addressed their concerns. Similarly, research on high school classrooms associated high quality instruction with teachers' use of authentic questions. In response to their teachers' authentic questions and responses, students were able to discuss and build on their previous conceptions.

This literature suggests that Socratic dialogues which are tightly controlled by the professor may be less effective than authentic discussions. . . . [D]ialogues which are tightly controlled by the questioner tend to track the questioner's thinking, not the respondent's. Such dialogues do not necessarily facilitate the respondent's efforts to link the new material to his or her previous conception. [Davis/Steinglass at 273-74.]

(2)   Ask all students to jot down their thoughts while engaging one student in dialogue.

Principle: The teacher asks students to jot down their thoughts while she is engaging in Socratic dialogue with other students.

Comments:
[During a Socratic dialogue, a teacher uses] a variety of techniques with the potential to engage many students at many levels. But inevitably, many students have not participated in the dialogue; some, overwhelmed by the relief that they were not the one called on, have not even listened attentively. To ensure that her observers are learning, [a teacher] may want to incorporate other methods into her repertoire. By asking students to jot down their thoughts (and not just take notes), she may ensure that every student is actively participating and thinking. These jottings might then provide a basis for discussion, perhaps encouraging those who rarely speak to do so. Students might also bring written responses to class where they could share them in pairs or small groups. [Davis/Steinglass at 275.]

(3)   Use variations on the Socratic dialogue and casebook method.

Principle: The teacher uses variations on the Socratic dialogue and case method.

Comments:
[If law teachers do not replace the Socratic dialogue and case method entirely with discussion and context-based instruction, they should consider using variations on the Socratic dialogue and casebook method. Some law teachers have developed innovative and creative techniques that make the case method come alive for students. Other teachers have extended considerable energy on breaking down the

ambiguous term "to think like a lawyer" into concrete objectives such as teaching how to read a complicated statute.

Judith Wegner observed law teachers who incorporated variations into the traditional use of the Socratic dialogue and case method that seemed to produce more engaging and educationally effective classes.

> Taken individually, these variations demonstrate the flexibility inherent in the case-dialogue method, a flexibility whose potential is infrequently realized. Taken together, they reveal the flexibility and the limitations of the case-dialogue method, the importance of teachers' backgrounds and values in shaping their instructional choices, and the powerful ways in which characteristics and expectations of students can shape the learning that takes place.[632]

Wegner described three variations that she thought were particularly effective. The first variation "involves an intensified focus on the needs of diverse learners, evidenced by professors' conscious use of a wider range of instructional materials, expanded forms of classroom dialogue, and explicit efforts to make the thinking process visible to all concerned."[633] Wegner reported that many of the teachers she observed "seem to foster learning throughout the class by endeavoring to draw a substantial portion of the class into active participation."[634]

> Sometimes, for example, classes are asked to engage in collective brainstorming, generating lists of possible questions or possible meanings for the term "mistake" in order to ground the group's understanding in their shared and diverse experience, and warm up for further interaction with lower stakes and a lesser sense of threat. Faculty members may compliment or thank students for their mistakes in recitation, observing in subsequent interviews that it's harder to teach to the class as a whole if they receive quick, correct answers, than if they can see and work with students' potential misunderstandings. In other classes, the traditional roles of faculty and students may be reversed at least at times, with students actively asking a multitude of questions and faculty building on these questions to illuminate difficult points. All of these forms of expanded or reconfigured dialogue appear geared to engaging students actively in the process of comprehension and analysis. They stand in sharp contrast to the alternative that is also well-represented across the range of schools in classes in which the professor continues to use more traditional Socratic questioning that focuses at length on a single student, but shifts into more extended lectures if a series of students displays limited comprehension, preparation, or analytical skill.[635]

The second variation "involves the introduction of imaginative instructional techniques that build on principles previously discussed in order to ask more of

---

[632] Wegner, Theory and Practice, *supra* note 46, at 34.

[633] *Id.*

[634] *Id.* at 37.

[635] *Id.*

and draw more from students as they envision their responsibilities in full-fledged professional roles."[636] These teachers "stretch their students' horizons by causing them to imagine themselves in significant professional roles."[637]

> In important ways, learning is thus "situated" in a demanding context that requires students to ask a good deal of themselves either on an occasional or recurring basis . . . . While attention continues to be paid to important intellectual tasks such as analysis and synthesis, students seem especially engaged, suggesting that instructional tactics such as these may hold larger lessons from which more faculty learn.[638]

The final variation "concerns some faculty members' deliberate efforts to stretch the perimeter of the traditional case-dialogue method by integrating additional disciplinary, professional, and social perspectives into traditional intellectual tasks."[639] These teachers endeavored "to address not only 'legal reasoning' but also other central aspects of 'thinking like a lawyer' – the roles of lawyers and the broader intellectual world of law. . . ."[640] The teachers talked explicitly about what lawyers do and important questions about professional norms.

Although she noted that few professors have the experience and interest to focus students' attention on professional roles and that casebooks often lack the kind of materials that would provide a meaningful context for discussion of professional roles, Wegner also recognized the vital importance of having such discussions.

> Students are often unformed in their understanding of lawyers and the law and may not know their own goals or possibilities implicit in new roles, yet become set in their impressions and attitudes very early. In the absence of other leavening influences, they may conclude, based on their first year experience, that lawyers are two-dimensional beings whose values, responsibilities, and struggles are not worth knowing about since they are invisible from view.[641]

We encourage teachers who employ Socratic dialogue to use the variations described by Wegner.]

(4)   Use other methods of instruction to complement Socratic dialogue.

Principle: **The teacher uses small group discussions, on-line discussions, roleplaying, in-class discussions of problems, and other methods of instruction in addition to Socratic dialogue.**

Comments:
[A teacher] might also use what are called "break-out groups," organizing her classes to include small group discussions in which students can speak more

---

[636] *Id.* at 34.
[637] *Id.* at 38.
[638] *Id.*
[639] *Id.* at 34.
[640] *Id.* at 45.
[641] *Id.* at 47.

comfortably and develop ideas that can then be discussed in the larger group. [Davis/Steinglass at 275.]

[A teacher] might also experiment with the use of on-line discussions. . . . [O]n-line formats elicit different kinds of discussions than classroom contexts. On-line discussions appeal to a broader group of students: students who are wary of speaking in public or of speaking extemporaneously are often more comfortable sharing ideas that they have composed in private and at their leisure. We have also found that on-line discussions allow us to address a broader range of subject matter than can be addressed in time-limited classes. [Davis/Steinglass at 275.]

[A teacher] might also foster a wider-ranging class discussion, and the development of a greater range of capacities, by asking students to analyze cases in role. By looking at cases from the perspectives of the parties, of their lawyers, of other individuals who might be involved or might be in similar situations in the future, and of the appellate court, students are more likely to grasp the significance – and learn the techniques – of interpretive, interactive, narrative, and problem-solving work. [Davis/Steinglass at 275.]

[A teacher] might also choose to develop [a greater range of] capacities by assigning problems, such as those commonly used in evidence courses. [Davis/Steinglass at 275.]

[Although Davis and Steinglass suggest that law teachers should add simulation and clinical teaching to their repertoire] "outside the constraints of a large, lecture class" [Davis/Steinglass at 276], [we encourage the use of simulations in large enrollment classes. The scope of the simulations and whether to have students participate in them during class or outside of class will depend on the educational goals of the course and the purposes of the simulations. However, simulations in which students assume the roles of lawyers, parties, witnesses, or judges can be designed for any size course without significantly affecting other classroom activities.

A teacher might also have students experience real life situations related to subjects being studied in the course. This was not among the suggestions made by Davis and Steinglass, but exposure to actual law practice can benefit students in ways that cannot be duplicated by other methods of instruction. Exposure to real life situations can range from something as simple as requiring students to observe judicial or administrative proceedings related to the subject of the course to something as complex as coordinating a course with an in-house clinic in which students assume responsibility for providing legal services to clients.]

Conclusion

[When a law teacher chooses to use the Socratic dialogue method of instruction, she should ensure that she is skilled in its use, she should demystify the process as much as possible by explaining its goals and techniques, she should not intentionally humiliate students, and she should not rely exclusively on the Socratic dialogue and case method of instruction.]

B.   Discussion.

1.   Introduction to Discussion.

Discussion is a technique used to some extent by all law school teachers, even in courses currently dominated by the Socratic dialogue and case method. We believe it should be used more often.

Discussion is a non-hierarchical technique, unlike Socratic dialogue and lecture. Students' opinions, ideas, and experiences are valued as well as their understanding of assigned readings. Discussion features "two-way spoken communication between students and teacher and direct interaction among students themselves."[642]

Some of the positive attributes of discussion were described by Lynn Daggett:[643]
- it provides an active learning role for students.
    Research shows that students learn more and retain learned information longer when their role in the learning process is active. Discussion provides a more active role for more students than lecture, in which the student role is passive, and Socratic teaching (in which only one student at a time may have an active role).

- it encourages students to listen and to learn from each other.

- it involves high level thinking, perhaps like Socratic teaching and unlike lecture.

- it exposes students to viewpoints other than their own.

- it helps students develop oral advocacy and other skills.

- it makes learning less teacher centered and more student centered.

- it provides feedback to the teacher about the level of student learning.
    During a lecture, the teacher must rely on student questions and nonverbal cues to determine if the lecture is effective. During a Socratic dialogue, the teacher tacitly assumes that the knowledge and skill displayed by the student being questioned is representative of the class. In contrast in discussion, because a wide variety of students participate, and because of the opportunities for the teacher to probe responses, the teacher gets substantial feedback about levels of student performance.

- it gives students a chance to bring their opinions and feelings to the study of law.

---

[642] HESS & FRIEDLAND, *supra* note 304, at 55.

[643] Lynn Daggett, *Using Discussion as a Teaching Method in Law School Classes, in* THE SCIENCE AND ART OF LAW TEACHING: CONFERENCE MATERIALS (1995).

Discussion gives students a chance to explore and air their affective responses to the law. Teacher feedback during discussion can help students to integrate their affective and cognitive responses to the material.

• it teaches the teacher.

For all its merits, however, discussion involves risks that require skill and planning to avoid. For example, a teacher can lose control of the class or get sidetracked or bogged down. Sometimes, the teacher's efforts to provoke discussion may be met with silence or produce poor quality discussion, and discussions can become unstructured if not carefully planned and guided.[644] Therefore, careful preparation and thoughtful execution are required for effective use of discussion.

2. Best Practices for Discussion.

This section contains a preliminary description of best practices for using discussion as a teaching method.[645]

a. Use discussion for appropriate purposes.

Principle: The teacher uses discussion to achieve clearly articulated educational goals more effectively and efficiently than other methods of instruction could achieve.

Comments:
Discussion is a good method for engaging students and helping them learn a subject more deeply. Discussions help students "to retain information at the end of the course, to develop problem-solving and thinking skills, to change attitudes, and to motivate additional learning about a subject."[646]

Discussion not only helps students develop cognitive abilities, it has benefits in the affective domain as well. Through effective discussions, students are exposed to diverse viewpoints, which helps students develop values and change attitudes. In addition, for many students, discussion makes learning more interesting and increases their motivation to work harder to learn more.[647]

As mentioned in the section on the Socratic dialogue and case method, educational theory suggests that discussion is a more effective method than Socratic dialogue for helping students acquire and retain new knowledge and understanding.

---

[644] The potential problems with discussion are described in more detail in *id.* at 4-8, and HESS & FRIEDLAND, *supra* note 304, at 56.

[645] The principles in this section are drawn from Daggett, *supra* note 643, at 4-8, and HESS & FRIEDLAND, *id.* The Hess & Friedland book also describes some specific discussion techniques, beginning on page 64.

[646] HESS & FRIEDLAND, *supra* note 304, at 55.

[647] *Id.* at 55-56.

b.   **Ask effective questions.**

Principle: **The teacher asks effective questions.**

Comments:
   Questions should be clear. Questions should be open-ended, not calling for yes or no answers. Questions should be asked one at a time. Various types of questions should be used. Teachers should consider giving students questions in advance and asking them to prepare to discuss them in an upcoming class.

   Perhaps the most important attribute of an effective questioner is patience. After asking the question, the teacher needs to be silent and wait for students to process the question and formulate responses. Research reveals that most teachers wait less than one second after asking the question before answering it themselves, rephrasing the question, or calling on a student. However, research shows that if the teacher waits three to five seconds after the question is posed, more students will respond, the complexity of the responses will increase, and more students will ask questions. One way teachers can increase the "wait time" and make the silence less uncomfortable is to tell students to jot down notes of their responses and questions before taking oral responses.[648]

c.   **Encourage students to ask questions.**

Principle: **The teacher encourages students to ask thoughtful questions.**

Comments:
   Teachers should encourage students to ask thoughtful questions. Teachers can facilitate student questions by expressly asking for questions, by giving students sufficient time to formulate thoughtful questions, and by giving positive reinforcement to students who ask good questions.

   When answering student questions, teachers can shape the discussion and create an environment that encourages student participation. Make sure the class can hear the question. If necessary, have the student, rather than the teacher, repeat the question so that students learn to listen to one another, not only to the teacher. Either the teacher or another student should answer the student's question directly – when students do not get direct answers, they quit asking questions. When the teacher is responding, talk to the entire class so that all students feel part of the conversation. Finally, check back with the student to see whether the question was addressed adequately.[649]

---

[648] *Id.* at 60-61.

[649] *Id.* at 62 (they also give some advice for handing troublesome questions).

d.   Maintain a somewhat democratic classroom.

Principle: **The teacher maintains a somewhat democratic classroom.**

Comments:
"Classes where the teacher keeps all the power to herself are unlikely to be good ones for discussion. Students are unlikely to take the risk of speaking candidly in classes where the teacher is authoritarian."[650]

e.   Validate student participation.

Principle: **The teacher validates students' efforts to join the discussion and praises students when it is deserved.**

Comments:
"Give positive reinforcement for appropriate responses. If at all possible, find some positive aspect of the student's comment. Memorialize the contribution. Refer to the comment by the student's name ("Mary's idea" or "John's theory"). Acknowledge new ideas ("Gee, I never thought of that before. I appreciate the new way of looking at this problem.")."[651]

f.   Use caution in responding to students' errors.

Principle: The teacher uses care in responding to wrong information in student comments.

Comments:
"Students should not be left with the wrong impression, but the teacher also should not exacerbate the loss of face for the student whose comment includes something inaccurate. Find something worthwhile and positive in what was said, and praise the student for that at the same time you correct the wrong part."[652]

"Handle 'wrong' answers tactfully. Focus on the answer not the student. See if the mistake is common to other students. Demonstrate that it is acceptable to make mistakes in the classroom because mistakes can lead to learning. Admit your own mistakes."[653]

g.   Keep your views to yourself.

Principle: **The teacher keeps her views to herself at the beginning of the discussion of a topic.**

Comments:
At least until the students have a chance to express their views without being influenced by the teacher's views. "Limit your own comments. Teachers need not respond to every student contribution. Otherwise the focus of the discussion rests on the teacher."[654]

---

[650] Daggett, *supra* note 643, at 14-16.
[651] HESS & FRIEDLAND, *supra* note 304, at 62.
[652] Daggett, *supra* note 643, at 14-16.
[653] HESS & FRIEDLAND, *supra* note 304, at 62.
[654] *Id.*

h.   **Do not talk too much or allow the discussion to go on too long.**

Principle: **The teacher does not talk too much or let the discussion go on too long.**

Comments:
"Inexperienced discussion leaders tend to make two mistakes: talking too much themselves or letting the discussion go on too long."[655]

i.   **Announce when the discussion is about to end.**

Principle: **The teacher announces when the discussion is about to end.**

Comments:
"When ready to close the discussion, the teacher announces that it is about to end so that students can make final comments. Then the teacher can provide closure to the discussion by summarizing key points, comparing student ideas to the ones the teacher prepared before class, referring students to material that is on point for the key ideas discussed, and giving students a bit of time to add to their notes."[656]

j.   **Establish an environment conducive to discussion.**

Principle: **The teacher establishes an environment conducive to discussion.**

Comments:
If students feel intimidated or do not believe their views will be respected, they will not participate meaningfully in discussions.

> Teachers need to establish a social environment conducive to discussion and rapport with their students to facilitate student participation. Teacher behavior that promotes rapport with students includes demonstrating an interest in each student and each student's learning, encouraging students to share their thoughts about class assignments or policy, and encouraging students to ask questions and to express personal views. Perhaps the single most important step that a teacher can take to improve the classroom environment is to learn the students' names.[657]

k.   **Give students time to reflect on the questions being discussed.**

Principle: **The teacher gives students time to reflect on the questions being discussed.**

Comments:
Not all learners process information the same way. Some

---

[655] Daggett, *supra* note 643, at 21.

[656] HESS & FRIEDLAND, *supra* note 304, at 62.

[657] *Id.* at 57 (some techniques for learning students' names are included in the book).

learners process information visually; some orally. Some think best by talking through a concept; others through hands on activities. Some learners think well on their feet; others need time to reflect on issue before discussing it.

Provide the class with the next discussion question at the end of the previous class. This allows reflective learners to digest the topic so they can effectively participate in the discussion. As a bonus, giving all students time to reflect often raises the level of the discussion.[658]

C.   Lecture.

1.   Introduction to Lecture.

If we can avoid lecturing students, we should. "One of the most common mistakes by lecturers is to use the lecture method at all."[659] Unfortunately, lectures are an indispensable and unavoidable part of any academic enterprise. Lectures are where we explain things to students.

Lectures do not have to be boring or ineffective. Lectures are the primary method of law school instruction in countries other than the United States. In some countries, lecture is used for economic reasons. Lecturing hundreds of students in large lecture halls is the only way for students to acquire information about the law. Printed course materials are not available; therefore, students create their own study materials by writing down what teachers read to them. Students who are able to gain access to published materials need not attend lectures. The roll is not taken, and the faculty neither call on students to answer questions nor try to engage students in a discussion of the subjects being studied.

Even in some countries with above average resources where students are able to acquire course materials, the lecture method is the traditional and preferred method of instruction. As expressed by Eckart Klein:

> In Germany, in contrast to the United States, law professors use the systemic presentation of material. This method which developed during the medieval period, involves lectures by the faculty.
>
> . . . .
>
> Even though the external realities mentioned above [the unfavorable student-teacher ratio and the exclusive focus on teaching theoretical, not practical, aspects of law] in the university encourage German law teachers to present material in a systematic fashion, most German law professors would be inclined to present the material in this way whether or not the external pressures existed.[660]

---

[658] Daggett, *supra* note 643, at 17.

[659] BLIGH, *supra* note 389, at 148.

[660] Eckart Klein, *Legal Education in Germany*, 72 OR. L. REV. 953, 953 (1993).

The strengths of the lecture method when it is properly utilized were described by Clive Walker as follows:

> [A] good lecture will do more than paraphrase a textbook. It can provide a helpful updating service on the latest cases and developments. In some cases the lecturer may be a leading researcher in the subject and therefore be able to impart expert insights and information not yet available in the books. . . . The lecturer may choose to put forward challenging views or criticisms which stimulate more debate than the private study of books is likely to achieve.[661]

Nigel Savage, however, points out that students in lecture halls are usually passive learners, and the large sizes of the audiences and lecture halls make it difficult to engage in any dialogue.[662] There is no data available about the effectiveness of the average lecturer, but the norm seems to be that most do little more than dictate from their notes to the students, and there is almost no opportunity for contact between students and lecturers.[663]

In some countries, lectures are supplemented by tutorials in which relatively small groups of students meet to discuss legal issues with a member of the faculty, most notably in England and Wales.[664] This is the exception, however, not the rule.

We recommend limiting the use of lecture because of its passive learning nature. To the extent that lectures are unavoidable, however, we should use best practices for lecturing.

2.   Best Practices for Lecture.

This section provides a few tips on best practices for using lectures, though one must keep in mind that effective lecturing is as much an art as any other form of teaching. "Except on obvious points, such as the need to face the class, to be audible and to avoid irritating mannerisms, there are few rules to lecturing."[665]

a.   Use lecture for appropriate purposes.

Principle: The teacher uses lecture for appropriate purposes.

Comments:
Lectures should be used to elaborate on the assigned material, give examples, or help put the material into context.[666] "Also, because texts often lag behind current

---

[661] Clive Walker, *Legal Education in England and Wales*, 72 OR. L. REV. 943, 946 (1993).

[662] Nigel Savage, *The System in England and Wales*, 43 S. TEX. L. REV. 597 (2002).

[663] *See, e.g.*, Joanne Felder, *Legal Education in South Africa*, 72 OR. L. REV. 999, 1002 (1993) (reporting that "lecturers [in South Africa] stand in front of groups ranging from 40 to 250 (depending on the law school) and dictate. There is thus almost no opportunity for contact between students and lecturers").

[664] *See* Walker, *supra* note 661, at 947.

[665] BLIGH, *supra* note 389.

[666] Florida State University, *Lecturing Effectively, in* INSTRUCTION AT FSU: A GUIDE TO TEACHING AND LEARNING PRACTICES 7-1 (2005) [hereinafter *Lecturing Effectively*], *available at* http://online.fsu.edu/learningresources/handbook/instructionatfsu/PDF-Chptr7.pdf.

knowledge, lectures are valuable methods for presenting new information."[667] Lectures are also good for quickly giving students specific information or facts.[668]

Donald Bligh concluded that while lecture is as effective as any other method for transmitting information, but not more effective than some, it is not as effective as more active methods for promoting thought, changing students' attitudes, or teaching behavioral skills.[669]

b. Limit the length of lectures.

Principle: The teacher limits the length of lectures.

Comments:
"[R]esearch has shown that after 10 to 20 minutes of continuous lecture, assimilation falls off rapidly."[670]

c. Do not read the text.

Principle: The teacher does not read the text.

Comments:
Too many professors make the mistake of lecturing the text, that is, they read the important parts of the text to the students.[671] This discourages students from reading the material themselves because they know the professor will give them the information they need in class.[672]

d. Organize the lecture.

Principle: The teacher organizes the lecture.

Comments:
Prepare a loose outline or notes for yourself, using the "tell them what you going to tell them, tell them, and tell them what you told them" format, and also prepare a brief outline of the lecture for the students to follow.[673] Make sure to emphasize and repeat key points and be able to link them to each other so that students can assimilate the items in their own minds.[674]

---

[667] *Id.*

[668] Grayson H. Walker Teaching Resource Center, University of Tennessee at Chattanooga, *Lecturing with Style!* [hereinafter Walker Center], http://www.utc.edu/Administration/WalkerTeachingResourceCenter/FacultyDevelopment/Lecture/index.html.

[669] BLIGH, *supra* note 389, at 3.

[670] Drummond, *supra* note 143.

[671] *Lecturing Effectively, supra* note 666, at 7-1.

[672] *Id.*

[673] Teaching Resources Office (TRACE), University of Waterloo, *Lecturing Effectively in the University Classroom*, http://www.adm.uwaterloo.ca/infotrac/tips/lecturingeffectively.pdf (last visited June 1, 2005).

[674] *Id.*

e. Employ effective delivery techniques.

Principle: The teacher employs effective delivery techniques.

Comments:

Be enthusiastic, speak loudly and clearly so that everyone can hear, vary your tone of voice, and maintain eye contact with the audience.[675] When possible, lecture by storytelling as this actively draws students into the material. Another benefit of storytelling is that because interest in the subject is piqued and the students are more personally involved, they can listen longer and the 10 to 20 minute rule does not apply.[676]

f. Use other techniques in conjunction with lecture.

Principle: The teacher does not rely on lecture alone.

Comments:

"The idea that lecturers should use the lecture method and no other for fifty minutes on end is absurd . . . ."[677] "[T]he inherent defects of the lecture method mean that, on its own, it is rarely adequate. Therefore, if not replaced, it will need to be combined with other methods in some way."[678]

g. Have reasonable expectations.

Principle: The teacher has reasonable expectations.

Comments:

Remember that the "less is more" mentality is especially true for lecturing.[679] Do not try to present too much information as most of it will be "lost in translation." "Unless the learner can encode the information in a rich context with good examples and reasons for remembering it, the information won't stay in memory very long."[680] It is more important to make sure students are learning the material than to "cover ground."

One suspects that law teachers in the United States lecture more than we care to admit. If so, this is all the more reason to use best practices whenever we decide that using lecture is the most effective way to teach our students.

---

[675] Walker Center, *supra* note 668.

[676] Drummond, *supra* note 143.

[677] BLIGH, *supra* note 389, at 70.

[678] *Id.* at 252.

[679] *Lecturing Effectively, supra* note 666, at 7-1.

[680] *Id.*

Chapter Seven
Best Practices for Assessing Student Learning

A.   The Importance and Purposes of Assessments.

Grades are important in law school, particularly for first year students. After one semester, grades determine which students are eligible for Law Review, Moot Court, and other significant opportunities in law school, which students are most likely to pass the bar examination, and which students will compete for the most highly compensated jobs. Students who fare most poorly are forced to leave law school, and they lose their opportunity to become lawyers. These are high stakes.

The main purpose of assessments in educational institutions is to discover if students have achieved the learning outcomes of the course studied.[681] In other words, we use assessments to find out whether students are learning what we want them to learn.

In law schools, as in medical schools, one purpose of assessment is to determine which students should receive degrees, but other purposes of assessment are more important.

> Aside from the need to protect the public by denying graduation to those few trainees who are not expected to overcome their deficiencies, the outcomes of assessment should be to foster learning, inspire confidence in the learner, enhance the learner's ability to self-monitor, and drive institutional self-assessment and curricular change.[682]

An institution's decisions about what and how it assesses student learning reflect the values of the institution.

> Assessment is also a statement of institutional values. Devoting valuable curricular time to peer assessment of professionalism, for example, can promote those values that are assessed while encouraging curricular coherence and faculty development, especially if there are corresponding efforts at the institution toward self-assessment and change.[683]

The goals and methods we select for assessment directly affect student learning. "Assessment methods and requirements probably have a greater influence on how and what students learn than any other single factor. This influence may well be of greater importance than the impact of teaching materials."[684]

---

[681] ALISON BONE, NATIONAL CENTRE FOR LEGAL EDUCATION, ENSURING SUCCESSFUL ASSESSMENT 3 (Roger Burridge & Tracey Varnava eds., 1999), *available at* http://www.ukcle.ac.uk/resources/assessment/bone.pdf (last visited April 27, 2006).

[682] Epstein & Hundert, *supra* note 150, at 226.

[683] *Id.* at 231.

[684] BONE, *supra* note 681, at 2.

[C]hanging the assessment procedure is one of the most effective ways of changing how and what students learn. Surface approaches are induced by excessive workloads, a narrow band of assessment techniques and undue emphasis upon knowledge reproduction. Deep approaches are influenced by choice, a variety of assessment methods, project work and an emphasis upon tasks that demand demonstration of understanding.[685]

Thus, legal educators should consider carefully what we are trying to assess and how we are doing it.

B.   The Shortcomings of Current Assessment Practices in the United States.

In the traditional law school course, especially in the all important first year, the only evaluation of how well a student is learning, and the entire basis for the student's grade for the course, is a three hour end-of-the-semester essay exam that requires students to apply memorized legal principles to hypothetical fact patterns. The practice of basing the assessment of student learning on a single test was initiated in the early 1870's at Harvard Law School by Dean Christopher Langdell.[686] Prior to that date, other American law schools relied upon frequent oral quizzes, evaluation of moot court performances, and, in jurisdictions that accorded graduates of local law schools diploma privileges, comprehensive written examinations requiring descriptive essays on relevant points of law.[687] American law schools quickly copied the Harvard way and "by the end of the nineteenth century, the use of single exams to assess student performance had become widespread among American law schools."[688] The single exam tradition remains with us today, despite long-standing criticisms from academics, practitioners, and students.[689]

The primary reason to administer assessments is to find out whether our students are learning what we want them to learn. Judith Wegner's study of legal education determined that the current grading practices of legal educators in the United States function less as a means for measuring student learning than as a means for sorting and ranking students and for "weeding out" students who are not

---

[685] *Id.* at 4.

[686] Aizen, *supra* note 313, at 768-69 (citing Steven Friedland, *A Critical Inquiry into the Traditional Uses of Law School Evaluation*, 23 PACE L. REV. 147 (2002); Steve Sheppard, *An Informal History of How Law Schools Evaluate Students, With a Predictable Emphasis on Law School Final Exams*, 65 UMKC L. REV. 657 (1997); John J. Costonis, *The MacCrate Report: Of Loaves, Fishes, and the Future of American Legal Education*, 43 J. LEGAL EDUC. 157 (1993); Russell L. Weaver, *Langdell's Legacy: Living with the Case Method*, 36 VILL. L. REV. 517 (1991)).

[687] Sheppard, *supra* note 686.

[688] Aizen, *supra* note 313, at 768-69.

[689] For a collection of scholarship documenting the dissatisfaction with the single exam practice and supporting an increase in the number, variety, and quality of law school assessments, see *id* at 769 nn.19 & 20. Recommendation 6 of the ABA's Task Force on Lawyer Competency was that "[l]aw schools and law teachers should develop and use more comprehensive methods of measuring law student performance than the typical end-of-the-term examination. Students should be given detailed critiques of their performance." CRAMTON REPORT, *supra* note 275, at 4.

developing the requisite knowledge, skills, and values to pass a bar examination.[690] She concluded that our emphasis on using assessments as a sorting device impedes the effectiveness of our educational efforts. "Since the point of law school is to foster learning and to develop learning habits such as professionals need, the cost of confounding learning in order to engage in incessant sorting seems very large indeed."[691]

The Carnegie Foundation's study of legal education discovered that current first year assessment practices have harmful effects on students' motivation and opinions of law school.

> Students' comments about assessment in their first year of law school often expressed puzzlement, frustration, and anguish. A recurring theme in their comments, striking in its frequency, was that they were not being tested on what they studied for and what they knew. Many felt that the testing was unfair, counterproductive, demoralizing, and arbitrary. Students saw little or no relation between their classroom experience and the end-of-the-semester examinations, or between learning to be a good lawyer and doing well on exams – a criticism that has been leveled at the cognitive apprenticeship in many professional and graduate schools. As our earlier chapters showed, law schools' heavy emphasis upon academic training, in contrast to the education in settings of practice typical of preparation for the health professions, heightens the likelihood of a disparity between learning to be a law student and learning to be a lawyer.

> A number of students complained that the quality and quantity of their studying was unrelated to their performance on the final examination. They claim to have had little feedback during the semester and no basis on which to gauge whether they were mastering the material or making adequate progress toward the desired proficiencies.[692]

The scaled grading system allows law schools to sort students for legal employers, but it impedes learning, community building, and moral development.

> The current scaled grading system in most law schools, which is based solely upon comparison to and competition with other students, is not a system designed to promote either community or the broader ideal of justice. It is a prime example of the hierarchical systems Mary Rose O'Reilly places on moral notice . . . . It is entirely individual-focused and rights based. It is judgmental and exclusive rather than compassionate and inclusive. It is essentially designed to rank students in an important but limited area of legal skills (while ignoring other important indices of qualifications as a lawyer) for the convenience of firms who are in the job market. If it has a

---

[690] Wegner, Assessment, *supra* note 24, at 19-22 and 34. We are only somewhat successful in preparing students for bar examinations, given that only 50% to 80% of law school graduates pass a state bar examination on their first attempt.

[691] *Id.* at 33.

[692] SULLIVAN ET AL., *supra* note 7, at 206.

pedagogical purpose, it is only to spur students to study for grades in competition with their fellow students, a "benefit" which is lost on many students after the first year when they see where they stand in the class and give up on trying to rise any higher. The competitive grading system is a primary instrument separating students from faculty in law schools and separating students from other students. It is a central impediment to construction of an effective law school community.[693]

Despite its long history as a part of legal education, the end-of-the-semester essay exam is an inadequate method for assessing student learning, and fundamental aspects of our current practice are significantly flawed. As Sandy D'Alemberte put it, "Is there any educational theorist who would endorse a program that has students take a class for a full semester or a full year and get a single examination at the end? People who conduct that kind of educational program are not trying to educate."[694]

As currently used, the end-of-the-semester essay exam is neither valid, nor reliable, nor fair. The problems with our current practice were summarized by Judith Wegner as follows:

> In sum, the current assessment system has a number of significant costs worth reconsidering: compromised efficacy that results from conflating sorting students and evaluating learning; perpetuation of past advantages and disadvantages in unintentional ways; confusion that impedes learning; and deployment of faculty time in relatively ineffective ways. In light of these costs, it is worth endeavoring to develop new systems of assessment deliberately designed to foster learning.[695]

Most of the preceding comments relate to assessment practices in traditional doctrinal courses. Unfortunately, current assessment practices are also flawed in experiential education courses such as simulation-based courses, in-house clinics, and externships.

In simulation-based courses, the primary and sometimes sole method of assessment is for a single teacher to observe a student performing a limited number of lawyering tasks. Sometimes, self- or peer-evaluation is also used. Frequently, students are given a grade on every performance, often without any opportunity to receive formative feedback before the summative assessment and without any opportunity to continue practicing until the appropriate level of proficiency is achieved. For that matter, almost no effort has been made to describe appropriate levels of proficiency.

In many in-house clinics and externships, grades are based mostly on the subjective opinion of one teacher who supervises the students' work. Grades in these courses tend to reflect an appraisal of students' overall performance as lawyers, not necessarily what they learned or how their abilities developed during the course. When written criteria are given to students, they tend to be checklists that cover the

---

[693] BENNETT, *supra* note 70, at 170.
[694] D'Alemberte, *supra* note 14, at 52.
[695] Wegner, Assessment, *supra* note 24, at 33.

entire spectrum of lawyering activities without any descriptions of different levels of proficiency.[696]

Virtually no experiential education courses give written tests or otherwise try to find out if students are acquiring the knowledge and understandings that the courses purport to teach. Items that could be clearly subjected to more objective testing include students' understanding of theories of practice or particular aspects of law, procedure, ethics, and professionalism. A students' understanding of many aspects of law practice as well as his or her lifelong learning skills could also be assessed, for example, by asking students to analyze recordings or transcripts of lawyers' performances. Serious efforts to assess student learning in experiential learning courses are not being made on any large scale.

In sum, except perhaps in legal writing and research courses, the current assessment practices used by most law teachers are abominable. We share Judith Wegner's conclusion that "[a] better assessment system would find ways to stimulate student reflection on future professional paths, strengths and weaknesses and guide students toward relevant learning opportunities; provide incentives that lead students to take more active responsibility for their own learning as they undertake increasingly sophisticated work throughout students' law school careers; and document information that would attest to graduates' professional capabilities while assisting employers in making efficient and informed hiring decisions."[697]

Legal educators in the United States "need to clarify the purposes of grading systems, reconsider practices that perpetuate advantages and disadvantages associated with high-stakes testing early in students' law school careers, find ways to stimulate rather than skew student learning and reallocate faculty time spent on semester-end grading to better use."[698]

C.   Best Practices for Assessing Student Learning.

Effective assessment exhibits qualities of validity, reliability, and fairness.[699] Validity means that an assessment tool must accomplish the purpose for which it was intended. Reliability means the test or measuring procedure yields the same results on repeated trials. A single do-or-die final essay exam given under time pressure at the end of the semester fails all three criteria.[700] It is neither valid, nor reliable, nor fair.

The best practices described in this section reflect recommendations for improving assessment practices arising from the work of numerous scholars, including Judith Wegner's study of legal education for the Carnegie Foundation for the Advancement of Teaching. They incorporate the five key principles that Wegner believes should influence the design process of an improved assessment system:

---

[696] *See, e.g.,* Appendix A and B in Stacy L. Brustin & David F. Chavkin, *Testing the Grades: Evaluating Grading Models in Clinical Legal Education*, 3 CLINICAL L. REV. 299 (1997).

[697] Wegner, Assessment, *supra* note 24, at 63.

[698] *Id.* at 30.

[699] MICHAEL JOSEPHSON, LEARNING AND EVALUATION IN LAW SCHOOL 7 (1984).

[700] Gregory S. Munro, *How Do We Know If We Are Achieving Our Goals?: Strategies for Assessing the Outcome of Curricular Innovation, in* ERASING LINES, *supra* note 38, at 229, 237.

- learning is the point,
- learning must be made visible in order to be assessed,
- learning is multifaceted and develops over time,
- assessment must reflect the particular purposes being served (such as evaluating, educating, assuring quality, conferring distinction, and documenting professional capability), and
- assessment occurs in context.[701]

The principles described in this section are only the beginning of the work that is needed to improve assessments in law schools. Experimentation with new methods of assessment will reveal the need to modify and add to the principles and proposals set forth below.

1.   Be Clear About Goals of Each Assessment.

Principle: **The teachers are clear about the goals of each assessment.**

Comments:
It is important to know what we are trying to evaluate. The goals of a particular assessment may be to evaluate a student's knowledge, behavior (what a student does before and after a learning experience), performance (ability to perform a task), attitudes and values, or a combination of these.

> *Cognitive assessment* means assessment of learning or knowledge.[702] For example, this could entail assessment of whether a student in Property has acquired the applicable knowledge of the substantive law. This is different from assessment of behavioral change and performance,[703] which is characterized by the student's ability to use knowledge.[704]

> *Behavioral assessment* measures change in what a student does before and after a course of learning.[705] "This 'observation' is made concerning an event in the student's life which is not regulated, contrived, or designed for the purposes of assessment or grading."[706] An example would be examining whether students who studied attorney engagement agreements in their professional skills and contracts courses later recorded in the file and warned clients of the statute of limitations during their clinical internships.

> *Performance assessment* measures the student's ability in a task that the student is asked to perform for the purposes of the assessment (for example, having the student find the errors in a civil complaint).[707]

---

[701] Wegner, Assessment, *supra* note 24, at 55.
[702] NICHOLS, *supra* note 111, at 37.
[703] *Id.* at 42.
[704] *Id.* at 37.
[705] *Id.* at 42.
[706] *Id.*
[707] *Id.* at 43.

Attitudinal assessment can measure differences in students' attitudes before and after a course of learning.[708] For instance, we can measure change in student attitude after a Professional Responsibility course. Law schools may want to know the attitude of incoming students on a host of issues or their perception about the law school or its programs. As student education progresses, the faculty may wish to know how particular parts of the program change student attitudes. On graduation, exit interviews may reveal attitudes the student has about her legal education, social issues, or moral issues. Finally, attitudes of practitioners toward the law school or any other relevant issues might be measured.[709]

2.   Assess Whether Students Learn What is Taught (validity).

Principle: **The assessment tools used by the teachers evaluate whether students learn what is being taught.**

Comments:

An assessment tool should be valid. An assessment tool is valid if it allows the teacher to draw inferences about the matters that the test purports to assess.[710] Congruence is a necessary aspect of validity, that is, the goals of the test must agree with the goals of the instruction.[711] For example, a professor who seeks to test students' ability to apply and distinguish cases might administer an essay question that raises issues testing the outer limits of a set of precedents. On its face, the exam appears to be a valid test of the skill. If, however, students must take the test in a closed-book setting or without sufficient time to review the relevant authorities while taking the exam, students who have developed the ability to apply and distinguish cases, but possess poor memorization skills, would likely perform poorly. Thus, the exam would not be valid.

The validity issue requires law teachers to consider carefully what law school exams measure. Referring to first year law school and other similar exams, Judith Wegner determined that "law school exams can best be understood as attempts to measure students' law-related problem-solving expertise."[712] Problem-based essay exams require students to perform three principle functions – spotting issues, identifying relevant authorities, and applying legal authorities to complex fact patterns – and on occasion a possible fourth, evaluating competing policies or principles.[713] Wegner concluded that such exams, as are typically used in the first year, "appear forthrightly directed to discerning the existence of student expertise as legal analysts confronted with a problem-solving task."[714]

Although essay exams appear to be a sound way to assess some aspects of problem-solving expertise, the manner in which we use them undermines their effectiveness. Law professors do not clearly explain that the purpose of the essay

---

[708] *Id.* at 44.

[709] Munro, *supra* note 4, at 115-17.

[710] Hess & Friedland, *supra* note 304, at 289. *See also* Smith & Ragan, *supra* note 201, at 95.

[711] Smith & Ragan, *surpa* note 197, at 95.

[712] Wegner, Assessment, *supra* note 24, at 3.

[713] Phillip Kissam, *Law School Examinations*, 42 Vand. L. Rev. 433, 440-42 (1989).

[714] Wegner, Assessment, *supra* note 24, at 9.

exam is to test problem-solving expertise, and most first year courses fail to provide instruction designed to help students develop such expertise.

> [C]lassroom teaching in first-year courses tends to focus primarily on certain intellectual tasks, including comprehension, analysis, application of legal principles to simple fact patterns, synthesis of related cases, and limited forms of "internal" evaluation concerning logic and doctrinal consistency. On the other hand, classes (or reading assignments) give students relatively little opportunity to observe models or experiment with application of law to complex fact patterns, synthesis across broader fields, or evaluation against the backdrop of social concerns. Students carefully observe how *others* (most notably judges) solve problems, but rarely work through how *they* (or the lawyers in key cases) might actually do so themselves. Strikingly, however, strong performance on examination essays requires demonstrated skill in just those matters that are not directly taught.[715]

This pattern of unintentional omission has important implications. It is extremely frustrating to some students and has a negative impact on their self-efficacy and motivation to learn.

> In the view of these students, there is a significant mismatch between what professors say and do in classes and what is tested on exams. Students are not given a chance to practice what will actually be tested, and don't get feedback to gauge how they might do when the day of reckoning arrives. They don't understand how what is tested relates to what is expected of lawyers. The impression is one of enormous frustration, of effort expended to little avail, of talented learners trying their hardest, of profound puzzlement without recourse.[716]

The situation also gives an unfair advantage to students who have strong analytical skills when they begin law school.

> Students who will be most likely to perform well under such circumstances are those who have had prior experience with (and who have internalized approaches to) similar academic tasks, those who are "expertlike" in their approaches at the same time of entry (as many faculty members probably were during their own student days), and those who have well-developed expertise in and self-awareness about learning in some other complex field that was once unknown. Others will not fare as well.[717]

Once the more "expert' students gain the advantage by receiving the highest grades, their expertise continues developing, and it is difficult for their peers to ever catch up.

> Thus, the incongruence between what is taught and what is tested is a serious problem that legal educators should address if they want to claim that law

---

[715] *Id.* at 14.

[716] *Id.* at 6.

[717] *Id.* at 14.

school problem-based essay exams are fair to all students. Ensuring that law school exams test what law professors teach is an issue to consider in all courses, of course, not just those in the first year.

Before each assessment, we should consider what we expect students to learn in our courses and what is important for us to assess. Different assessment methods may be required to assess each of the following educational objectives that we might be trying to achieve:

- self-reflection and life-long learning skills,
- intellectual and analytical skills,
- core knowledge of the law,
- core understanding of the law,
- professionalism, and
- professional skills.

Our most difficult challenge, of course, is to assess the overall level of professional competence that our students possess.

3. Conduct Criteria-Referenced Assessments, Not Norm-Referenced (reliability).

Principle: **The teacher conducts criteria-referenced assessments.**

Comments:

An assessment tool should be reliable, that is, it should accurately rate those who have learned as having learned and those who have not learned as having not learned.[718] It should not matter whether a student is being assessed first or last or whether one teacher or another is conducting the assessment. We join Judith Wegner and other scholars in encouraging law professors to develop and apply explicit grading criteria to minimize the risk of unreliability in assigning grades.[719]

Assessments can be norm-referenced or criteria-referenced. Assessments in the United States tend to be norm-referenced; assessments in the United Kingdom are typically criteria-referenced. Norm-referenced assessments are based on how students perform in relation to other students in a course rather than how well they achieve the educational objectives of the course. Normative assessment is often done to ensure that certain grade curves can be achieved.

Norm-referenced evaluations inform students how their performance relates to other students, but they do not help students understand the degree to which they achieved the educational objectives of the course. This can have a negative effect on student motivation and learning.

> [S]tudents . . . perceive that something different is going on in the current circumstance, and wonder whether the "sorting" process reflects an artificial or arbitrary allocation of rewards. In the absence of a clearly stated explanation of the actual standards to be achieved,

---

[718] SMITH & RAGAN, *supra* note 197, at 97.

[719] *See* N. R. Madhava Menon, *Designing a Simulation-Based Clinical Course: Trial Advocacy, in* A HANDBOOK ON CLINICAL LEGAL EDUCATION 177, 181 (N. R. Madhava Menon ed., 1998) ("Students and evaluators need a clear understanding of the criteria on which performances will be graded.").

it is easy to become frustrated, then angry, wasting energy that might otherwise be invested in meaningful efforts to learn.

Students also powerfully articulate their hunger to link assessment and learning. They want to learn to take exams, and they want feedback so they can improve.[720]

Norm-referenced assessment allows grades to be distributed along a bell curve. We should not be concerned about whether students' performances will be distributed along a normal "bell curve" because one should not expect it to be.[721] Mandatory grade curves are not consistent with best practices for assessing student learning. A bell curve outcome actually reflects a failure of instruction.

What matters is whether students adequately achieve the learning outcomes of the course. Our goal should be to achieve the learning outcomes we establish for our courses, whether those are to learn certain information, understand key concepts, or develop skills to a specified level of proficiency.

[T]he primary goal is to help students learn to think about their own thinking so they can use the standards of the discipline or profession to recognize shortcomings and correct their reasoning as they go. It isn't to rank students. Grading on a curve, therefore, makes no sense in this world. Students must meet certain standards of excellence, and while none of those standards may be absolute, they are not arbitrary either. Grades [should] represent clearly articulated levels of achievement.[722]

Some students will achieve the objectives of our courses faster or easier than other students, but if our teaching is effective and successful, all students should learn what we want them to learn and earn high marks on assessments. If a student is incapable of learning what we are trying to teach, the student should not be allowed to become a lawyer. If a student is capable of learning, but fails to do so, we may want to ask whether the fault is the student's or our own.

We can improve the quality of our assessments by following the approach used in other disciplines of developing and disclosing criteria-referenced assessments. Criteria-referenced assessments rely on detailed, explicit criteria that identify the abilities students should be demonstrating (for example, applying and distinguishing cases) and the bases on which the instructor will distinguish among excellent, good, competent, or incompetent performances.[723] "Ideally, criteria should be subject-based and geared specifically to the assessment to which it relates."[724]

The use of criteria minimizes the risk of unreliability in assigning grades.[725] Criteria-referenced assessment enables teachers to "judge whether certain criteria have been satisfied and normally operates on a pass/fail basis: an example would be

---

[720] Wegner, Assessment, *supra* note 24, at 26.

[721] *Id.* at 30.

[722] BAIN, *supra* note 299, at 160.

[723] Sophie Sparrow, *Describing the Ball: Improve Teaching by Using Rubrics – Explicit Grading Criteria*, 2004 MICH. ST. L. REV. 1, 6-15.

[724] BONE, *supra* note 681, at 11.

[725] *See* Menon, *supra* note 719, at 181.

the driving test. It is not important to establish whether more or less drivers pass this test in any one year (or at any one center) but only to ensure that the national pass standard is maintained."[726] "[T]he implicit pedagogical philosophy underlying criterion-referenced assessment is that the fundamental purpose of professional education is not sorting, but producing as many individuals proficient in legal reasoning and competent practice as possible."[727]

The use of clear criteria helps students understand what is expected of them as well as why they receive the grades they receive. Even more importantly, it increases the reliability of the teacher's assessment by tethering the assessment to explicit criteria rather than the instructor's gestalt sense of the correct answer or performance.[728] The criteria should be explained to students long before the students undergo an assessment. This enhances learning and encourages students to become reflective, empowered, self-regulated learners.[729]

4. Use Assessments to Inform Students of Their Level of Professional Development.

Principle: **The teacher uses assessments to inform students of their level of professional development.**

Comments:

The development of expertise takes time, and there are stages with discernable differences: novice, advanced beginner, competent, proficient, and expert.[730] Therefore, our assessments should communicate to students where their development of professional expertise stands. Defining the level of proficiency that we want law students to achieve at each stage of their professional development is a task that warrants the attention of legal educators.

In communicating with students about their level of expertise in legal analysis, for example, one might want to articulate assessments for students in terms of levels of proficiency, perhaps linked to characteristics of student performance in the following way:

> *Limited proficiency:* overly simplistic, incomplete analysis that misses key issues and fails to use relevant legal rules, facts and policy;

> *Basic competence:* formalistic analysis that recognizes many issues, distinguishes relevant and irrelevant principles, and makes substantial but incomplete use of relevant rules, facts and policy;

> *Intermediate competence:* integrated analysis that addresses nearly all issues, focusing on and developing relevant rules, facts and policy in a meaningful way that reflects conceptual understanding rather than a formulaic approach, and spots but does not work extensively or effectively with issues involving substantial uncertainty or novelty;

---

[726] BONE, *supra* note 681, at 4.

[727] SULLIVAN ET AL., *supra* note 7, at 210-11.

[728] Sparrow, *supra* note 723, at 28-29.

[729] *Id.* at 22-25.

[730] Wegner, Assessment, *supra* note 24, at 11.

Advanced proficiency: demonstrates characteristics of intermediate proficiency, but also considers implications of analysis more fully, brings to bear sound and creative approaches, works extensively and effectively with issues involving substantial uncertainty or novelty.[731]

Another way of indicating students' progress toward expertise is illustrated by the following scale that the Law Society of England and Wales requires Legal Practice Course providers to use. It not only indicates whether a student can perform a task, transaction, or skill, but also assesses the level of supervision that the student requires. "Course providers could then provide the student with a graduated record indicating the level of achievement demonstrated. The student should then be able to identify the level of supervision required in the future and be able to plan his or her future learning needs accordingly."[732]

- the student is familiar with the skill, task or transaction, but not able to perform it.
- the student can perform the skill, task or transaction, but requires closely supervised practice.
- the student can perform the skill, task or transaction with minimal supervision.
- the student can perform the skill, task or transaction adequately without further training.
- the student can perform the skill, task or transaction in an outstanding manner with virtually no supervision and could provide assistance to others.

Similar descriptions can be developed for any of the competencies that we want students to develop during law school. For example, an on-going project by faculty at Georgia State University College of Law, the Glasgow Graduate School of Law, and the Dundee Medical School is developing assessment criteria for evaluating lawyer-client communication skills, beginning with client interviewing.[733] The project breaks down the components of effective client interviewing skills into discrete segments with descriptions of various levels of proficiency.

The project's emerging assessment tool was used as part of the summative Interviewing Assessment at the Glasgow Graduate School of Law in January, 2006, which also involved standardized clients.[734] The analysis of data following that assessment indicated a close correlation among ratings of the interviews made by standardized clients, practicing lawyers serving as evaluators, and academic staff.[735]

The form used in the Glasgow assessment posed the following eight questions which were rated on a scale of 1 to 5.

1. The greeting and introduction by the student lawyer was appropriate.
2. I felt the student lawyer listened to me.
3. The student lawyer approach to questioning was helpful.
4. The student lawyer accurately summarized my situation.

---

[731] *Id.* at 12.

[732] Legal Practice Course, *supra* note 142, at 25-26.

[733] Karen Barton, Clark D. Cunningham, Gregory Todd Jones & Paul Maharg, *Valuing What Clients Think: Standardized Clients and the Assessment of Communicative Competence,* 13 CLINICAL L. REV. 1 (Fall 2006).

[734] *Id.* at 33-41.

[735] *Id.* at 41-50.

5. I understood what the student lawyer was saying.
6. I felt comfortable with the student lawyer.
7. I would feel confident with the student lawyer dealing with my situation.
8. If I had a new legal problem I would come back to this student lawyer.

Explicit criteria described how many points to award for each of the eight topics. For example, the following criteria were used for awarding points on number 6, "I felt comfortable with the student lawyer:"

1 point:	Lawyer was bored, uninterested, rude unpleasant, cold, or obviously insincere.
2 points:	Lawyer was mechanical, distracted, nervous, insincere, or used inappropriate remarks.
3 points:	Lawyer was courteous to you and encouraged you to confide in him or her.
4 points:	Lawyer was generally attentive to and interested in you. You felt confident to confide in him/her.
5 points:	Lawyer showed a genuine and sincere interest in you. There was a sense of connection between you and the lawyer.

Hopefully, more collaborations like the Glasgow/Georgia State project will lead to the development of additional descriptions of levels of proficiency in professional expertise and a growing consensus about what we should be teaching students and how we can measure success.

Our greatest challenge is finding effective ways to assess the overall competence of our students. If our program of instruction aims to develop competence, we should be concerned about how best to evaluate the level of competence of each student. In order to do this, we must put students in the roles of lawyers.

Legal analysis alone is only a partial foundation for developing professional competence and identity. It is not enough even to develop analytic knowledge plus merely skillful performance. The goal has to be integration into a whole greater than the sum of its parts. Assessment of students' learning and growth need to be consistent with the goal of this integration: professional judgment and the ability to continue to learn and develop toward the highest standards of the legal profession. These broader aspects of professional development can be assessed in ways that can help students, but the assessment must take place "in role," rather than in the more detached mode that "law of lawyering" courses typically foster.[736]

Assessments of competence would not only assess students' knowledge and capabilities but also their professionalism. This is not easy to achieve, but the medical profession has demonstrated that it is possible.

Assessing the more complex goal of students' professionalism or ability to embody good ethical and professional judgment is more

---

[736] SULLIVAN ET AL., *supra* note 7, at 225.

difficult to achieve . . . . Significant evidence from medical schools, however, suggests that some basic aspects of professionalism can be assessed and that, moreover, such assessments yield highly significant predictions about which students are likely to exhibit problematic behaviors as practitioners.[737]

Medical educators are much more advanced than legal educators in thinking about assessment issues and developing tools and methods to assess student leaning. "Medical educators, hearing the call of public accountability, are adapting educational programs to teach apprentice practitioners in a way that ensures competent practice."[738] We can learn from their experience.

> The measurement of professional behavior is one of the greatest challenges in medical education today. Professional behaviors are very difficult to measure with paper-and-pencil tests because of the likelihood that students will respond with socially desirable, as opposed to personally realistic, choices. As a result, the best measures of professional behavior lie in the context of clinical activity and involve a conflict that the student or resident must resolve under supervision.[739]

According to Drs. Ronald Epstein and Edward Hundert,[740] the three most commonly used assessment methods in medical schools are subjective assessments by supervising clinicians, multiple-choice examinations, and standardized patient assessments.

> 1.   *Subjective assessments by supervising clinicians.* During clinical experiences, faculty physicians observe students' performance and rate them not only on their scientific and technical competence, but also on "dimensions of professionalism, including compassion, respect, interprofessional relationships, and conscientiousness."[741] These ratings can lack reliability for numerous reasons.
>
> > [E]valuators often do not observe trainees directly. They often have different standards and are subject to halo effects and racial and sex bias. Because of interpatient variability and low interrater reliability, each trainee must be subject to multiple assessments for patterns to emerge. Standardized rating forms for direct observation of trainees and structured oral examination formats have been developed in response to this criticism.[742]
>
> > Another format being used to evaluate professional competence is to have trainees present several best-case videotapes of their performance in real clinical settings to a trained examiner who uses

---

[737] *Id.* at 222.

[738] David Stern, MD, PhD, *Outside the Classroom: Teaching and Evaluating Future Physicians*, 20 GA. ST. U. L. REV. 877, 903 (2004).

[739] *Id.* at 902 (citations omitted).

[740] Epstein & Hundert, *supra* note 150, at 226.

[741] Stern, *supra* note 738, at 902.

[742] Epstein & Hundert, *supra* note 150, at 230 (citations omitted).

specified criteria for evaluation.[743] "Although the face validity of such a measure is high and the format is well-accepted by physicians, the number of cases that should be presented to achieve adequate reliability is unclear."[744]

2. *Multiple-choice examinations.* Multiple choice examinations have been proven to be a highly reliable way to evaluate factual knowledge and problem-solving skills and to assess some aspects of context and clinical reasoning.[745]

3. *Standardized patient assessments.* The use of standardized patients in an Objective Structured Clinical Examination (OSCE) can produce reliable ratings of communication, physical examination, counseling, and technical skills if there is a sufficiently large number of standardized patient cases and if criteria for competence are based on evidence.[746] "Although few cases are needed to assess straightforward skills, up to 27 cases may be necessary to assess interpersonal skills reliably in high stakes examinations."[747] It is difficult to define pass/fail criteria for OSCEs, and there is a debate about whether to use standardized patients or external raters.[748] "The OSCE scores may not correlate with multiple-choice examinations and academic grades, suggesting that these tools measure different skills."[749]

Peer ratings can provide accurate and reliable assessments of physician performance, especially professionalism.[750] Peers may be in the best position to evaluate professionalism; people often act differently when not under direct scrutiny. Anonymous medical student peer assessments of professionalism have raised awareness of professional behavior, fostered further reflection, helped students identify specific mutable behaviors, and been well-accepted by students. Students should be assessed by at least 8 of their classmates. The composite results should be edited to protect the confidentiality of the raters.[751]

Self-assessment is another tool that has helped evaluate the competency of physicians. Self-assessments have been used with some success in standardized patient exercises and in programs that offer explicit training in the use of self-assessment instruments. Among trainees who did not have such training, however, self-assessment was neither valid nor accurate. Rather, it was more closely linked to the trainee's psychological sense of self-efficacy and self-confidence than to appropriate criteria, even among bright and motivated individuals.[752]

The various types of assessments make it difficult to rank students, because a student may excel in some dimensions and struggle in others. "However, one rarely

---

[743] *Id.*

[744] *Id.*

[745] *Id.* at 230 (citations omitted).

[746] *Id.*

[747] *Id.* (citations omitted).

[748] *Id.*

[749] *Id.* (citations omitted).

[750] *Id.* at 231.

[751] *Id.* (citations omitted).

[752] *Id.* (citations omitted).

needs this process of ranking in a field where competence, rather than comparative excellence, is the essential characteristic."[753]

In the medical profession, many people are supporting the development of more comprehensive licensing examinations that add structured direct observations, OCSE standardized patient (SP) stations, real patient cases, case-based questions, peer assessments, and essay-type questions to the traditional computer-gradable formats.[754]

> Comprehensive assessments link content across several formats. Post-encounter probes immediately after SP exercises using oral, essay, or multiple-choice questions test pathophysiology and clinical reasoning in context. Triple-jump exercises – consisting of a case presentation, an independent literature search, and then an oral or written postencounter examination – test the use and application of medical literature. Validated measures of reflective thinking have been developed that use patient vignettes followed by questions that require clinical judgment. These measures reflect students' capacity to organize and link information; also, they predict clinical reasoning ability 2 years later. Combining formats appears to have added value with no loss in reliability.[755]

The website of the Accreditation Council for Graduate Medical Education (ACGME)[756] reflects an effort by that organization to assist medical professionals in expanding their repertoire of assessment tools and thereby expand the range and diversity of skills assessed. For example, the website details a range of tools for assessing students' development of interpersonal and communication skills, including rating forms completed by patients, coding of videotaped patient interviews, and self-rating on a humanism scale.[757]

The ACGME Outcome Project's TOOLBOX OF ASSESSMENT METHODS©,[758] includes descriptions and examples of instruments recommended for use by programs as they assess the outcomes of their educational efforts. These include:

1. *360-Degree Evaluation Instrument.* Ratings forms completed by supervisors, peers, subordinates, and patients and families to provide feedback about a person's performance on several topics (e.g., teamwork, communication, management skills, decision-making).

2. *Chart-Stimulated Recall Oral Examination (CRS).* A trained and experienced physician examiner questions the examinee about the care provided probing for reasons behind the work-up, diagnoses, interpretation of clinical findings, and treatment plans.

---

[753] Stern, *supra* note 738, at 903.

[754] Epstein & Hundert, *supra* note 150, at 232.

[755] *Id.* (citations omitted).

[756] ACGME Outcome Project, *supra* note 124, at Competencies to Assess, Complete List, http://www.acgme.org/outcome/assess/complist.asp.

[757] *Id.* at Interpersonal and Communication Skills Assessment Approaches, http://www.acgme.org/outcome/assess/IandC_Index.asp.

[758] *Id.* at Toolbox of Assessment Methods (Version 1.1 2000), http://ACGME.org/Outcome/assess/Toolbox.pdf.

3. *Checklist Evaluation of Live or Recorded Performance.* Checklists consist of essential or desired specific behaviors, activities, or steps that make up a more complex competency or competency component.

4. *Global Rating of Live or Recorded Performance.* Global rating forms are distinguished from other rating forms in that (a) the global rater judges general categories of ability (e.g., patient care skills, medical knowledge, interpersonal and communication skills) instead of specific skills, tasks, or behaviors; and (b) the ratings are completed retrospectively based on general impressions collected over a period of time (e.g., end of a clinical rotation) derived from multiple sources of information (e.g., direct observations or interactions; input from other faculty, residents, or patients; review of work products or written materials).

5. *Objective Structured Clinical Examination (OSCE).* One or more assessment tools are administered at 12 to 20 separate standardized patient encounter stations, each station lasting 10-15 minutes. Between stations candidates may complete patient notes or a brief written examination about the previous patient encounter. All candidates move from station to station in sequence on the same schedule. Standardized patients are the primary assessment tool used in OSCEs, but OSCEs have included other assessment tools such as data interpretation exercises using clinical cases, and clinical scenarios with mannequins to assess technical skills.

6. *Procedure, Operative, or Case Logs.* These logs document each patient encounter by medical conditions seen and surgical operations or procedures performed.

7. *Patient Surveys.* Surveys of patients to assess satisfaction with hospital, clinic, or office visits typically include questions about the physician's care. The questions often assess satisfaction with general aspects of the physician's care, (e.g., amount of time spent with the patient, overall quality of care, physician competency (skills and knowledge), courtesy, and interest or empathy). More specific aspects of care can be assessed including: the physician's explanations, listening skills and provision of information about examination findings, treatment steps, and drug side effects.

8. *Portfolios.* A collection of products prepared by the resident that provides evidence of learning and achievement related to a learning plan. A portfolio typically contains written documents but can include video- or audio-recordings, photographs, and other forms of information. Reflecting upon what has been learned is an important part of constructing a portfolio.

9. *Record Review.* Trained staff in an institution's medical records department or clinical department perform a review of patients' paper or electronic records.

10.　*Simulations and Models.* Simulations used for assessment of clinical performance closely resemble reality and attempt to imitate but not duplicate real clinical problems. Key attributes of simulations are that: they incorporate a wide array of options resembling reality, allow examinees to reason through a clinical problem with little or no cueing, permit examinees to make life-threatening errors without hurting a real patient, provide instant feedback so examinees can correct a mistaken action, and rate examinees' performance on clinical problems that are difficult or impossible to evaluate effectively in other circumstances. Simulation formats have been developed as paper-and-pencil branching problems (patient management problems or PMPs), computerized versions of PMPs called clinical case simulations (CCX®), role-playing simulations (e.g., standardized patients (SPs), clinical team simulations), anatomical models or mannequins, and combinations of all three formats.

11.　*Standardized Oral Examination.* A type of performance assessment using realistic patient cases with a trained physician examiner questioning the examinee. The examiner begins by presenting the examinee with a clinical problem in the form of a patient case scenario and asks the examinee to manage the case. Questions probe the reasoning for requesting clinical findings, interpretation of findings, and treatment plans.

12.　*Standardized Patient Examination.* Standardized patients (SPs) are well persons trained to simulate a medical condition in a standardized way or actual patients who are trained to present their condition in a standardized way.

13.　*Written Examination.* A written or computer-based MCQ examination is composed of multiple-choice questions (MCQ) selected to sample medical knowledge and understanding of a defined body of knowledge, not just factual or easily recalled information.

Other innovations that are being used to assess the professional competence of physicians include:

1. Multimethod assessment.
2. Clinical reasoning in situations that involve clinical uncertainty.
3. Standardized patient exercises linked to postencounter probes of pathophysiology and clinical reasoning.
4. Exercises to assess the use of medical literature.
5. Long-station standardized patient exercises.
6. Simulated continuity.
7. Teamwork exercises.
8. Unannounced standardized patients in clinical settings.
9. Assessments by patients.
10. Peer assessment of professionalism.
11. Portfolios of videotapes.
12. Mentored self-assessment.

13. Remediation based on a learning plan.[759]

It would be a worthwhile project for legal educators to investigate the feasibility of applying the techniques mentioned in this section to assessments during law school, as part of the bar examination, and after entry into practice.

5.   Be Sure Assessment is Feasible.

Principle: The teacher uses assessments to measure outcomes that are reasonably possible to assess validly, reliably, and fairly.

Comments:
    Feasibility is an additional consideration. There may be some desirable outcomes that are impossible or too difficult to assess. For example, it may not be feasible to assess a student's commitment to justice. This does not mean law schools should stop trying to instill a commitment to seek justice in students, but we may not be able to measure how well we are succeeding. Therefore, we should be careful to distinguish between desired outcomes and measurable outcomes.

    On the other hand, if law teachers make the effort, we may discover ways to evaluate some things that we might initially consider unmeasurable. For example, Laurie Morin and Louise Howells believe they found a way to measure the development of students' reflective judgment.[760] We should closely monitor the progress of Marge Shultz and Sheldon Zedeck's effort to create a new Law School Admissions Test (see the section on various statements of desirable outcomes of legal education in Chapter Two). If they succeed in developing tests that measure some or all of the twenty-six factors related to effective lawyering, their project will have implications for assessing law student learning, not just their qualifications for law school admission.

    There may be some desirable outcomes that we could assess, but it is not feasible to do so because of the time and training required to implement the assessment, equipment or technology required, number of assessments required per examinee, or financial cost. We should not stop trying to achieve desirable outcomes because they are difficult to assess, but we should be realistic about what we can assess and whether it is imperative that we do so.

6.   Use Multiple Methods of Assessing Student Learning.

Principle: The teachers use multiple methods of assessing student learning.

Comments:
    "A valid, reliable, and fair picture of the student's ability is much more likely to exist if the measures are done several times using different modes of evaluation."[761]

    An assessment may take the form of a final exam, a test administered after

---

[759] Epstein & Hundert, *supra* note 150, at 232.

[760] Laurie Morin & Louise Howells, *The Reflective Judgment Project*, 9 Clinical L. Rev. 623 (2003).

[761] Munro, *supra* note 700, at 238.

a unit of instruction is covered, a paper, an observation of performance, a discussion between student and teacher, portfolio (profile) reviews, or some other method of determining what a student has learned. Before selecting an assessment tool, we should be clear about the goals of the assessment and the purposes for which it will be used.

The problem-based essay exam is the primary assessment tool used by legal educators in the United States. New methods could improve the quality of our assessments of student learning. One of the reasons why law teachers do not conduct formative assessments or more frequent summative assessments is the length of time it takes to read and evaluate large numbers of problem-based essay exams. Therefore, improvements in law school assessment would be enhanced by finding alternative forms of assessing learning.

Greg Sergienko makes a persuasive case for expanding the use of multiple choice exams, including the results of his study demonstrating that multiple choice tests can be more sophisticated tools than essay questions for analyzing students' abilities to read facts and cases as well as their ability to apply an unfamiliar rule of law to a legal problem.[762] Sergienko and Wegner agree that even problem-based essay exams can be scored much more quickly if they are criteria-referenced.[763]

We should not, however, overlook the value of helping students develop self-assessment skills.

> A most important aspect of assessment is student self-assessment. Throughout an attorney's professional life after law school, her success in practice will depend on the ability to self-assess professional performance, behavior, and attitudes. "An indispensable trait of the truly competent lawyer, at whatever stage of career development, is that of knowing the extent and limits of his competence: what he can do and what requires the assistance of others." [CRAMTON REPORT, *supra* note 280, at 8.] Yet law students are trained in a tradition in which all assessment is external so that she never must assess herself. Early in law school, students need to be taught the essentials of assessment and need to be introduced to self-assessment. They need to assess their own work and then compare their assessment with that of their instructor. They need feedback on their ability to self-assess so that they can improve. Teachers can provide students with assessment instruments that reflect explicit criteria for the performance so that the students can judge their own performance. As Cramton said, we should view legal education "in long-run terms as preparation for a lifetime career involving continuous growth and self-development over a forty-year period." [CRAMTON REPORT, *supra* note 280, at 10.][764]

Students would benefit from instruction in and application of peer-assessment and self-assessment methods. Law schools should also explore expanding the involvement of teaching assistants in assessments, at least for helping

---

[762] Greg Sergienko, *New Modes of Assessment*, 38 SAN DIEGO L. REV. 463, 493-505 (2001).

[763] Wegner, Assessment, *supra* note 24, at 33.

[764] MUNRO, *supra* note 4, at 124.

provide feedback on formative assessments.

Computerized testing and scoring holds great promise for the future in providing formative and summative assessments. Existing technology can help prepare assessment tools and evaluate the results. For example, there is a web-based platform called "Cyber Workbooks" that allows faculty to publish their course materials by integrating learning outcomes such as critical thinking, applied reasoning, and creative problem-solving. The platform consists of an authoring tool for developing course modules with lessons, questions, and answers, a user website accessible by students with a user name and password, and an administrative site for generating reports and allowing faculty to evaluate course modules. The platform has built-in assessment features that will identify, measure, validate, and report on learning outcomes and identify student weaknesses, without any special training. The program will time, grade, and record student responses to minimize faculty time and burden.[765]

7.   Distinguish Between Formative and Summative Assessments.

Principle: The teacher distinguishes between formative and summative assessments.

Comments:

It is important to know what we will do with the information our assessments will produce. The purpose of an assessment can be formative, summative, or both. Formative assessments are used to provide feedback to students and faculty. Their purpose is purely educational, and while they may be scored, they are not used to assign grades or rank students. A summative assessment is one that is used for assigning a grade or otherwise indicating a student's level of achievement. "Summative assessment occurs at the end of a course of study and is primarily used for the purpose of making a final judgment of the student alongside his or her peers – final in the sense that (unless there are mitigating circumstances) it is how a student performs in this assessment that will be used to decide whether a student can proceed, e.g., to the next level of the course or be admitted to a vocational course."[766]

8.   Conduct Formative Assessments Throughout the Term.

Principle: The teachers conduct formative assessments throughout the term.

Comments:

As mentioned above, formative assessments are used to provide feedback to students and faculty. Their purpose is purely educational, and while they may be scored, they are not used to assign grades or rank students. Current practices in the United States are uneven and inadequate. Some law teachers give practice exams and others use a variety of techniques to find out whether students are learning what we think we are teaching. The norm, however, is to give a final exam at the end of the semester without conducting any formative assessments during the course.

---

[765] For more information about "Cyber Workbooks" go to http://www.cyberworkbooks. com.

[766] BONE, *supra* note 681, at 4.

Providing formative feedback to students ought to be the primary form of assessment in legal education.

> Contemporary learning theory suggests that efficient application of educational effort is significantly enhanced by the use of formative assessment. For educational purposes, summative devices have their place primarily as devices to protect the public by ensuring basic levels of competence. Formative practices directed toward improved learning ought to be the primary forms of assessment.[767]

Formative assessments are especially important for first year students.

> For many students what is needed is time – time to adjust, grapple with hidden difficulties, and gain an intellectual home – and assistance – feedback that lets them know where they stand and how to move ahead more quickly. But time and assistance are exactly what is missing. Instead, first-year students are ranked and sorted at the end of each semester with profound consequences for the rest of their lives.[768]

The authors of the Carnegie Foundation's report explained why formative assessment is critical for educating professionals.

> [T]he essential goal of professional schools must be to form practitioners who are aware of what it takes to become competent in their chosen domain and equips them with the reflective capacity and motivation to pursue genuine expertise. They must become "metacognitive" about their own learning, to use the psychologists' term. This is why effective means of formative assessment are so critical for training professionals.[769]

Formative assessments also help teachers know whether their coverage of a topic is sufficient or whether they need to review the material again or present it in a different manner. Educational experts advocate assessing student learning throughout the learning process and afterwards for the purpose of determining how to improve instruction and whether to continue or discard it. "If it becomes apparent that all or most of the students fail to comprehend a particular area of a course or a particular point made by the professor, this data indicates that the problem may be attributable to the professor."[770] This information allows us to make corrections before any failures to learn become real problems.[771]

Formative assessments can take many forms. Giving practice exams is one example. Assigning short homework problems that could be reviewed by teaching assistants is another. There are various forms of peer-assessment or self-assessment exercises that can be used in class or between classes. Self-scoring computer quizzes can be created to help students practice taking exams and evaluate their strengths

---

[767] SULLIVAN ET AL., *supra* note 7, at 242.

[768] Wegner, Assessment, *supra* note 24, at 31.

[769] SULLIVAN ET AL., *supra* note 7, at 217.

[770] HESS & FRIEDLAND, *supra* note 304, at 286.

[771] SMITH & RAGAN, *supra* note 197, at 338.

and weaknesses.

Various forms of classroom assessments are gaining popularity in law schools. "'Classroom assessment' focuses on 'small scale assessments conducted continuously by . . . teachers to determine what students are learning in that class.'Classroom assessment is integral to learning and valuable because it is so proximate in time, providing immediate feedback to teacher and student."[772] After class, the teacher can quickly review the students' responses, determine whether the students have learned the intended lessons, report the results to the students, and plan remediation if necessary.[773]

Barbara Glesner-Fines encourages law teachers to use classroom assessment techniques for improving student learning and helping students build self-regulated learning skills.[774] Glesner-Fines identifies traditional methods of classroom assessment, such as watching student non-verbal cues, polling students, pop quizzes, and "The Minute Paper." Another technique is to have students during or at the end of class submit written answers to questions such as "What is the most important point you learned today?" "What was the muddiest point in . . . . ?" Paraphrase the ____ [rule or holding]." "Give an example of ____." [775]

Thomas A. Angelo and K. Patricia Cross's seminal work on this subject describe fifty effective techniques to assess student learning and faculty teaching in the classroom, including the ones mentioned above.[776] According to Greg Munro, these include techniques for assessing prior knowledge, recall, and understanding. The following techniques can be employed successfully in virtually any class:[777]

1.   *Misconception/preconception check:* This classroom assessment technique uncovers prior knowledge or beliefs that may hinder or block learning. For example, law students studying auto casualty insurance in an insurance class often believe that Uninsured Motorist coverage applies only when the insured is driving or riding as a passenger in a vehicle, when, in fact, the policy language covers the insured as a pedestrian hit by an uninsured motorist, which coverage accords with the legislative intent to protect the public from injury by uninsured motorists. Students also believe that Bodily Injury Liability coverage will provide benefits to a driver injured in a single-vehicle rollover, when, in fact, it covers the driver only for liability to others. These misconceptions can be revealed and dealt with by means of the misconception/preconception check before

---

[772] Munro, *supra* note 700, at 241 (quoting K. Patricia Cross, *Feedback in the Classroom: Making Assessment Matter* 5 (AAHE Assessment Forum, AM. ASSN. FOR HIGHER EDUC. 1988)). *See also* HESS & FRIEDLAND, *supra* note 304, at 261 (encouraging the use of classroom feedback as formative assessments).

[773] Barbara Glessner-Fines, *Classroom Assessment Techniques for Law School Teaching, in* ASSESSMENT, FEEDBACK, AND EVALUATION: EIGHTH ANNUAL CONFERENCE OF THE INSTITUTE FOR LAW SCHOOL TEACHING (2001). For information about using technology to facilitate asking questions and tabulating answers, see the section "Enhance Learning With Technology."

[774] *Id.*

[775] *Id.*

[776] THOMAS A. ANGELO & K. PATRICIA CROSS, CLASSROOM ASSESSMENT TECHNIQUES: A HANDBOOK FOR COLLEGE TEACHERS (1993).

[777] The following descriptions of assessment techniques were copied almost verbatim from Munro, *supra* note 700, at 242-44 (citations omitted).

covering the material.

2.   *Minute papers:* The "one-minute paper" or "half-sheet response" asks students in a couple of minutes or on a half sheet of paper some variation of the questions, "What is the most important thing you learned during this class?" and "What important question remains unanswered?" This allows the professor to assess whether students are getting the main theme around which the material is based or are meeting learning objectives. It also lets the professor know what students do not understand. This is especially important, since faculty often assume students have learned or have a base of knowledge when, in fact, they do not.

3.   *Empty outlines:* The professor gives the students a partially completed outline and asks them to fill in the outline for the material covered in the reading, lecture, or other materials.

4.   *Categorizing grids:* This technique requires students to sort information in appropriate conceptual categories.

5.   *Defining features matrix:* This assessment matrix requires students to categorize concepts according to the presence or absence of certain defining features. For example, students in a securities or business regulation course might be asked to categorize transactions on a matrix defining features that determine whether the transaction constitutes a security for purposes of regulation. Students in an insurance class might categorize on a matrix various forms of contract to determine whether they are "insurance" for purposes of insurance regulation.

6.   *Classroom opinion polls:* This device helps students to be aware of their own opinions, weigh them in light of those of their peers, and test them against evidence and expert opinion.

7.   *Course-related self-confidence surveys:* The professor designs this survey with a few simple questions designed to determine the students' self-confidence in an ability or skill. This allows the professor to evaluate the best approach to student learning and the needs of the students. For example, a professor in a trial advocacy class might design a survey asking students their level of confidence that, in this class, they will gain the ability to speak publicly, conduct voir dire, make a prepared statement of what their evidence will show, perform cross-examination, or make a closing argument. The survey may reveal that students lack confidence in their ability to cross-examine a witness or to carry on a voir dire dialogue with a jury. The professor can then work with students on strategies to overcome that lack of confidence.

8.   *Electronic mail feedback:* The professor asks a single question by e-mail to the class. Each student responds with a personal, anonymous message to the professor's electronic mailbox. This provides a fast method of receiving immediate feedback on an issue regarding

teaching or teacher.

9.   *Group instructional feedback technique:* This method provides a peer reviewed but anonymous form of teaching evaluation.[778] Generally, a facilitator from outside the school visits the class, which has been divided into small groups. The facilitator asks the groups three questions regarding the course and instruction: (1) What works? (2) What does not work? (3) What can be done to improve the course or instruction? The facilitator then presides over reporting by the groups to help them arrive at consensus on the three questions. The facilitator reports the results to the professor, allowing the process to remain anonymous but providing valid, reliable, and fair feedback to the professor.

Angelo and Cross point out several positive characteristics of classroom assessment. They note that, although it is teacher directed, "depending on the judgment, wisdom and experience of the teacher," it is simultaneously learner centered. Moreover, it is mutually beneficial to both teacher and students. Classroom assessment is formative, not designed to be "evidence for grading," but part of the learning process. It is ongoing and can become part of the "daily feedback loop between students and teacher."[779]

Technology is presenting some new ways to conduct classroom assessments. For example, classroom performance systems use "clickers," in which each student is given a keypad to respond to in-class multiple choice questions. The software records and reports on the results as a tool for responding to students' diverse ways of learning and serves as a classroom assessment technique that informs the teachers whether the students are learning and informs the students whether their learning strategies are working productively. Another technological innovation is the use of recording systems which automatically make video and sound records of students' classroom answers and performances for subsequent review.

Legal educators should strive to provide students with formative feedback on their progress in every course before administering summative evaluations. Our students need it, and they deserve it.

9.   **Conduct Multiple Summative Assessments Throughout the Term, When Possible.**

Principle: **The school conducts multiple summative assessments of student learning throughout the term, when possible.**

Comments:
Although law school exams provide a mechanism for assigning grades and ranking students, a single examination is an inadequate tool for determining which students have learned and which have not. The stakes of evaluation are high: grades serve to rank students for prospective employers and reflect on students'

---

[778] For a more detailed description, see Gregory S. Munro, *More Effective Evaluation of the Course and Instructor, in* HESS & FRIEDLAND, *supra* note 304, at 281.

[779] Munro, *supra* note 700, at 244 (citations omitted).

chances for admission to other educational programs.[780] Multiple evaluations of student learning increase the accuracy of the conclusions about student performance, improve student performance on the final examination, and increase the range of skills, values, and knowledge that the instructor may evaluate.[781]

A single assessment has significant potential for error because a student might be ill or have other personal issues that can distort the accuracy of the evaluation. The potential for distortion is exacerbated by the fact that a single assessment produces higher levels of stress because of its significance to the student's grade in the course and future. Similarly, there is a greater potential for teacher error if only one summative assessment is administered per term, particularly when problem-based essay exams are used.

There may be some justification for delaying summative assessments to the end of the semester if it would be unfair to evaluate students earlier. For example, first year students' analytical skills may not be sufficiently developed until the end of the first semester, or even the first year, to administer summative assessments sooner. However, it may be that some aspects of first year learning should be summatively assessed during the term, particularly students' understand of legal doctrine or their ability to read and understand appellate cases (both of which could be assessed with multiple choice tests). In upper level courses where the transmission of legal doctrine or other knowledge is a significant objective of the course, there is no excuse for not conducting summative assessments throughout the term.

Legal educators in the United States should also reconsider the current practice of allowing individual professors to draft and grade their own exams without any oversight. Summative assessments should be collaboratively created and graded, as is the common practice in British Commonwealth jurisdictions. To the extent that resources permit, summative assessments should be vetted by learning experts, at least periodically.

10. Ensure That Summative Assessments Are Also Formative Assessments.

Principle: **The school ensures that summative assessments are also formative assessments.**

Comments:
Students cannot learn unless the results of their summative assessments are explained to them. Assigning a student a grade or even describing the level of professional development does not help the student understand how to improve. For example, a summative evaluation might indicate that a student's performance on an exam demonstrated *limited proficiency*, that is, it showed overly simplistic, incomplete analysis that misses key issues and fails to use relevant legal rules, facts and policy. This conclusion, however, does not provide any basis upon which the student can understand the shortcomings of the student's analysis or how it could be improved. As the ABA's Task Force on Lawyer Competency recommended in 1979, "[l]aw schools and law teachers should develop and use more comprehensive methods of measuring law student performance than the typical end-of-the-term examination.

---

[780] HESS & FRIEDLAND, *supra* note 304, at 285.
[781] *Id.* at 290.

Students should be given detailed critiques of their performance."[782] Students learn with feedback.

In American law schools, final exams are not returned to students unless students ask to see theirs, and most law teachers do not try to explain the results of final examinations to the entire class. This tradition is inconsistent with best practices, because it misses an opportunity to use final examinations to enhance student learning.

> How did the student answer the question? Did he grasp the problem? Did he analyse the facts properly? Did he argue effectively? What are his weaknesses? The student never knows. I have in my files 143 [scripts]; not one of my students knows anything other than the final mark. The [scripts] were not to be returned. I defy anyone to tell me this is proper educational process . . . . [M]arginal comments on the returned [script] would certainly serve as a teaching device. Individual or group discussion of the examination should be part of the teaching process.[783]

Teachers should return all written exams and papers to students, with notes indicating specific strengths and shortcomings. Teachers should explain to students how they fared on other forms of summative evaluations. Teachers should provide model answers to exams, and encourage students to seek guidance about how to improve, either through internet correspondence, one on one meetings, class debriefings, or other methods.[784]

Michael Hunter Schwartz developed a form designed to facilitate student reflection and self-regulation with respect to law school exams, papers and other graded work. The form asks the student to: (1) compare how well she did with how well she expected to have done (to improve student self-assessment), (2) identify what she did incorrectly, in part by identifying the professorial comments most frequently appearing on her paper, (3) identify the causes of any errors in her work, focusing on correctable causes such as incorrect learning strategy choices or insufficient persistence, and (4) plan how she will avoid the error(s) in the future.[785]

11.   Require Students to Compile Educational Portfolios

Principle: **The school requires students to compile educational portfolios.**

Comments:
     Educational portfolios are seldom used in the United States, although they are required throughout the system of higher education in the United Kingdom. They can take many forms, but essentially they are compilations of materials that

---

[782] CRAMTON REPORT, *supra* note 275, at 4.

[783] BONE, *supra* note 681, at 15 (citing Albert Orschel, *Is Legal Education Doing its Job?*, 40 ABA J. 121, 124 (Feb. 1954)).

[784] *See* Richard Henry Seamon, *Lightening and Enlightening Exam Conferences*, 56 J. LEGAL EDUC. 122 (2006) (describing how exam conferences can help students learn the law, write better exam answers, and avoid discouragement and cynicism and how they can help faculty teach better, write better exam questions and grade them more fairly and accurately, and avoid discouragement and cynicism).

[785] Exercise 16-2, SCHWARTZ, *supra* note 406.

document a student's academic achievement and personal development.[786] Their perceived benefits include "making the results of learning in higher education more explicit, placing greater responsibility on students to understand and direct their own learning and personal growth, integrating academic and extracurricular development, creating more effective means to track student progress and enhance program quality, and assisting students in their search for employment."[787]

A system of student portfolios addresses many of the assessment principles previously discussed. They focus both teachers' and learners' attention on learning, and make multi-faceted learning that progresses throughout students' educational lifetimes visible in fresh and meaningful ways. Portfolios place responsibility squarely on learners to consider how diverse academic and outside learning relate, and bring them into closer, meaningful contact with advisers who can monitor and encourage their work. Portfolios also provide a convenient means both for documenting professional capability in the interest of future employment, and encouraging and recognizing distinguished work.[788]

Portfolios can be particularly helpful for students who do not get off to the best start but whose expertise and academic achievement mature as they proceed through law school. In fact, portfolios can facilitate a student's development by causing the student to reflect on her personal and professional objectives and by providing a tool for demonstrating that first semester grades do not accurately reflect her potential as a lawyer. Examples of materials that might be included in a student's educational portfolio include:

short reflective essays on personal and professional goals at the start of law school and each successive year; writing samples and work product of various sorts; resumes; certificates of academic distinction awarded for advanced proficiency in the first year or honors performance thereafter; "learning logs" associated with certain courses or work experiences; evidence of extracurricular activities that demonstrate effective work in teams or special professional contributions; statements regarding volunteer service of various sorts; letters of reference from faculty or work supervisors; evidence of research skills and use of advanced technology; and transcripts.[789]

A student might also use the portfolio to demonstrate her progress toward

---

[786] American Association for Higher Education, Electronic Portfolios: Emerging Practices in Student, Faculty, and Institutional Learning (2001). While he was at Western State University College of Law, Michael Hunter Schwartz, now at Washburn University School of Law, designed and led a portfolio assessment process. The faculty identified the skills, knowledge, and values that Western States students should possess upon graduation, created a curriculum map identifying where in the curriculum students are introduced to, practice and must master those skills, knowledge, and values, and required students to create electronic web portfolios to which they submit evidence of attainment of the skills, knowledge, and values and reflect on those submissions. Schwartz expects to complete a law review article dealing with this project by the fall of 2006.

[787] Wegner, Assessment, *supra* note 24, at 70. *See also* Aaronson, *supra* note 33, at 6-7 (discussing the content and benefits of student portfolios).

[788] Wegner, Assessment, *supra* note 24, at 72-73.

[789] *Id.* at 71.

developing the fundamental skills and values needed for law practice. If a school records student performances in simulation-based courses or competitions, copies of a student's best performances could be included in the portfolio. This is made all the easier if the school uses digital recording devices. In fact, in this digital age, the entire portfolio can be electronic.[790]

Students would be able to provide selected materials from the portfolio to prospective employers, and schools could consider giving special academic recognition to students whose portfolios demonstrate outstanding achievement. "Criteria for such recognition would be made available well in advance to all interested students. Criteria would ideally be developed by faculty, in consultation with students, using the opportunity to articulate the meaning of excellence in light of the school's mission and goals, and the aspirations and potential of its students."[791]

---

[790] *See* BARBARA L. CAMBRIDGE, ELECTRONIC PORTFOLIOS: EMERGING PRACTICES IN STUDENT, FACULTY, AND INSTITUTIONAL LEARNING (2001).

[791] Wegner, Assessment, *supra* note 24, at 72.

Chapter Eight
Best Practices for Assessing Institutional Effectiveness

A.   Evaluate Effectiveness Regularly.

Principle: The school regularly evaluates the program of instruction to determine if it is effective at preparing students for the practice of law.

Comments:
        Information about educational effectiveness is necessary for law schools to make informed judgments about their inputs, resources, and outcomes in order to improve instruction and accountability to all stakeholders in the educational process. Educational effectiveness is a "core commitment" of institutions committed to excellence.[792] Any institution committed to learning and improvement should investigate the effectiveness of its program of instruction on a regular basis.

        The American Association of Higher Education makes it clear that educational institutions need to evaluate their effectiveness longitudinally, repeatedly, and as part of the institutions' process of doing business:

> Assessment works best when it is ongoing not episodic. Assessment is a process whose power is cumulative. Though isolated, "one-shot" assessment can be better than none, improvement is best fostered when assessment entails a linked series of activities undertaken over time. This may mean tracking the progress of individual students, or of cohorts of students; it may mean collecting the same examples of student performance or using the same instrument semester after semester. The point is to monitor progress toward intended goals in a spirit of continuous improvement. Along the way, the assessment process itself should be evaluated and refined in light of emerging insights.[793]

        The ABA accreditation standards require schools to evaluate the effectiveness of their programs of instruction, including how well they prepare students for the practice of law.

> Each law school shall engage in a periodic review of the curriculum to ensure that it prepares the school's graduates to participate effectively and responsibly in the practice of law.[794]

        The ABA also requires law schools to develop self-studies before sabbatical inspections and, since 2006, to engage in a continuing process of setting goals, selecting means for achieving goals, monitoring success in achieving goals, and appropriately reexamining goals.

---

[792] WESTERN ASSOCIATION ACCREDITATION HANDBOOK, *supra* note 18, at 44.

[793] American Association of Higher Education (AAHE), *Nine Principles of Good Practice for Assessing Student Learning* [hereinafter *Nine Principles*], http://www.aahe.org/assessment/principl.htm.

[794] Interpretation 302-3, ABA STANDARDS, *supra* note 28, at 19.

SELF-STUDY. Before each site evaluation visit, the dean and
faculty of a law school shall develop a written self-study, which
shall include a mission statement. The self-study shall describe the
program of legal education, evaluate the strengths and weaknesses
of the program in light of the school's mission, set goals to improve
the program, and identify the means to accomplish the school's
unrealized goals.[795]

STRATEGIC PLANNING AND ASSESSMENT. In addition to the
self-study described in Standard 202, a law school shall demonstrate
that it regularly identifies specific goals for improving the law
school's program, identifies means to achieve the established goals,
assesses its success in realizing the established goals and periodically
reexamines and appropriately revises its established goals.[796]

In other words, best practices preclude law schools from simply assuming
that, just because students complete the law schools' degree requirements, they
will possess the skills, values, and knowledge described as the school's educational
outcomes. Rather, law schools need to develop and identify evidence that their
graduates regularly attain each of the law school's intended outcomes.

B.   Use Various Methods to Gather Information.

Principle: **The school uses various methods to gather quantitative
and qualitative information about the effectiveness of the program of
instruction.**[797]

Comments:
Assessment experts refer to the goal of creating a "set" of assurance measures
as creating a "culture of evidence."[798] For example, the Western Association of
Schools and Colleges requires that an institution employ "a deliberate *set* of quality
assurance processes at each level of institutional functioning . . . . These processes
involve assessments of effectiveness, track results over time, and use the results of
these assessments to revise and improve structures and processes, curricula and
pedagogy."[799] The Association's standards also indicate that an institution committed
to learning and improvement "conducts sustained, evidence-based, and participatory
discussions about how effectively it is accomplishing its purposes and achieving its

---

[795] Standard 202, *id.* at 11.

[796] Standard 203, *id.*

[797] This principle was adapted from a definition of assessment in research on standards for the conduct of quality assessment in higher education. Alice M. Thomas, Standards
for the Conduct of Quality Assessment in Higher Education, Paper Presented at the Annual
Meeting of the Association for the Study of Higher Education (Oct. 31, 1991).

[798] *See* A. Darlene Pacheco, *Culture of Evidence*, 9 Assessment and Accountability Forum 14 (Summer 1999). Pacheco, who is the Associate Director of the Accrediting Commission
for Community and Junior Colleges, Western Association of Schools and Colleges, explains the
culture of evidence idea by asserting that "[d]eveloping a program for assessing institutional
effectiveness requires an institutional commitment to assessment that is a 'broad-based and
integrated system of research, evaluation and planning.' Institutional assessment is expected
to include program reviews that demonstrably leads to improvement of programs and services." *Id.*

[799] Western Association Accreditation Handbook, *supra* note 18, at 29.

educational objectives."[800]

Evidence of educational effectiveness may be direct or indirect. The Council for Higher Education Accreditation (CHEA) explains that direct evidence of student learning outcomes is the result of a process deliberately designed for this purpose and may include such approaches as:
- *capstone performances* (typified by traditional doctorate dissertation experiences),
- *professional/clinical performances* (using students' performances in clinical settings to evaluate student attainment of the student learning outcomes),
- *third-party testing* (licensing examinations, such as bar examinations), and
- *faculty-designed examinations* (competency tests, for example).

Indirect evidence of student learning outcomes may include:
- *portfolios and work samples* (students select samples from course, externship and clinical work as evidence of their attainment of each outcome),
- *follow-up of graduates* (surveys),
- *employer ratings for performance* (surveys), and
- *self-reported growth by graduates* (surveys).[801]

The Council for Higher Education Accreditation identifies four criteria for determining whether a set of assessment practices are sufficient.
1. *Comprehensiveness.* Submitted evidence should cover knowledge and skills taught throughout a course or program.
2. *Multiple Judgments.* Submitted evidence should involve more than one source or involve multiple judgments of student performance.
3. *Multiple Dimensions.* Submitted evidence should provide information on multiple dimensions of student performance – i.e., they should yield more than a summative grade.
4. *Directness.* Submitted evidence should involve at least one type based on direct observation or demonstration of student capacities – i.e., they should involve more than simply a self-report.[802]

Greg Munro identified the following methods for assessing the success of the law school in meeting its mission and institutional outcomes.

Self-study: A law school's self-study done in preparation for an accreditation visit can be an excellent form of institutional self-assessment if it is a collaborative task performed by the faculty. If the self-study is window dressing performed by the deans or a small committee of the faculty, it will have less value. Also, the self-study can be effective if those conducting it make the right inquiries regarding the state of the school's mission, outcomes, teaching methods, curriculum, assessment program, strategies for achieving goals, and obstacles to those goals. It can be much less useful if it focuses only on such things as library size, staff size, level of funding,

---

[800] Standard 4, Creating an Organization Committed to Learning and Improvement, *id.* at 28.

[801] *Student Learning Outcomes Workshop*, 5 The CHEA Chronicle 2 (2002).

[802] *Id.*

and faculty characteristics.

Accreditation and site visits: To a certain extent, accreditation teams constitute an outside objective source for institutional self-assessment. Site visits and accreditation reviews are the most intensive form of institutional assessment most law schools undergo. Nevertheless, accreditation will generally reveal whether the school meets minimum accreditation standards and is not necessarily focused on whether the school meets its own institutional mission and outcomes.

Interviews: Law schools can use interviews to ask specific questions of any of the school's constituencies to glean answers that will allow the school to evaluate its success in any area. For example, students, upon admission to the law school, might be interviewed to determine effectiveness in marketing the law school; likewise, students might be interviewed upon graduation to determine effectiveness in meeting institutional outcomes. Lawyers, judges, or virtually any constituency that has a chance to observe the school or its students, faculty, or alumni are appropriate candidates for carefully designed interviews.

Questionnaires and surveys: These can be sent to any constituency of the law school. Most commonly, schools survey their alumni or the bench and bar for perspectives or opinions about some aspect of the institutional mission. The student body can be surveyed quickly for feedback on many issues of institutional outcomes.

Statistical information: Those engaged in institutional assessment will find useful statistical data readily accessible in the school's own files. Admission files contain LSAT scores, information on prior occupation and education, reasons for entering law school, bar exam results, and a host of other statistics that can be used for assessment. Student files can answer many questions about the nature of the school's students and the value added during their tenure in law school. Fund development has caused schools increasingly to develop and retain alumni records, which are a source of much information on institutional outcomes.

Bar exam results: Though bar exam results are a form of statistical information discussed above, such results merit separate mention. One of the most obvious measures of student and institutional outcomes in law schools is bar exam results and trends that may be reflected in such results over time. They are limited in their usefulness and valid only on particular questions, but they are an important measure of whether the school is providing students with that body of knowledge and skills deemed necessary by bar examiners. The bar exams are unique forms of institutional assessment, because they are administered and evaluated by a body outside the law school and require graduates to demonstrate a certain level of proficiency in those skills the exams address. Some bar exams now require demonstration of drafting and other professional skills.

Faculty portfolios: Faculty curriculum vitae are the prime source of data on the success of the institution in promoting faculty achievement in the area of teaching, public service, and scholarship. Faculty can also develop portfolios for purposes of promotion and tenure that would supplement a CV by addition of teaching videotapes, class syllabi, and other materials by which the faculty's performance and qualities can be assessed.

Placement records: One measure of success in student learning and institutional outcomes is the school's success in placing its graduates. Hence, review of placement records is a valuable assessment tool for the institution.[803]

The bar examination is, as mentioned above, one form of direct evidence of institutional effectiveness. ABA accreditation practices have used first-time bar pass rates on the bar examination most commonly taken by a law school's graduates as the primary, if not exclusive, measure of educational effectiveness. This approach results in accreditation decisions that are both over-inclusive and under-inclusive.

The decisions are over-inclusive because, if a law school has a high bar pass rate, its ABA approval is assured even though that bar pass rate may be the product of factors that do not bear on the quality of a law school's educational program. For example, a law school may achieve a very high bar pass rate if the law school admits only students with excellent entrance credentials and does not make the students so much worse that they fail the bar exam. In the alternative, a law school's bar pass rates may be high, and its ABA approval secure, simply because its graduates take a bar examination that is, relative to all bar examinations, easier. The ABA only looks at the bar exam results in the state where most of a school's students take the bar exam. It does not matter is if a high percentage of the law school's students fail other states' examinations.

The decisions are under-inclusive because a law school that admits high risk students and is situated in a state with a relatively more difficult bar examination will have difficulty obtaining or retaining its ABA approval, even if nearly all of its graduates pass the bar examination eventually and even if the first-time rate, after controlling for entrance credentials, is better than other law schools in the jurisdiction. This issue is compounded by the fact that the bar examination, does not necessarily test the skills and knowledge most important to the success of novice lawyers. For example, one standard for evaluating an assessment tool is whether it is valid. "An assessment measure is valid if it actually assesses or measures what it claims to assess or measure."[804] The MBE portion of the bar exam, to which many states give the greatest weight, does not really measure students' ability to write the kinds of documents lawyers typically write or analyze the kinds of problems lawyers typically analyze, making the validity of the instrument dubious. While the essays and performance tests at least require students to analyze and write, lawyers in practice never base their analyses on their memory of legal doctrine, never cite rules without using court opinions and statutes to support their discussions, and very

---

[803] Munro, *supra* note 700, at 244-46.

[804] Smith & Ragan, *supra* note 197, at 95.

infrequently have only a half hour, hour, or even three hours to think through legal problems.

For these reasons, law schools and law school accrediting bodies should work together to adopt methodologies to supplement bar examination results as a measure of institutional effectiveness.

C.   Use Student Performance and Outcome Assessment Results.

Principle: The school uses student performance and outcome assessment results in its evaluation of the educational effectiveness of the school's program of instruction.[805]

Comments:
The Council for Higher Education Accreditation makes the following observation in its Statement of Mutual Responsibilities for Student Learning Outcomes: Accreditation, Institutions, and Programs:

> Institutions and programs have their own responsibilities for developing and using evidence of student learning outcomes. Specifically, institutions and programs should . . . [d]etermine and communicate clearly to constituents:
> • what counts as evidence that these outcomes have been achieved, and
> • what level of attainment of these outcomes is required to assure the quality of institutional or program offerings.

> Develop recognizable processes for regularly collecting and interpreting evidence of student learning outcomes.

> Use the results of this process to identify strengths and weaknesses or gaps between expected and actual performance and to identify and overcome barriers to learning. [806]

Similarly, the Council of Regional Accrediting Agencies states that accrediting agencies should expect that institutions, among other things, provide:

> 1. *Documentation of student learning.* The institution demonstrates that student learning is appropriate for the certificate or degree awarded and is consistent with the institution's own standards of academic performance. The institution accomplishes this by:
> • setting clear learning goals, which speak to both content

---

[805] This principle was adapted from the accreditation standards of the Accreditation Council for Graduate Medical Education, *available at* http://www.acgme.org/Outcome/. The ACGME's shift to outcome assessments is discussed in Chapter Two, in the section "The Global Movement Toward Outcomes-Focused Education." The ACGME and the American Board of Medial Specialties are collaborating on the development of an assessment toolbox. The toolbox will include descriptions recommended for use by programs as they assess the outcomes of their educational efforts.

[806] Council for Higher Education, Statement Of Mutual Responsibilities for Student Learning Outcomes: Accreditation, Institutions, and Programs, http://www.chea.org/pdf/StmntStudentLearningOutcomes9-03.pdf (2003).

and level of attainment,
* collecting evidence of goal attainment using appropriate assessment tools,
* applying collective judgment as to the meaning and utility of the evidence, and
* using this evidence to effect improvements in its programs.

2. *Compilation of evidence.* Evidence of student learning is derived from multiple sources, such as courses, curricula, and co-curricular programming, and includes effects of both intentional and unintentional learning experiences. Evidence collected from these sources is complementary and portrays the impact on the student of the institution as a whole.[807]

Thus, this principle encourages law schools to create a feedback loop in which the law school regularly collects data about student achievement of the law school's desired student outcomes; disseminates that information to faculty, administration, alumni, employers and other interested parties; and uses the information to reach conclusions about the effectiveness of the law school's overall curriculum and individual programs. In short, law schools need to adopt assessment programs that result in data that helps the law schools evaluate whether their students are learning what they need to be learning.

D.   Meet Recognized Standards for Conducting Assessments.

Principle: The school's processes for conducting assessments of student performance and educational outcomes meet recognized standards for conducting assessments in higher education.[808]

Comments:

The Accreditation Council of Graduate Medical Education identified five key considerations for selecting assessment instruments and implementing assessment systems. The assessment approach must provide valid data, yield reliable data, be feasible, have external validity, and provide valuable information.[809]

Alice M. Thomas identified forty assessment standards judged by experts as the most important standards in the practice of quality assessment in undergraduate higher education.[810]

Together, these two works suggest that law schools not only should be creating assessment systems but also should be assessing those systems themselves. An assessment system, in other words, is valuable only if it really does result in good information on which a law school can justifiably rely. Consequently, law schools

---

[807] Council of Regional Accrediting Agencies, Regional Accreditation and Student Learning: Principles for Good Practices,http://www.msche.org/publications/regn-isl050208135331.pdf.

[808] This principle was adapted from the accreditation standards of the Accreditation Council for Graduate Medical Education, *available at* http://www.acgme.org/Outcome/.

[809] Key Considerations for Selecting Assessment Instruments and Implementing Assessment Systems, http://www.acgme.org/outcome/assess/keyconsider.asp (last visited 9/19/06).

[810] Thomas, *supra* note 797.

should make sure that their data, collectively, genuinely and accurately assesses the skills, values, and knowledge it is purporting to assess, such that the results could be replicated by an outside assessor. The data should provide the law school with guidance as to which courses, programs and instructional methodologies the law school should retain, which it should alter, and which it should discard.

E.   Solicit and Incorporate Opinions from Outside of the Academy.

Principle: The school solicits and incorporates the opinions of its alumni as well as other practicing judges and lawyers who hire and interact with graduates of the school.

Comments:

Many law schools make curriculum decisions, even significant decisions, without consulting with practitioners. This approach is precisely contrary to best practices in curriculum development. For example, the Western Association of Schools and Colleges uses the following criterion for evaluating its member institutions: "Appropriate stakeholders, including alumni, employers, practitioners, and others defined by the institution, are involved in the assessment of the effectiveness of the institution."[811]

Likewise, the Council for Higher Education Accreditation includes "employer ratings of performance" and "self-reported growth by graduates" as recommended types of evidence that institutions can use to prove educational effectiveness. [812]

This approach treats employers and alumni as stakeholders in the educational product produced by the law school.

F.   Demonstrate How Data is Used to Improve Effectiveness.

Principle: The school demonstrates how educational outcomes data is used to improve individual student and overall program performance.[813]

Comments:

It is not enough that a school simply collects data on educational outcomes. There is a general consensus that institutions must not only conduct assessments but also use the resulting data to determine whether they are delivering an effective educational program. The school should demonstrate how the collected evidence is used to improve instruction both at an individual student level and in furtherance of the overall educational mission of the school.

The accreditation standards of the Western Association of Schools and Colleges require that the results from institutional research be "used to . . . revise institutional . . . approaches to teaching and learning . . . ."[814]

---

[811] Western Association Accreditation Handbook, *supra* note 18, at 30.

[812] *Student Learning Outcomes Workshop, supra* note 801, at 2.

[813] This principle was adapted from the accreditation standards of the Accreditation Council for Graduate Medical Education, *available at* http://www.acgme.org/Outcome/.

[814] Standard 4, Western Association Accreditation Handbook, *supra* note 18.

A commitment to continuous improvement is a duty owed by educators to the general public. The ninth principle in the American Association of Colleges and Schools *Nine Principles of Good Practice in Student Assessment* states that:

> *Through assessment, educators meet responsibilities to students and to the public.* There is a compelling public stake in education. As educators, we have a responsibility to the public that support or depend on us to provide information about the ways in which our students meet goals and expectations. But that responsibility goes beyond the reporting of such information; our deeper obligation – to ourselves, our students, and society – is to improve. Those to whom educators are accountable have a corresponding obligation to support such attempts at improvement.[815]

The Association of American Colleges expresses a similar vision for the future of evaluating the success of American higher education: "the institution itself becomes a life-long learner, continuously assessing itself at all levels, then feeding the results back into improvement loops for both student learning and campus processes."[816]

Peggy L. Maki, a Senior Scholar with the American Association of Higher Education explains that a commitment to student learning requires institutions to develop and use data:

> Accreditors are increasingly interested in learning about what an institution has discovered about student learning and how it intends to improve student outcomes . . . .
>
> If an institution aims to sustain its assessment efforts to continually improve the quality of education, it needs to develop channels of communication whereby it shares interpretations of students' results and incorporates recommended changes into its budgeting, decision making, and strategic planning as these processes will likely need to respond to and support proposed changes. Most institutions have not built into their assessment plans effective channels of communication that share interpretations of student achievement with faculty and staff, as well as with members of an institution's budgeting and planning bodies – including strategic planning bodies. Assessment is certain to fail if an institution does not develop channels that communicate assessment interpretations and proposed changes to its centers of institutional decision making, planning, and budgeting.[817]

In short, data collection about student outcomes is meaningful only to the extent that a law school *distributes* data to all interested parties and *uses* that data to improve itself, to change the curriculum, to change teaching and learning methods, and even to change the assessment methods themselves.

---

[815] *Nine Principles, supra* note 793.
[816] *Principles of Good Practice in the New Academy, supra* note 270, at 36.
[817] Maki, *supra* note 130, at 8.

Chapter Nine
Components of a "Model" Best Practices Curriculum

This chapter describes one vision of a curriculum that seeks to implement best practices for legal education. The purpose of including it is simply to present ideas for consideration, discussion, and debate. We do not intend to suggest that this is the only way to design an effective program of instruction.[818]

We know there are components of many law schools' existing programs of instruction that are consistent with our recommendations. We considered naming those schools and describing what they are doing in some detail. In the end, however, the Steering Committee decided against the proposal because we did not feel we had valid selection criteria, and we did not want to unintentionally offend people at law schools we overlooked that might have equally good or superior programs than the ones we included. Compiling and sharing descriptions of innovative programs is a worthy project for someone to undertake.

The vision of legal education described in this chapter is consistent with that of the authors of the Carnegie Foundation's report on legal education. We envision a curriculum with three parts that interact with and influence each other.

Those elements are first, the teaching of legal doctrine and analysis, which provides the basis for professional growth; second, introduction to the several facets of practice included under the rubric of lawyering, leading to acting with responsibility for clients; and third, a theoretical and practical emphasis upon inculcation of the identity, values, and dispositions consonant with the fundamental purposes of the legal profession.[819]

We particularly like the description of best practices for developing students' professional identity and values contained in the Carnegie Foundation's report.

[I]t is possible to imagine a continuum of teaching and learning experiences concerned with the apprenticeship of professional identity. At one end of the continuum would be courses in legal ethics, in particular those directly oriented to the "law of lawyering" that students must master in order to pass the bar examination. A bit further along would fall other academic courses, including those of the first year, into which issues concerning the substantive ends of law, the identity and role of lawyers, and questions of equity and purpose are combined with the more formal, technical issues of legal reasoning. Approaches of this sort are often called the "pervasive method" of teaching ethics. Further along the continuum we encounter courses that directly explore the identity and roles of lawyers, the difficulties of adhering to larger purposes amid the press of practice, and the way professional ideals become manifest in legal careers. Further still fall lawyering courses that

---

[818] For a somewhat different vision of a problem-solving curriculum that is consistent with best practices, see Menkel-Meadow, *supra* note 45.

[819] SULLIVAN ET AL., *supra* note 7, at 250.

bring questions of both competence and responsibility to clients and to the legal system into play. Finally, at the continuum's other end, we find externships and clinical courses in which direct experience of practice with clients becomes the focus.[820]

Whether a school chooses to pursue this vision of legal education or a different one, it should plan its program of instruction deliberately to achieve its mission and produce its desired educational outcomes. A variety of approaches should be expected, even among schools with similar missions and goals. Regardless of the particular mission of a school, however, best practices considerations require that there be a vision driven by goals and a coherent program of instruction designed to implement that vision.

A.   The First Year Program of Instruction.

The first year should provide the building blocks for the progressive acquisition of knowledge, skills, and values in the upper class curriculum and in law practice. The program of instruction should continue the current practice of emphasizing the development of analytical skills (how to think like a lawyer), research and writing skills, and basic legal knowledge.[821] The goals of the first year should also include beginning the process of helping students develop their legal problem-solving expertise, self efficacy, and self-reflection and lifelong learning skills.[822] First year students should be introduced to jurisprudence, the history and values of the legal profession and professions in general, notable figures in the law, the roles of lawyers, the ways in which legal problems arise and are resolved in our society and other societies, and challenges facing the legal profession such as commercialization, accountability, and access to justice.[823] This instruction should occur in the classrooms and co-curricular programs.

First year students should be given an overview of the program of instruction and how it is designed to prepare them for practice by progressively building their knowledge, skills, and values toward competence.[824] All teachers should explain their educational objectives and their methods of instruction.[825]

The Socratic dialogue and casebook method should be used sparingly.[826] Context-based instruction, especially discussion of problems should be the prevalent method of instruction.[827] While habits of objective legal analysis should be taught, students should also be taught when and how justice, morality, and good sense should control the outcomes of legal problems.[828]

All teachers should create and maintain healthy learning environments.[829] Teachers should coordinate reading and project assignments to ensure that student

---

[820] *Id.* at 180-81.

[821] *See* Chapter Two, §§ E & F.

[822] *See* Chapter One, § B. 4. a.; Chapter Two, § F; Chapter Four, § C. 11.

[823] *See* Chapter One, §§ B. 4. a & b (1); Chapter Two, §§ F. 3, 4, & 6.

[824] *See* Chapter Two, §§ A, C, E, & F; Chapter Three.

[825] *See* Chapter Two, §§ A & B; Chapter Four, §§ B & F. 2.

[826] *See* Chapter Four, § F.

[827] *See* Chapter Four, § G.

[828] *See* Chapter One, § B. 4. b. (3); Chapter Two, § F. 6.

[829] *See* Chapter Four, § C.

workloads are manageable and not overly stressful.[830] The school should encourage and aid students in nurturing the quality of their lives and help them experience self-esteem, relatedness to others, autonomy, and authenticity.[831] The administration, faculty, and staff should model professional behavior.[832]

Simulations should be incorporated into every course to strengthen students' understanding of legal concepts and to give them opportunities to assume professional roles.[833] Some simulations can be conducted during class time, while others may be conducted outside of class. Ideally, the simulations should be video recorded and students should receive feedback,[834] but the method, extent, and even the existence of feedback will depend on the educational goals of the simulations and the resources of the school. All simulations conducted outside of class should be debriefed at the beginning of the next class meeting.[835]

Participation in study groups should be required or strongly suggested, and students should be assigned group projects, some to take place during class meetings and others outside of class. Students should be trained how to work in collaborative groups and be closely supervised to ensure these experiences reflect aspects of law practice collaboration and build their collaborative skills.[836]

Students should also receive instruction in how to be expert self-regulated learners so they develop the skills of controlling their learning process; managing their workload, time, and stress; self-monitoring their learning process while it is in progress; and reflecting on their learning afterward, thereby continuously improving themselves as learners.[837] Students should be required to maintain reflective journals in at least one course.[838]

Academic responsibility should be taken seriously by everyone at the school, and students should be expected to conduct themselves as professionals from the moment they enter law school guided by a student code of professionalism. A similar code of professionalism should apply to faculty and staff.

Students should have contact with practicing lawyers and judges from orientation throughout their first year in law school.[839] This can occur through a variety of methods, including preceptorships or other forms of mentoring arrangements, inviting practitioners to be guest speakers in classes or at events open to all students, and requiring students to participate in "field trips" which at a minimum should include observations of actual appellate court arguments.[840] Students should write reflective journals about their experiences and observations during field trips, which ideally would be reviewed by an instructor.[841]

---

[830] *See* Chapter One, § B. 4. c; Chapter Four, §§ C. 1 & 4.
[831] *See* Chapter Two, § F. 6. e.
[832] *See* Chapter Three, § D; Chapter Four, § C. 12.
[833] *See* Chapter Four, § G; Chapter Five, §§ A. 1. & 2. b. and B. 1. & 2. a.
[834] *See* Chapter Four, § C. 10; Chapter Five, § A. 2. e.
[835] *See* Chapter Five, § B. 2. e.
[836] *See* Chapter Four, § C. 6.
[837] *See* Chapter Four, § C. 11; Chapter Five, § A. 1.
[838] *See* Chapter Four, § C. 11.
[839] *See* Chapter Four, § H.
[840] *See* Chapter Four, §§ G & H.
[841] *See* Chapter Four, § C. 11.

Multiple methods of assessing student learning should be used throughout law school.[842] All assessments should be criteria-referenced.[843] Mandatory or suggested grade curves should not be used.[844] Formative assessments should begin early and continue throughout each semester.[845] Intermittent summative assessments should be conducted, leading up to final exams.[846] Every summative assessment should also be a formative assessment.[847] This means that students should receive feedback on all academic work during law school. For example, final exams should be returned to students with notations indicating strengths and deficiencies, along with model answers and scoring keys. Students should be encouraged to seek clarification of feedback they do not understand.

Students who encounter difficulty with summative or formative assessments should receive assistance from the faculty and, when appropriate, from academic support personnel. At the end of the first semester, the only grades should be pass or fail, with perhaps an honors designation for truly outstanding achievement. Alternatively, schools should articulate grades in terms of levels of proficiency reflecting characteristics of student performance, for example, limited proficiency, basic competence, intermediate competence, and advanced proficiency.[848] Every student should begin compiling a portfolio that will be expanded throughout law school.[849]

A law school should not allow a student to stay enrolled beyond the first semester unless the student demonstrates the intellectual skills expected of a first semester student or the school has reason to believe that, with academic support, the student will achieve an acceptable level of proficiency by the end of the second semester.

The intellectual skills to be demonstrated are those that constitute the ability to "think like a lawyer." This includes the ability to understand the holdings of appellate cases, to distinguish among appellate cases, and to apply legal doctrine to a set of facts and predict what a court would decide. More generally, "thinking like a lawyer" involves broader problem-solving skills, including the grounding of analysis in facts, the comprehensive spotting of relevant issues and concerns, the search for governing rules, principles, or standards by which to make decisions, the weighing of competing policy considerations in light of their consequences, the value placed on consistency and deference to past decisions, the utility of reasoning by analogy, the importance of reasoned justification, and the need to reach a conclusion and make a decision even if not perfect.[850]

These are core abilities that are essential to continued learning in law school and the practice of law. If a student cannot demonstrate these abilities by the end of the first semester, it would likely be a waste of the student's time and money to continue in law school.

---

[842] *See* Chapter Seven, § C. 6.

[843] *See* Chapter Seven, § C. 3.

[844] *See* Chapter Seven, § C. 3.

[845] *See* Chapter Seven, § A. 8.

[846] *See* Chapter Seven, § A. 9.

[847] *See* Chapter Seven, § A. 10.

[848] *See* Chapter Seven, § C. 4.

[849] *See* Chapter Seven, § C. 11.

[850] *See* Chapter Two, §§ E & F. 2.

B.   The Second Year Program of Instruction.

The second year should continue helping students develop legal problem-solving expertise, self efficacy, and self-reflection and lifelong learning skills.[851] Whereas the first year focuses on legal analysis, the second should focus on fact analysis. The school should continue providing instruction about core legal knowledge, including knowledge that is essential to all lawyers and foundational information that students will need to pursue specialized interests or tracks in the third year.[852] Schools should consider developing courses that provide an overview of various related subject areas that give students an acquaintance with multiple subjects rather than a more in depth understanding of one subject.[853] This will enable students to acquire a general understanding of a wider range of subjects, any of which they could learn in more depth if needed in practice.

Emphasis in the second year should be placed on helping students develop their knowledge and understanding about professional skills and values, including sensitivity to client-centered practice.[854] Basic introductory courses in professional skills, especially transactional and pretrial skills, should be offered to all students during both semesters. Instruction in legal writing, drafting, and research should continue. Pre- or co-requisite courses might include professional responsibility, evidence, remedies, and civil procedure.

Casebooks should be abandoned altogether and replaced with treatises and problems.[855] More sophisticated, complex, and challenging problems and simulations should be used in all courses.[856] Co-curricular and extra-curricular programs, including competitions and the pro bono program, should be coordinated with curricular offerings.

Externship courses or required observation programs should be organized to give students opportunities to observe and reflect on law practice.[857] The primary educational goal of such experiences should be to develop students' understanding of professional values and commitment to those values, including seeking justice, fostering respect for the rule of law, and dealing sensitively and effectively with diverse clients and colleagues.[858] In furtherance of these objectives, a school might select externships with public interest lawyers and lawyers who handle pro bono cases to give students role models of lawyers who take seriously the profession's obligation to provide access to justice.[859] Another option is to place students at agencies that provide services to under-represented segments of society or perhaps in disciplinary counsels' offices. Schools with sufficient resources should offer students opportunities to enroll in in-house clinics that provide legal services to under-represented members of our society, either as second chairs to third year students or as lead counsel on cases they are qualified to handle.

---

[851] *See* Chapter Two, § F; Chapter Three, § B.

[852] *See* Chapter Two, §§ F. 3 & 4.

[853] *See* Chapter Two, §§ F. 3 & 4.

[854] *See* Chapter Two, §§ F. 5 & 6; Chapter Four, § G.

[855] *See* Chapter Two, §§ F. 3 & 4.

[856] *See* Chapter Three, § B.

[857] *See* Chapter Four, § G. 3.

[858] *See* Chapter Two, § F. 6; Chapter Three, § D; Chapter Four, § G. 3; Chapter Five, § D. 2. a.

[859] *See* Chapter Two, § F. 6; Chapter Three, § D; Chapter Four, § G. 3.

Students should be required to write reflective journals or papers in all experiential education courses.[860] Assessment practices should continue as in the first year.

C.   The Third Year Program of Instruction.[861]

The emphasis in the third year should be to continue helping students develop their problem-solving expertise and cultivate "practical wisdom."[862] The school should give special attention to helping students refine their self-reflection and lifelong learning skills.[863] Rather than having discrete subject specific courses, multiple subjects should be taught in integrated contexts.[864] Most courses could be organized as simulated law firms in which students work individually and in groups to resolve legal problems.[865] For example, one course might be organized as a general practice firm, while others might be organized, for example as a corporate firm, a family law firm, a criminal defense firm, or prosecutor's office. The specific subjects should reflect the most probable settings in which the school's students are likely to enter practice. Practicing or retired lawyers should be recruited to assist in these courses.

Students should be required to participate in externship courses or in-house clinics in which students represent clients or participate in the work of lawyers and judges, not just observe it.[866] Care should be taken to ensure that the externships and in-house clinics have clear, achievable educational objectives that cannot be adequately replicated in the simulated law firm courses or other courses.[867] One option is to continue giving students opportunities to participate in the public interest practice settings such as those described in the second year curriculum. Another option would be to give students opportunities to work in the types of legal settings in which they are most likely to find themselves in their first years of practice.

Students should be required to write reflective journals or papers in all experiential education courses.[868]

Assessments during the third year should not only measure what students are learning in each course, they should also evaluate the overall competencies of students to help students understand the degree to which they are ready for their first day in law practice.[869] Students who are significantly deficient in the knowledge, skills, or values required to practice law effectively and responsibly should be counseled about these deficiencies and assisted in developing plans to remedy the problems. If a student is able to graduate without remedying significant deficiencies, the law school should inform relevant bar admissions authorities about the student's deficiencies.

---

[860] *See* Chapter Four, § F. 11.

[861] In schools that have part-time programs, the recommendations in this section might constitute the third and fourth years of instruction.

[862] *See* Chapter Two, § E; Chapter Four, § G. 3.

[863] *See* Chapter Two, § F. 1. & 2. a; Chapter Four, § C. 11.

[864] *See* Chapter Three, § C.

[865] *See* Chapter Four, § C. 6.

[866] *See* Chapter Four, § G. 3.

[867] *See* Chapter Five, §§ A. 2. b, C. 2. a, & D. 2. a.

[868] *See* Chapter Four, § C. 11.

[869] *See* Chapter Five, §§ A. 2. b & C. 2. a; Chapter Seven, § C. 4.

Third year students should have access to affordable programs to prepare them for the bar examination, perhaps offered by the school as part of the third year curriculum for credit. Law schools should at least help students understand what they are expected to know to succeed on bar examinations and help them locate relevant treatises on bar exam subjects.[870]

---

[870] *See* Chapter One, § B. 1.

Conclusion: The Road Ahead

This document contains proposed solutions to many of the problems with legal education in the United States. Three principles of best practices are particularly important:

1.   The school is committed to preparing its students to practice law effectively and responsibly in the contexts they are likely to encounter as new lawyers.
2.   The school clearly articulates its educational goals.
3.   The school regularly evaluates the program of instruction to determine if it is effective in preparing students for the practice of law.

Adherence to these principles is essential for improving our system of legal education. It is unlikely that any real progress can be made until legal educators declare what they are trying to do and evaluate how well they are succeeding.

While one may fairly disagree with some of our proposals or conclude that other alternatives would be more effective or viable, one cannot change the fact that our system of legal education has severe deficiencies. Law schools are not adequately preparing most students for practice, and licensing authorities are not adequately protecting clients from unprepared new lawyers.

The resistence of the legal academy to change is so well-entrenched that we hesitated to undertake this project. Some thought it would be a total waste of time or, at best, an academic exercise. "The likelihood of coherent and productive change is not great. Law teachers are amazingly good at denial and at perceiving the world in ways they prefer regardless of how it really is."[871] The authors of the Carnegie Foundation's report concluded that, although "[l]aw schools have been sent stern messages about these issues for decades,"[872]

> efforts to improve legal education have been more piecemeal than comprehensive. Few schools have made the overall practices and effects of their educational effort a subject for serious study. Too few have attempted to address these issues on a systematic basis. This relative lack of responsiveness by the law schools, taken as a group, to the well-reasoned pleas of the national bar antedates our investigation.[873]

Why have legal educators consistently resisted change for so many years? The reasons have included pressures to conform to norms brought about by hiring, retention, promotion, and tenure practices that value scholarship over teaching; limited textbook options; economics of large class teaching; and an accreditation process that encourages conformity with the norm.[874] Additional barriers to change have included inertia, faculty autonomy, and the narrow, unquestioned, and damaging paradigm that teaching students to think like lawyers is what

---

[871] David Barnhizer, An Essay on Strategies for Facilitating Learning 7 (June 2006), Cleveland-Marshall Legal Studies Paper No. 06-127, *available at* SSRN: http://ssrn.com/abstract=906638.

[872] SULLIVAN ET AL., *supra* note 7, at 242.

[873] *Id.* at 243.

[874] Schwartz, *supra* note 396, at 360-62.

legal education is all about. John Mudd made the following comments about the impediments to reform that existed in 1988:

> The first [barrier to change] is the law school counterpart to the physics principle that a body at rest tends to stay at rest. Complex organizations like law schools are bound by institutional inertia. We do not move swiftly in any direction, and it is difficult to begin movement at all. When we initiated a process of change at our school, I sometimes felt like a few of us were trying to push a parked boxcar. To borrow another metaphor, it is helpful to keep in mind that turning a battleship requires more time and energy than turning a speedboat, and law schools are more like battleships than speedboats.
>
> Another factor inhibiting movement is faculty autonomy, the tradition under which individual professors determine the content of their courses. Roger Cramton calls this the Lone Ranger theory of legal education. A generation ago Karl Llewellyn noted that each law professor "loves his baby, thinks his darling more important than any other darling, works out his gospel, and argues, fights, and sometimes intrigues for more hours per semester to spread the Perfect Word. . . . Still it is not good doctrine that 'What is fun for the law professor is good for the country.'" In law schools we are often confronted with something approaching a paralytic democracy. There is just enough diffusion of power to prevent movement on matters that encompass major portions of the academic program.
>
> Another barrier to change is our inherited ideology, the view that thinking like a lawyer is what legal education is all about. As a former logic teacher, I would not for a moment suggest that we do anything but promote careful, critical thinking in law schools. Nevertheless, we perform a disservice to our schools and our students if we substitute a time-worn phrase for a careful examination of our educational goals. . . . It has been said that a change in world view changes the world viewed. I offer a corollary: intransigence in thinking results in intransigence in action. We must guard against the tendency to accept uncritically someone else's statement of our educational purpose.[875]

We do not know the extent to which the impediments described by Mudd still exist. We do expect it will be difficult to motivate some law teachers to change their attitudes and practices. Traditions die hard, even traditions that are clearly out of step with best practices.

Most law schools have been faculty-centered, not student-centered, and the law faculties have controlled what they taught and how they taught it. Law teachers in the United States are reasonably well paid, have relatively light teaching loads (9 to 12 credit hours per year), have little contact with students outside of class, grade on the basis of one final exam at the end of the semester (an exam that individual

---

[875] John O. Mudd, Remarks at the ABA Section of Legal Education and Admissions to the Bar's National Conference on Legal Education for a Changing Profession 68, Mar. 25, 1988.

teachers prepare and grade with no oversight), and have their summers off, often with stipends to write law review articles. There has been little accountability, especially after a law teacher receives tenure (typically in the sixth year of teaching). There have been very few incentives to engage in curricular innovations or to develop excellent teaching skills.

For the reasons outlined above, Michael Schwartz fears that "[l]aw professors not only have no incentive to change their teaching methods, they have no incentive to change at all."[876] While this may be true of some law teachers, we know it is not true of all law teachers. We learned during this project that many academics understand the need for change and see the potential that exists today for significantly improving the quality of legal education. A growing body of scholarship acknowledges the shortcomings of legal education and proposes new approaches for educating law students. Evidence of this is apparent in the large number of citations in this document to materials that were published just before, or since, our project was initiated in 2001, in addition to numerous documents that were shared with us before they were published.

Although the challenges to implementing best practices for legal education are quite significant, we are hopeful that progress will be made. The need is great.

Developing a more balanced and integrated legal education that can address more of the needs of the legal profession than the current model seems highly desirable on its merits. However, as we have seen, there are major obstacles such a development will have to overcome. A trade-off between higher costs and greater educational effectiveness is one. Resistance to change in a largely successful and comfortable academic enterprise is another. However, in all movements for innovation, champions and leaders are essential factors in determining whether or not a possibility becomes realized. Here, the developing network of faculty and deans concerned with improving legal education is a key resource waiting to be developed and put to good use.

We believe that it is well worth the effort. The calling of legal educators is a high one. It is to prepare future professionals with enough understanding, skill, and judgment to support the vast and complicated system of the law needed to sustain the United States as a free society worthy of its citizens' loyalty. That is to uphold the vital values of freedom with equity and extend these values into situations as yet unknown but continuous with the best aspirations of our past.[877]

It will take many leaders to change legal education. As John Mudd wrote, "[c]hange has been described as the process of modifying the culture of an organization and leadership as the moving force in creating and shaping a new culture."[878] Leadership may come from people outside of law schools who have a responsibility to protect the public's interest such as chief justices, bar examiners,

---

[876] Schwartz, *supra* note 396, at 360-62.

[877] SULLIVAN ET AL., *supra* note 7, at 261.

[878] John O. Mudd, *Academic Change in Law Schools*, 29 GONZ. L. REV. 29, 73 (1993/94) (citing EDGAR H. SHEIN, ORGANIZATIONAL CULTURE AND LEADERSHIP 317 (1985)).

accrediting bodies, legislators, and alumni who see our new graduates in practice and truly understand the need to improve their preparation for practice.

Leadership from within law schools is essential, however, and there are signs that it may be emerging. There are growing numbers of talented people in law schools who care about the quality of their teaching and the success and satisfaction of their students. They are engaging in innovative and positive work that may eventually transform legal education. Perhaps something in this document will encourage more law teachers to reexamine their assumptions and traditions about legal education and become leaders for change, and perhaps law school deans will support and reward them for doing so.

It may turn out that Harvard Law School will lead the way out of the quagmire that it inadvertently led legal education into 130 years ago. Elena Kagan appointed a curriculum review committee when she became Dean of Harvard Law School in 2003 and charged it with rethinking how the law is taught in America.[879] The committee recommended changes that would "push students to take a more practical, problem-solving approach to the law beginning in their first year . . . . The changes are meant to prepare graduates better for the modern legal world . . . ."[880]

In the Spring of 2006, the Harvard Law School faculty approved changes in the second- and third-year programs of study, then unanimously approved changes to the first-year course offerings in October, 2006.[881] Three new courses were added to the first-year curriculum, including a course focusing on problem-solving. To make room for the new courses, the school reduced the amount of time that students will spend studying the five traditional doctrinal courses – contracts, torts, property, civil procedure, and criminal law. The program of instruction in the second and third years is designed to provide the students with expanded opportunities for clincial work, internships, and study abroad. The changes to Harvard's curriculum "reflect a belief that problem-solving exercises should be a critical component of legal education and that hands-on training should be central to many students' law school experience."[882] While Harvard's actions do not approach the more fundamental changes called for in this document, they are steps in the right direction.

If legal educators can find a way to move forward together and build a system of legal education that respects appropriate traditions and embraces sound educational practices, perhaps we can realize the outcomes envisioned in the following paragraph.

> [T]he Socratic method will give way to a more collaborative
> mode of learning between faculty and students, just as appellate

---

[879] Marcella Bombardieri, *Harvard Law Dean's Goal is a Revolution*, THE BOSTON GLOBE, Sept. 21, 2003, http://boston.com/news/local/articles/2003/09/21/law_deans_goal_is_a_revolution/. *See also,* Beth Potier, *Big Plans Highlight Elena Kagan's 2L*, HARVARD UNIVERSITY GAZETTE, Sept. 16, 2004, http://hno.harvard.edu/gazette/2004/09.16/03-kagan.html.

[880] Sacha Pfeiffer, THE BOSTON GLOBE, *Mired in Past, Law Schools in U.S. Rethink Role*, INTERNATIONAL DAILY TRIBUNE (Paris), May 10, 2006, http://www.iht.com/articles/2006/05/10/business/harvard.php. *See also* Sephanie Frances Ward, *A Push For Problem-Solving: As Harvard Ponders, Others Embrace Change in Law School Approach*, ABA JOURNAL EREPORT, May 26, 2006, http://abanet.org/journal/ereport/my26harvard.html.

[881] Rethinking Langdell, HARVARD LAW TODAY 5 (December, 2006).

[882] *Id.*

case analysis will be replaced by case studies and a greater number of simulation exercises in substantive law courses. Law schools will treat the teaching of essential lawyering skills and professional values as part of the core curriculum, and law faculty will coordinate what is taught throughout the entire curriculum to insure that students have sufficient opportunities to acquire and develop the skills and values they will need as twenty-first century practitioners.[883]

The Clinical Legal Education Association (CLEA) intends to continue working with other organizations and individuals to encourage and support efforts to implement changes that are consistent with the proposals in this document. CLEA welcomes all the help it can get.

---

[883] Barry et al., *supra* note 283, at 72.